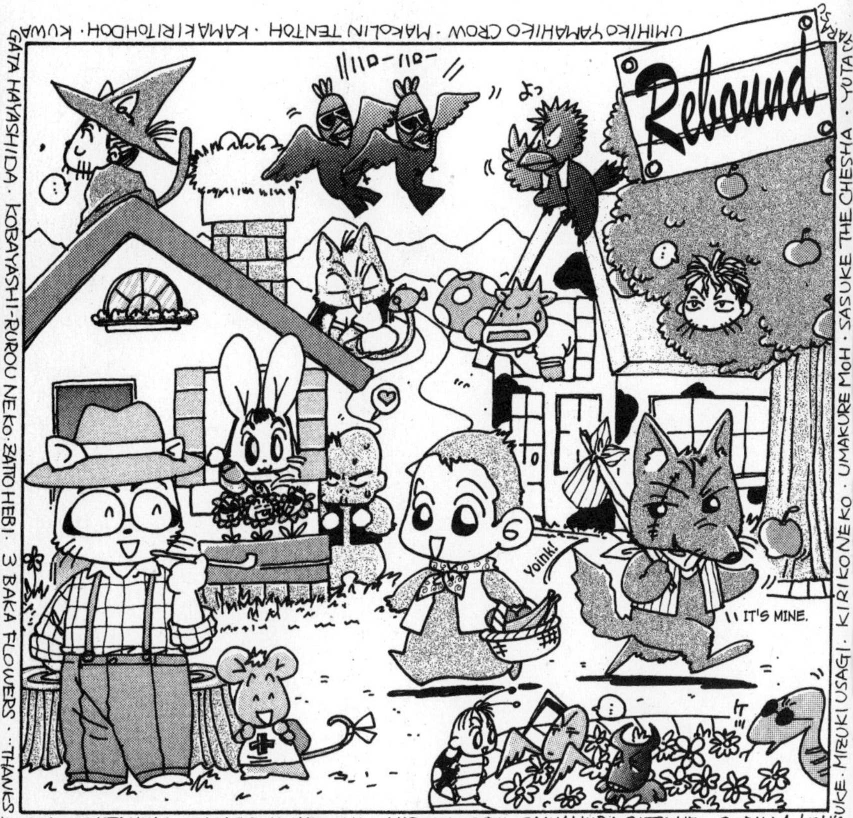

Rebound
Yoink!
IT'S MINE.
SAKURAI TANUKI · IMAGAWA NEZUMI · NARUCHO SARU · SAWAMURA GITSUNE · GORILLA KOHSUKE · MIZUKI USAGI · KIRIKONEKO · UMAKURE MOH · SASUKE THE CHESHA · YUTA KARASU
UMIHIKO YAMAHIKO CROW · MAKOLIN TENTOH · KAMAKIRITOHDOH · KUWAGATA HAYASHIDA · KOBAYASHI-RUROU NEKO · ZATTO HEBI · 3 BAKA FLOWERS · ..THANKS!

Presented by
YURIKO NISHIYAMA

By Yuriko Nishiyama

Volume 7

Los Angeles • Tokyo • London

Translator - Shirley Kubo
English Adaption - Jordan Capell
Copy Edit - Aaron Sparrow
Retouch and Lettering - Steven Redd
Cover Layout - Patrick Hook
Graphic Designer - John Lo

Editor - Luis Reyes
Digital Imaging Manager - Chris Buford
Pre-Press Manager - Antonio DePietro
Production Managers - Jennifer Miller, Mutsumi Miyazaki
Art Director - Matt Alford
Managing Editor - Jill Freshney
VP of Production - Ron Klamert
President & C.O.O. - John Parker
Publisher & C.E.O. - Stuart Levy

E-mail: info@TOKYOPOP.com
Come visit us online at www.TOKYOPOP.com

A  Manga

TOKYOPOP Inc.
5900 Wilshire Blvd. Suite 2000
Los Angeles, CA 90036

Rebound Vol. 7

ISBN: 1-59182-531-8

First TOKYOPOP printing: April 2004

10 9 8 7 6 5 4 3 2 1

Printed in the USA

-Play by Play-
The Season So Far...

The Johnan High School Basketball team has worked hard all year and has finally gotten to the national championships in Sapporo. However, if the team loses just one game, they're on the first plane back to Tokyo.

The boys have proven to be quite a powerhouse at the tournament, winning their first round game against Kyan Industry High School and their second round game against Tsukuba, their once-bitter rivals. Luckily, they became friends with the two opposing teams and have enjoyed Sapporo's nightlife with both of them. Nate has even met a girl from one of the girls league teams, Tomomi, who may or may not be trying to make the moves on the little tike on their excursions around Sapporo. Sawamura, the pretty boy wiz kid of the Johnan team, ends up being reunited with his estranged father in Sappero after two years apart. Sapporo is proving to be a lucky town for Johnan...now will it stay that way? They may have made it to the third round...but here they have to face Yokohama High...and then, if their luck holds out, the tournament favorites Kanakita in round four. But maybe some help from old friends will get them a little more prepared for the challenges ahead of them.

Today on REBOUND

SEVEN

REBOUND

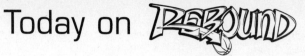

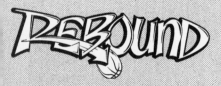

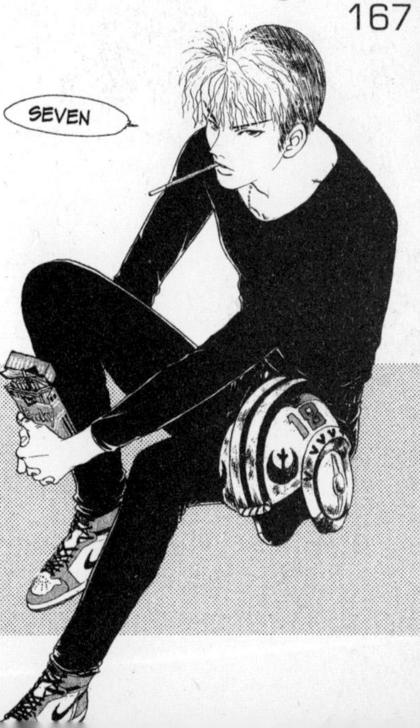

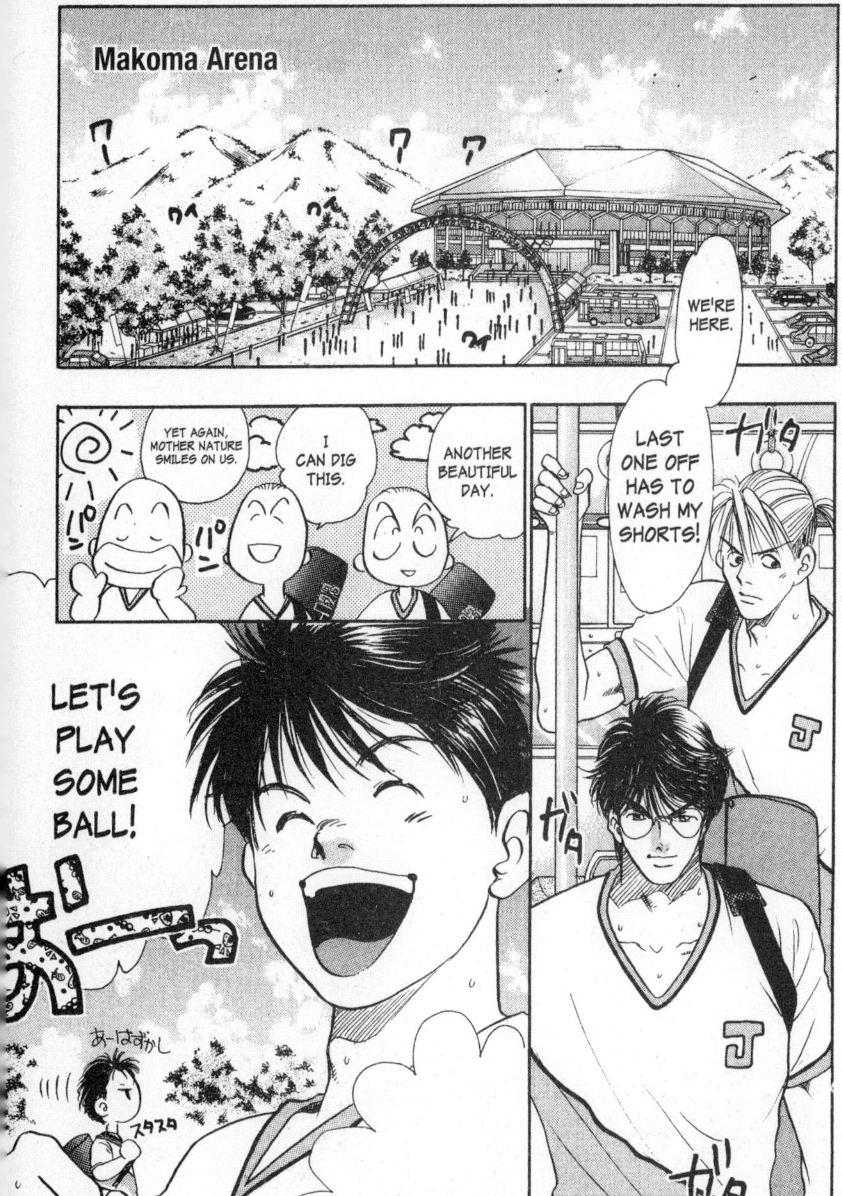
Makoma Arena
WE'RE HERE.
LAST ONE OFF HAS TO WASH MY SHORTS!
ガタ
ガタ
ANOTHER BEAUTIFUL DAY.
I CAN DIG THIS.
YET AGAIN, MOTHER NATURE SMILES ON US.
LET'S PLAY SOME BALL!
YEEAAH!
ガタ
あーはずかし
スタスタ

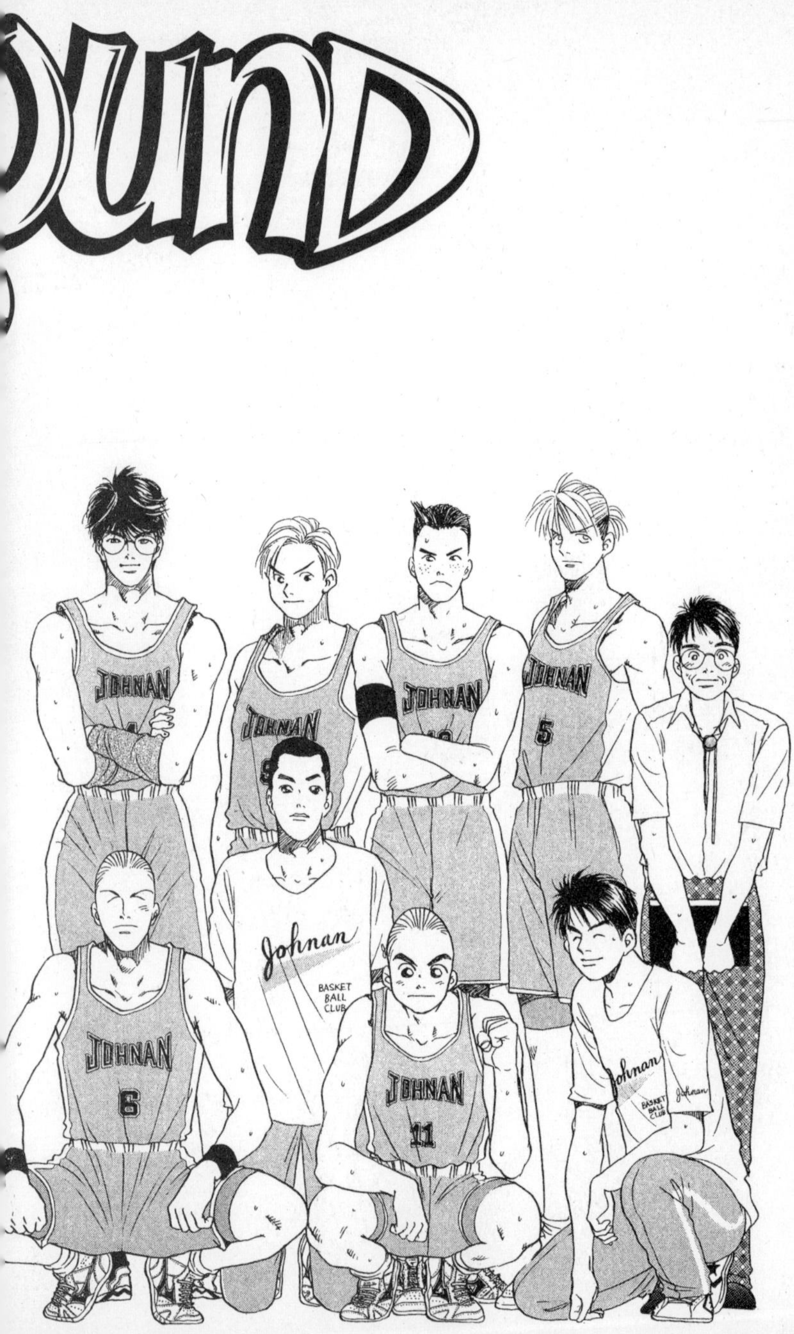
OUND
JOHNAN
JOHNAN
JOHNAN
JOHNAN
5
Johnan
BASKET
BALL
CLUB
JOHNAN
6
JOHNAN
11
Johnan
BASKET
BALL
CLUB

Episode 50 Cool Eyes

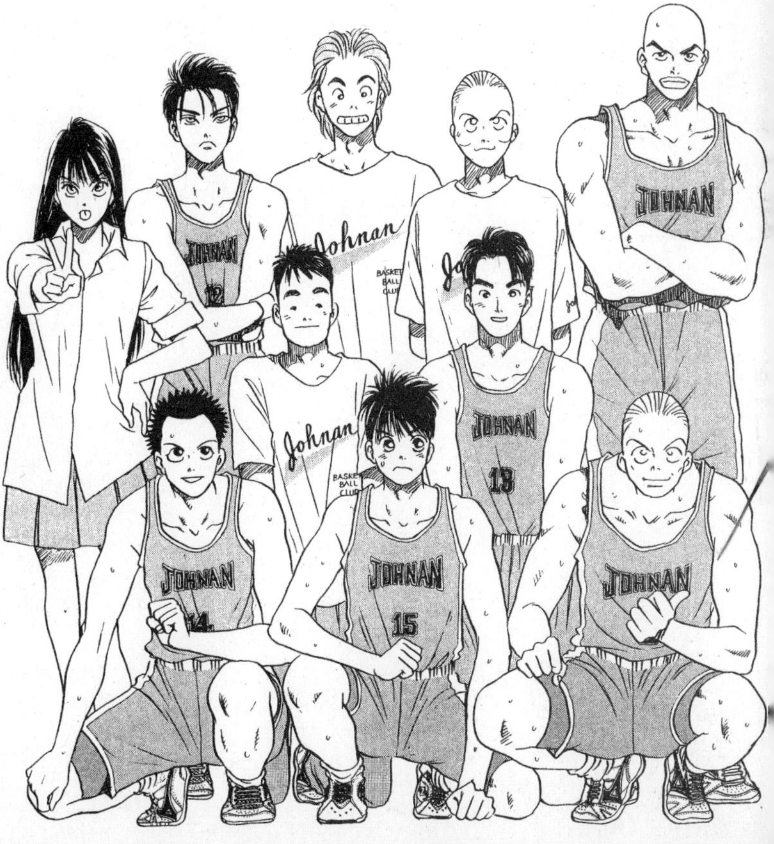
JOHNAN
12
Johnan
BASKETBALL CLUB
JOHNAN
13
JOHNAN
14
JOHNAN
15
JOHNAN

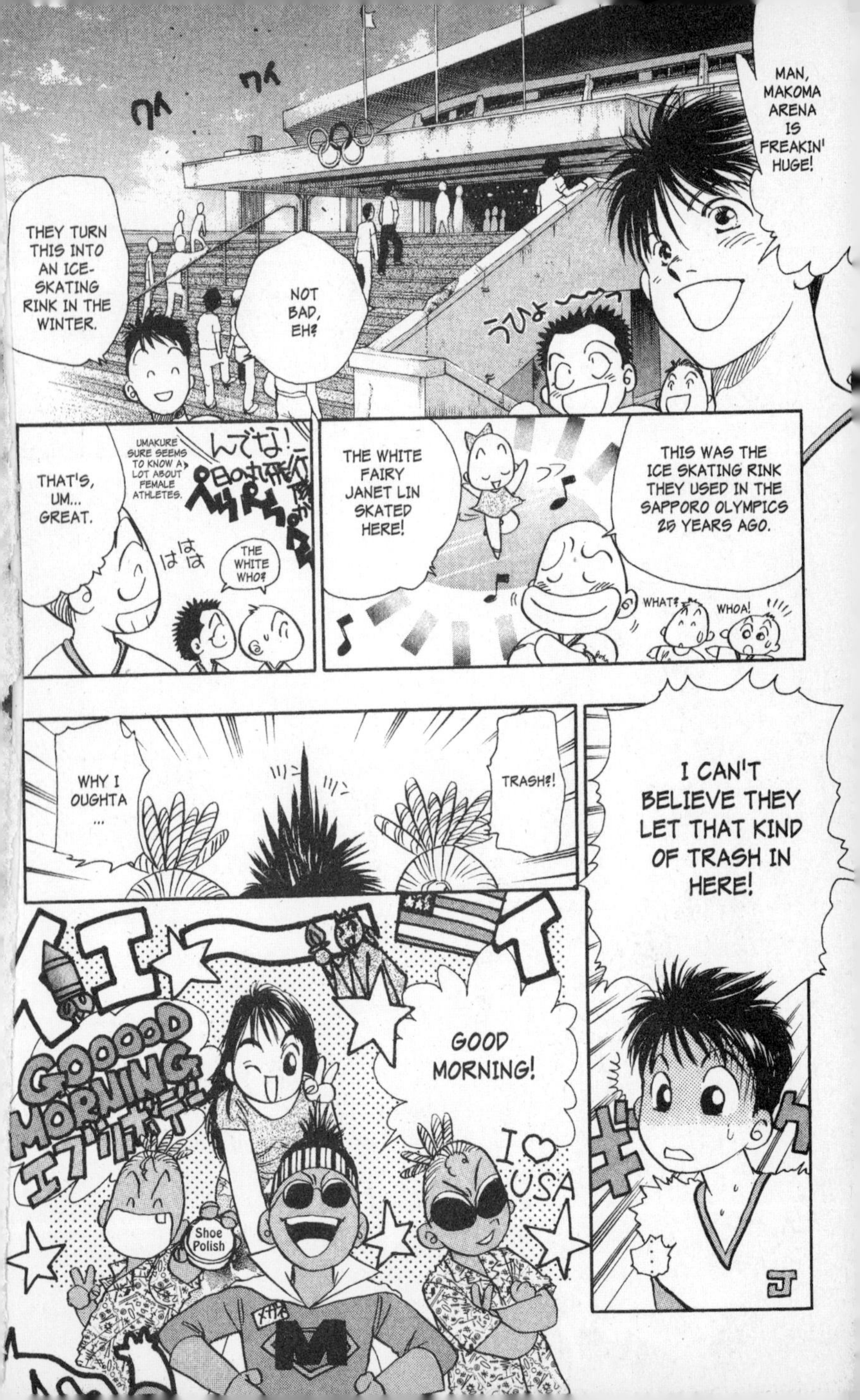
MAN, MAKOMA ARENA IS FREAKIN' HUGE!
NOT BAD, EH?
THEY TURN THIS INTO AN ICE-SKATING RINK IN THE WINTER.
THIS WAS THE ICE SKATING RINK THEY USED IN THE SAPPORO OLYMPICS 25 YEARS AGO.
THE WHITE FAIRY JANET LIN SKATED HERE!
WHOA!
WHAT?
UMAKURE SURE SEEMS TO KNOW A LOT ABOUT FEMALE ATHLETES.
THAT'S, UM... GREAT.
THE WHITE WHO?
I CAN'T BELIEVE THEY LET THAT KIND OF TRASH IN HERE!
TRASH?!
WHY I OUGHTA ...
GOOD MORNING!
GOOOOOD MORNING
I ♥ USA
Shoe Polish

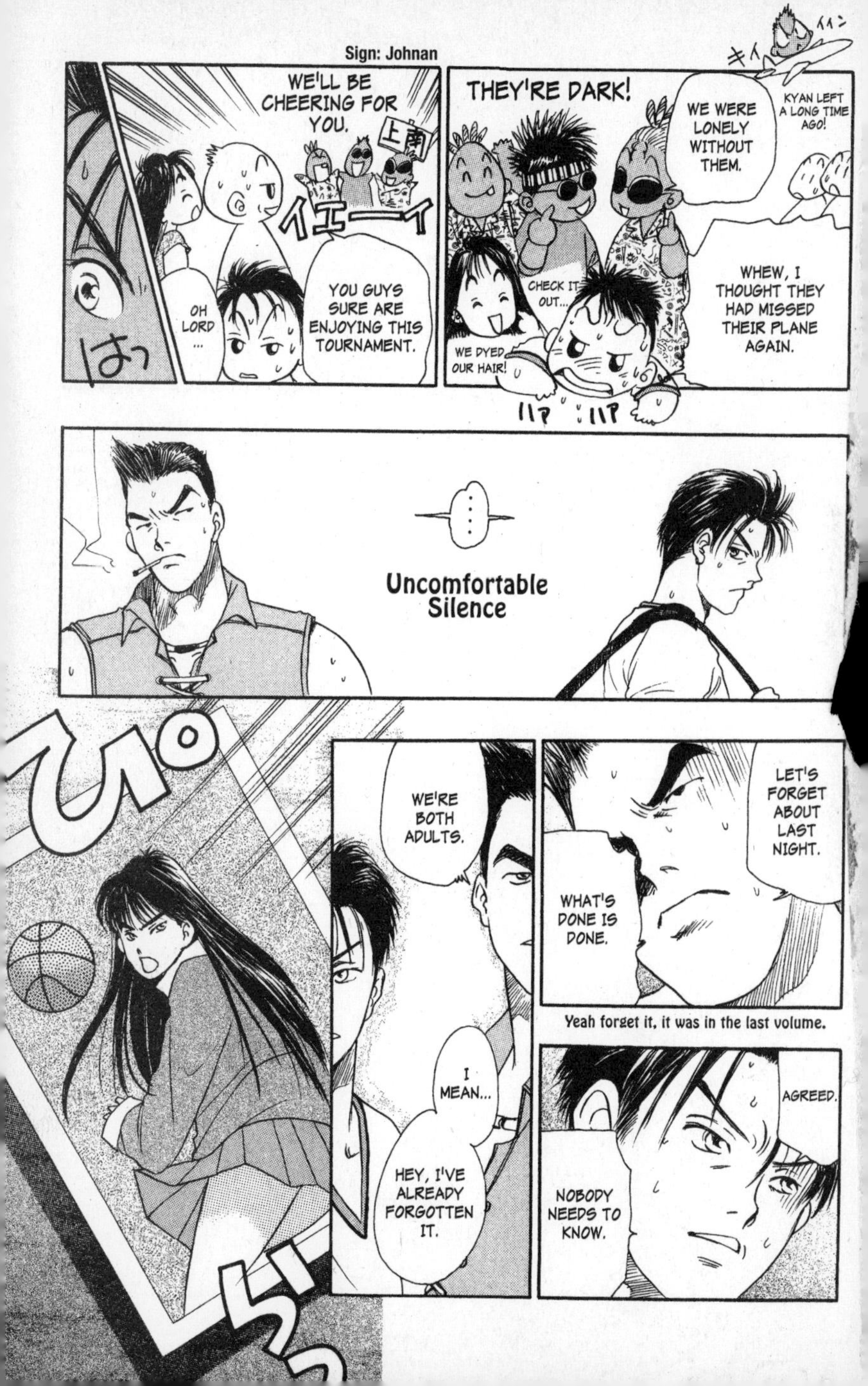
Sign: Johnan
キィ
イィン
KYAN LEFT A LONG TIME AGO!
WE WERE LONELY WITHOUT THEM.
THEY'RE DARK!
WHEW, I THOUGHT THEY HAD MISSED THEIR PLANE AGAIN.
CHECK IT OUT...
WE DYED OUR HAIR!
ハァ ハァ
WE'LL BE CHEERING FOR YOU.
上南
イエーイ
YOU GUYS SURE ARE ENJOYING THIS TOURNAMENT.
OH LORD ...
はっ
....
Uncomfortable Silence
LET'S FORGET ABOUT LAST NIGHT.
WHAT'S DONE IS DONE.
Yeah forget it, it was in the last volume.
AGREED.
NOBODY NEEDS TO KNOW.
WE'RE BOTH ADULTS.
I MEAN...
HEY, I'VE ALREADY FORGOTTEN IT.
ぴ

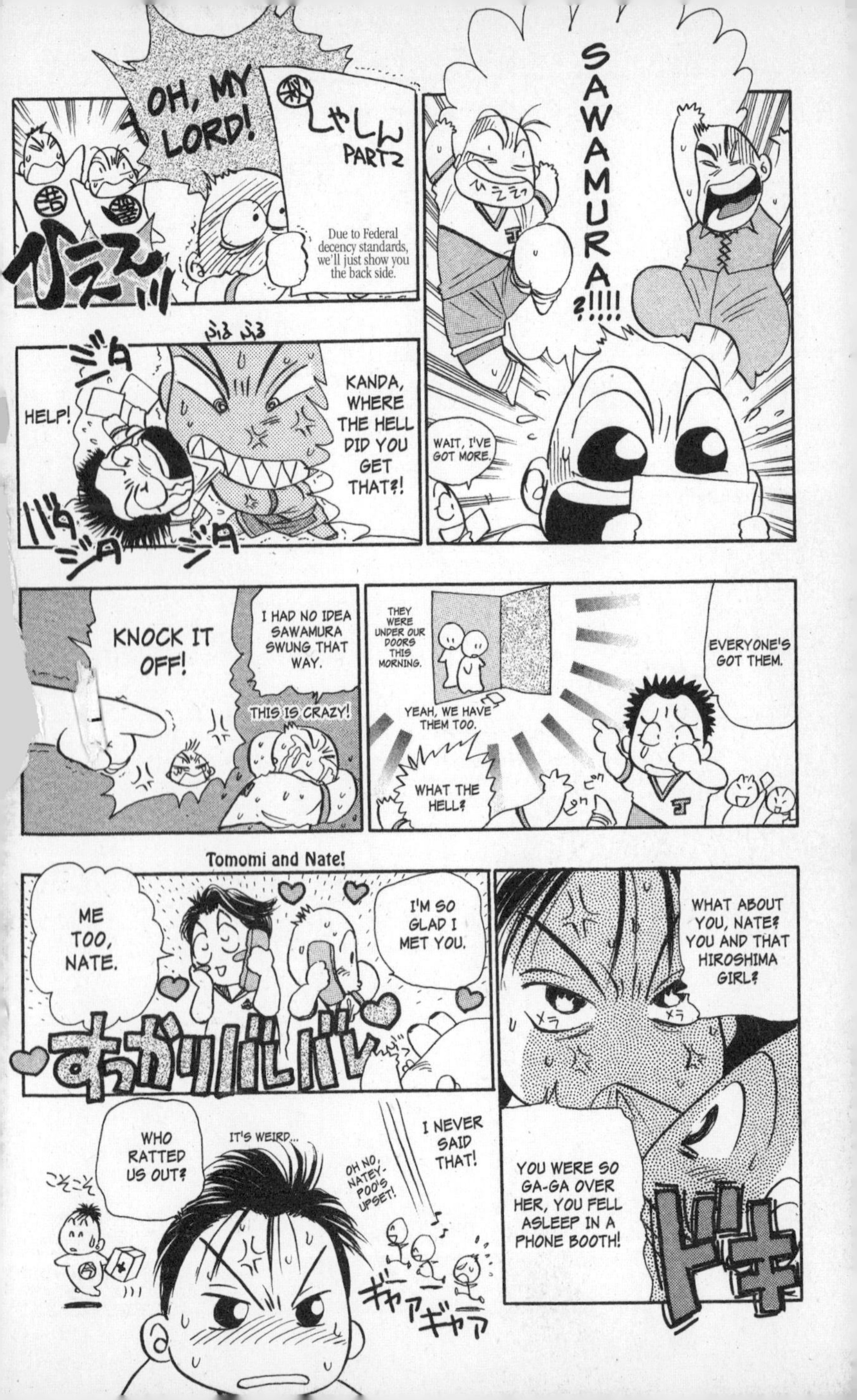
SAWAMURA?!!!!!
ひえぇ
WAIT, I'VE GOT MORE.
OH, MY LORD!
しゃしん PART2
Due to Federal decency standards, we'll just show you the back side.
ひえぇ
ふる ふる
KANDA, WHERE THE HELL DID YOU GET THAT?!
HELP!
ジタ
バタ ジタ ジタ
EVERYONE'S GOT THEM.
THEY WERE UNDER OUR DOORS THIS MORNING.
YEAH, WE HAVE THEM TOO.
ピク ピク
WHAT THE HELL?
I HAD NO IDEA SAWAMURA SWUNG THAT WAY.
KNOCK IT OFF!
THIS IS CRAZY!
Tomomi and Nate!
WHAT ABOUT YOU, NATE? YOU AND THAT HIROSHIMA GIRL?
メラ メラ
YOU WERE SO GA-GA OVER HER, YOU FELL ASLEEP IN A PHONE BOOTH!
ドキ
I'M SO GLAD I MET YOU.
ME TOO, NATE.
I NEVER SAID THAT!
OH NO, NATEY-POO'S UPSET!
IT'S WEIRD...
WHO RATTED US OUT?
こそこそ
ギャアギャア

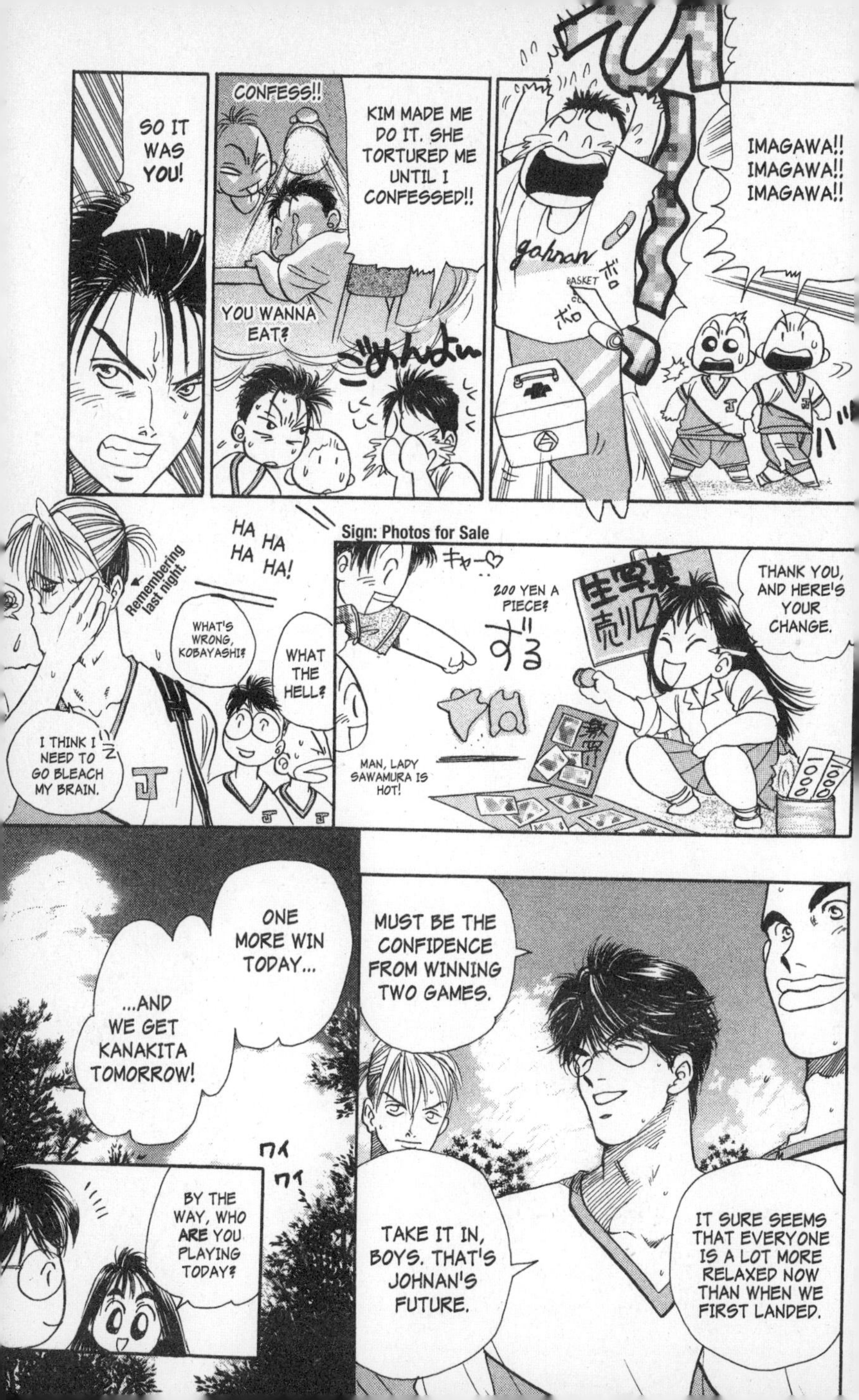
IMAGAWA!! IMAGAWA!! IMAGAWA!!
BASKET
ボロ
ボロ
KIM MADE ME DO IT. SHE TORTURED ME UNTIL I CONFESSED!!
CONFESS!!
YOU WANNA EAT?
ごめんよぉ
SO IT WAS YOU!
Sign: Photos for Sale
THANK YOU, AND HERE'S YOUR CHANGE.
キャー♡
200 YEN A PIECE?
ずる
MAN, LADY SAWAMURA IS HOT!
HA HA HA HA!
Remembering last night.
WHAT'S WRONG, KOBAYASHI?
WHAT THE HELL?
I THINK I NEED TO GO BLEACH MY BRAIN.
MUST BE THE CONFIDENCE FROM WINNING TWO GAMES.
IT SURE SEEMS THAT EVERYONE IS A LOT MORE RELAXED NOW THAN WHEN WE FIRST LANDED.
TAKE IT IN, BOYS. THAT'S JOHNAN'S FUTURE.
ONE MORE WIN TODAY...
...AND WE GET KANAKITA TOMORROW!
ワイ
ワイ
BY THE WAY, WHO ARE YOU PLAYING TODAY?

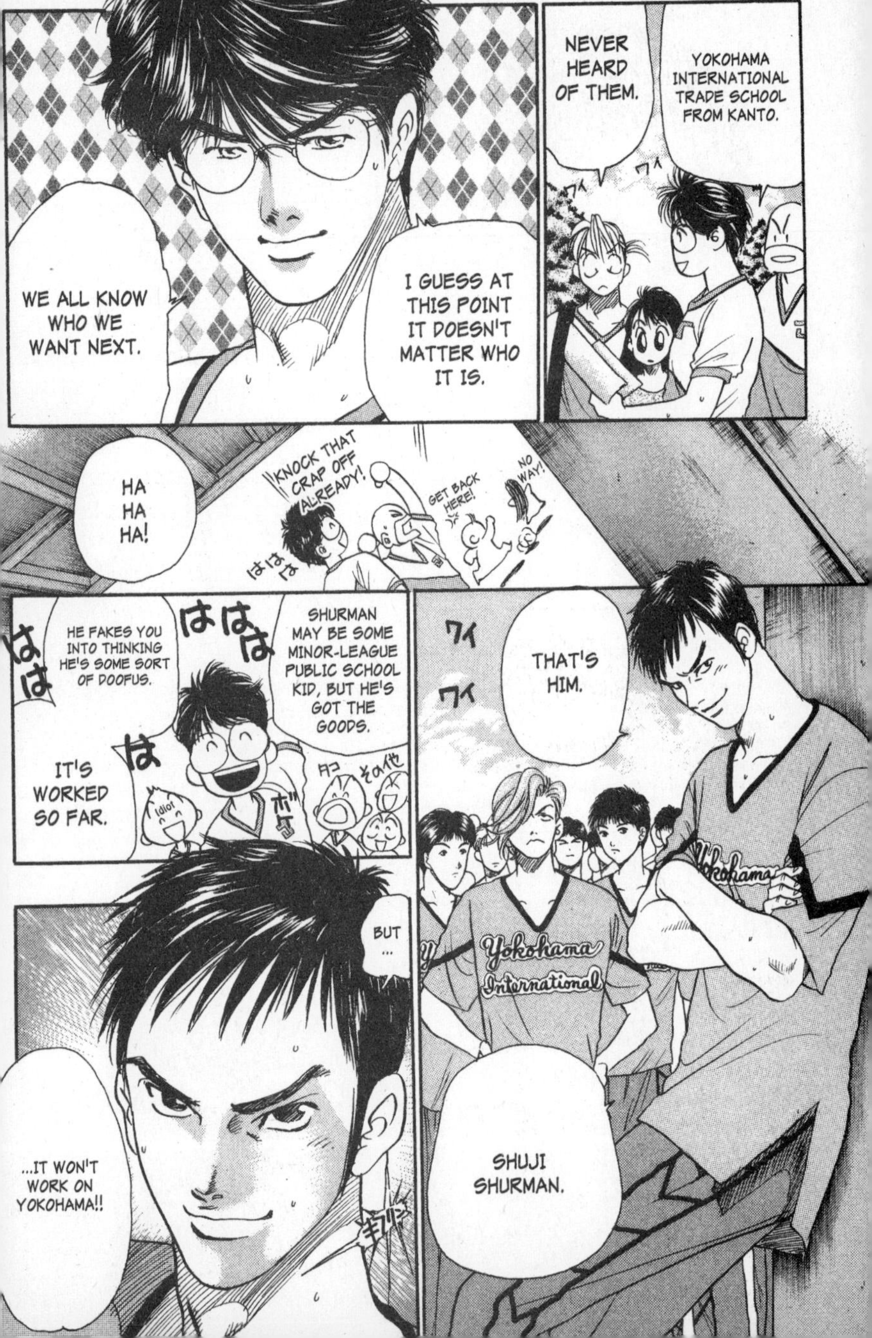
YOKOHAMA INTERNATIONAL TRADE SCHOOL FROM KANTO.
NEVER HEARD OF THEM.
ワイ
ワイ
I GUESS AT THIS POINT IT DOESN'T MATTER WHO IT IS.
WE ALL KNOW WHO WE WANT NEXT.
NO WAY!
GET BACK HERE!
KNOCK THAT CRAP OFF ALREADY!
HA HA HA!
ははは
ワイ
ワイ
THAT'S HIM.
SHUJI SHURMAN.
SHURMAN MAY BE SOME MINOR-LEAGUE PUBLIC SCHOOL KID, BUT HE'S GOT THE GOODS.
ははは
HE FAKES YOU INTO THINKING HE'S SOME SORT OF DOOFUS.
はは
は
IT'S WORKED SO FAR.
タコ
その他
ボケ
idiot
BUT ...
...IT WON'T WORK ON YOKOHAMA!!

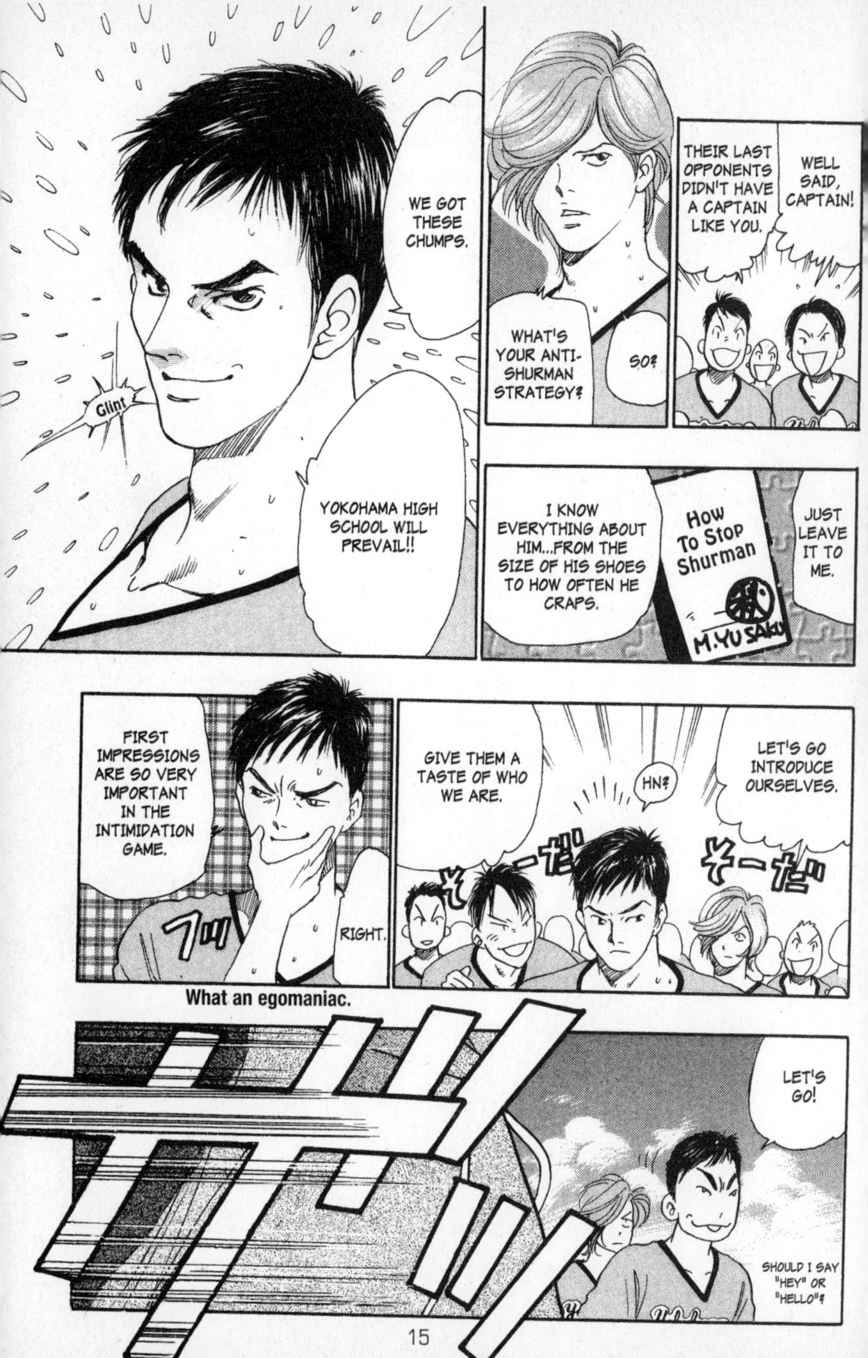
WELL SAID, CAPTAIN!
THEIR LAST OPPONENTS DIDN'T HAVE A CAPTAIN LIKE YOU.
SO?
WHAT'S YOUR ANTI-SHURMAN STRATEGY?
JUST LEAVE IT TO ME.
How To Stop Shurman
M.YU SAKU
I KNOW EVERYTHING ABOUT HIM...FROM THE SIZE OF HIS SHOES TO HOW OFTEN HE CRAPS.
WE GOT THESE CHUMPS.
Glint
YOKOHAMA HIGH SCHOOL WILL PREVAIL!!
LET'S GO INTRODUCE OURSELVES.
HN?
GIVE THEM A TASTE OF WHO WE ARE.
そーだ
そーだ
FIRST IMPRESSIONS ARE SO VERY IMPORTANT IN THE INTIMIDATION GAME.
RIGHT.
フッ
What an egomaniac.
LET'S GO!
SHOULD I SAY "HEY" OR "HELLO"?

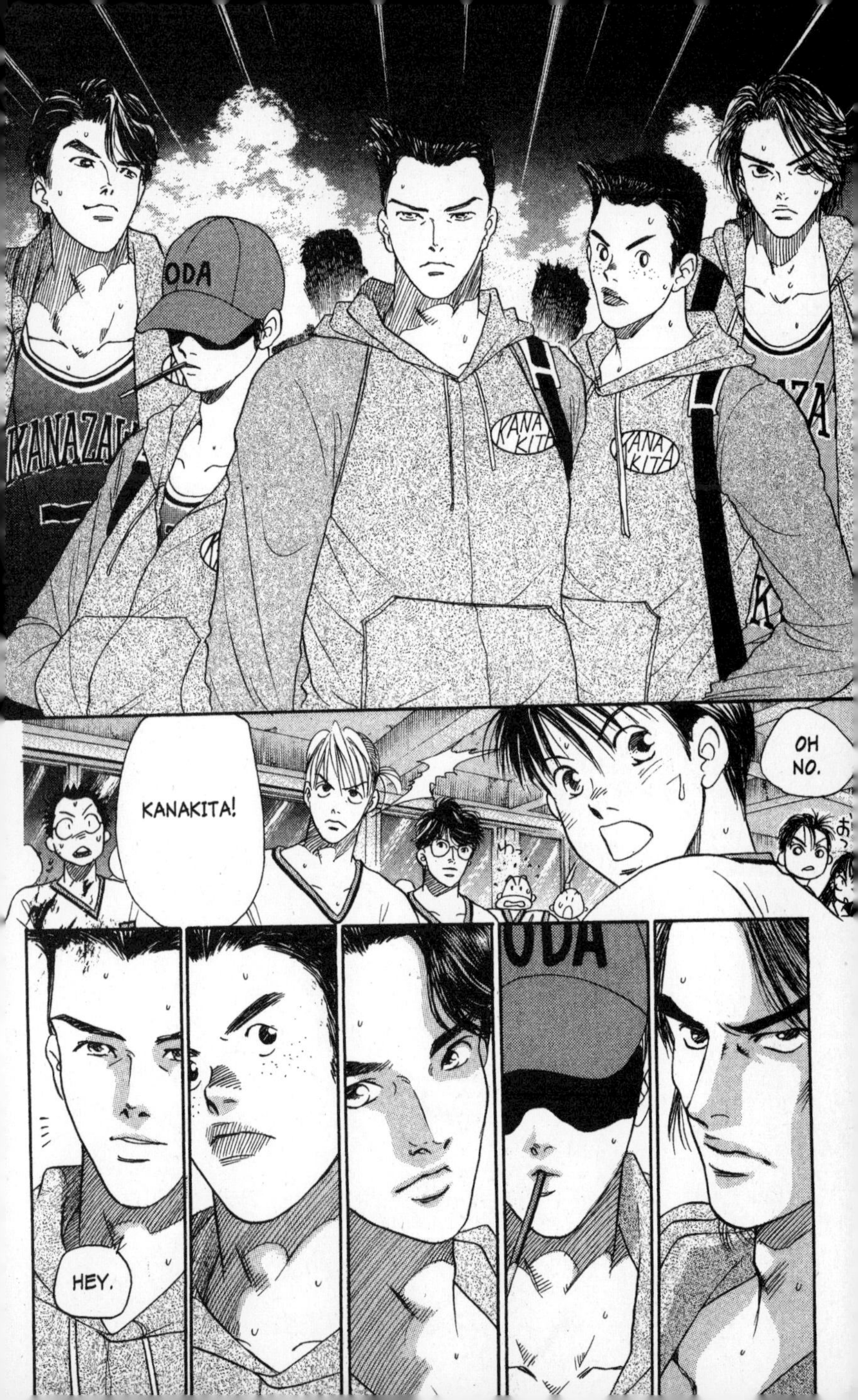
OH NO.
KANAKITA!
HEY.

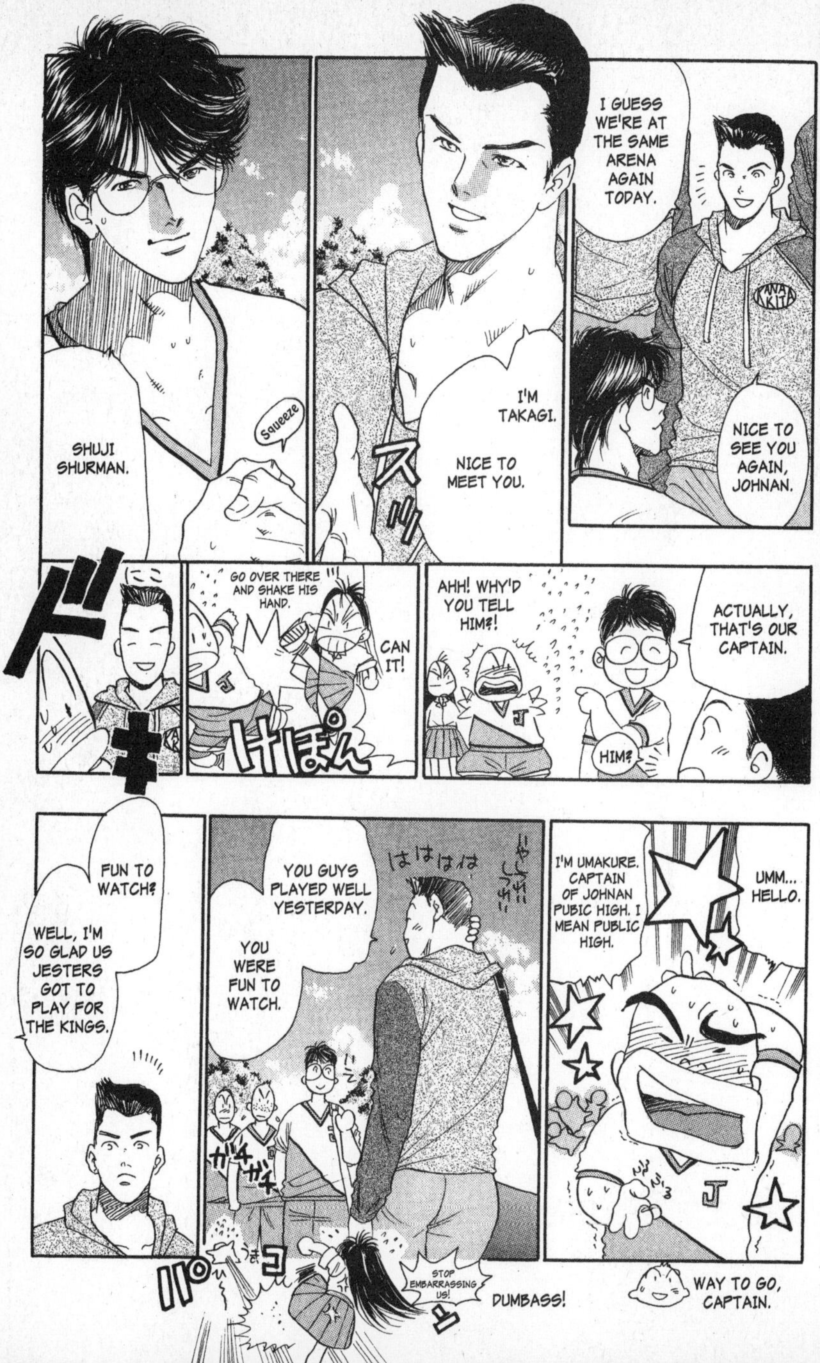
I GUESS WE'RE AT THE SAME ARENA AGAIN TODAY.
NICE TO SEE YOU AGAIN, JOHNAN.
I'M TAKAGI.
NICE TO MEET YOU.
スッ
SHUJI SHURMAN.
Squeeze
ACTUALLY, THAT'S OUR CAPTAIN.
HIM?
AHH! WHY'D YOU TELL HIM?!
GO OVER THERE AND SHAKE HIS HAND.
CAN IT!
けぽん
にこ
UMM... HELLO.
I'M UMAKURE. CAPTAIN OF JOHNAN PUBIC HIGH. I MEAN PUBLIC HIGH.
YOU GUYS PLAYED WELL YESTERDAY.
YOU WERE FUN TO WATCH.
ガチガチ
FUN TO WATCH?
WELL, I'M SO GLAD US JESTERS GOT TO PLAY FOR THE KINGS.
STOP EMBARRASSING US!
DUMBASS!
WAY TO GO, CAPTAIN.

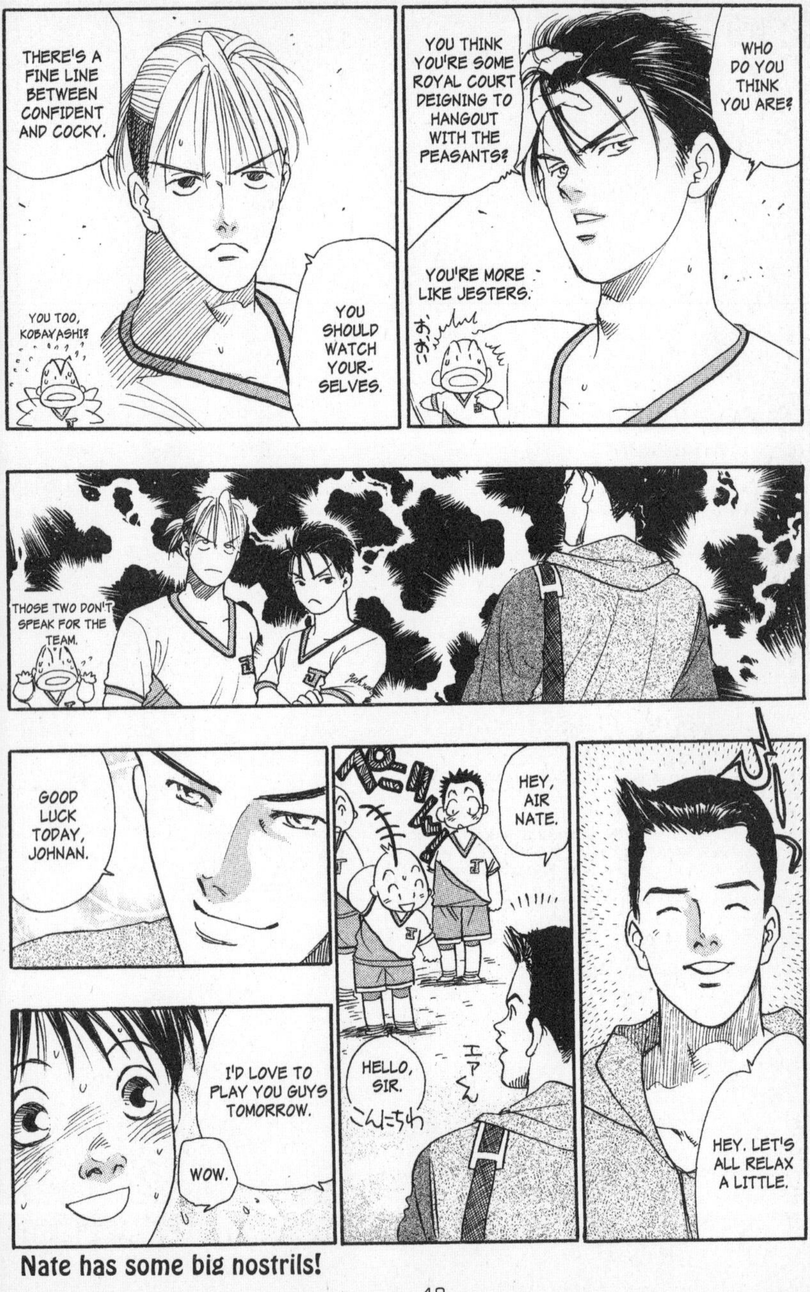
WHO DO YOU THINK YOU ARE?
YOU THINK YOU'RE SOME ROYAL COURT DEIGNING TO HANGOUT WITH THE PEASANTS?
YOU'RE MORE LIKE JESTERS.
THERE'S A FINE LINE BETWEEN CONFIDENT AND COCKY.
YOU SHOULD WATCH YOURSELVES.
YOU TOO, KOBAYASHI?
THOSE TWO DON'T SPEAK FOR THE TEAM.
HEY. LET'S ALL RELAX A LITTLE.
HEY, AIR NATE.
エアくん
HELLO, SIR.
こんにちわ
GOOD LUCK TODAY, JOHNAN.
I'D LOVE TO PLAY YOU GUYS TOMORROW.
WOW.

Nate has some big nostrils!

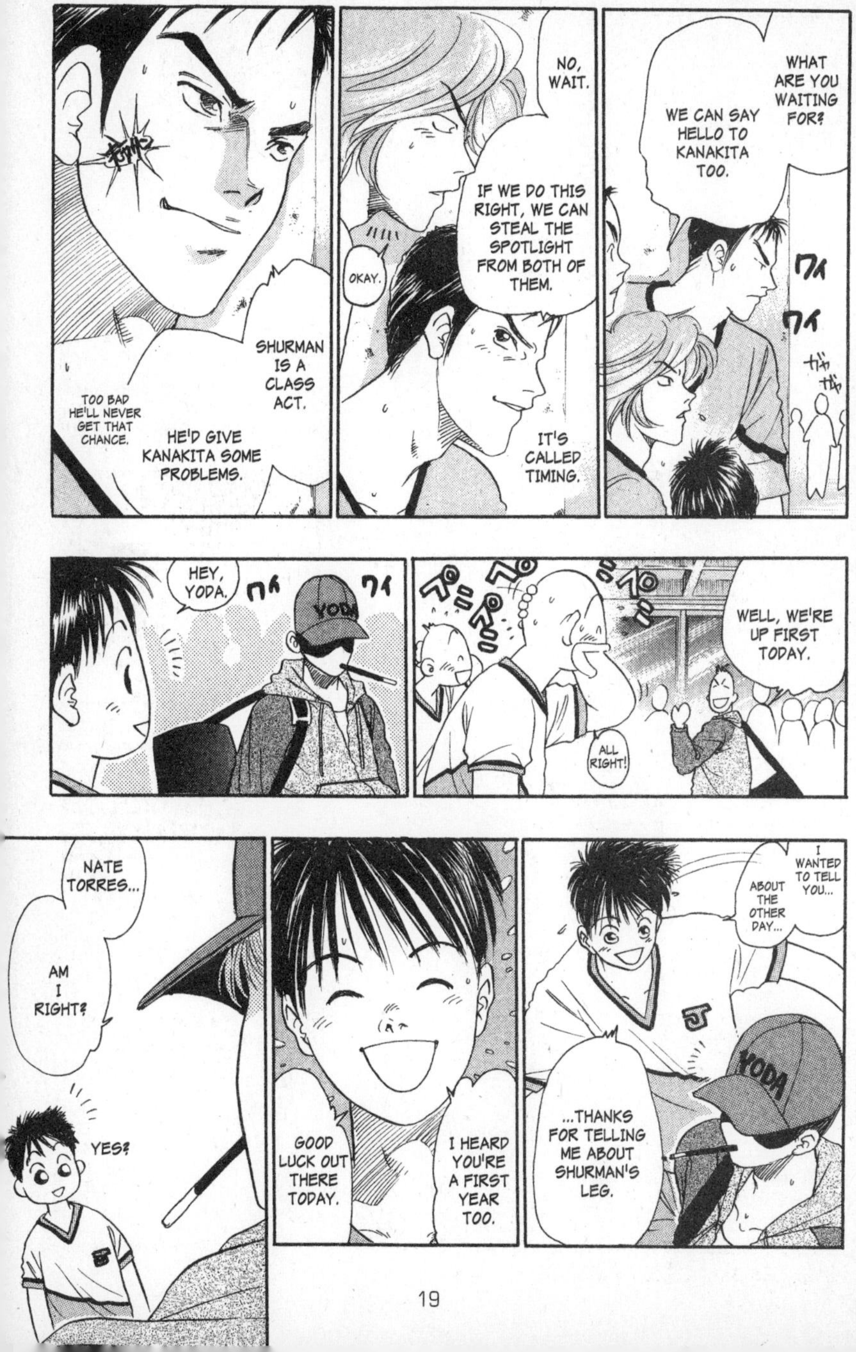
WHAT ARE YOU WAITING FOR?
WE CAN SAY HELLO TO KANAKITA TOO.
ワイ
ワイ
NO, WAIT.
IF WE DO THIS RIGHT, WE CAN STEAL THE SPOTLIGHT FROM BOTH OF THEM.
OKAY.
IT'S CALLED TIMING.
SHURMAN IS A CLASS ACT.
HE'D GIVE KANAKITA SOME PROBLEMS.
TOO BAD HE'LL NEVER GET THAT CHANCE.
WELL, WE'RE UP FIRST TODAY.
ALL RIGHT!
HEY, YODA.
ワイ
ワイ
YODA
I WANTED TO TELL YOU...
ABOUT THE OTHER DAY...
...THANKS FOR TELLING ME ABOUT SHURMAN'S LEG.
YODA
I HEARD YOU'RE A FIRST YEAR TOO.
GOOD LUCK OUT THERE TODAY.
NATE TORRES...
AM I RIGHT?
YES?

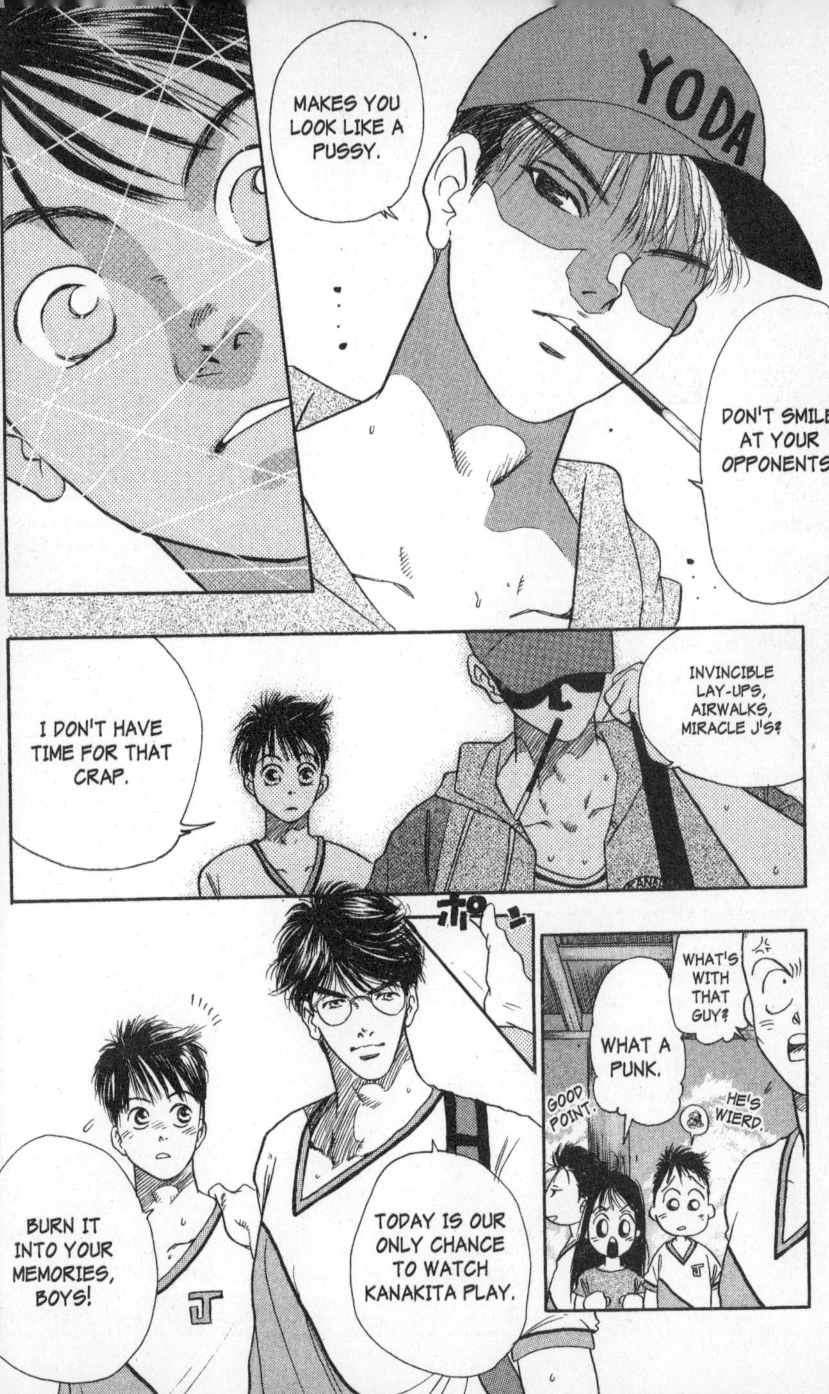
DON'T SMILE AT YOUR OPPONENTS.
MAKES YOU LOOK LIKE A PUSSY.
INVINCIBLE LAY-UPS, AIRWALKS, MIRACLE J'S?
I DON'T HAVE TIME FOR THAT CRAP.
WHAT'S WITH THAT GUY?
WHAT A PUNK.
HE'S WIERD.
GOOD POINT.
TODAY IS OUR ONLY CHANCE TO WATCH KANAKITA PLAY.
BURN IT INTO YOUR MEMORIES, BOYS!

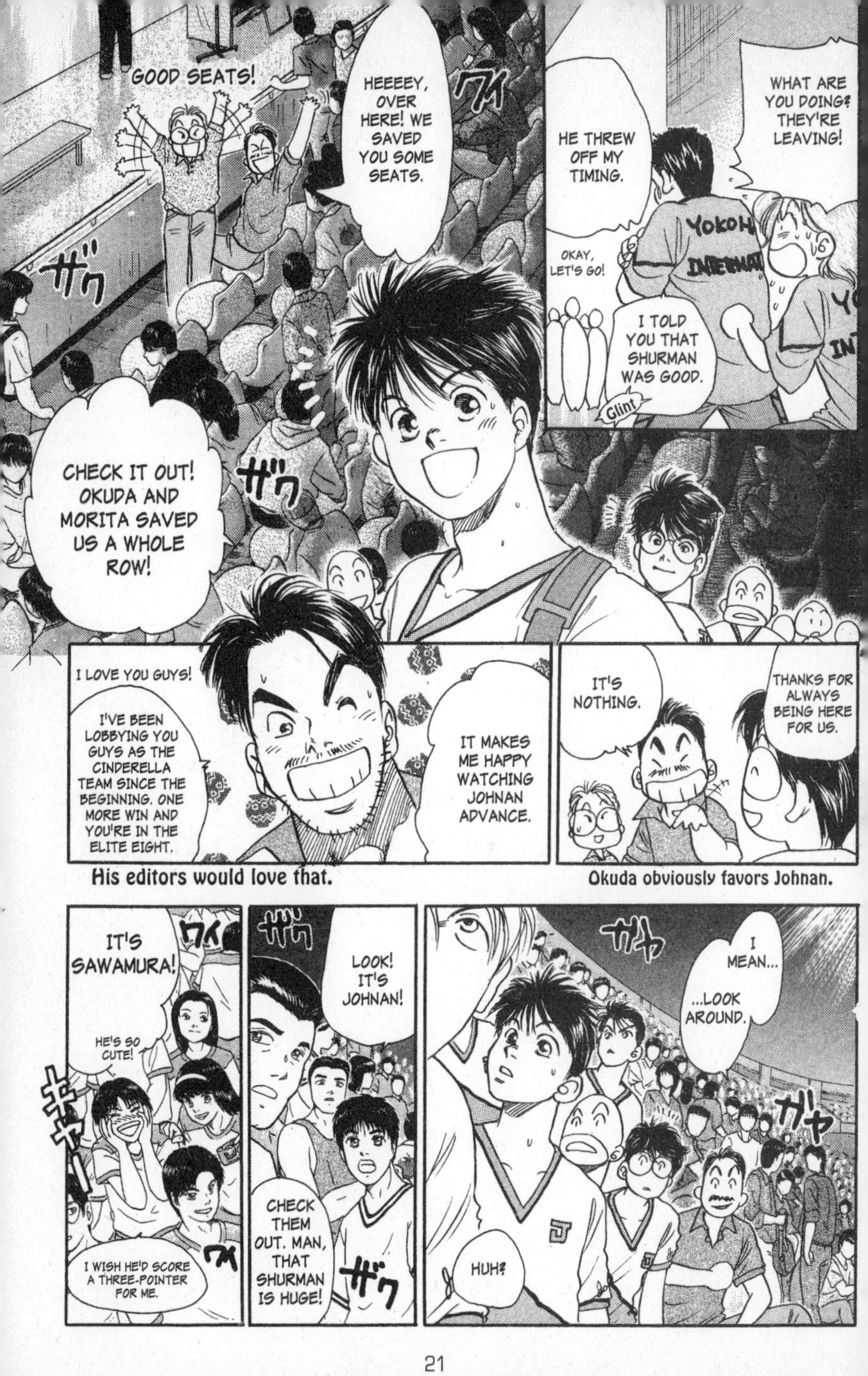
WHAT ARE YOU DOING? THEY'RE LEAVING!
HE THREW OFF MY TIMING.
OKAY, LET'S GO!
I TOLD YOU THAT SHURMAN WAS GOOD.
Glint
HEEEEY, OVER HERE! WE SAVED YOU SOME SEATS.
GOOD SEATS!
CHECK IT OUT! OKUDA AND MORITA SAVED US A WHOLE ROW!
THANKS FOR ALWAYS BEING HERE FOR US.
IT'S NOTHING.
IT MAKES ME HAPPY WATCHING JOHNAN ADVANCE.
I LOVE YOU GUYS!
I'VE BEEN LOBBYING YOU GUYS AS THE CINDERELLA TEAM SINCE THE BEGINNING. ONE MORE WIN AND YOU'RE IN THE ELITE EIGHT.
Okuda obviously favors Johnan.
His editors would love that.
I MEAN...
...LOOK AROUND.
HUH?
LOOK! IT'S JOHNAN!
CHECK THEM OUT. MAN, THAT SHURMAN IS HUGE!
IT'S SAWAMURA!
HE'S SO CUTE!
I WISH HE'D SCORE A THREE-POINTER FOR ME.

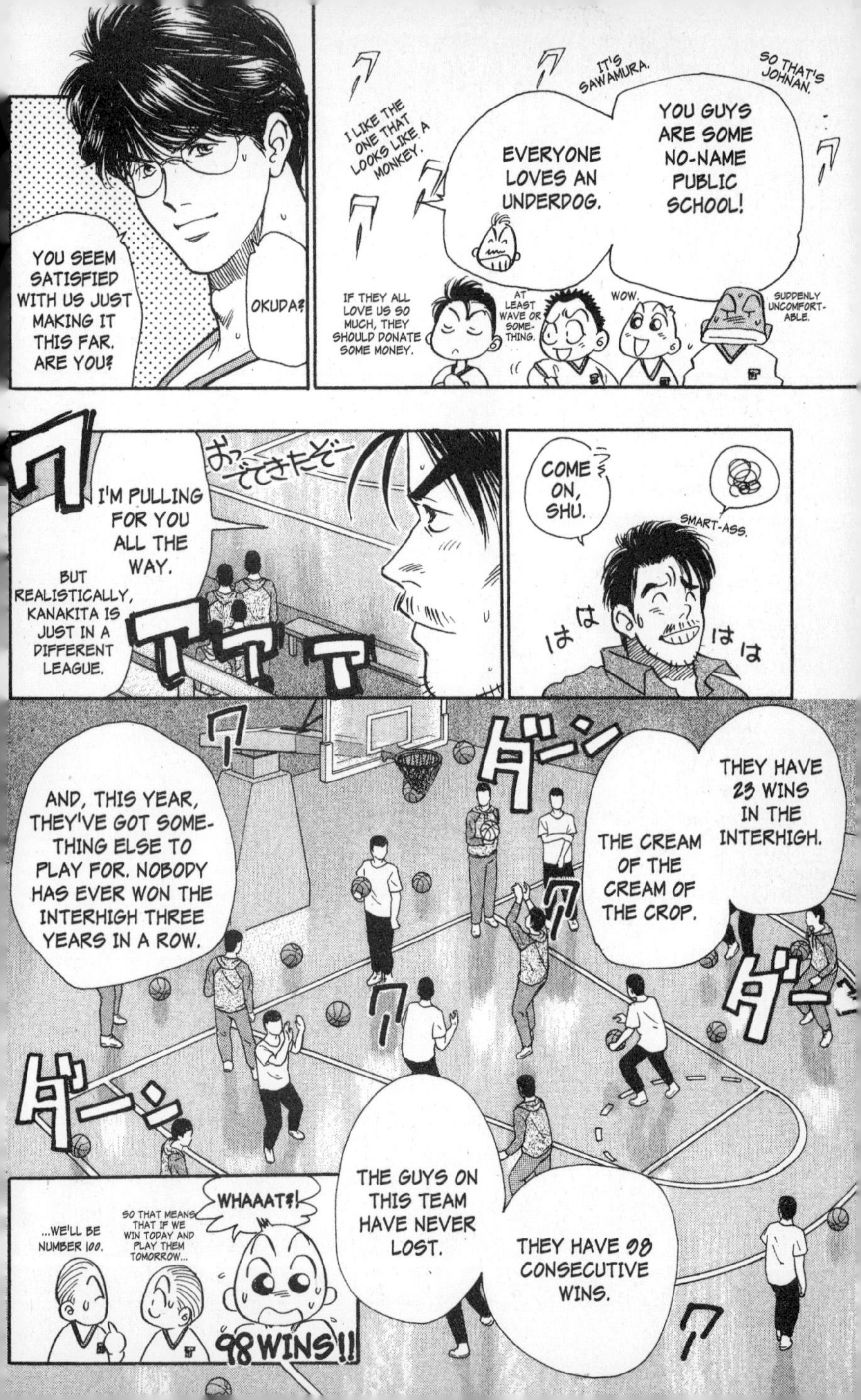
SO THAT'S JOHNAN.
IT'S SAWAMURA.
YOU GUYS ARE SOME NO-NAME PUBLIC SCHOOL!
EVERYONE LOVES AN UNDERDOG.
I LIKE THE ONE THAT LOOKS LIKE A MONKEY.
SUDDENLY UNCOMFORTABLE.
WOW.
AT LEAST WAVE OR SOMETHING.
IF THEY ALL LOVE US SO MUCH, THEY SHOULD DONATE SOME MONEY.
OKUDA?
YOU SEEM SATISFIED WITH US JUST MAKING IT THIS FAR. ARE YOU?
COME ON, SHU.
SMART-ASS.
はは はは
おっ でてきたぞ
I'M PULLING FOR YOU ALL THE WAY.
BUT REALISTICALLY, KANAKITA IS JUST IN A DIFFERENT LEAGUE.
ワァァァ
ダーン
THEY HAVE 23 WINS IN THE INTERHIGH.
THE CREAM OF THE CREAM OF THE CROP.
AND, THIS YEAR, THEY'VE GOT SOMETHING ELSE TO PLAY FOR. NOBODY HAS EVER WON THE INTERHIGH THREE YEARS IN A ROW.
ダーン
ダーン
THEY HAVE 98 CONSECUTIVE WINS.
THE GUYS ON THIS TEAM HAVE NEVER LOST.
WHAAAT?!
98 WINS!!
SO THAT MEANS THAT IF WE WIN TODAY AND PLAY THEM TOMORROW...
...WE'LL BE NUMBER 100.

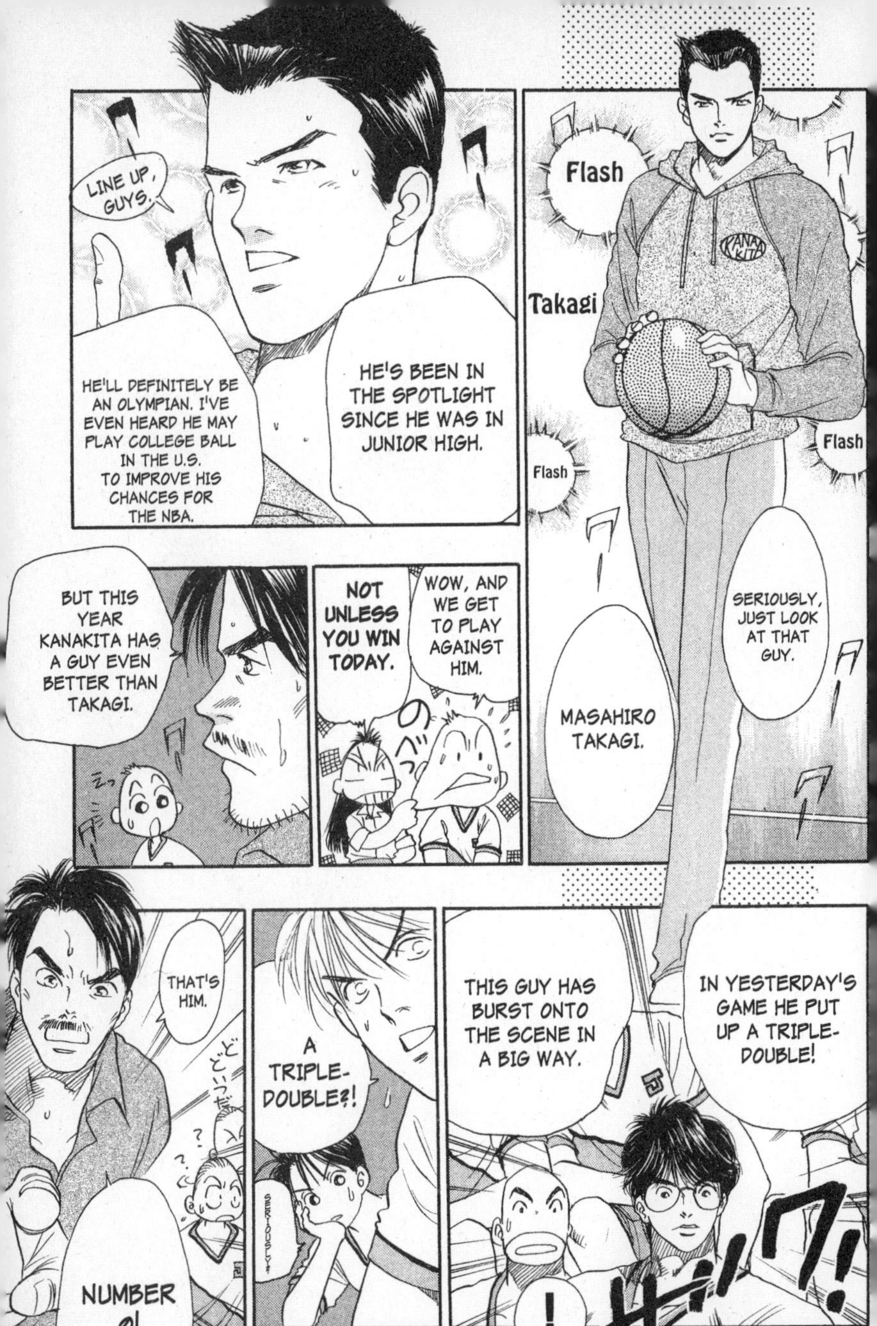
Flash
Takagi
Flash
Flash
SERIOUSLY, JUST LOOK AT THAT GUY.
MASAHIRO TAKAGI.
LINE UP, GUYS.
HE'S BEEN IN THE SPOTLIGHT SINCE HE WAS IN JUNIOR HIGH.
HE'LL DEFINITELY BE AN OLYMPIAN. I'VE EVEN HEARD HE MAY PLAY COLLEGE BALL IN THE U.S. TO IMPROVE HIS CHANCES FOR THE NBA.
WOW, AND WE GET TO PLAY AGAINST HIM.
NOT UNLESS YOU WIN TODAY.
BUT THIS YEAR KANAKITA HAS A GUY EVEN BETTER THAN TAKAGI.
IN YESTERDAY'S GAME HE PUT UP A TRIPLE-DOUBLE!
THIS GUY HAS BURST ONTO THE SCENE IN A BIG WAY.
!
A TRIPLE-DOUBLE?!
SERIOUSLY?!
THAT'S HIM.
どいつだ
NUMBER 9!

A triple-double is double figures in points, rebounds, and assists.

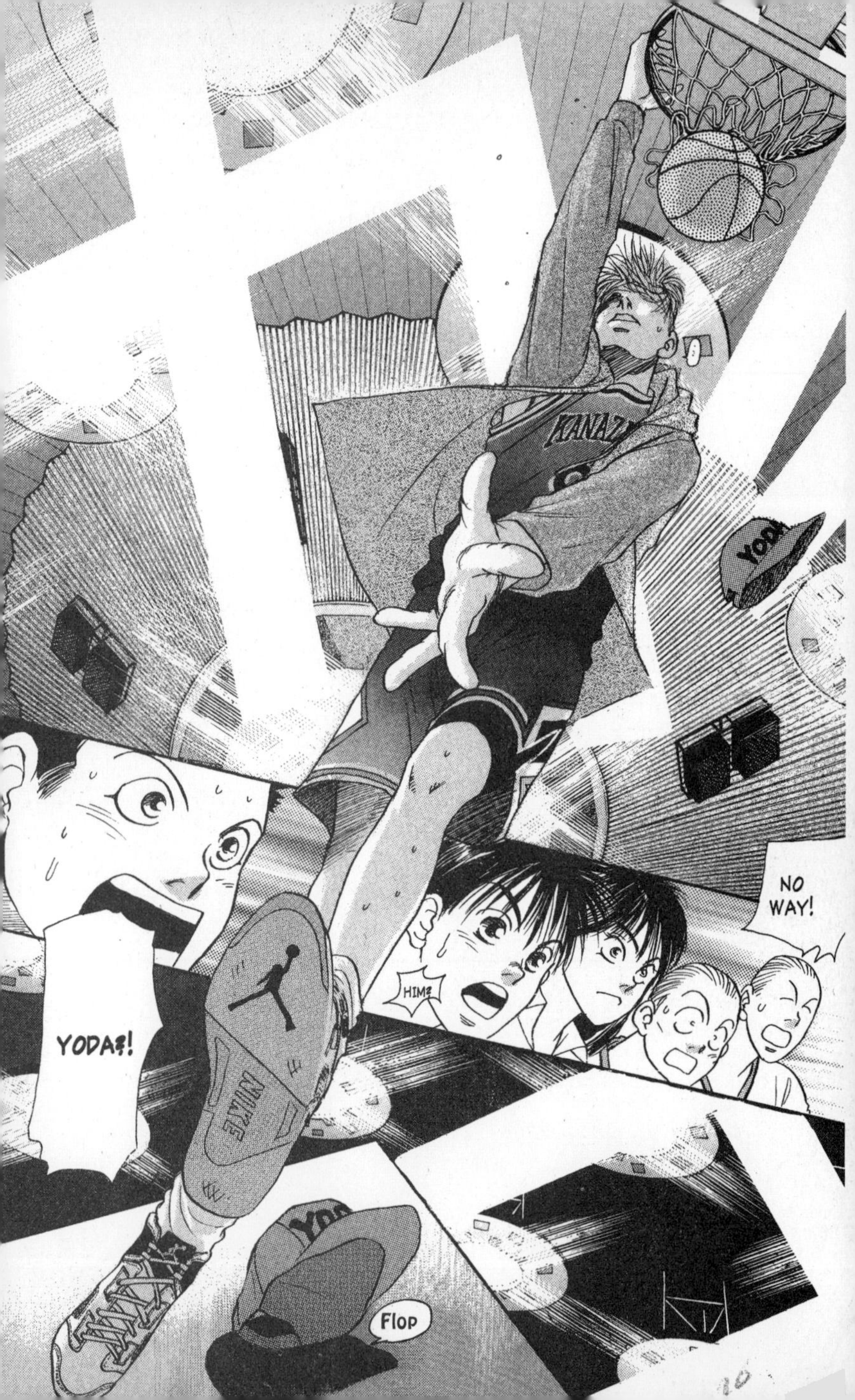
NO WAY!
HIM?
YODA?!
Flop

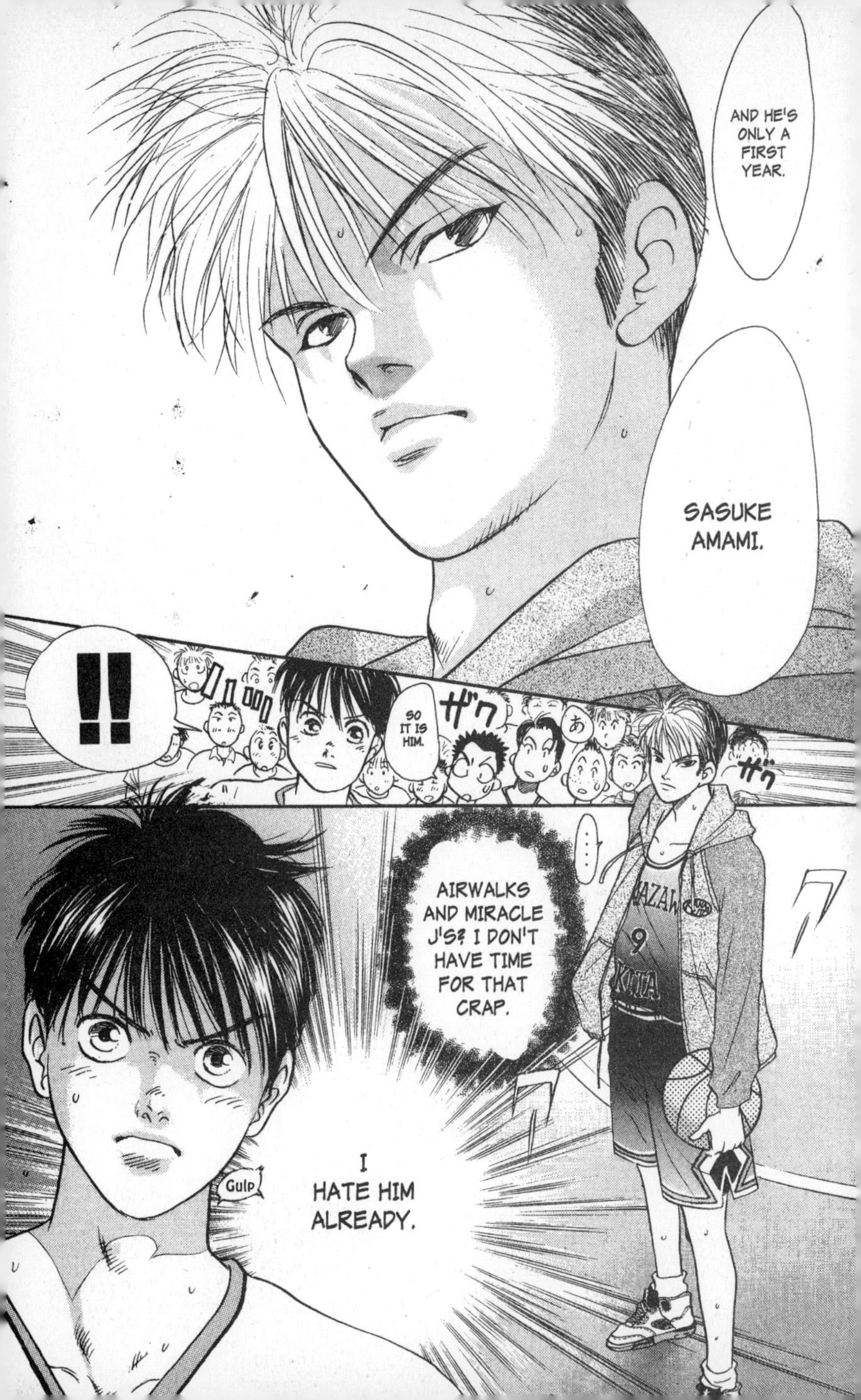
AND HE'S ONLY A FIRST YEAR.
SASUKE AMAMI.
ザワ
あ
ザワ
SO IT IS HIM.
!!
. . .
AIRWALKS AND MIRACLE J'S? I DON'T HAVE TIME FOR THAT CRAP.
I HATE HIM ALREADY.
Gulp

You're Reading...

REBOUND

And if you're enjoying the character of Nate, you'll love TOKYOPOP's new feature length film...THE MONKEY BOY WONDER, the thrilling tale of an aging caped crusader and his simian companion saving the world one banana at a time.

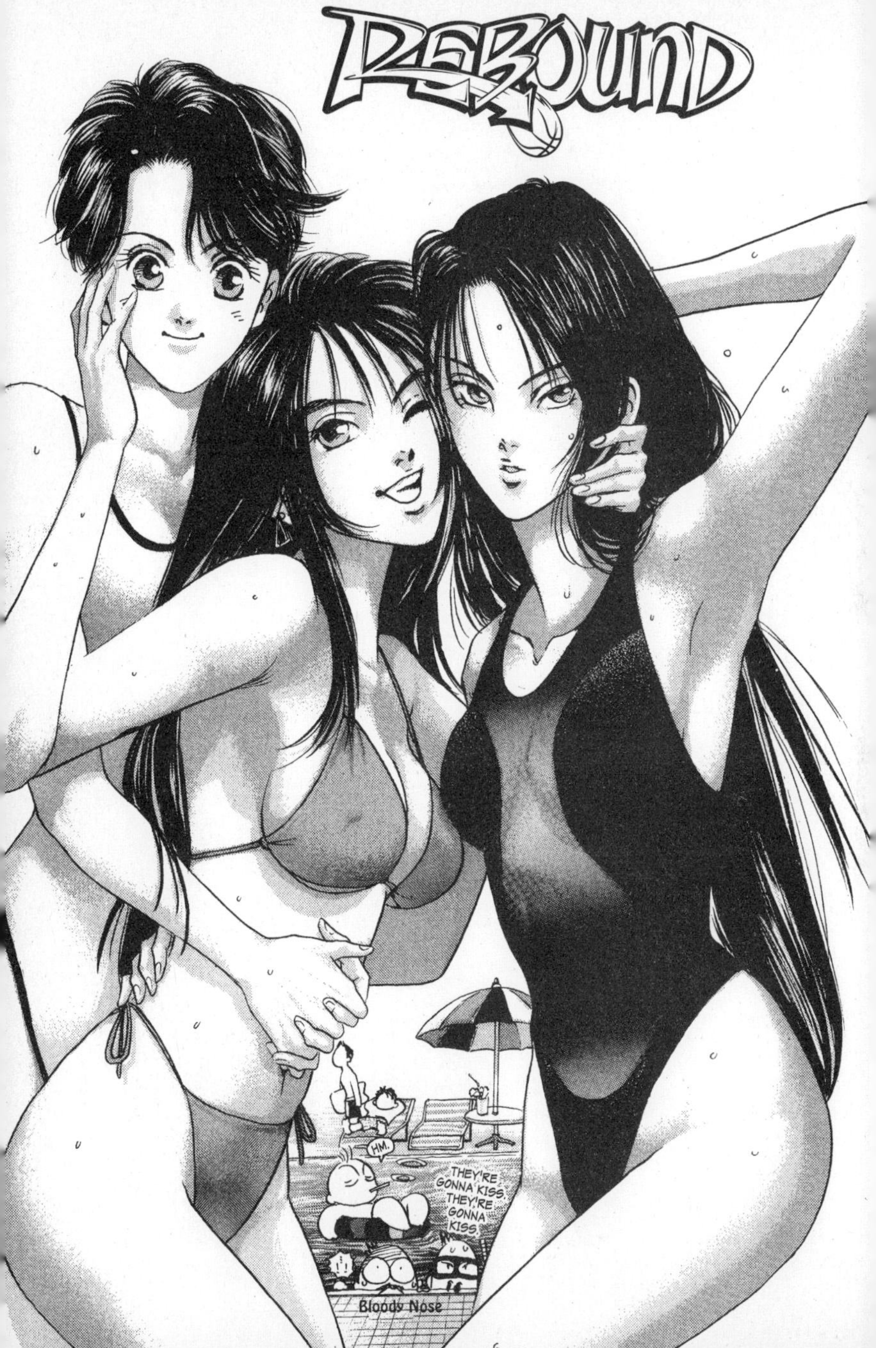
REBOUND
THEY'RE GONNA KISS. THEY'RE GONNA KISS.
HM.
Bloody Nose

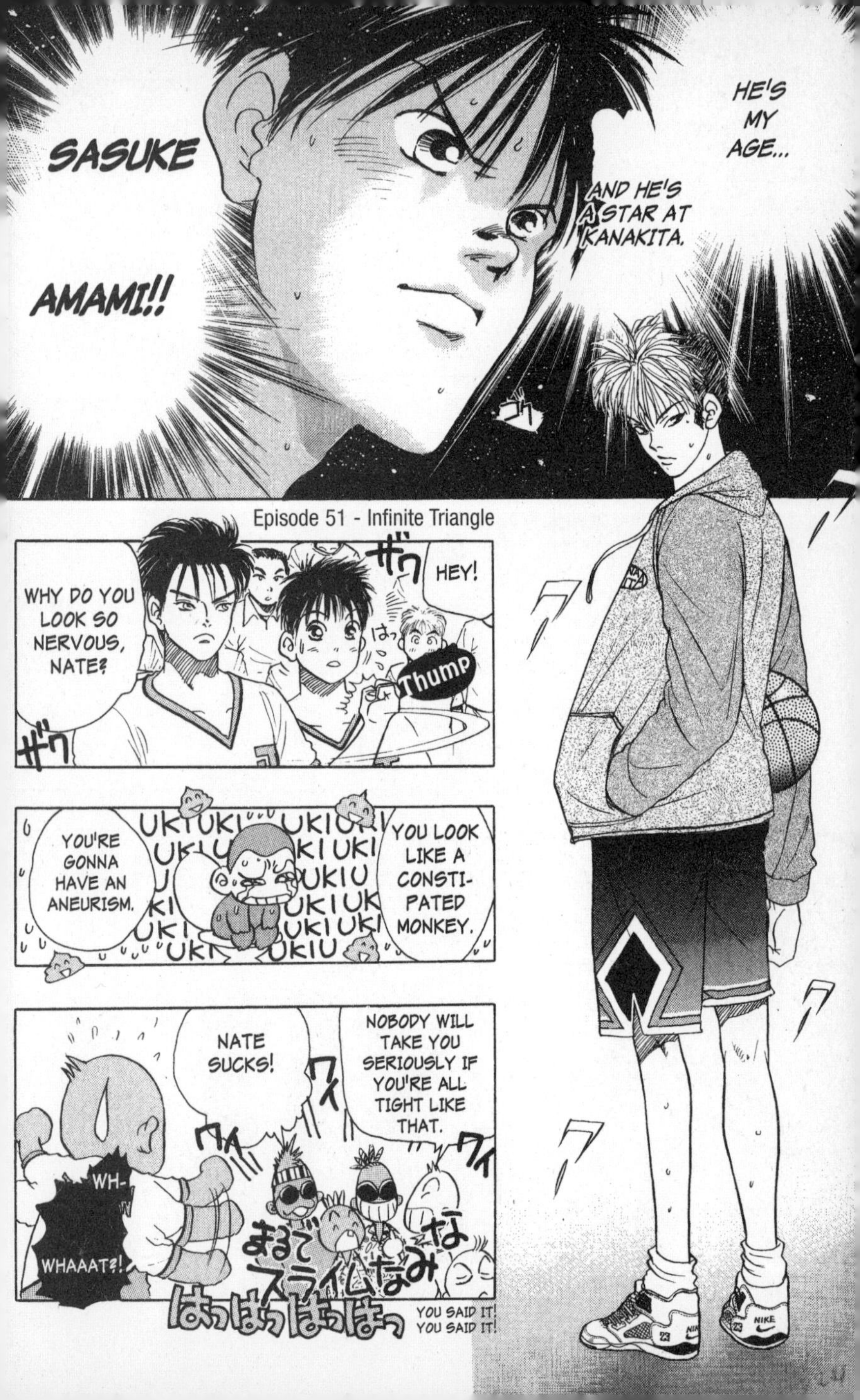
HE'S MY AGE...
AND HE'S A STAR AT KANAKITA.
SASUKE AMAMI!!
Episode 51 - Infinite Triangle
HEY!
ザワ
WHY DO YOU LOOK SO NERVOUS, NATE?
はっ
Thump
YOU LOOK LIKE A CONSTI-PATED MONKEY.
YOU'RE GONNA HAVE AN ANEURISM.
NOBODY WILL TAKE YOU SERIOUSLY IF YOU'RE ALL TIGHT LIKE THAT.
NATE SUCKS!
WH-
WHAAAT?!
まるでスライムなみな
はっはっはっはっ
YOU SAID IT! YOU SAID IT!

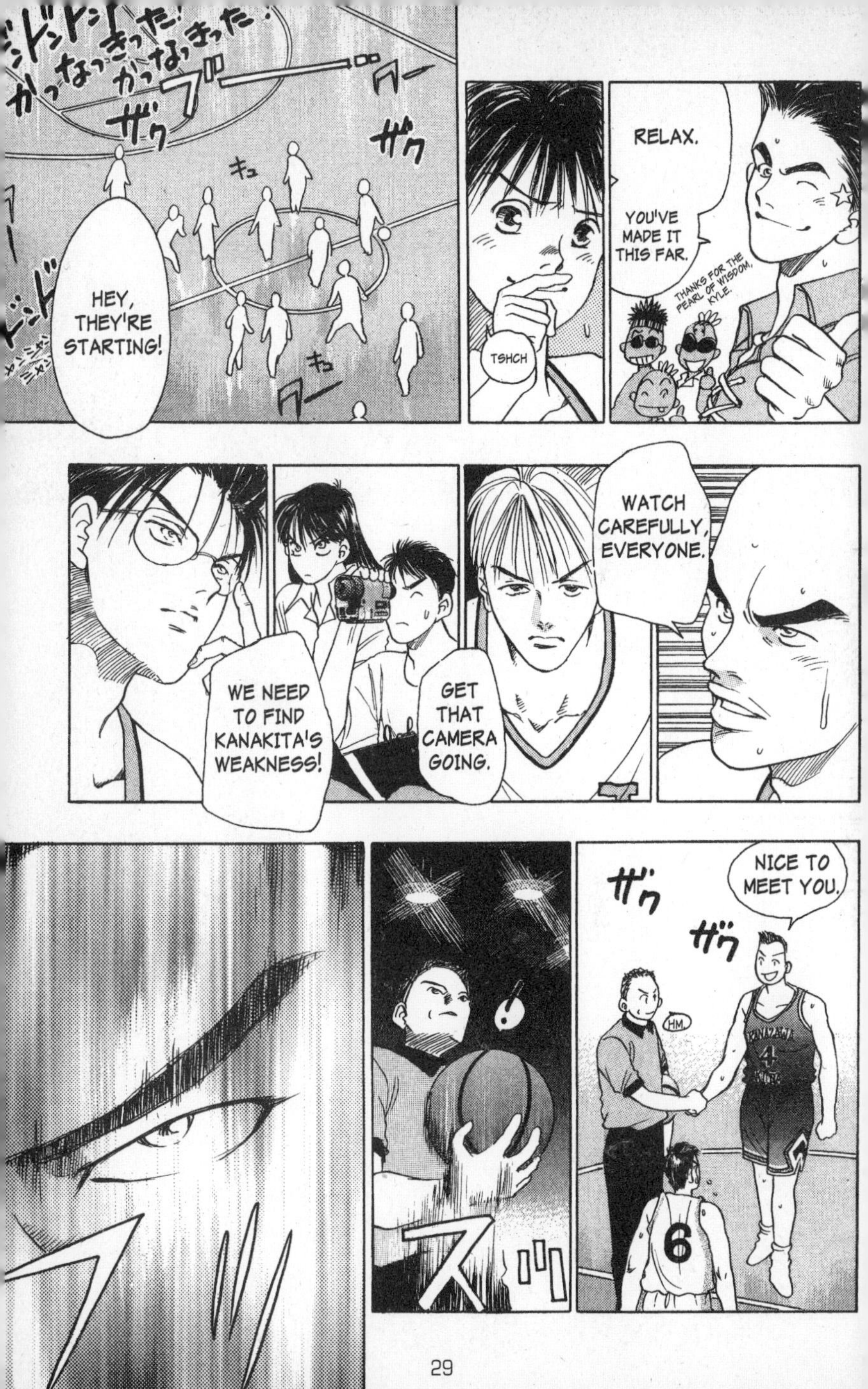
RELAX.
YOU'VE MADE IT THIS FAR.
THANKS FOR THE PEARL OF WISDOM, KYLE.
TSHCH
ザク
ザク
キュ
HEY, THEY'RE STARTING!
キュ
ワー
WATCH CAREFULLY, EVERYONE.
GET THAT CAMERA GOING.
WE NEED TO FIND KANAKITA'S WEAKNESS!
NICE TO MEET YOU.
ザク
ザク
HM.
ス

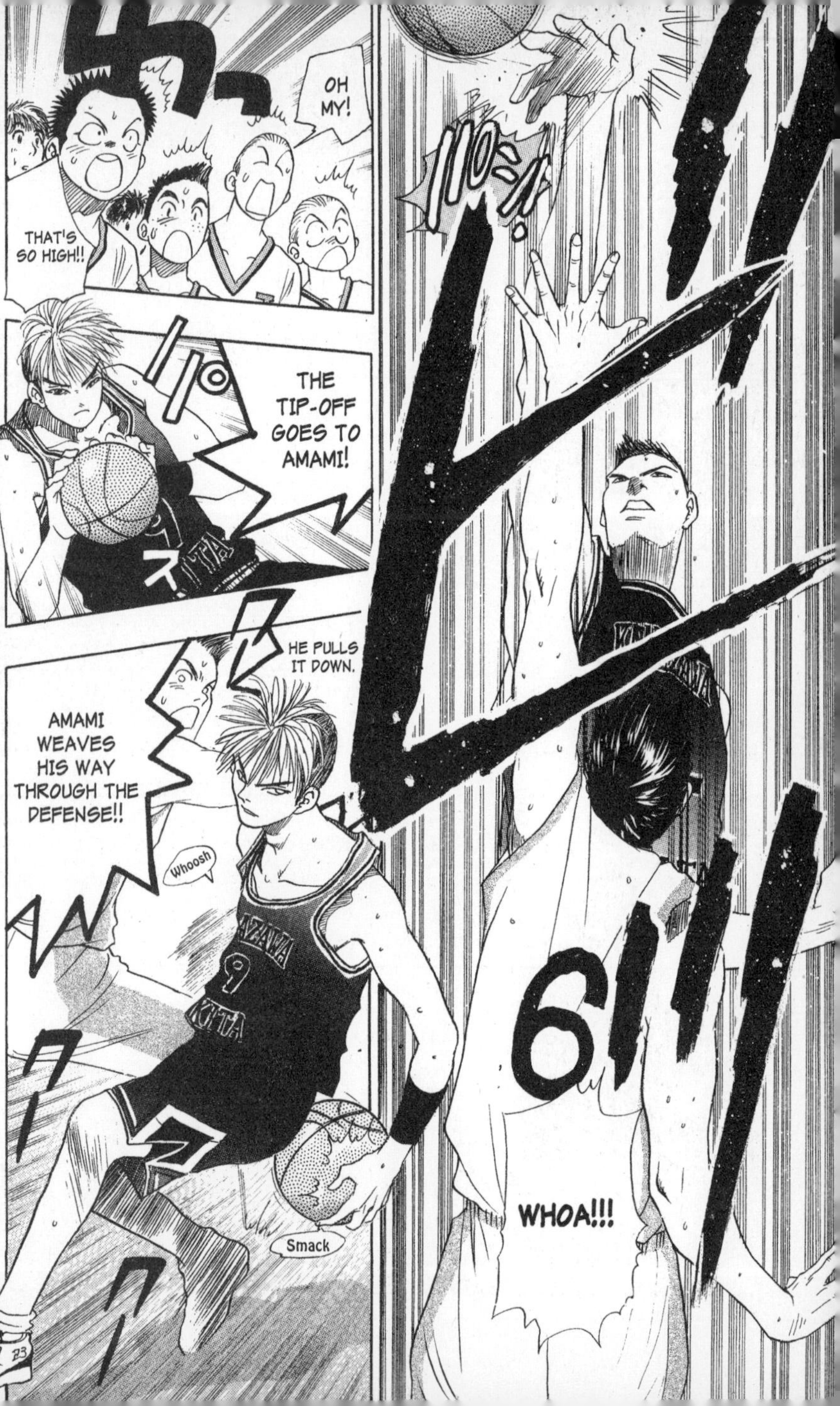
WHOA!!!
OH MY!
THAT'S SO HIGH!!
THE TIP-OFF GOES TO AMAMI!
HE PULLS IT DOWN.
AMAMI WEAVES HIS WAY THROUGH THE DEFENSE!!
Whoosh
Smack

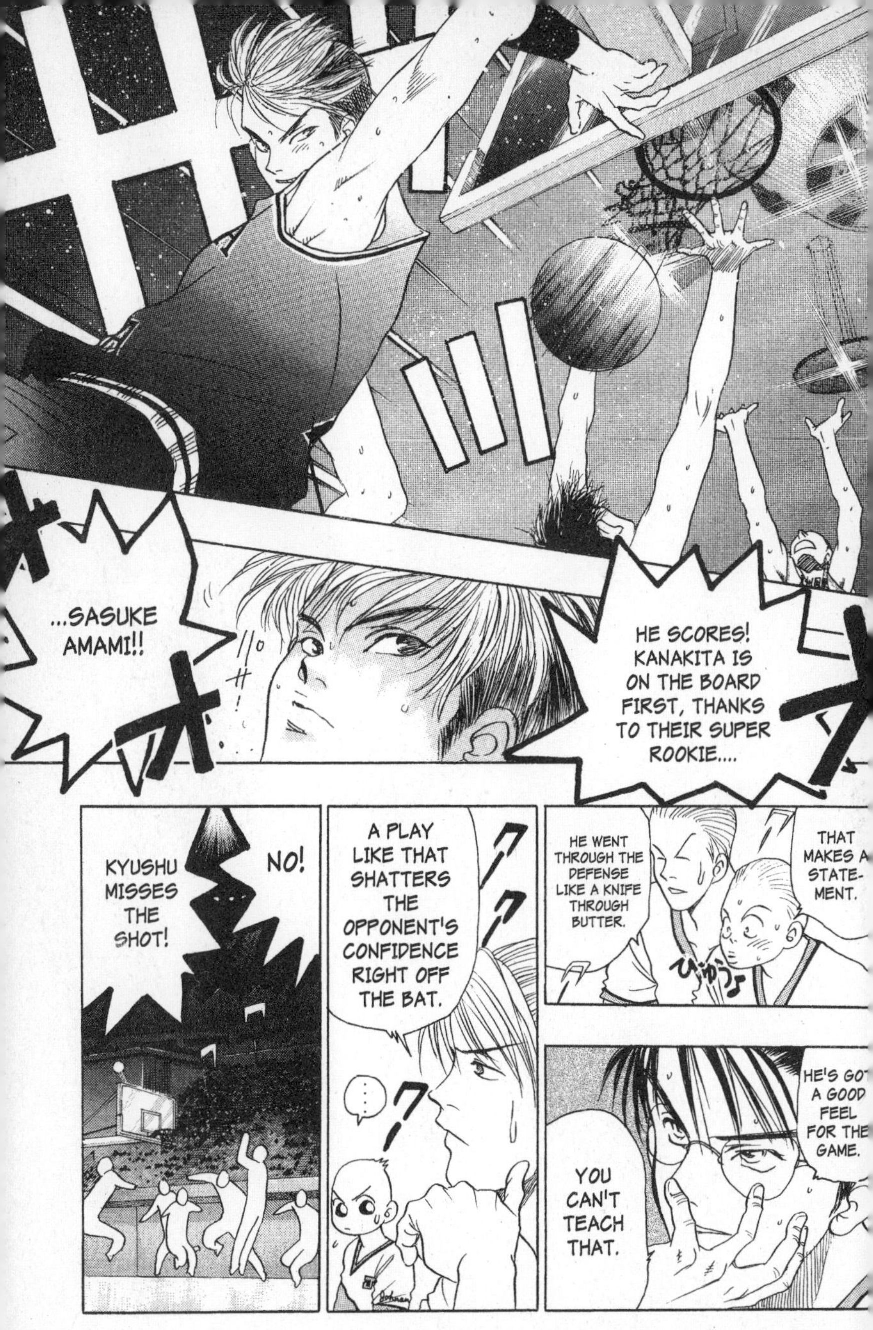
HE SCORES! KANAKITA IS ON THE BOARD FIRST, THANKS TO THEIR SUPER ROOKIE....
...SASUKE AMAMI!!
THAT MAKES A STATEMENT.
HE WENT THROUGH THE DEFENSE LIKE A KNIFE THROUGH BUTTER.
HE'S GOT A GOOD FEEL FOR THE GAME.
YOU CAN'T TEACH THAT.
A PLAY LIKE THAT SHATTERS THE OPPONENT'S CONFIDENCE RIGHT OFF THE BAT.
...
NO!
KYUSHU MISSES THE SHOT!

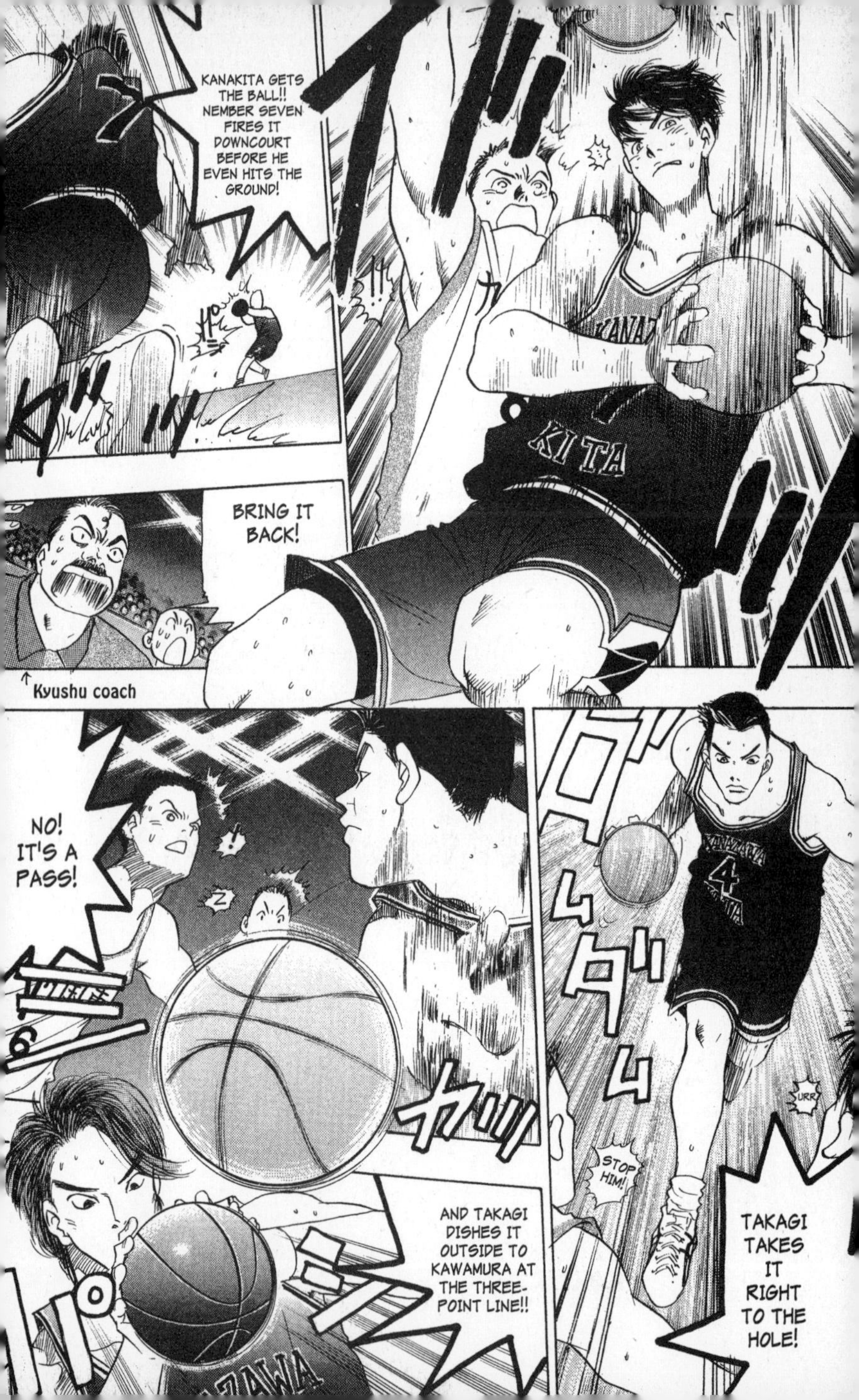
KANAKITA GETS THE BALL!! NEMBER SEVEN FIRES IT DOWNCOURT BEFORE HE EVEN HITS THE GROUND!
BRING IT BACK!
Kyushu coach
TAKAGI TAKES IT RIGHT TO THE HOLE!
URR
STOP HIM!
NO! IT'S A PASS!
AND TAKAGI DISHES IT OUTSIDE TO KAWAMURA AT THE THREE-POINT LINE!!

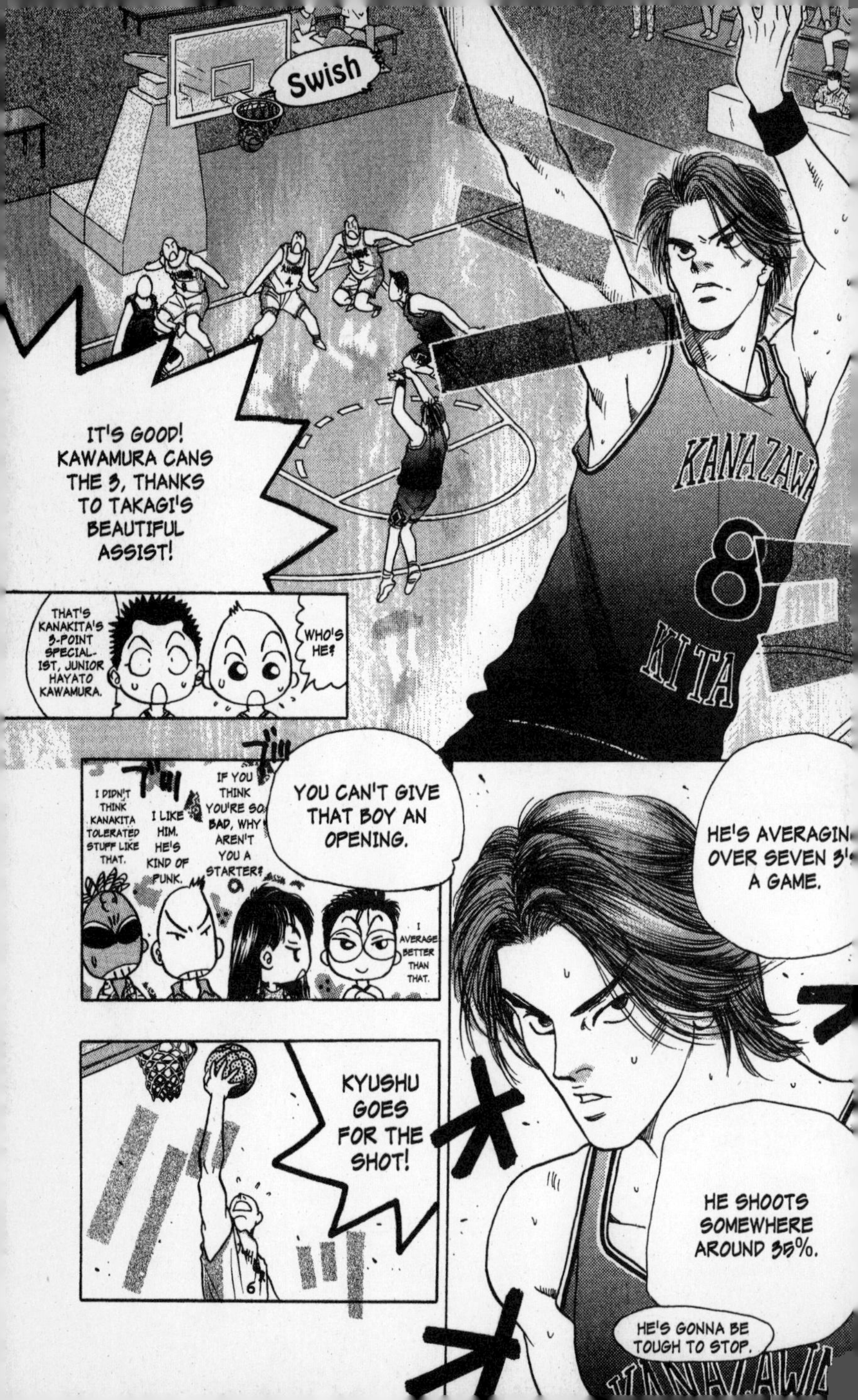
Swish
IT'S GOOD! KAWAMURA CANS THE 3, THANKS TO TAKAGI'S BEAUTIFUL ASSIST!
KANAZAWA 8 KITA
WHO'S HE?
THAT'S KANAKITA'S 3-POINT SPECIAL-IST, JUNIOR HAYATO KAWAMURA.
HE'S AVERAGIN OVER SEVEN 3' A GAME.
HE SHOOTS SOMEWHERE AROUND 35%.
HE'S GONNA BE TOUGH TO STOP.
YOU CAN'T GIVE THAT BOY AN OPENING.
I AVERAGE BETTER THAN THAT.
IF YOU THINK YOU'RE SO BAD, WHY AREN'T YOU A STARTER?
I LIKE HIM. HE'S KIND OF PUNK.
I DIDN'T THINK KANAKITA TOLERATED STUFF LIKE THAT.
KYUSHU GOES FOR THE SHOT!

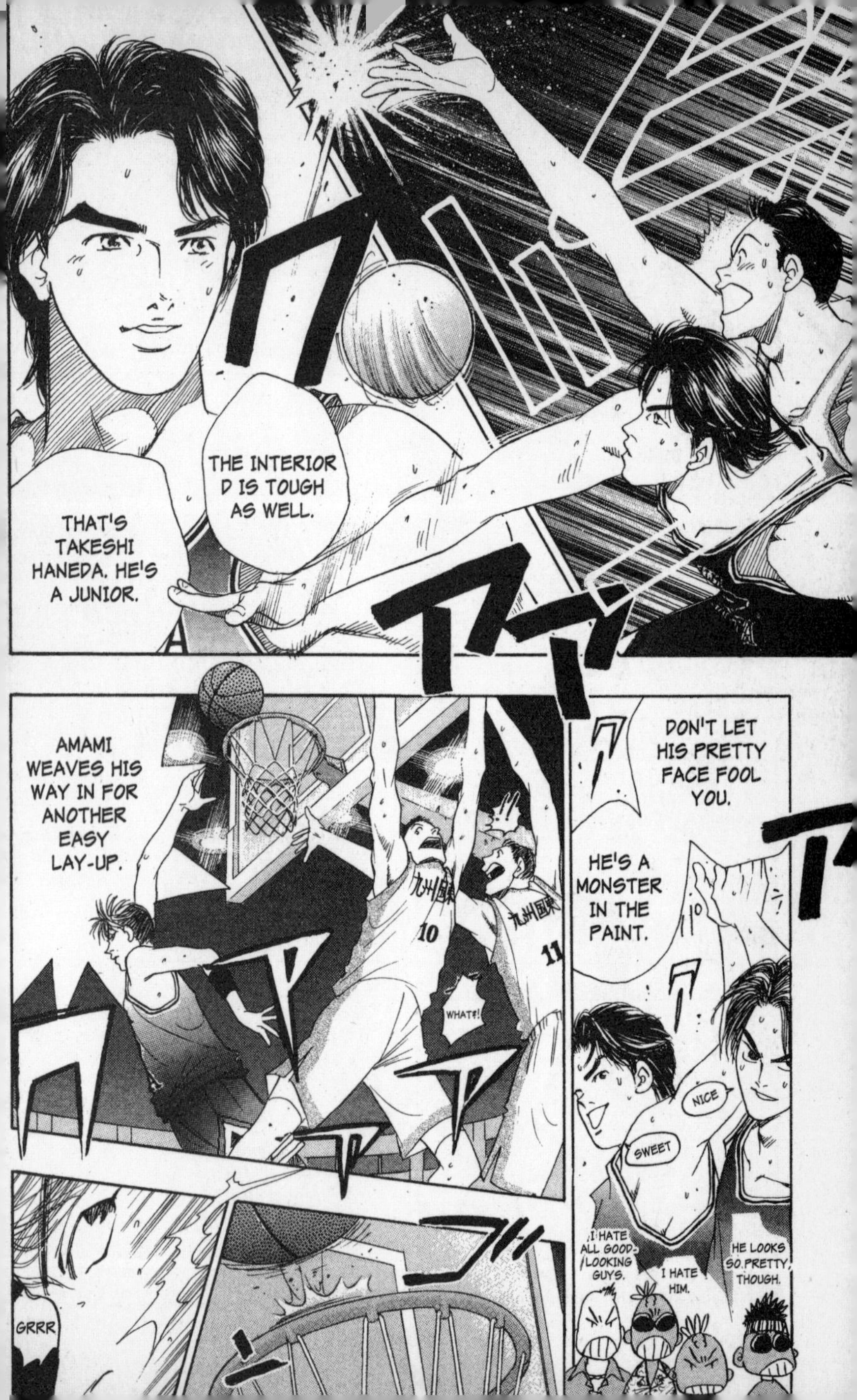
THE INTERIOR D IS TOUGH AS WELL.
THAT'S TAKESHI HANEDA. HE'S A JUNIOR.
DON'T LET HIS PRETTY FACE FOOL YOU.
HE'S A MONSTER IN THE PAINT.
NICE
SWEET
HE LOOKS SO PRETTY, THOUGH.
I HATE HIM.
I HATE ALL GOOD-LOOKING GUYS.
WHAT?!
AMAMI WEAVES HIS WAY IN FOR ANOTHER EASY LAY-UP.
10
11
GRRR

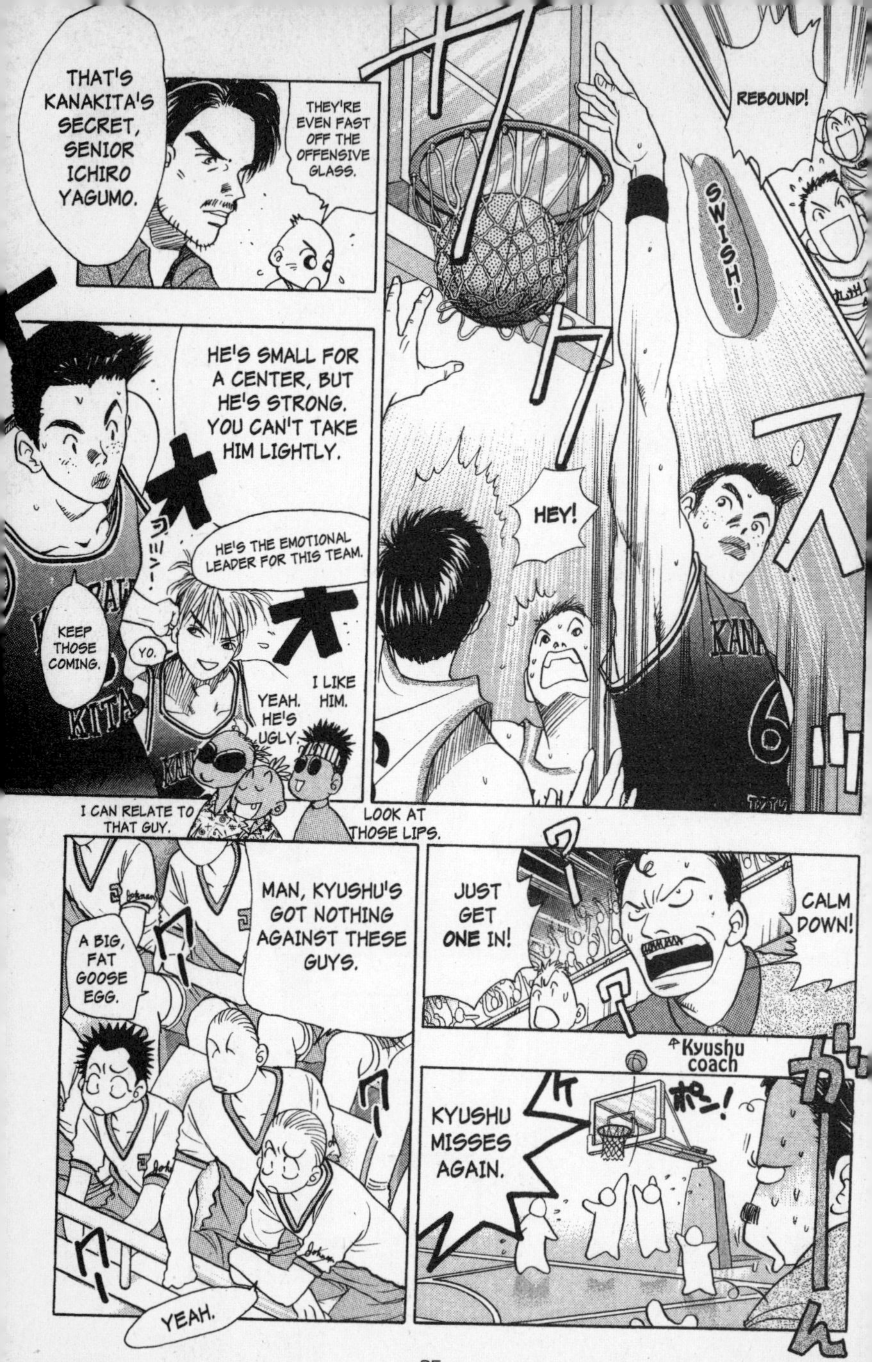
REBOUND!
SWISH!
HEY!
THEY'RE EVEN FAST OFF THE OFFENSIVE GLASS.
THAT'S KANAKITA'S SECRET, SENIOR ICHIRO YAGUMO.
HE'S SMALL FOR A CENTER, BUT HE'S STRONG. YOU CAN'T TAKE HIM LIGHTLY.
HE'S THE EMOTIONAL LEADER FOR THIS TEAM.
KEEP THOSE COMING.
YO.
I LIKE HIM.
YEAH. HE'S UGLY.
LOOK AT THOSE LIPS.
I CAN RELATE TO THAT GUY.
CALM DOWN!
JUST GET ONE IN!
↑Kyushu coach
KYUSHU MISSES AGAIN.
MAN, KYUSHU'S GOT NOTHING AGAINST THESE GUYS.
A BIG, FAT GOOSE EGG.
YEAH.

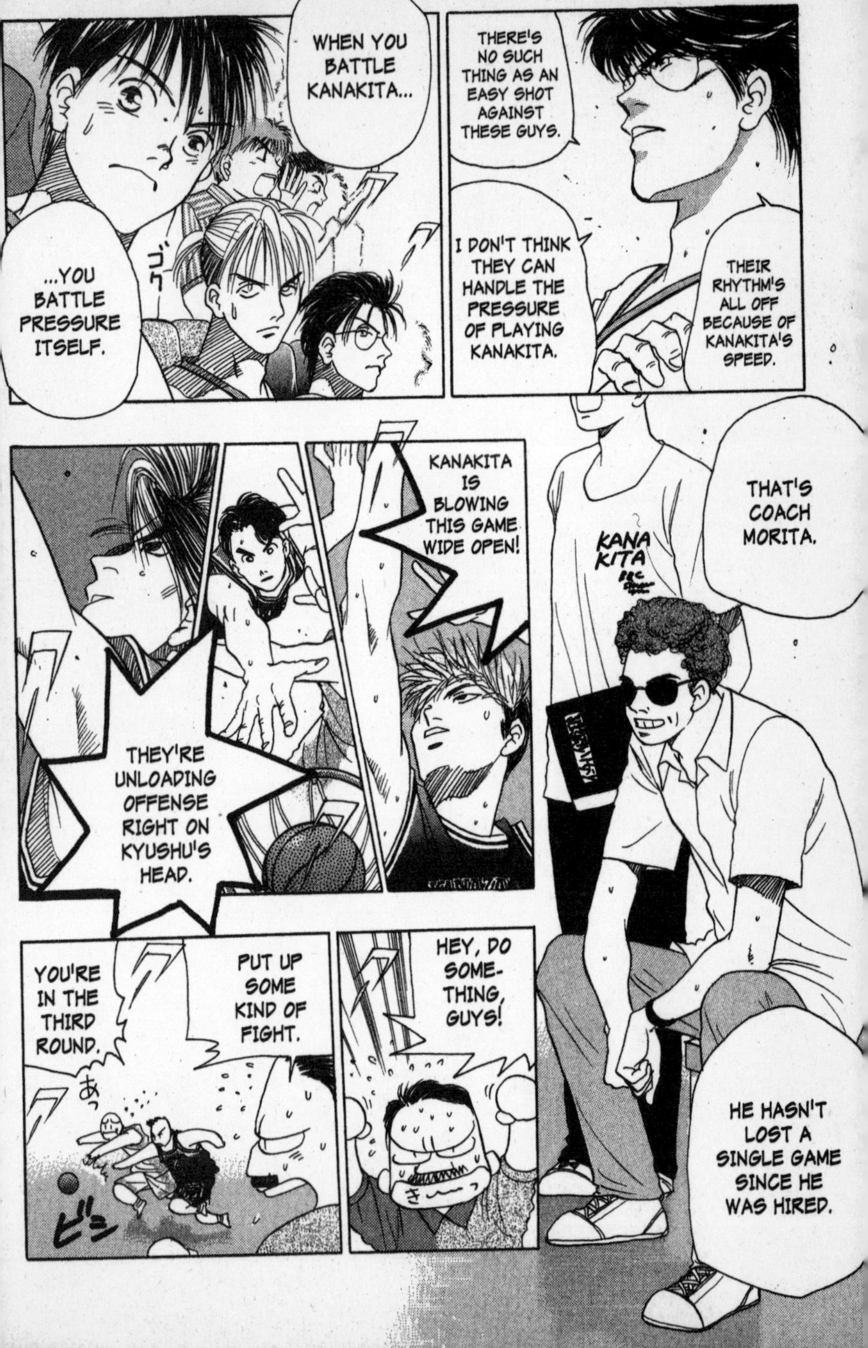
THERE'S NO SUCH THING AS AN EASY SHOT AGAINST THESE GUYS.
I DON'T THINK THEY CAN HANDLE THE PRESSURE OF PLAYING KANAKITA.
THEIR RHYTHM'S ALL OFF BECAUSE OF KANAKITA'S SPEED.
WHEN YOU BATTLE KANAKITA...
ゴク
...YOU BATTLE PRESSURE ITSELF.
THAT'S COACH MORITA.
KANA KITA
HE HASN'T LOST A SINGLE GAME SINCE HE WAS HIRED.
KANAKITA IS BLOWING THIS GAME WIDE OPEN!
THEY'RE UNLOADING OFFENSE RIGHT ON KYUSHU'S HEAD.
HEY, DO SOME-THING, GUYS!
き〜〜
PUT UP SOME KIND OF FIGHT.
YOU'RE IN THE THIRD ROUND.
あっ

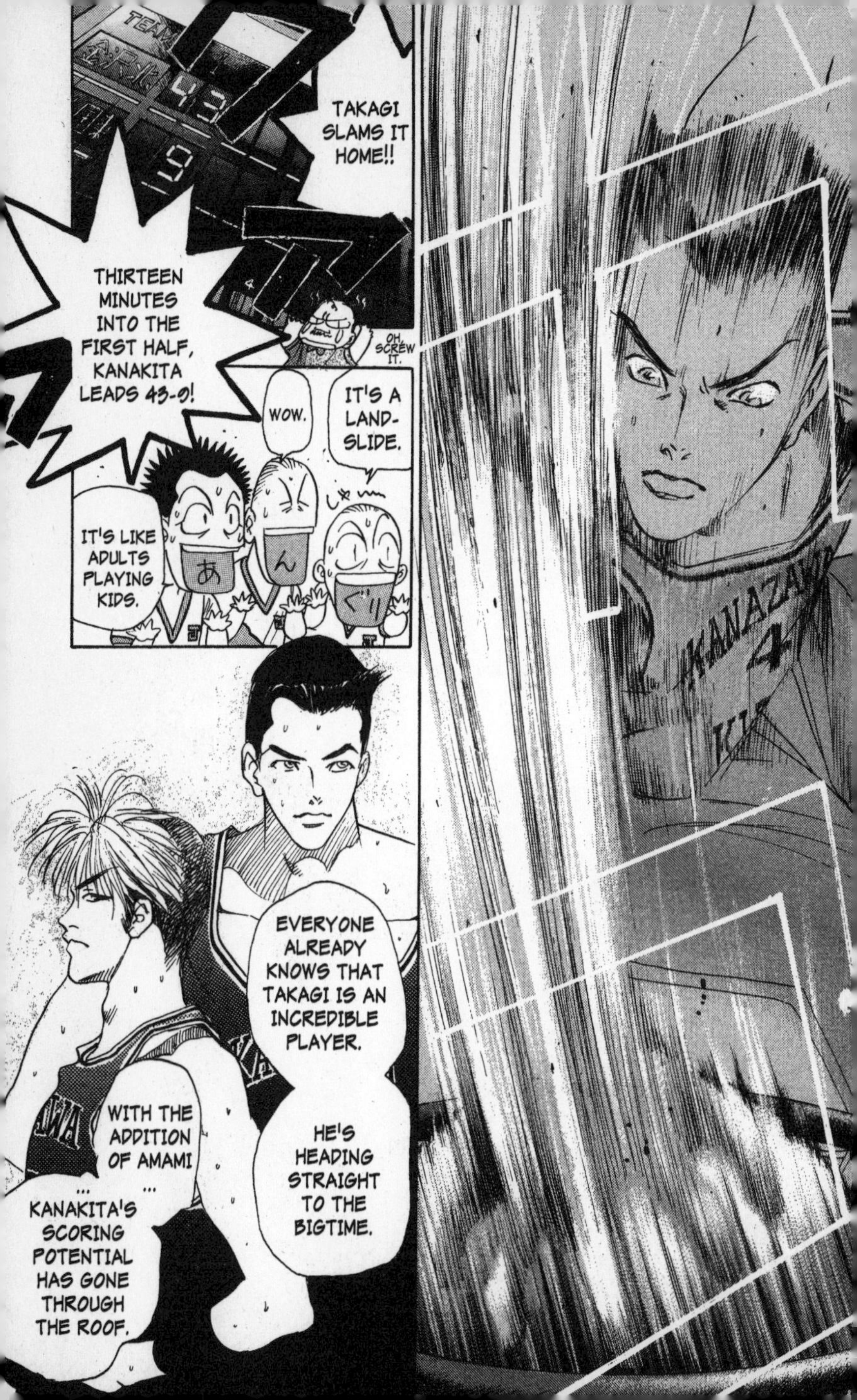
TAKAGI SLAMS IT HOME!!
THIRTEEN MINUTES INTO THE FIRST HALF, KANAKITA LEADS 43-9!
OH, SCREW IT.
IT'S A LANDSLIDE.
WOW.
IT'S LIKE ADULTS PLAYING KIDS.
EVERYONE ALREADY KNOWS THAT TAKAGI IS AN INCREDIBLE PLAYER.
HE'S HEADING STRAIGHT TO THE BIGTIME.
WITH THE ADDITION OF AMAMI ...
... KANAKITA'S SCORING POTENTIAL HAS GONE THROUGH THE ROOF.

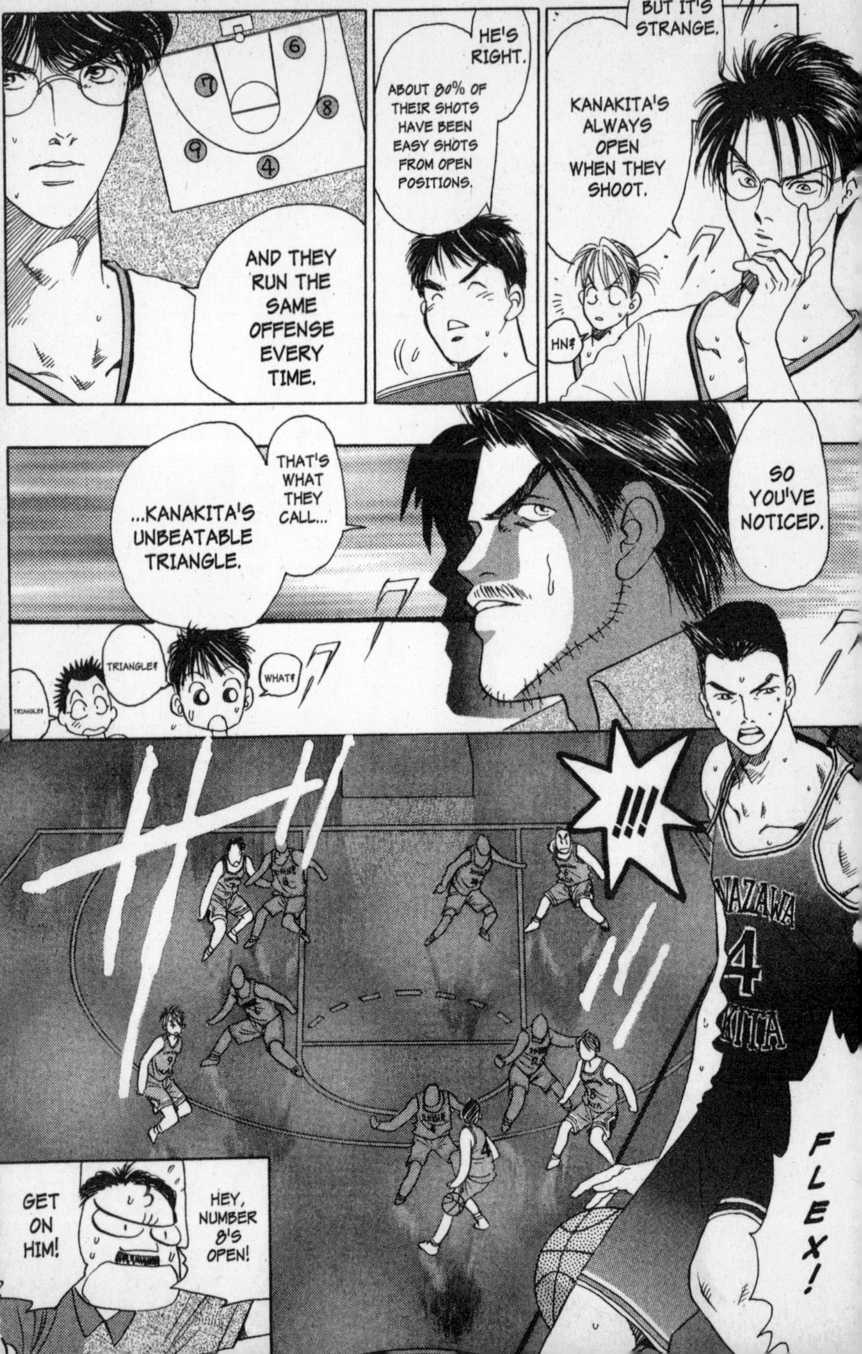
BUT IT'S STRANGE.
KANAKITA'S ALWAYS OPEN WHEN THEY SHOOT.
HN?
HE'S RIGHT.
ABOUT 80% OF THEIR SHOTS HAVE BEEN EASY SHOTS FROM OPEN POSITIONS.
AND THEY RUN THE SAME OFFENSE EVERY TIME.
SO YOU'VE NOTICED.
THAT'S WHAT THEY CALL...
...KANAKITA'S UNBEATABLE TRIANGLE.
WHAT?
TRIANGLE?
TRIANGLE?
!!!
FLEX!
HEY, NUMBER 8'S OPEN!
GET ON HIM!

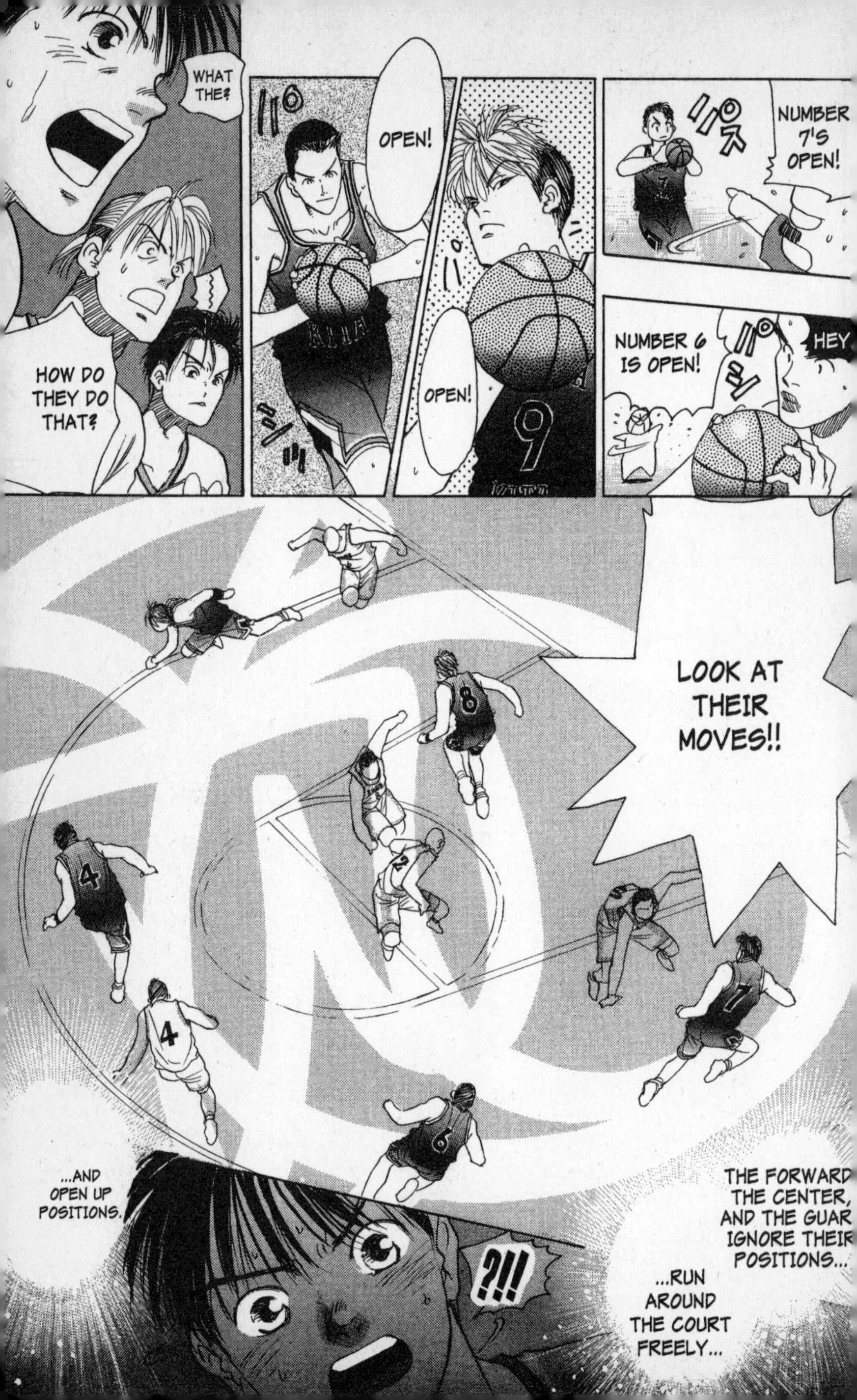
NUMBER 7'S OPEN!
HEY
NUMBER 6 IS OPEN!
OPEN!
OPEN!
WHAT THE?
HOW DO THEY DO THAT?
LOOK AT THEIR MOVES!!
THE FORWARD THE CENTER, AND THE GUAR IGNORE THEIR POSITIONS...
...RUN AROUND THE COURT FREELY...
?!!
...AND OPEN UP POSITIONS.

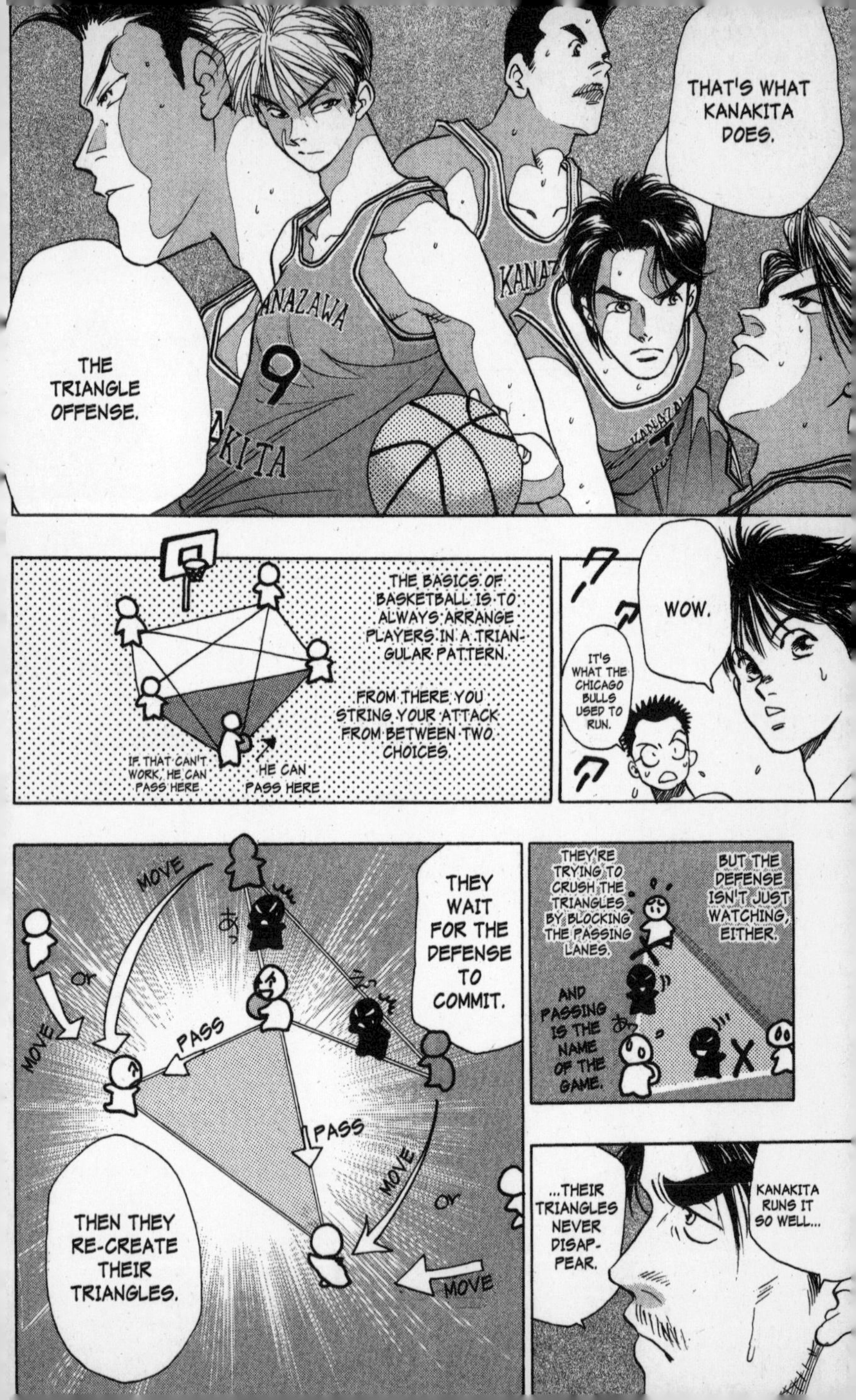
THAT'S WHAT KANAKITA DOES.
THE TRIANGLE OFFENSE.
WOW.
IT'S WHAT THE CHICAGO BULLS USED TO RUN.
THE BASICS OF BASKETBALL IS TO ALWAYS ARRANGE PLAYERS IN A TRIANGULAR PATTERN.
FROM THERE YOU STRING YOUR ATTACK FROM BETWEEN TWO CHOICES.
HE CAN PASS HERE
IF THAT CAN'T WORK, HE CAN PASS HERE
BUT THE DEFENSE ISN'T JUST WATCHING, EITHER.
THEY'RE TRYING TO CRUSH THE TRIANGLES BY BLOCKING THE PASSING LANES.
AND PASSING IS THE NAME OF THE GAME.
KANAKITA RUNS IT SO WELL...
...THEIR TRIANGLES NEVER DISAPPEAR.
THEY WAIT FOR THE DEFENSE TO COMMIT.
MOVE
or
MOVE
PASS
PASS
MOVE
or
MOVE
THEN THEY RE-CREATE THEIR TRIANGLES.

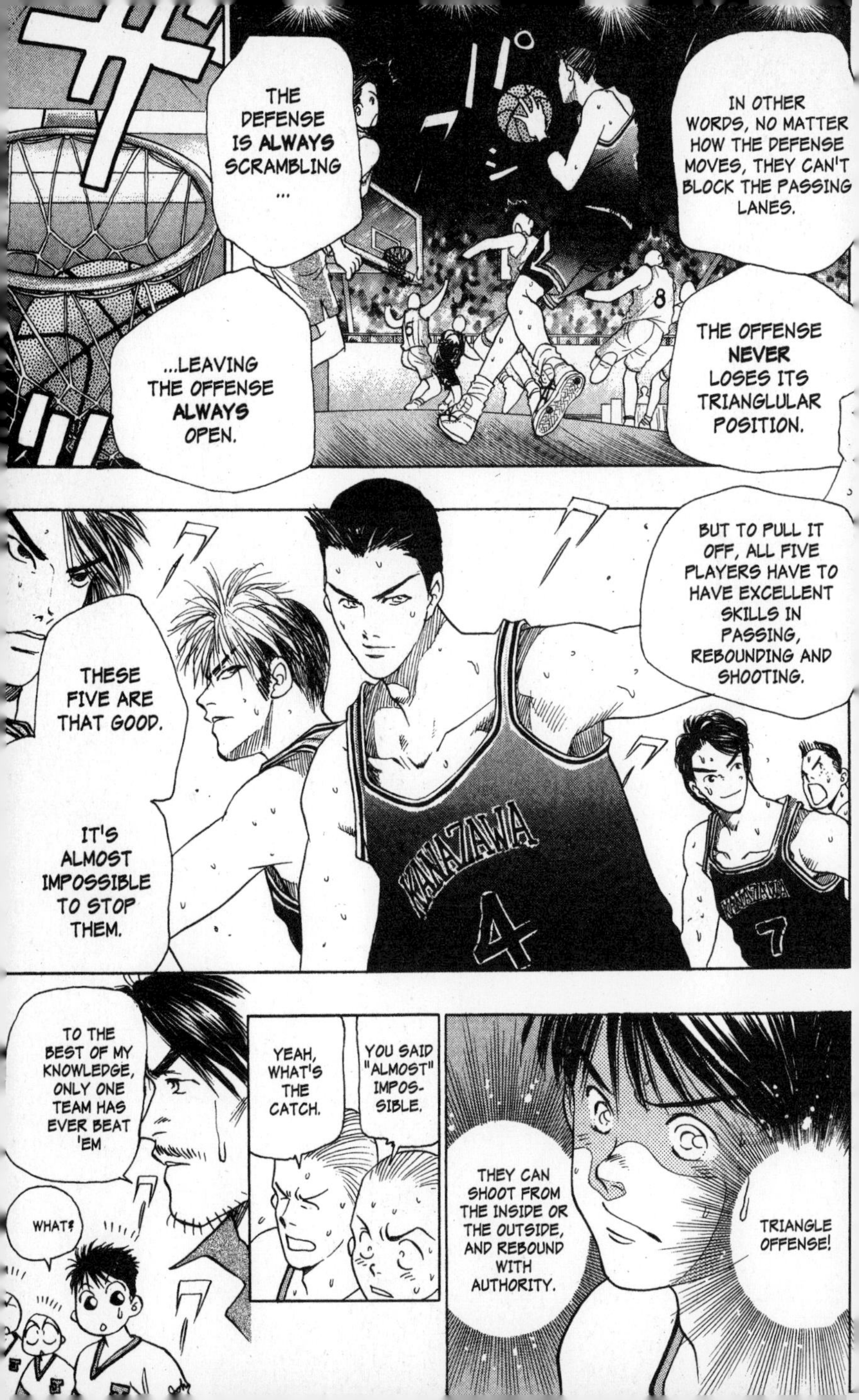
IN OTHER WORDS, NO MATTER HOW THE DEFENSE MOVES, THEY CAN'T BLOCK THE PASSING LANES.
THE OFFENSE NEVER LOSES ITS TRIANGLULAR POSITION.
THE DEFENSE IS ALWAYS SCRAMBLING ...
...LEAVING THE OFFENSE ALWAYS OPEN.
BUT TO PULL IT OFF, ALL FIVE PLAYERS HAVE TO HAVE EXCELLENT SKILLS IN PASSING, REBOUNDING AND SHOOTING.
THESE FIVE ARE THAT GOOD.
IT'S ALMOST IMPOSSIBLE TO STOP THEM.
TRIANGLE OFFENSE!
THEY CAN SHOOT FROM THE INSIDE OR THE OUTSIDE, AND REBOUND WITH AUTHORITY.
YOU SAID "ALMOST" IMPOS-SIBLE.
YEAH, WHAT'S THE CATCH.
TO THE BEST OF MY KNOWLEDGE, ONLY ONE TEAM HAS EVER BEAT 'EM
WHAT?

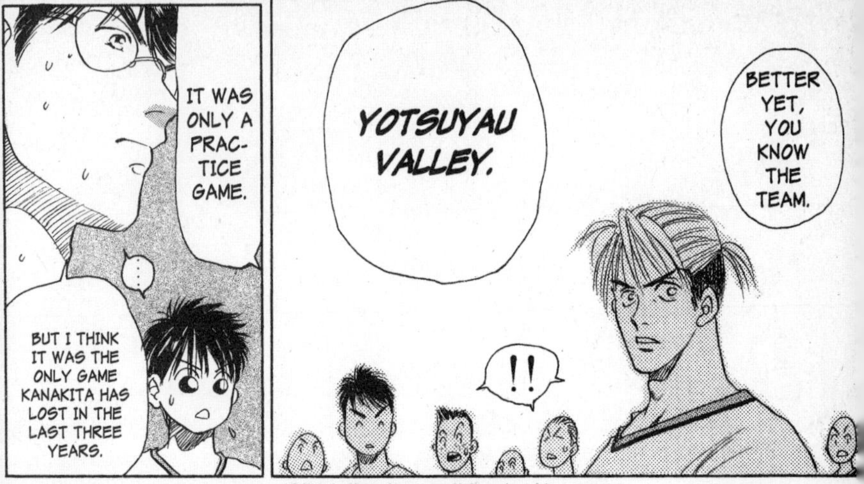
BETTER YET, YOU KNOW THE TEAM.
YOTSUYAU VALLEY.
!!
IT WAS ONLY A PRAC-TICE GAME.
...
BUT I THINK IT WAS THE ONLY GAME KANAKITA HAS LOST IN THE LAST THREE YEARS.

*Editor's Note: Yotsuyau Valley played in a summer league against Kanakita in Harlem Beat 11.

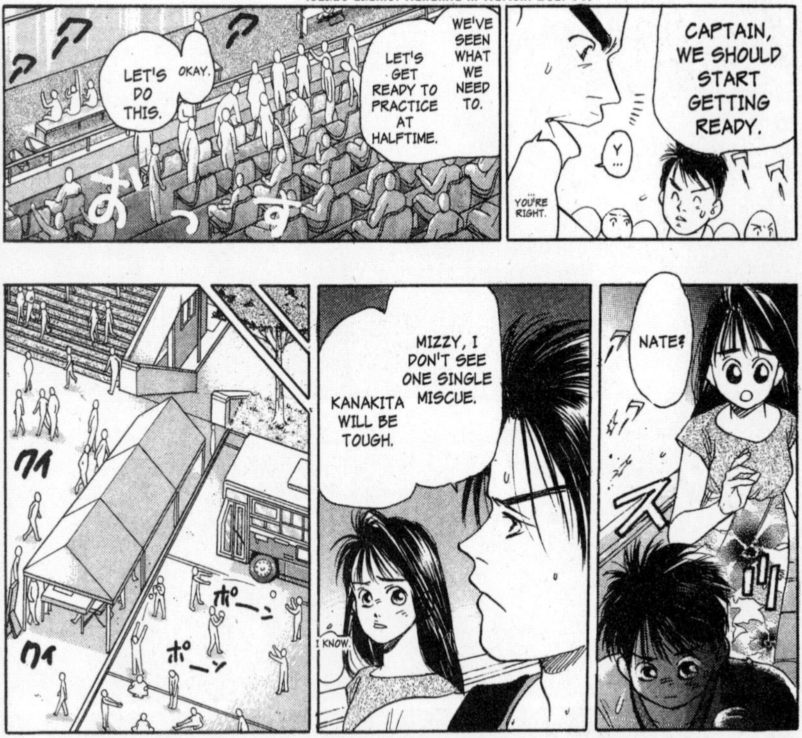
CAPTAIN, WE SHOULD START GETTING READY.
Y...
YOU'RE RIGHT.
WE'VE SEEN WHAT WE NEED TO.
LET'S GET READY TO PRACTICE AT HALFTIME.
OKAY.
LET'S DO THIS.
おっす
NATE?
MIZZY, I DON'T SEE ONE SINGLE MISCUE.
KANAKITA WILL BE TOUGH.
I KNOW.
ポーン
ポーン
ワイ
ワイ

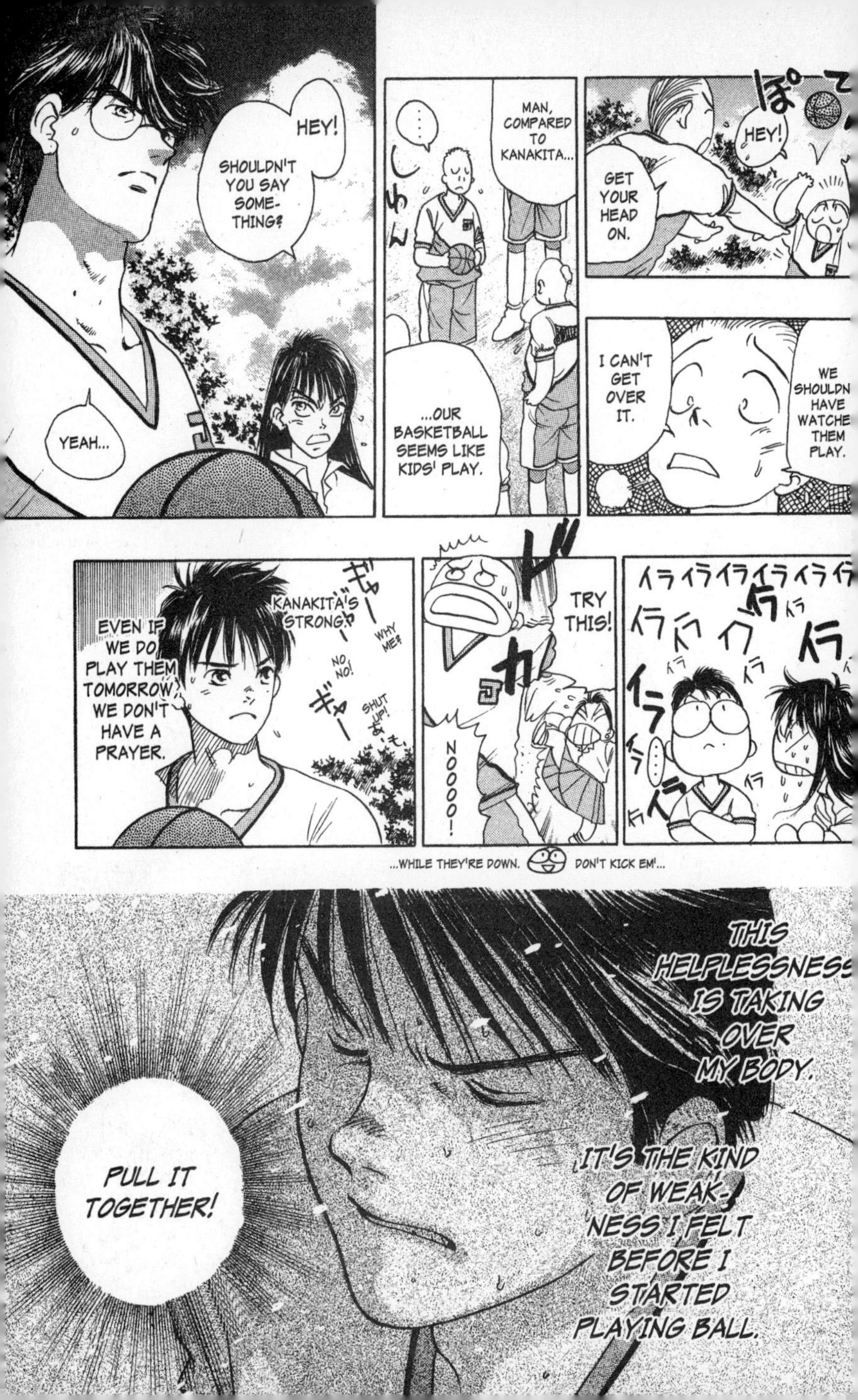
ぽて
HEY!
GET YOUR HEAD ON.
WE SHOULDN HAVE WATCHE THEM PLAY.
I CAN'T GET OVER IT.
MAN, COMPARED TO KANAKITA...
...OUR BASKETBALL SEEMS LIKE KIDS' PLAY.
...
しゅん
HEY!
SHOULDN'T YOU SAY SOME-THING?
YEAH...
イライライライライライライ
TRY THIS!
ドカ
NOOOOO!
KANAKITA'S STRONG.
EVEN IF WE DO PLAY THEM TOMORROW, WE DON'T HAVE A PRAYER.
ギャー
WHY ME?
NO NO!
SHUT UP!
ギャー
DON'T KICK EM'...
...WHILE THEY'RE DOWN.
THIS HELPLESSNESS IS TAKING OVER MY BODY.
IT'S THE KIND OF WEAK-NESS I FELT BEFORE I STARTED PLAYING BALL.
PULL IT TOGETHER!

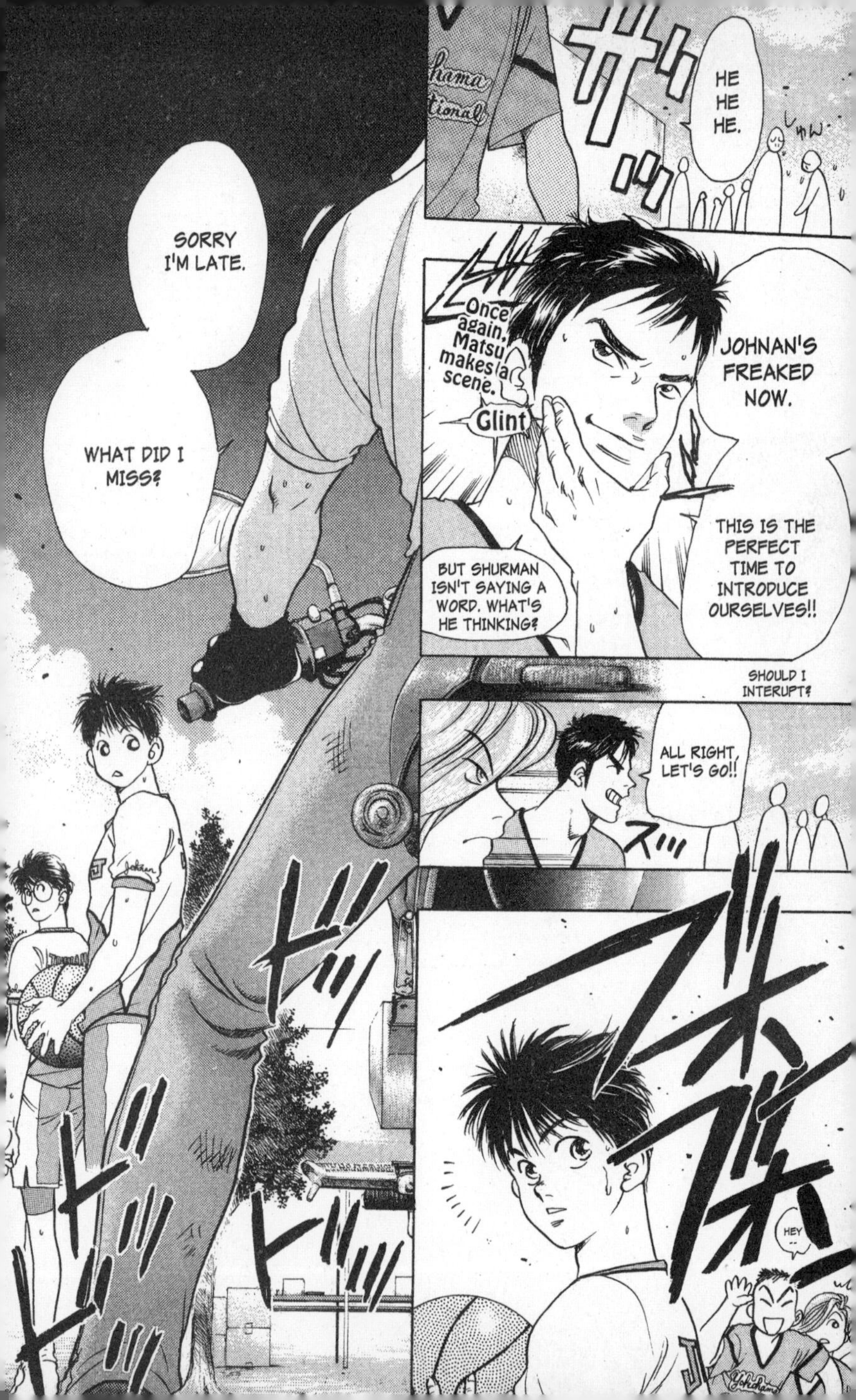
HE HE HE.
JOHNAN'S FREAKED NOW.
THIS IS THE PERFECT TIME TO INTRODUCE OURSELVES!!
Once again, Matsu makes a scene.
Glint
BUT SHURMAN ISN'T SAYING A WORD. WHAT'S HE THINKING?
SHOULD I INTERUPT?
ALL RIGHT, LET'S GO!!
HEY --
SORRY I'M LATE.
WHAT DID I MISS?

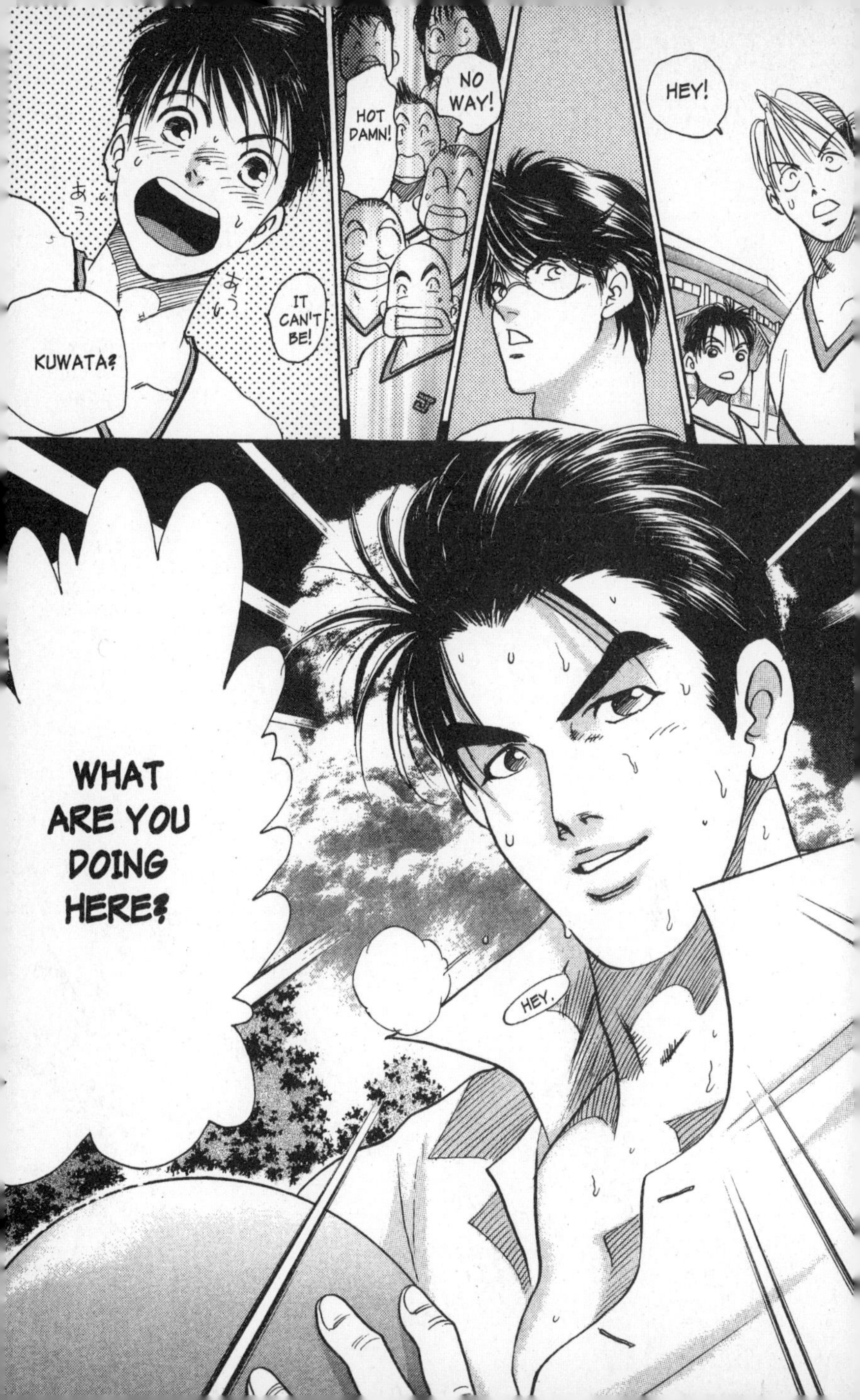
HEY!
NO WAY!
HOT DAMN!
IT CAN'T BE!
あう
あう
KUWATA?
WHAT ARE YOU DOING HERE?
HEY.

You're Reading...

REBOUND

REBOUND

Episode 52 – Regaining Courage

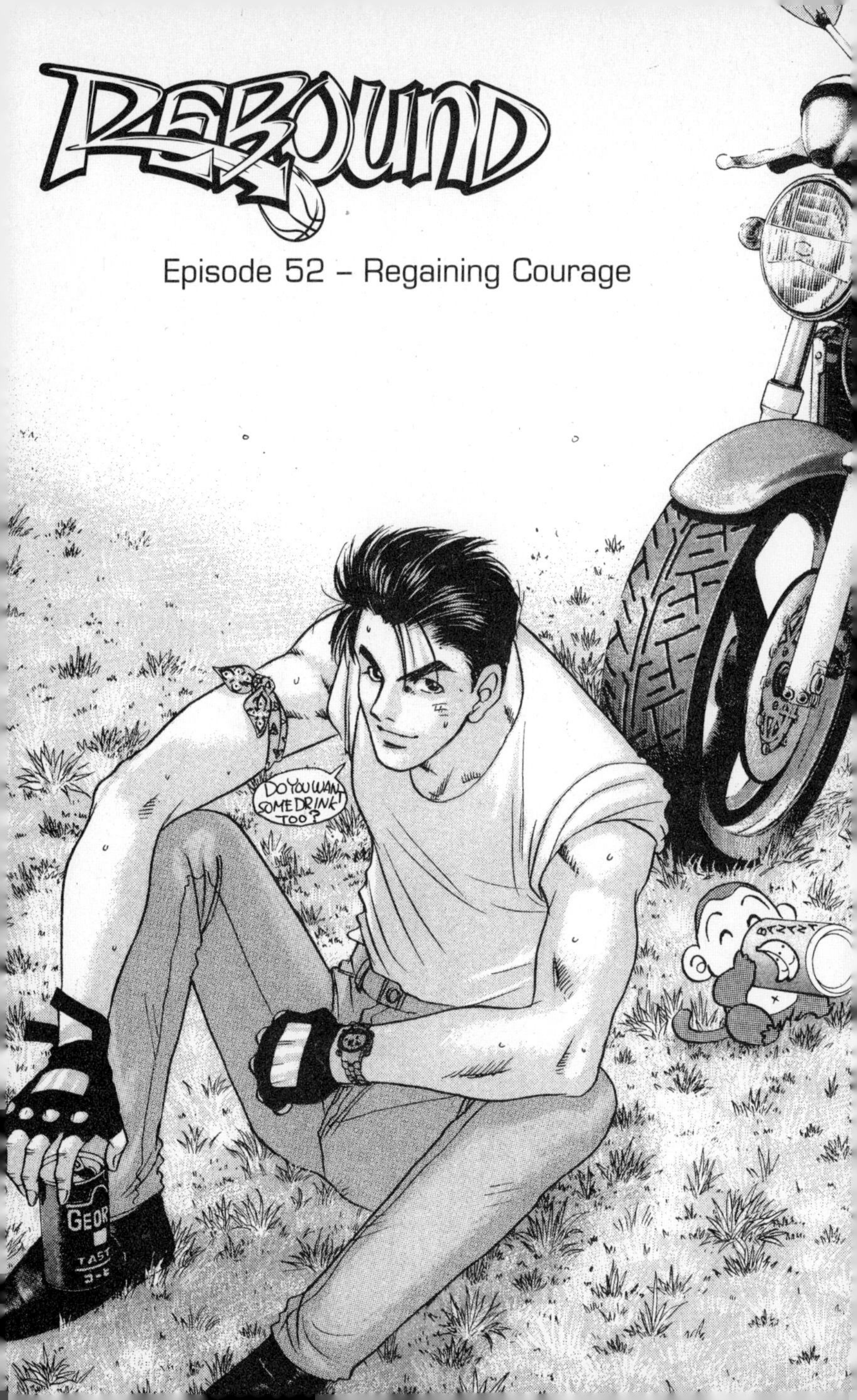
DO YOU WANT SOME DRINK TOO?

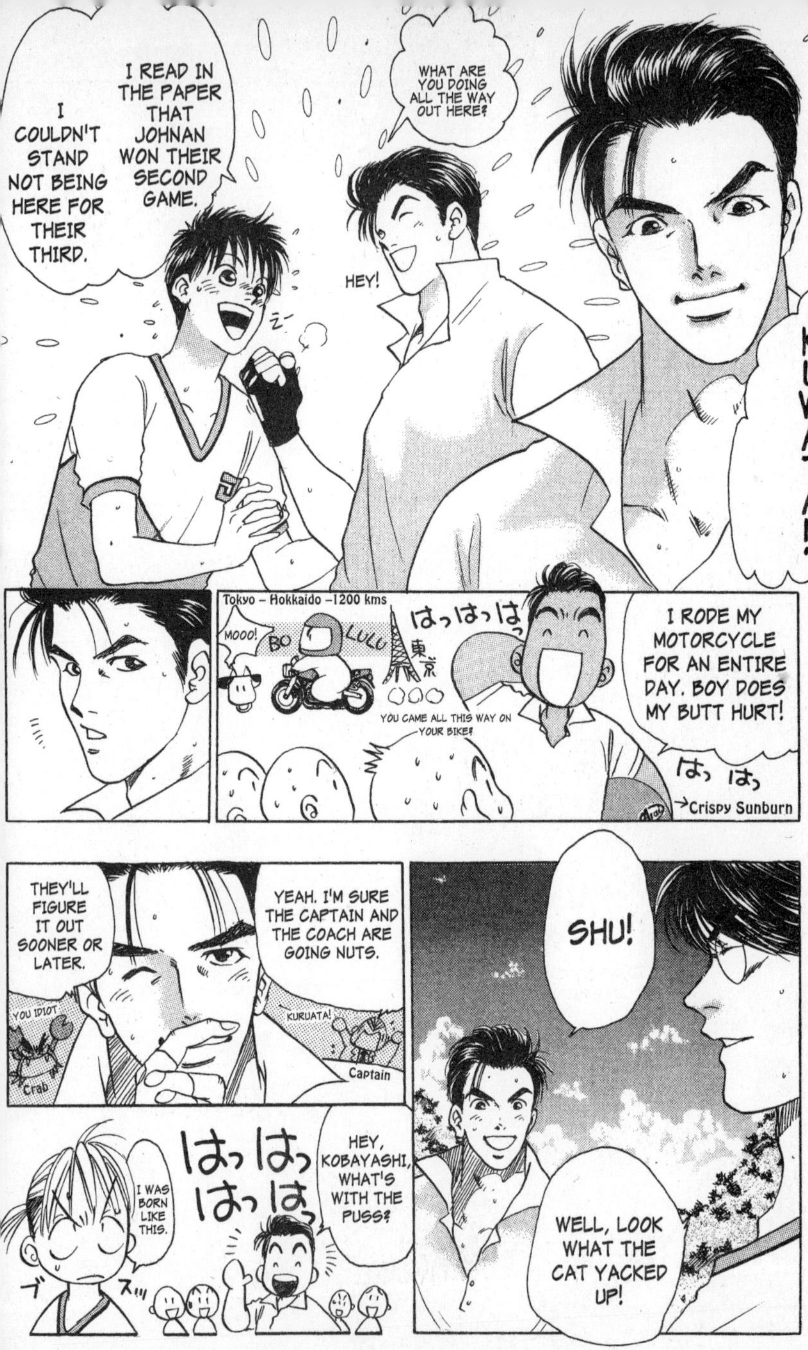
KUWATA!!
WHAT ARE YOU DOING ALL THE WAY OUT HERE?
HEY!
I READ IN THE PAPER THAT JOHNAN WON THEIR SECOND GAME.
I COULDN'T STAND NOT BEING HERE FOR THEIR THIRD.
I RODE MY MOTORCYCLE FOR AN ENTIRE DAY. BOY DOES MY BUTT HURT!
はっはっは
Tokyo – Hokkaido –1200 kms
東京
BOLULU
MOOO!
YOU CAME ALL THIS WAY ON YOUR BIKE?
はっはっ
→Crispy Sunburn
SHU!
WELL, LOOK WHAT THE CAT YACKED UP!
YEAH. I'M SURE THE CAPTAIN AND THE COACH ARE GOING NUTS.
THEY'LL FIGURE IT OUT SOONER OR LATER.
KURUATA!
Captain
YOU IDIOT
Crab
HEY, KOBAYASHI, WHAT'S WITH THE PUSS?
はっはっはっはっ
I WAS BORN LIKE THIS.
ブスッ

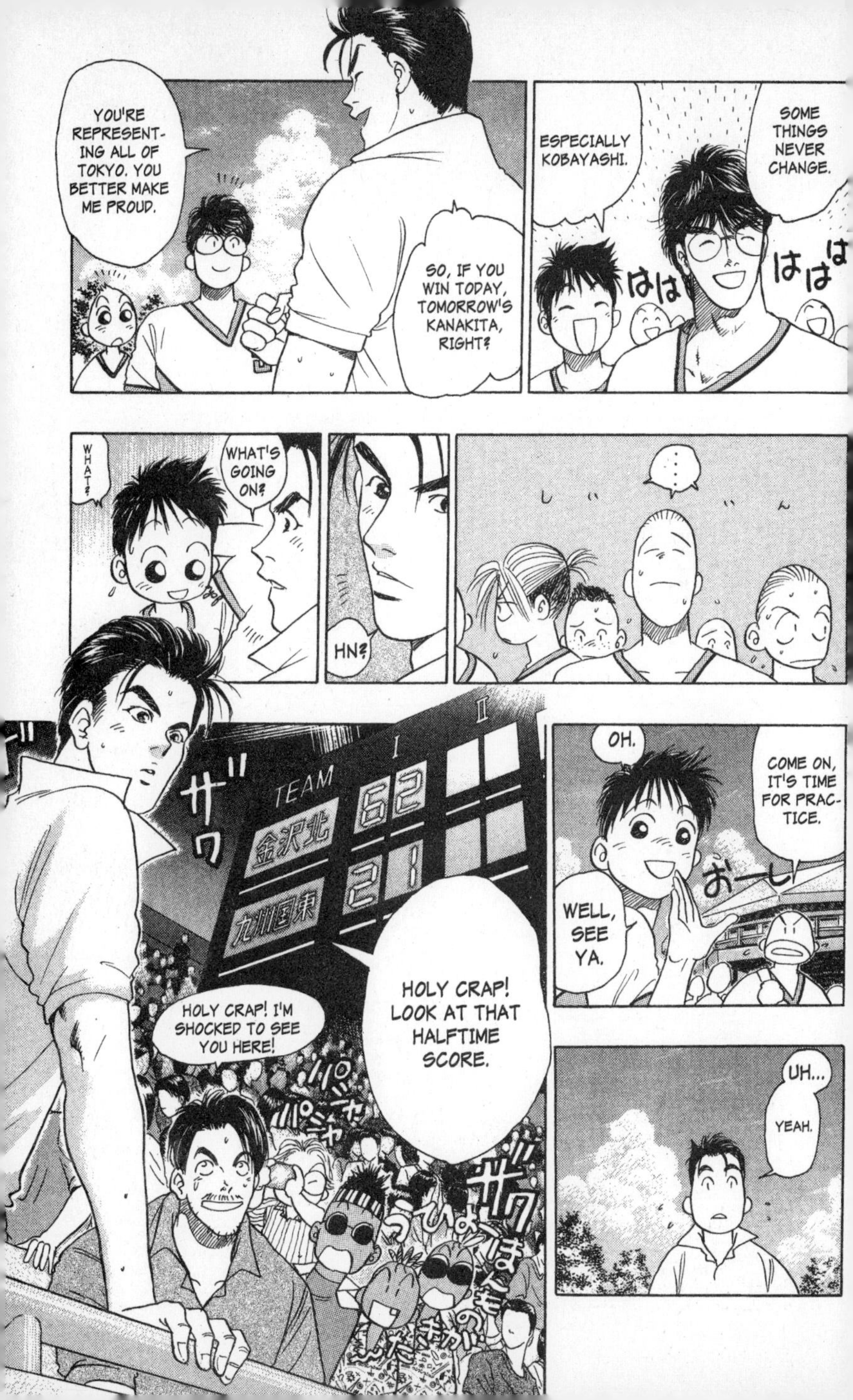
SOME THINGS NEVER CHANGE.
ESPECIALLY KOBAYASHI.
ははは
はは
YOU'RE REPRESENTING ALL OF TOKYO. YOU BETTER MAKE ME PROUD.
SO, IF YOU WIN TODAY, TOMORROW'S KANAKITA, RIGHT?
...
しいいん
HN?
WHAT'S GOING ON?
WHAT?
COME ON, IT'S TIME FOR PRACTICE.
おーい
OH.
WELL, SEE YA.
UH...
YEAH.
ザワ
TEAM
I
II
金沢北
62
九州国東
21
HOLY CRAP! LOOK AT THAT HALFTIME SCORE.
HOLY CRAP! I'M SHOCKED TO SEE YOU HERE!
パシャ
パシャ
ザワ

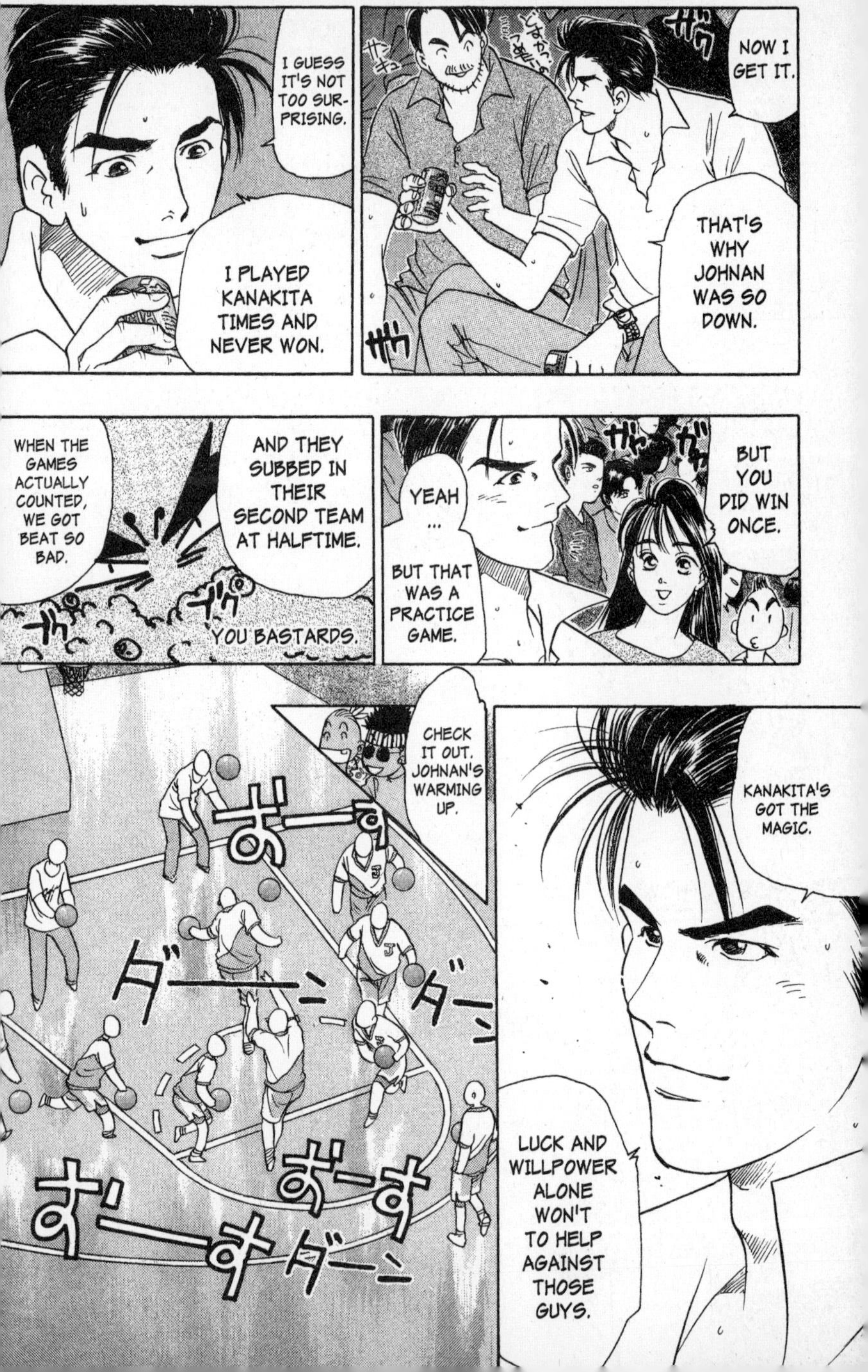
NOW I GET IT.
THAT'S WHY JOHNAN WAS SO DOWN.
I GUESS IT'S NOT TOO SUR-PRISING.
I PLAYED KANAKITA TIMES AND NEVER WON.
BUT YOU DID WIN ONCE.
YEAH ...
BUT THAT WAS A PRACTICE GAME.
AND THEY SUBBED IN THEIR SECOND TEAM AT HALFTIME.
WHEN THE GAMES ACTUALLY COUNTED, WE GOT BEAT SO BAD.
YOU BASTARDS.
KANAKITA'S GOT THE MAGIC.
LUCK AND WILLPOWER ALONE WON'T TO HELP AGAINST THOSE GUYS.
CHECK IT OUT. JOHNAN'S WARMING UP.
おーす
ダーン
おーす
すーす ダーン

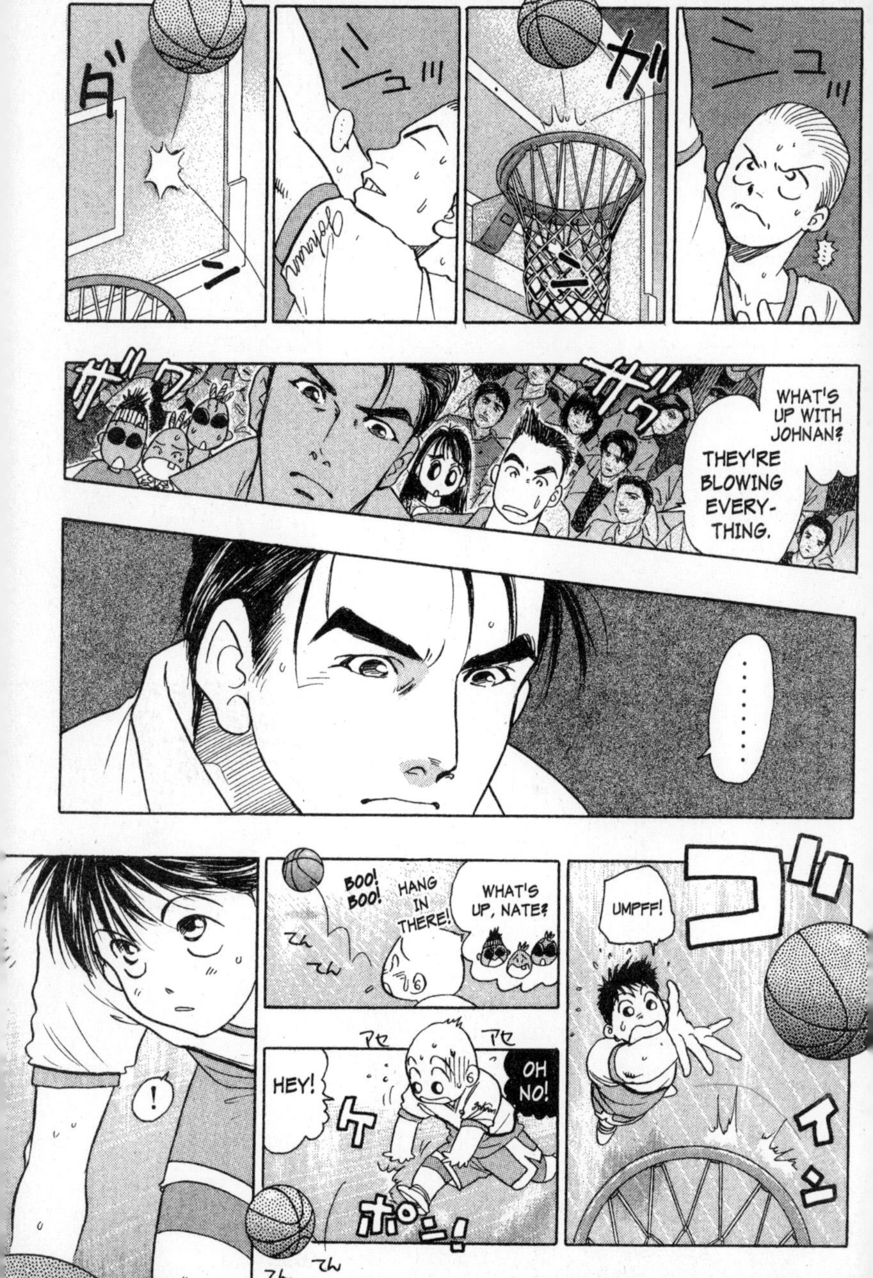
WHAT'S UP WITH JOHNAN?
THEY'RE BLOWING EVERY-THING.
....
UMPFF!
WHAT'S UP, NATE?
HANG IN THERE!
BOO! BOO!
OH NO!
HEY!
!

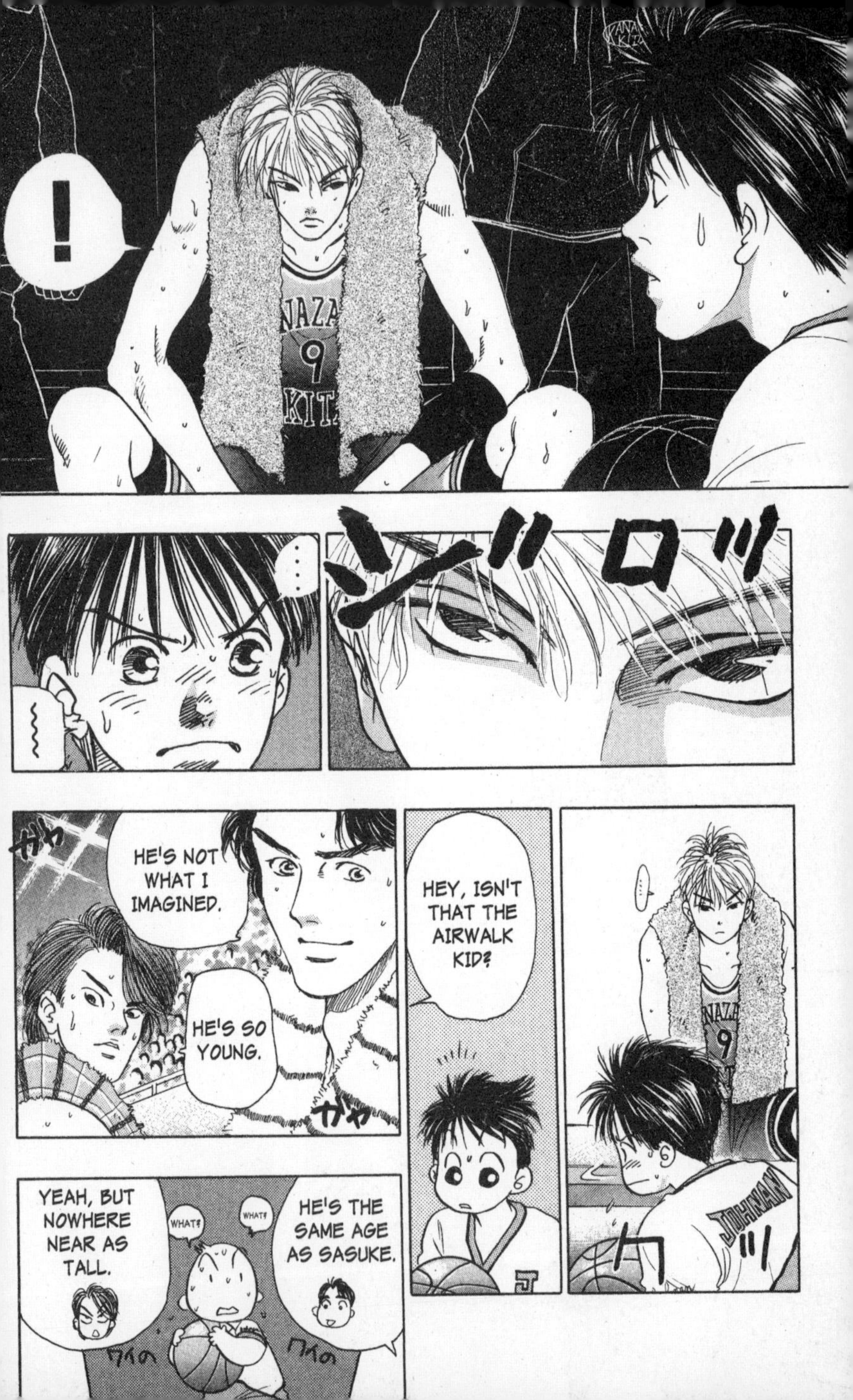
!
ジロッ
...
...
HEY, ISN'T THAT THE AIRWALK KID?
HE'S NOT WHAT I IMAGINED.
HE'S SO YOUNG.
ガヤ
ガヤ
HE'S THE SAME AGE AS SASUKE.
WHAT?
WHAT?
YEAH, BUT NOWHERE NEAR AS TALL.

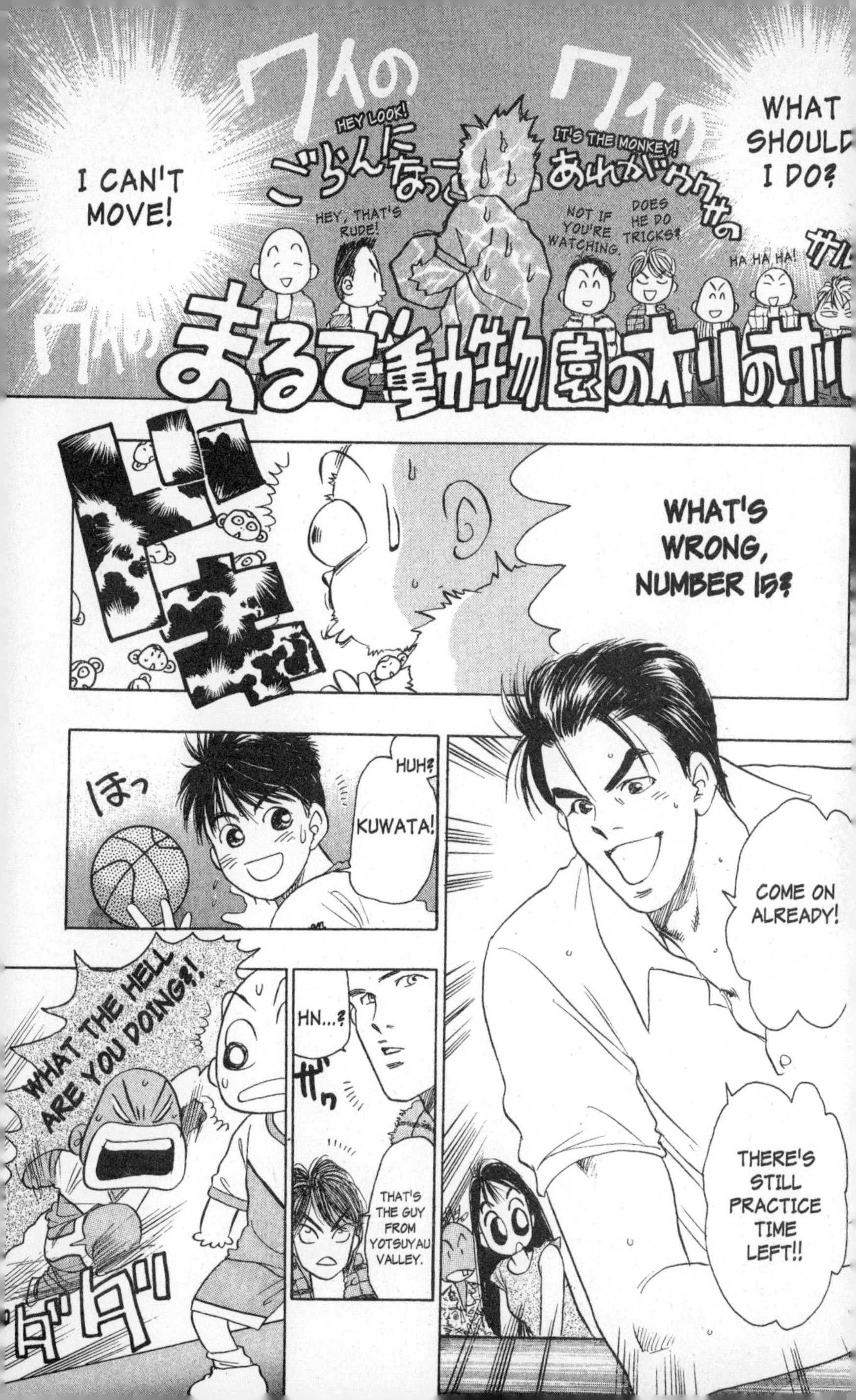
ワイのワイの
WHAT SHOULD I DO?
HA HA HA!
DOES HE DO TRICKS?
NOT IF YOU'RE WATCHING.
IT'S THE MONKEY!
HEY LOOK!
HEY, THAT'S RUDE!
I CAN'T MOVE!
まるで動物園のオリのサル
WHAT'S WRONG, NUMBER 15?
COME ON ALREADY!
THERE'S STILL PRACTICE TIME LEFT!!
HUH?
KUWATA!
ほっ
HN...?
ザッ
THAT'S THE GUY FROM YOTSUYAU VALLEY.
WHAT THE HELL ARE YOU DOING?!

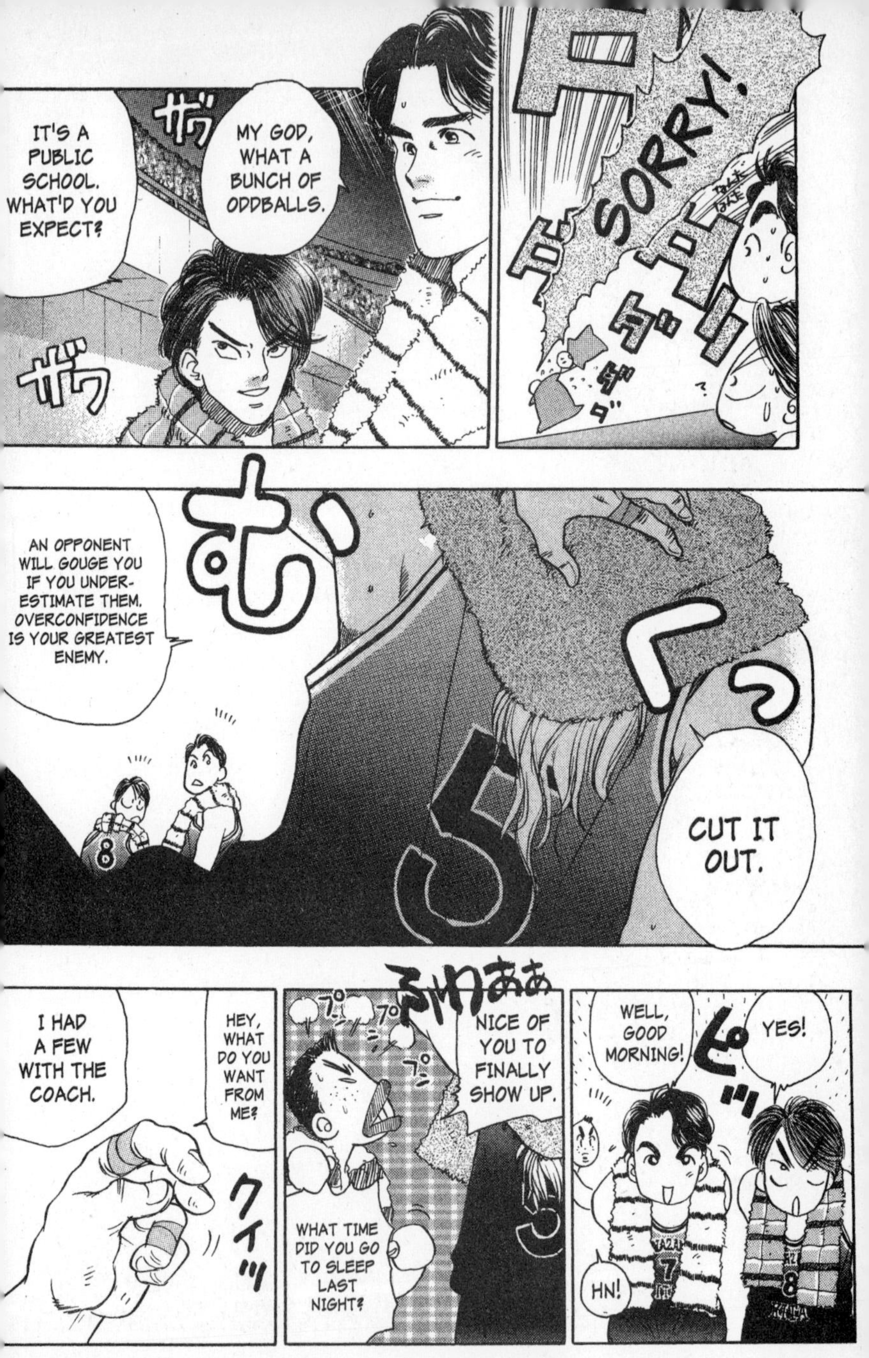
SORRY!
MY GOD, WHAT A BUNCH OF ODDBALLS.
IT'S A PUBLIC SCHOOL. WHAT'D YOU EXPECT?
CUT IT OUT.
AN OPPONENT WILL GOUGE YOU IF YOU UNDER-ESTIMATE THEM. OVERCONFIDENCE IS YOUR GREATEST ENEMY.
YES!
WELL, GOOD MORNING!
HN!
NICE OF YOU TO FINALLY SHOW UP.
WHAT TIME DID YOU GO TO SLEEP LAST NIGHT?
HEY, WHAT DO YOU WANT FROM ME?
I HAD A FEW WITH THE COACH.

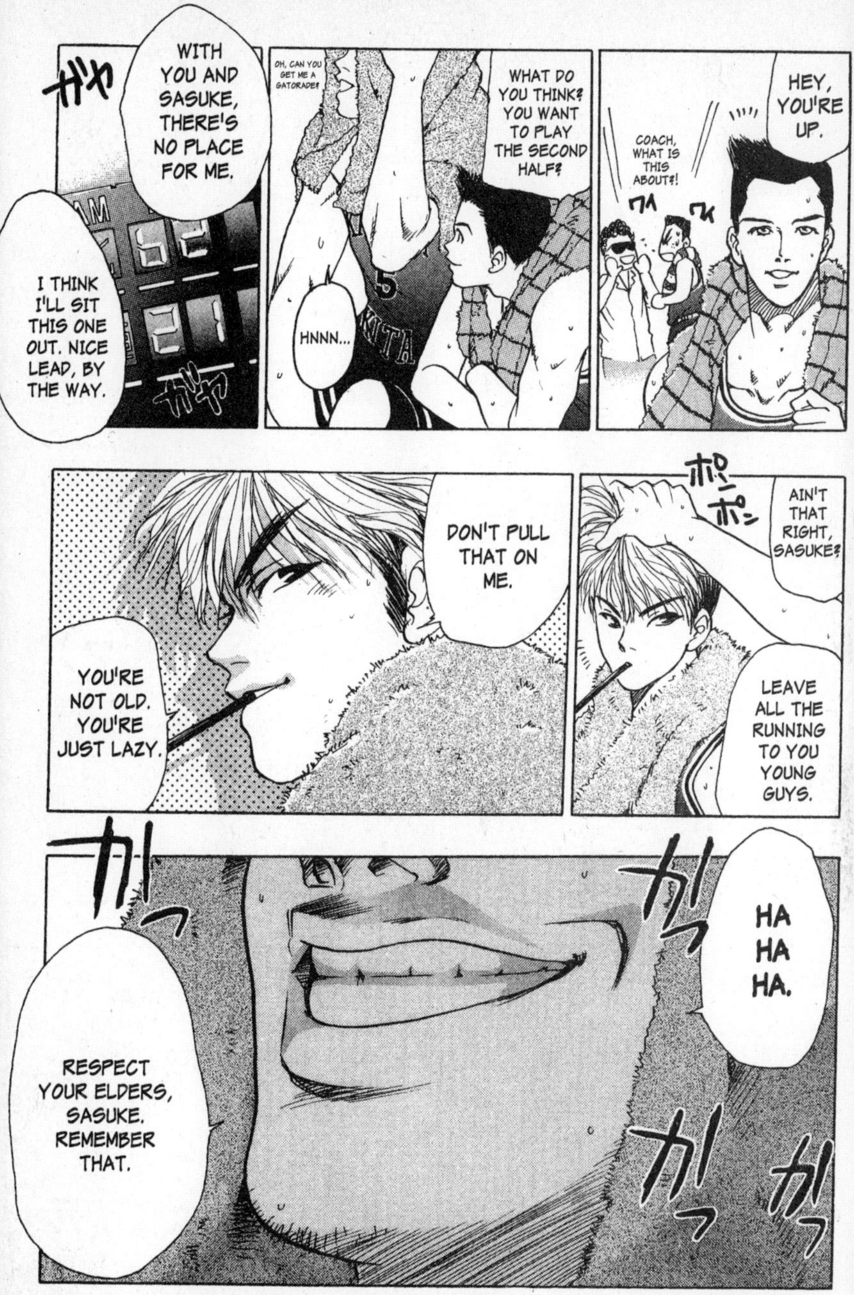
HEY, YOU'RE UP.
COACH, WHAT IS THIS ABOUT?!
WHAT DO YOU THINK? YOU WANT TO PLAY THE SECOND HALF?
OH, CAN YOU GET ME A GATORADE?
HNNN...
WITH YOU AND SASUKE, THERE'S NO PLACE FOR ME.
I THINK I'LL SIT THIS ONE OUT. NICE LEAD, BY THE WAY.
AIN'T THAT RIGHT, SASUKE?
LEAVE ALL THE RUNNING TO YOU YOUNG GUYS.
DON'T PULL THAT ON ME.
YOU'RE NOT OLD. YOU'RE JUST LAZY.
HA HA HA.
RESPECT YOUR ELDERS, SASUKE. REMEMBER THAT.

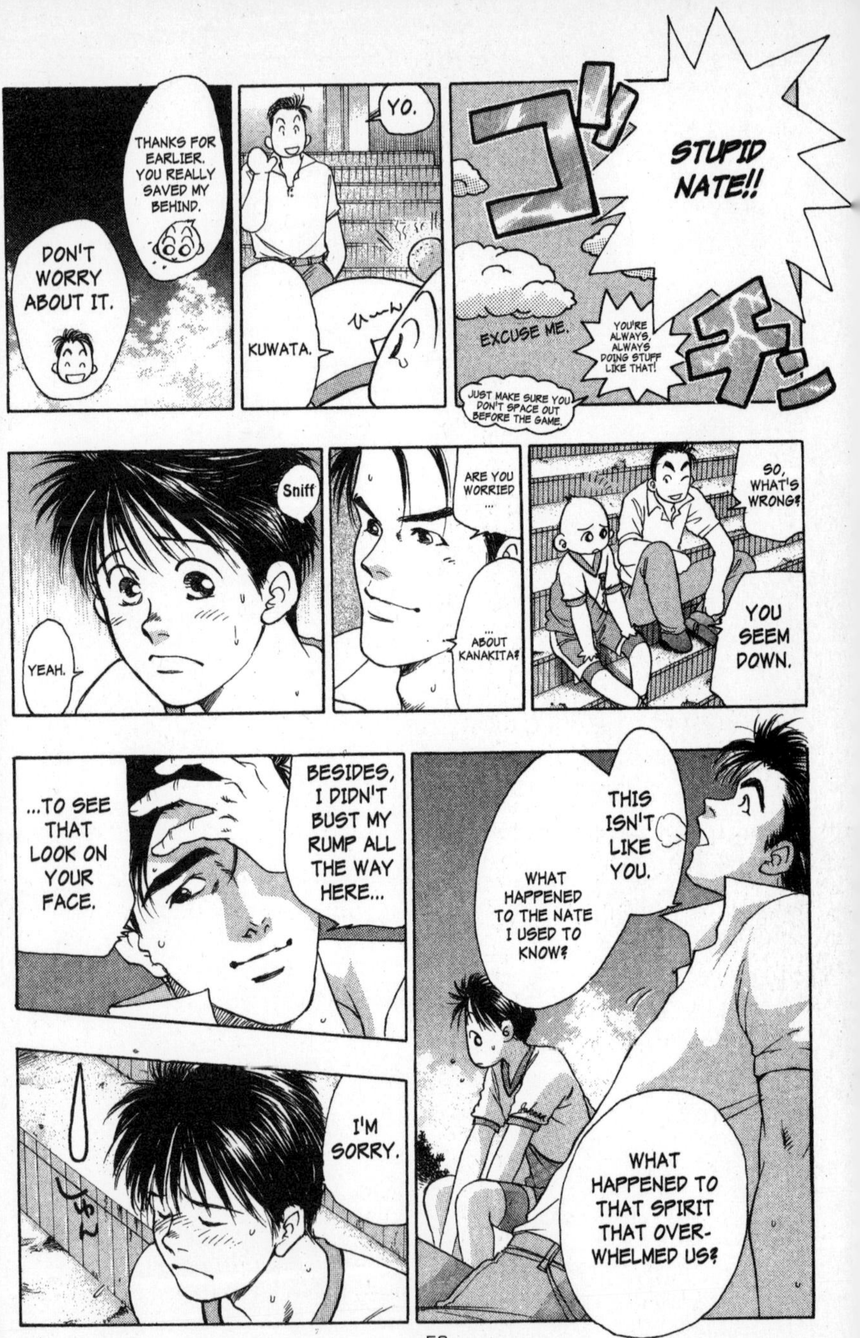
STUPID NATE!!
YOU'RE ALWAYS, ALWAYS DOING STUFF LIKE THAT!
EXCUSE ME.
JUST MAKE SURE YOU DON'T SPACE OUT BEFORE THE GAME.
YO.
KUWATA.
THANKS FOR EARLIER. YOU REALLY SAVED MY BEHIND.
DON'T WORRY ABOUT IT.
SO, WHAT'S WRONG?
YOU SEEM DOWN.
ARE YOU WORRIED ...
... ABOUT KANAKITA?
Sniff
YEAH.
THIS ISN'T LIKE YOU.
WHAT HAPPENED TO THE NATE I USED TO KNOW?
WHAT HAPPENED TO THAT SPIRIT THAT OVER-WHELMED US?
BESIDES, I DIDN'T BUST MY RUMP ALL THE WAY HERE...
...TO SEE THAT LOOK ON YOUR FACE.
I'M SORRY.

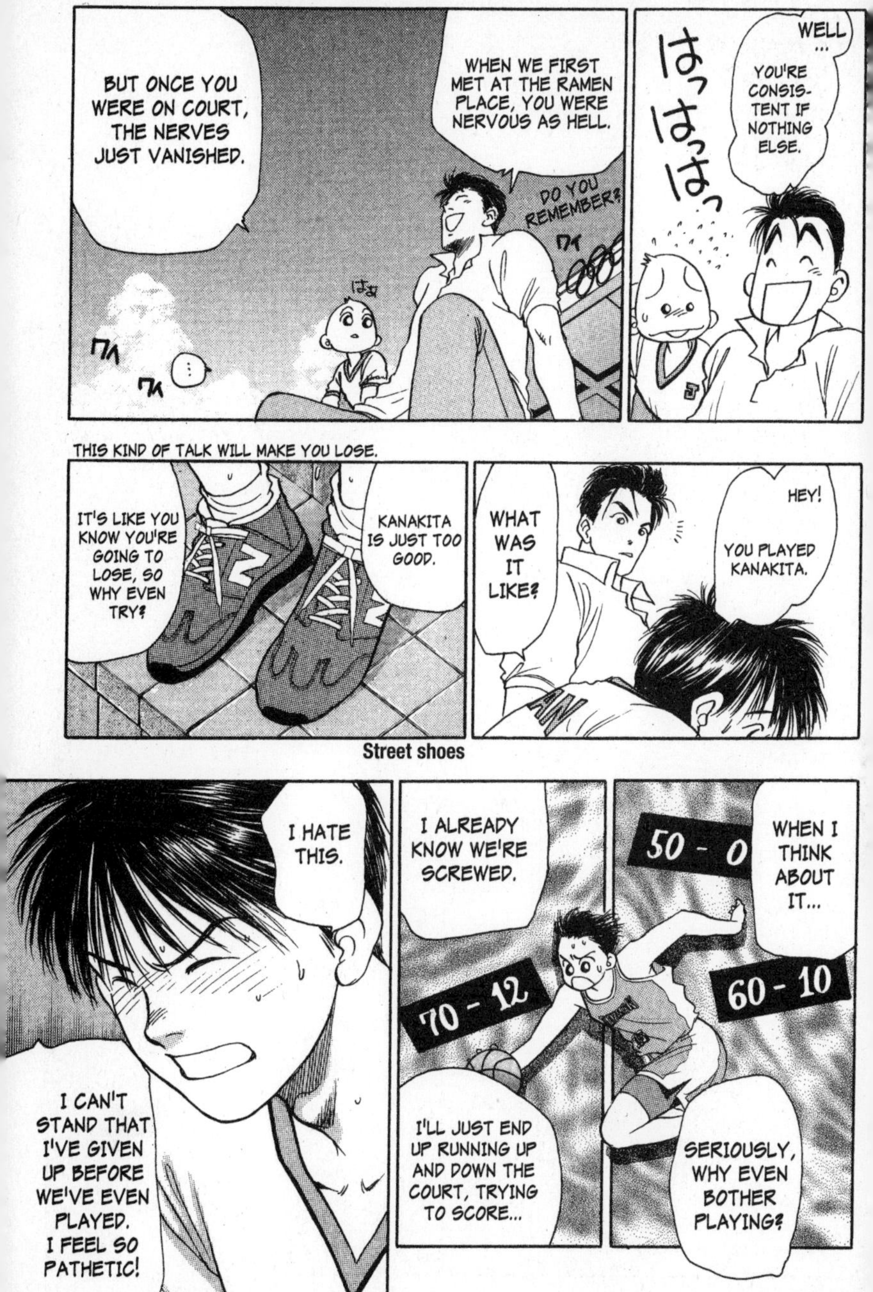

WELL... YOU'RE CONSIS-TENT IF NOTHING ELSE.
はっはっはっ
WHEN WE FIRST MET AT THE RAMEN PLACE, YOU WERE NERVOUS AS HELL.
DO YOU REMEMBER?
BUT ONCE YOU WERE ON COURT, THE NERVES JUST VANISHED.
...
THIS KIND OF TALK WILL MAKE YOU LOSE.
HEY!
YOU PLAYED KANAKITA.
WHAT WAS IT LIKE?
KANAKITA IS JUST TOO GOOD.
IT'S LIKE YOU KNOW YOU'RE GOING TO LOSE, SO WHY EVEN TRY?
Street shoes
WHEN I THINK ABOUT IT...
50 - 0
60 - 10
SERIOUSLY, WHY EVEN BOTHER PLAYING?
I ALREADY KNOW WE'RE SCREWED.
70 - 12
I'LL JUST END UP RUNNING UP AND DOWN THE COURT, TRYING TO SCORE...
I HATE THIS.
I CAN'T STAND THAT I'VE GIVEN UP BEFORE WE'VE EVEN PLAYED. I FEEL SO PATHETIC!

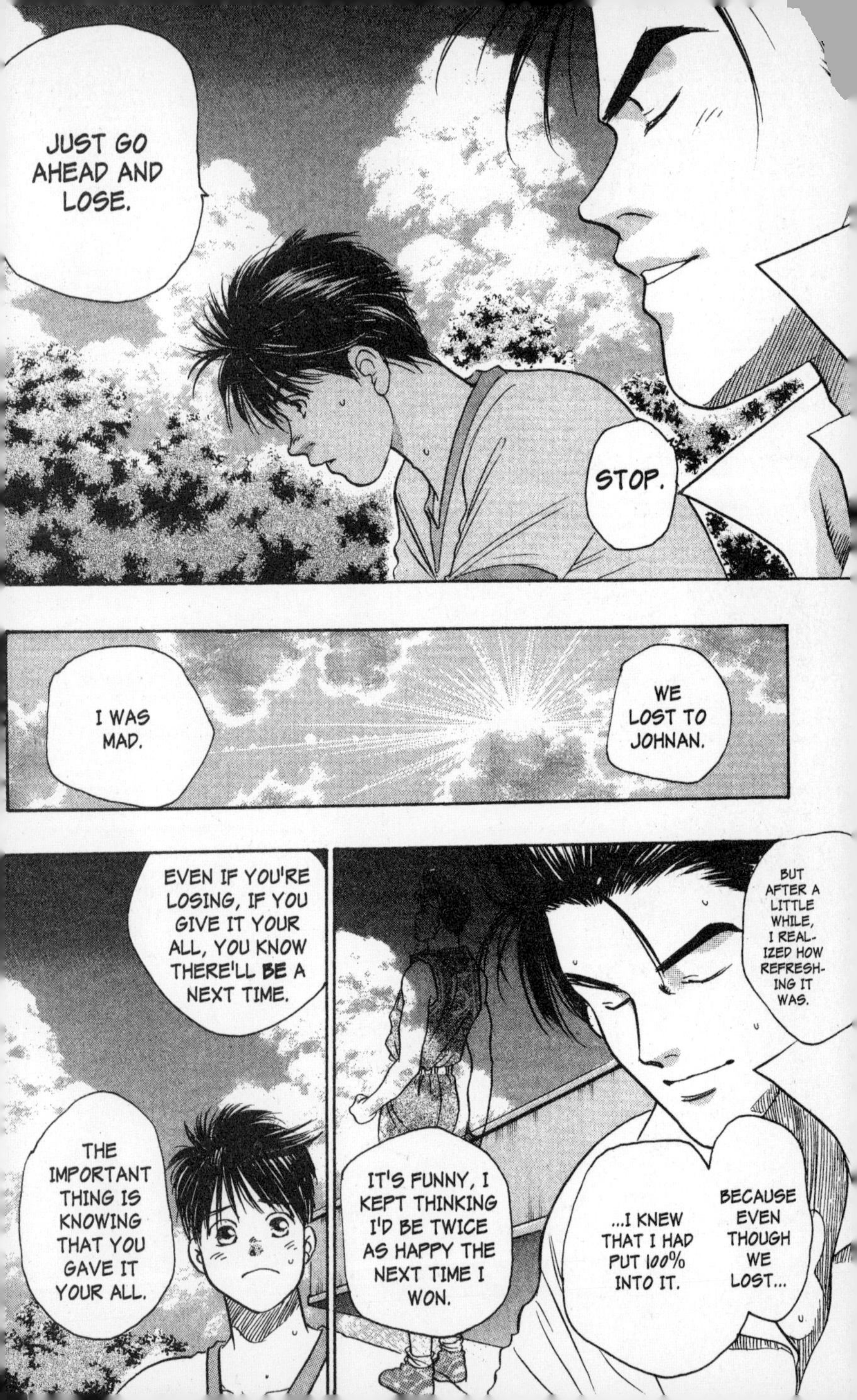
STOP.
JUST GO AHEAD AND LOSE.
WE LOST TO JOHNAN.
I WAS MAD.
BUT AFTER A LITTLE WHILE, I REAL-IZED HOW REFRESH-ING IT WAS.
BECAUSE EVEN THOUGH WE LOST...
...I KNEW THAT I HAD PUT 100% INTO IT.
IT'S FUNNY, I KEPT THINKING I'D BE TWICE AS HAPPY THE NEXT TIME I WON.
EVEN IF YOU'RE LOSING, IF YOU GIVE IT YOUR ALL, YOU KNOW THERE'LL BE A NEXT TIME.
THE IMPORTANT THING IS KNOWING THAT YOU GAVE IT YOUR ALL.

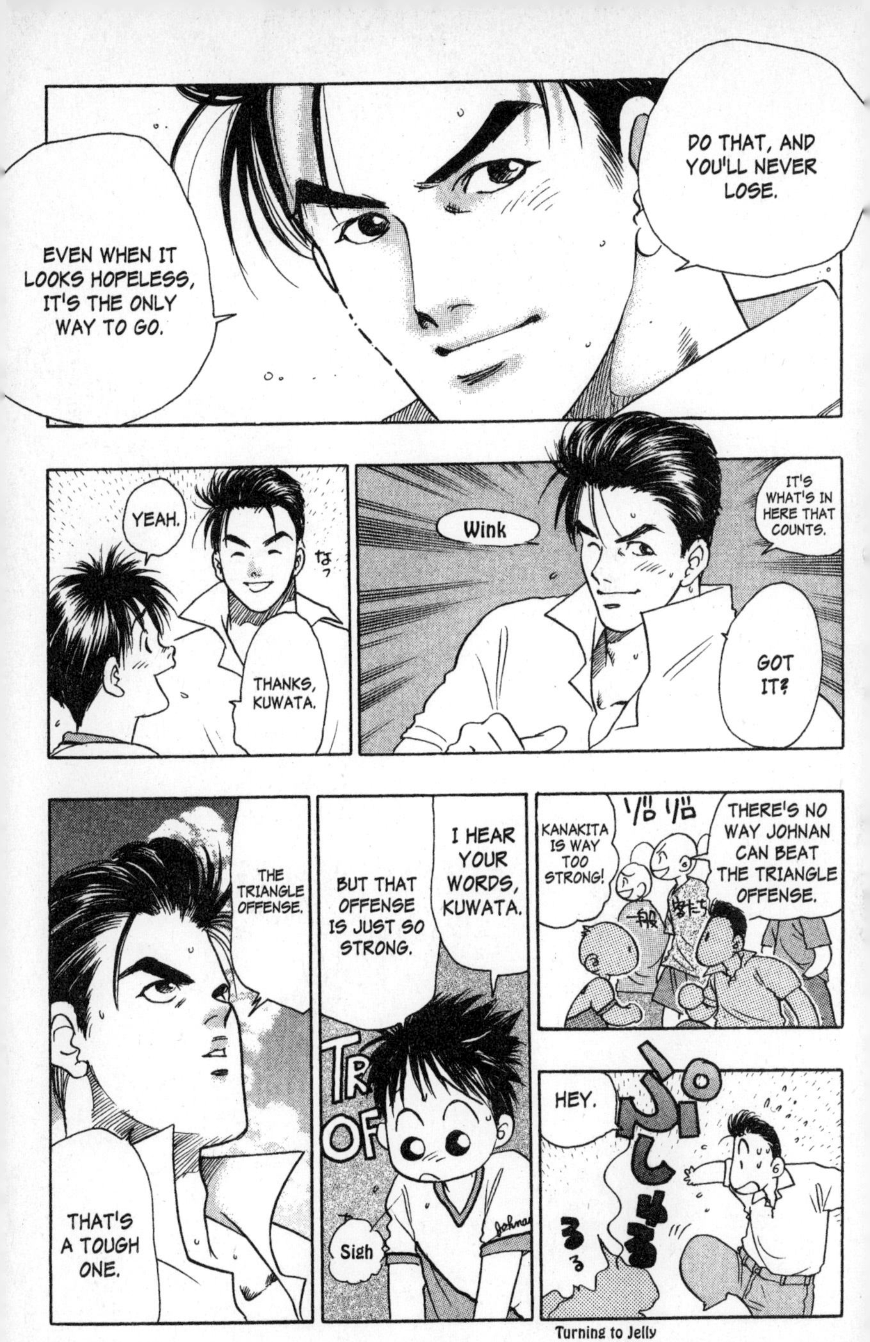
DO THAT, AND YOU'LL NEVER LOSE.
EVEN WHEN IT LOOKS HOPELESS, IT'S THE ONLY WAY TO GO.
IT'S WHAT'S IN HERE THAT COUNTS.
Wink
GOT IT?
THANKS, KUWATA.
YEAH.
なっ
THERE'S NO WAY JOHNAN CAN BEAT THE TRIANGLE OFFENSE.
KANAKITA IS WAY TOO STRONG!
HEY.
ぷしゅるるる
I HEAR YOUR WORDS, KUWATA.
BUT THAT OFFENSE IS JUST SO STRONG.
Sigh
THE TRIANGLE OFFENSE.
THAT'S A TOUGH ONE.
Turning to Jelly

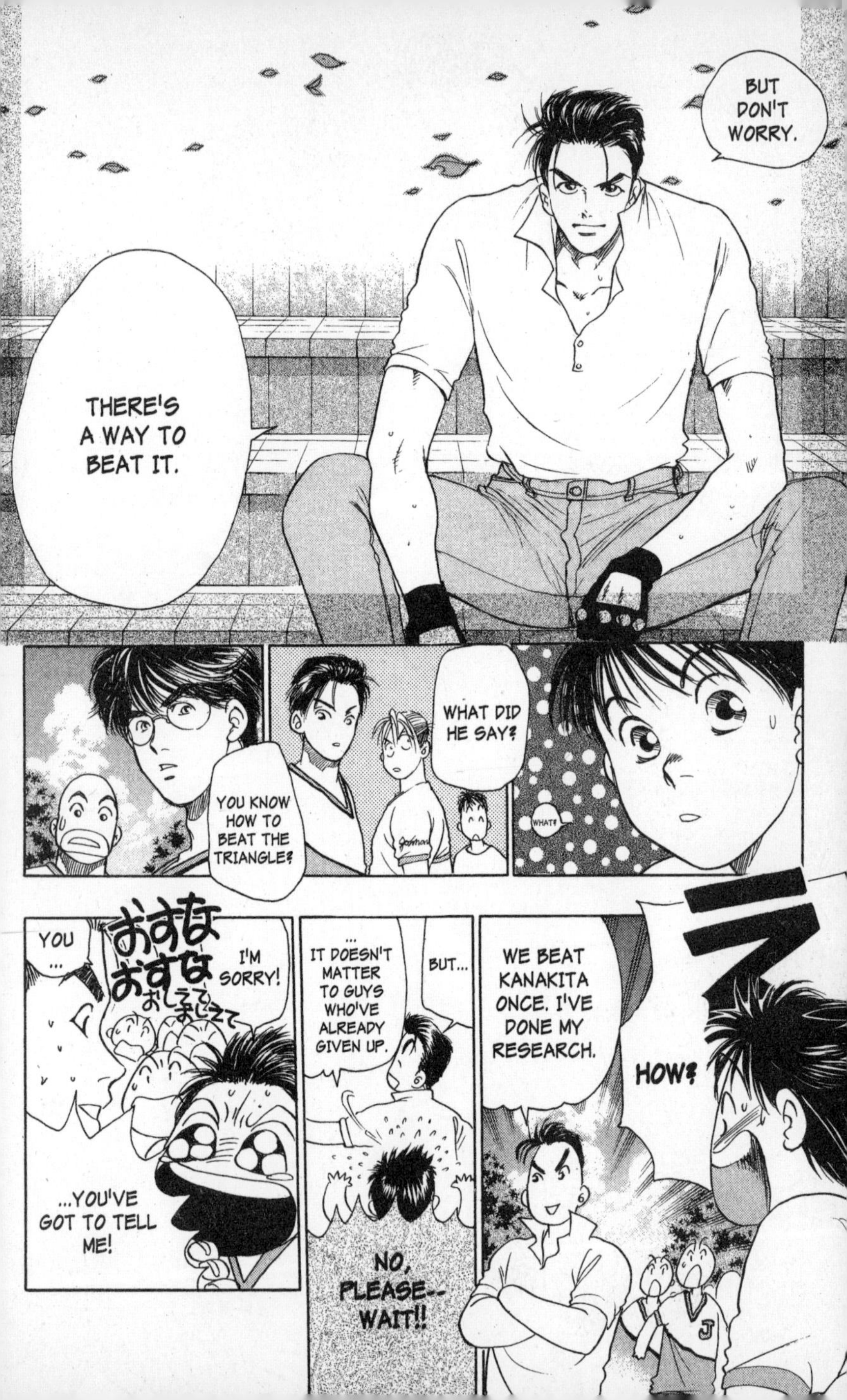
BUT DON'T WORRY.
THERE'S A WAY TO BEAT IT.
WHAT?
WHAT DID HE SAY?
YOU KNOW HOW TO BEAT THE TRIANGLE?
ラ
HOW?
WE BEAT KANAKITA ONCE. I'VE DONE MY RESEARCH.
BUT...
... IT DOESN'T MATTER TO GUYS WHO'VE ALREADY GIVEN UP.
NO, PLEASE-- WAIT!!
I'M SORRY!
おすな おすな
おしえて おしえて
YOU ...
...YOU'VE GOT TO TELL ME!

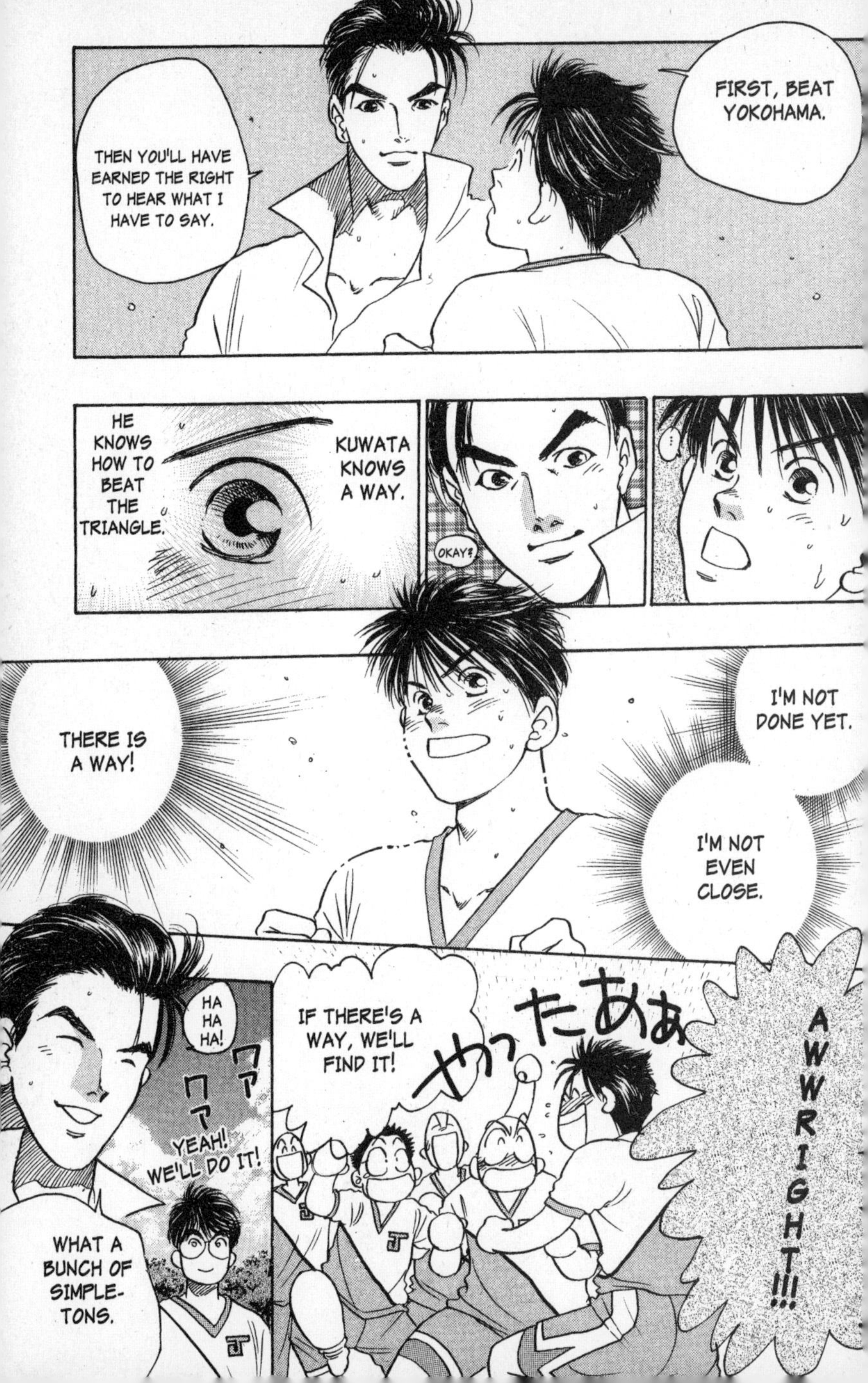
FIRST, BEAT YOKOHAMA.
THEN YOU'LL HAVE EARNED THE RIGHT TO HEAR WHAT I HAVE TO SAY.
OKAY?
KUWATA KNOWS A WAY.
HE KNOWS HOW TO BEAT THE TRIANGLE.
I'M NOT DONE YET.
I'M NOT EVEN CLOSE.
THERE IS A WAY!
AWWRIGHT!!!
やったぁぁ
IF THERE'S A WAY, WE'LL FIND IT!
HA HA HA!
ワア ワア
YEAH! WE'LL DO IT!
WHAT A BUNCH OF SIMPLE-TONS.

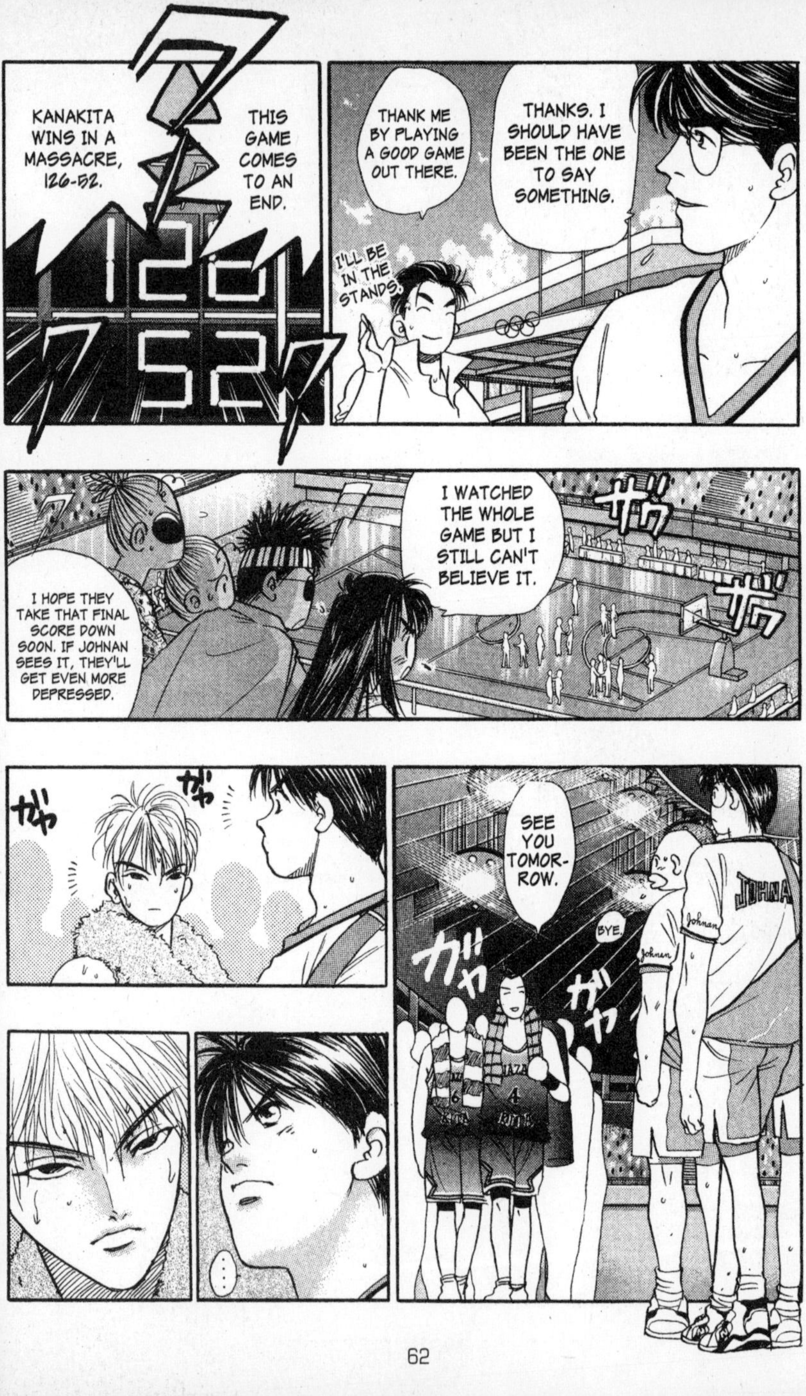
THANKS. I SHOULD HAVE BEEN THE ONE TO SAY SOMETHING.
THANK ME BY PLAYING A GOOD GAME OUT THERE.
I'LL BE IN THE STANDS.
THIS GAME COMES TO AN END.
KANAKITA WINS IN A MASSACRE, 126-52.
126
52
ザワ
ザワ
I WATCHED THE WHOLE GAME BUT I STILL CAN'T BELIEVE IT.
I HOPE THEY TAKE THAT FINAL SCORE DOWN SOON. IF JOHNAN SEES IT, THEY'LL GET EVEN MORE DEPRESSED.
SEE YOU TOMOR-ROW.
BYE.
ガヤ
ガヤ
ガヤ
ガヤ
...

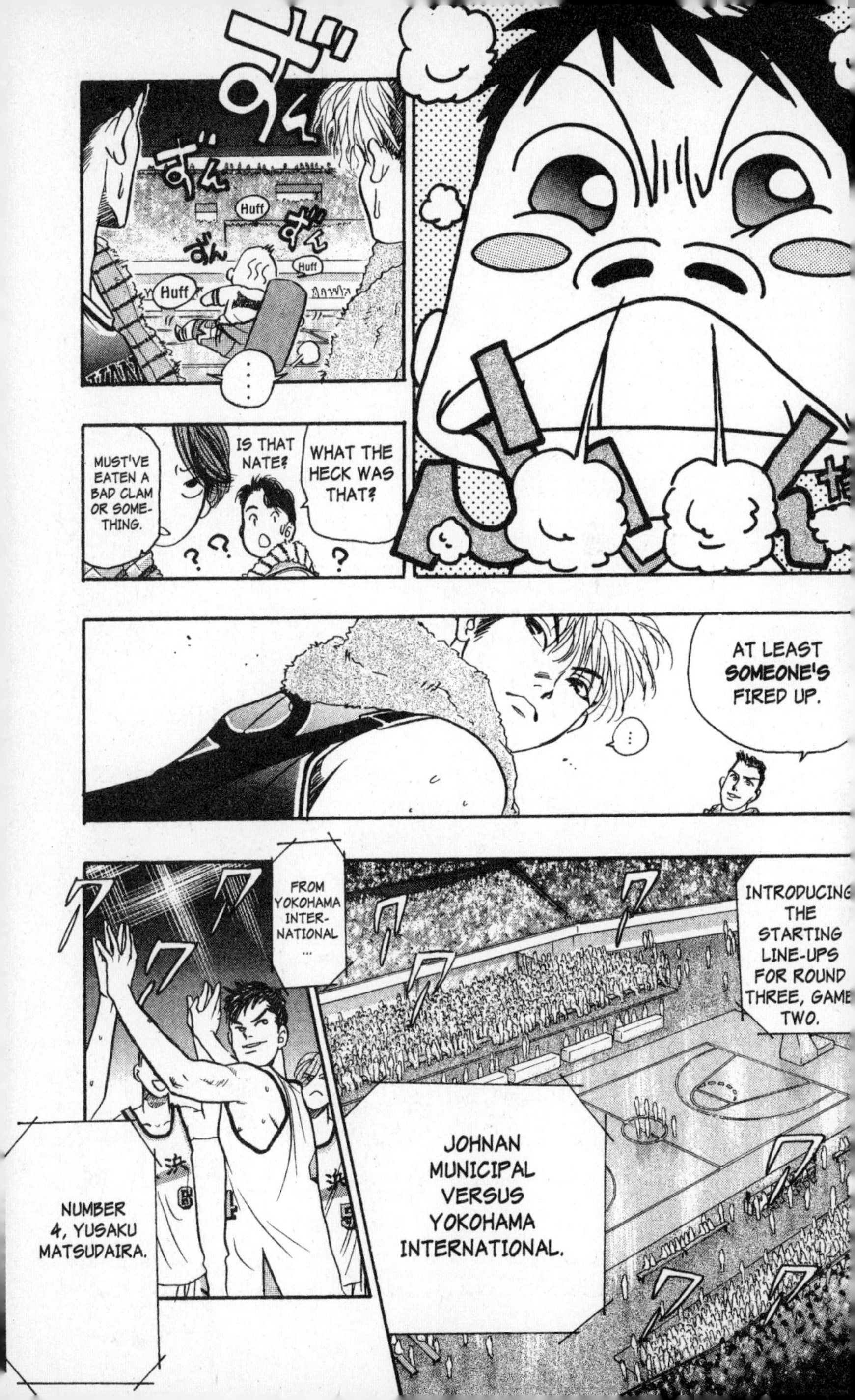
ずん
ずん
ずん
ずん
Huff
Huff
Huff
...
WHAT THE HECK WAS THAT?
IS THAT NATE?
MUST'VE EATEN A BAD CLAM OR SOMETHING.
AT LEAST SOMEONE'S FIRED UP.
...
INTRODUCING THE STARTING LINE-UPS FOR ROUND THREE, GAME TWO.
JOHNAN MUNICIPAL VERSUS YOKOHAMA INTERNATIONAL.
FROM YOKOHAMA INTERNATIONAL...
NUMBER 4, YUSAKU MATSUDAIRA.

Sign: Announcer's Booth

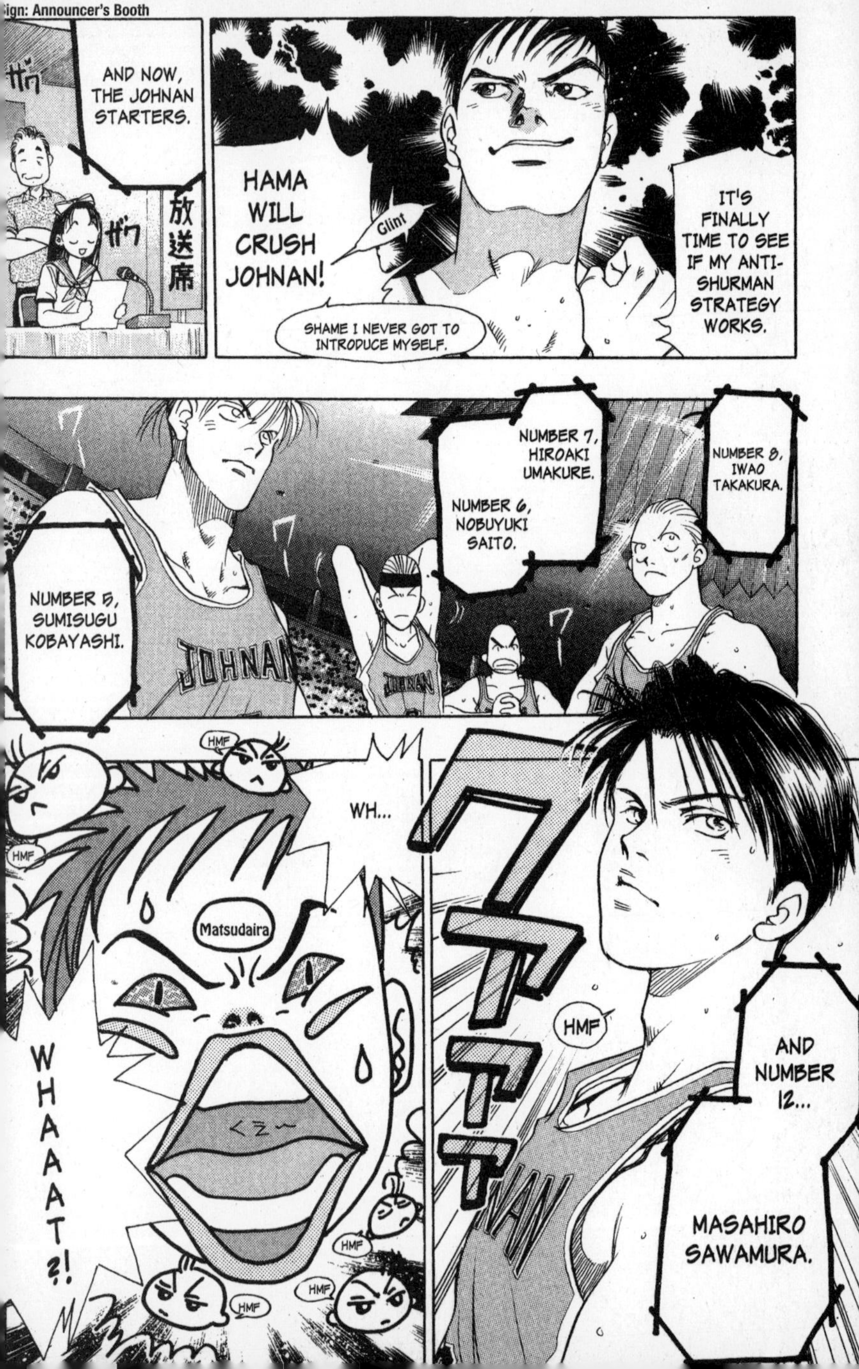
IT'S FINALLY TIME TO SEE IF MY ANTI-SHURMAN STRATEGY WORKS.
Glint
HAMA WILL CRUSH JOHNAN!
SHAME I NEVER GOT TO INTRODUCE MYSELF.
AND NOW, THE JOHNAN STARTERS.
ザワ
放送席
ザワ
NUMBER 8, IWAO TAKAKURA.
NUMBER 7, HIROAKI UMAKURE.
NUMBER 6, NOBUYUKI SAITO.
NUMBER 5, SUMISUGU KOBAYASHI.
JOHNAN
AND NUMBER 12...
MASAHIRO SAWAMURA.
HMF
WH...
Matsudaira
WHAAAAT?!
HMF
HMF
HMF
HMF
HMF

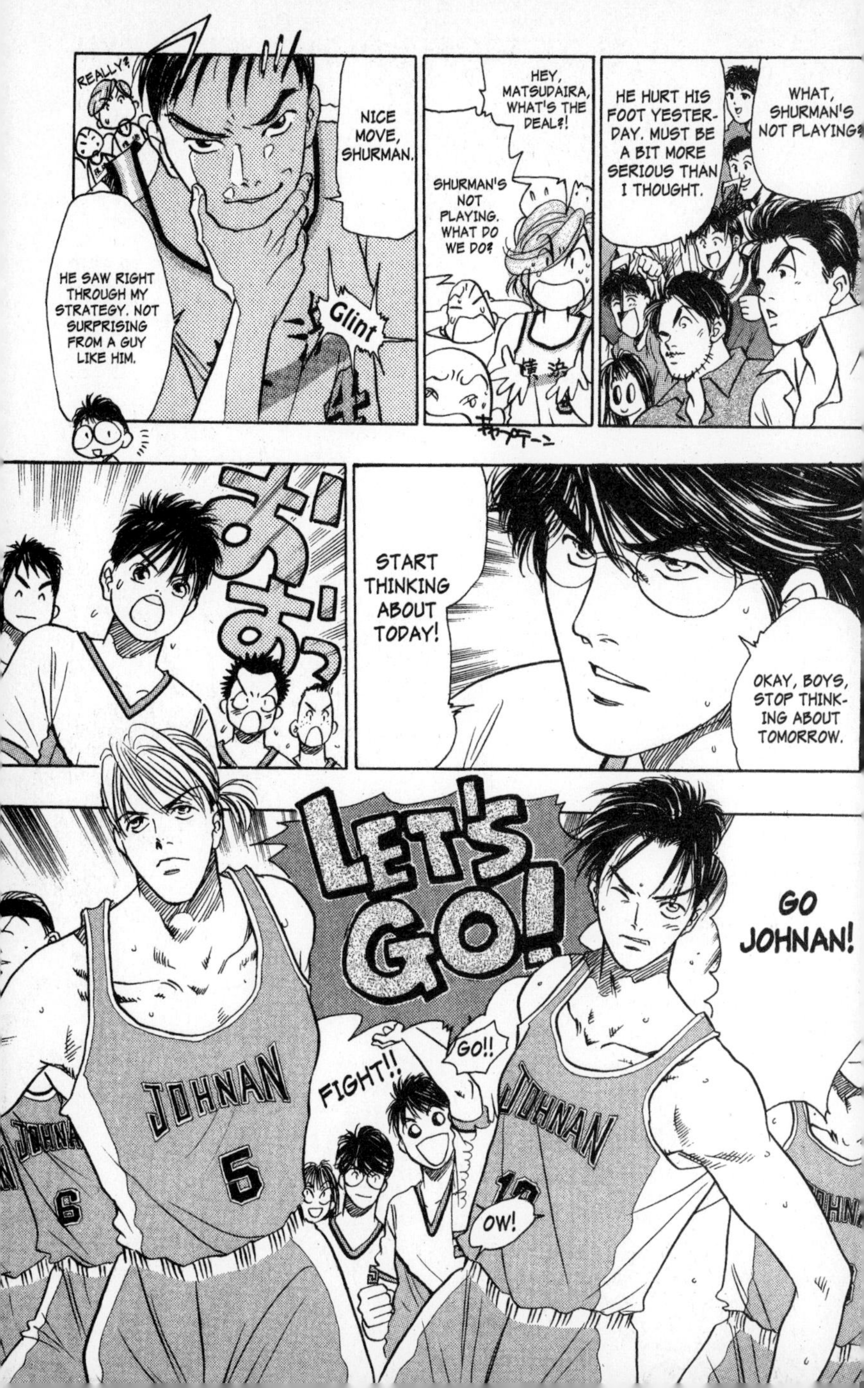
WHAT, SHURMAN'S NOT PLAYING?
HE HURT HIS FOOT YESTERDAY. MUST BE A BIT MORE SERIOUS THAN I THOUGHT.
HEY, MATSUDAIRA, WHAT'S THE DEAL?!
SHURMAN'S NOT PLAYING. WHAT DO WE DO?
NICE MOVE, SHURMAN.
REALLY?
Glint
HE SAW RIGHT THROUGH MY STRATEGY. NOT SURPRISING FROM A GUY LIKE HIM.
OKAY, BOYS, STOP THINKING ABOUT TOMORROW.
START THINKING ABOUT TODAY!
GO JOHNAN!
LET'S GO!
GO!!
FIGHT!!
OW!

You're Reading...

REBOUND

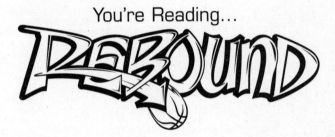

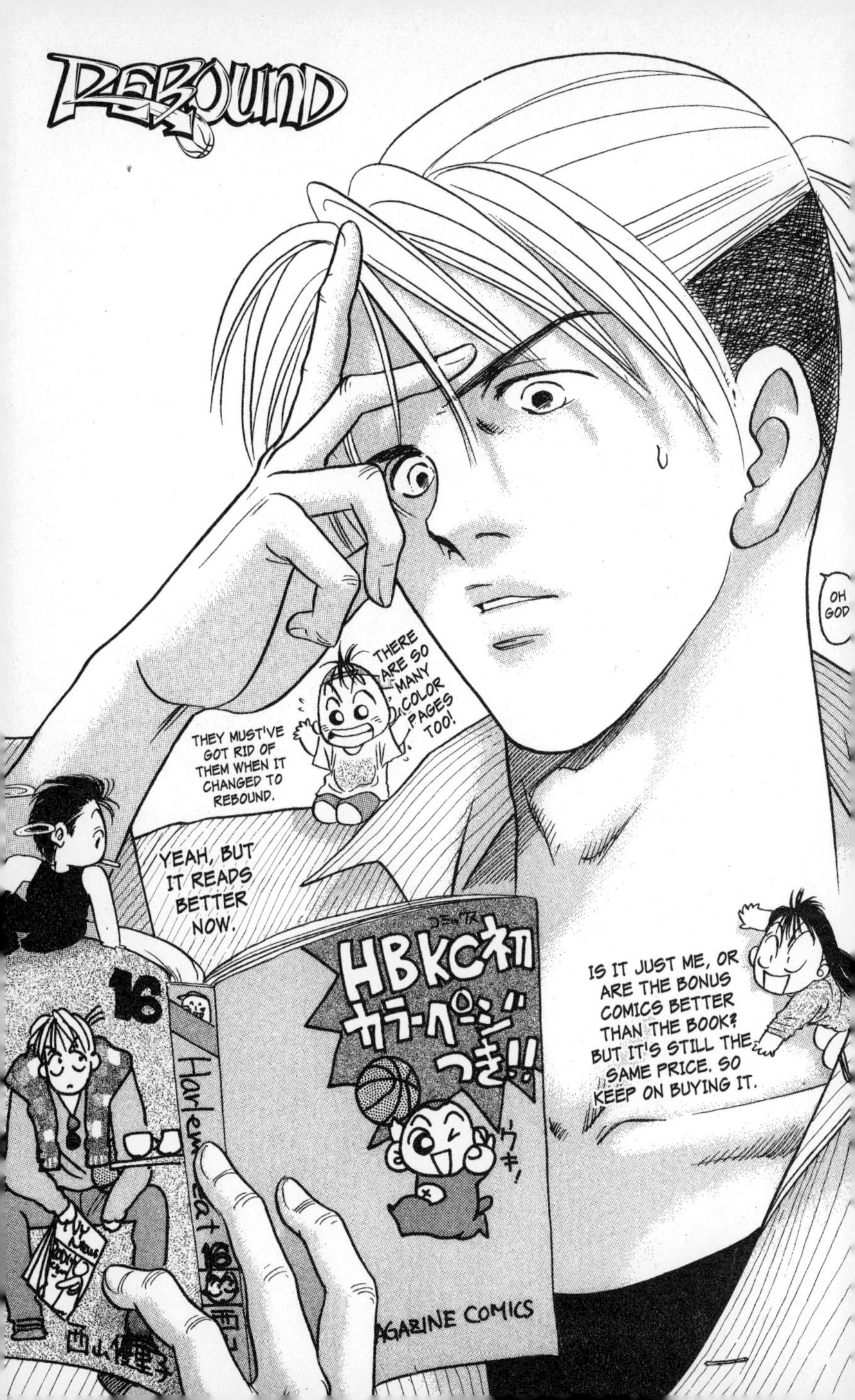
REBOUND
OH GOD
THERE ARE SO MANY COLOR PAGES TOO!
THEY MUST'VE GOT RID OF THEM WHEN IT CHANGED TO REBOUND.
YEAH, BUT IT READS BETTER NOW.
IS IT JUST ME, OR ARE THE BONUS COMICS BETTER THAN THE BOOK? BUT IT'S STILL THE SAME PRICE. SO KEEP ON BUYING IT.
HBKC初 カラーページつき!!
Harlem
16
AGAZINE COMICS

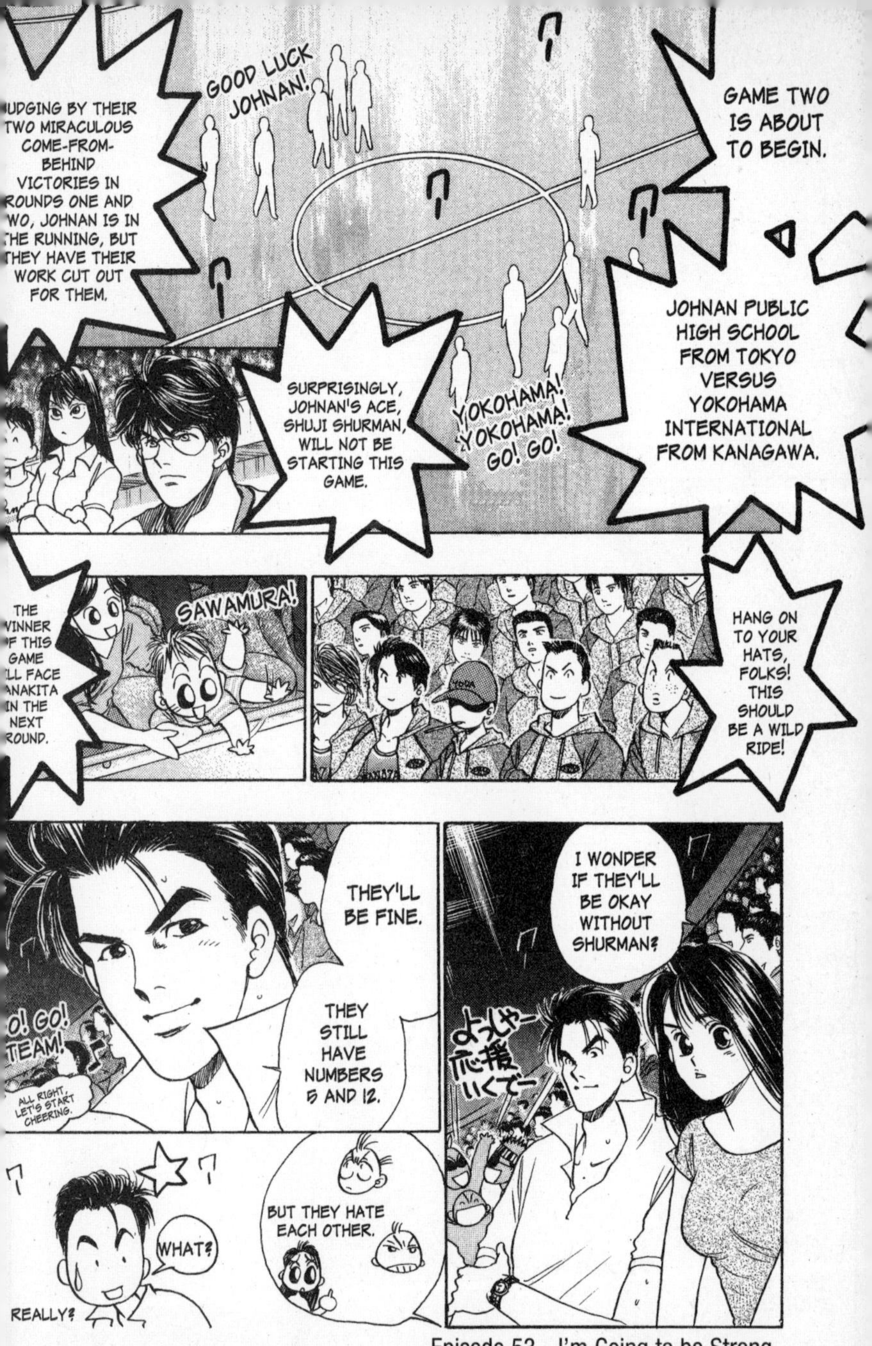
GAME TWO IS ABOUT TO BEGIN.
GOOD LUCK JOHNAN!
UDGING BY THEIR TWO MIRACULOUS COME-FROM-BEHIND VICTORIES IN ROUNDS ONE AND WO, JOHNAN IS IN HE RUNNING, BUT THEY HAVE THEIR WORK CUT OUT FOR THEM.
JOHNAN PUBLIC HIGH SCHOOL FROM TOKYO VERSUS YOKOHAMA INTERNATIONAL FROM KANAGAWA.
YOKOHAMA! YOKOHAMA! GO! GO!
SURPRISINGLY, JOHNAN'S ACE, SHUJI SHURMAN, WILL NOT BE STARTING THIS GAME.
HANG ON TO YOUR HATS, FOLKS! THIS SHOULD BE A WILD RIDE!
SAWAMURA!
THE VINNER F THIS GAME LL FACE ANAKITA IN THE NEXT ROUND.
I WONDER IF THEY'LL BE OKAY WITHOUT SHURMAN?
よっしゃー応援いくでー
THEY'LL BE FINE.
THEY STILL HAVE NUMBERS 5 AND 12.
O! GO! TEAM!
ALL RIGHT, LET'S START CHEERING.
BUT THEY HATE EACH OTHER.
WHAT?
REALLY?

Episode 53 - I'm Going to be Strong

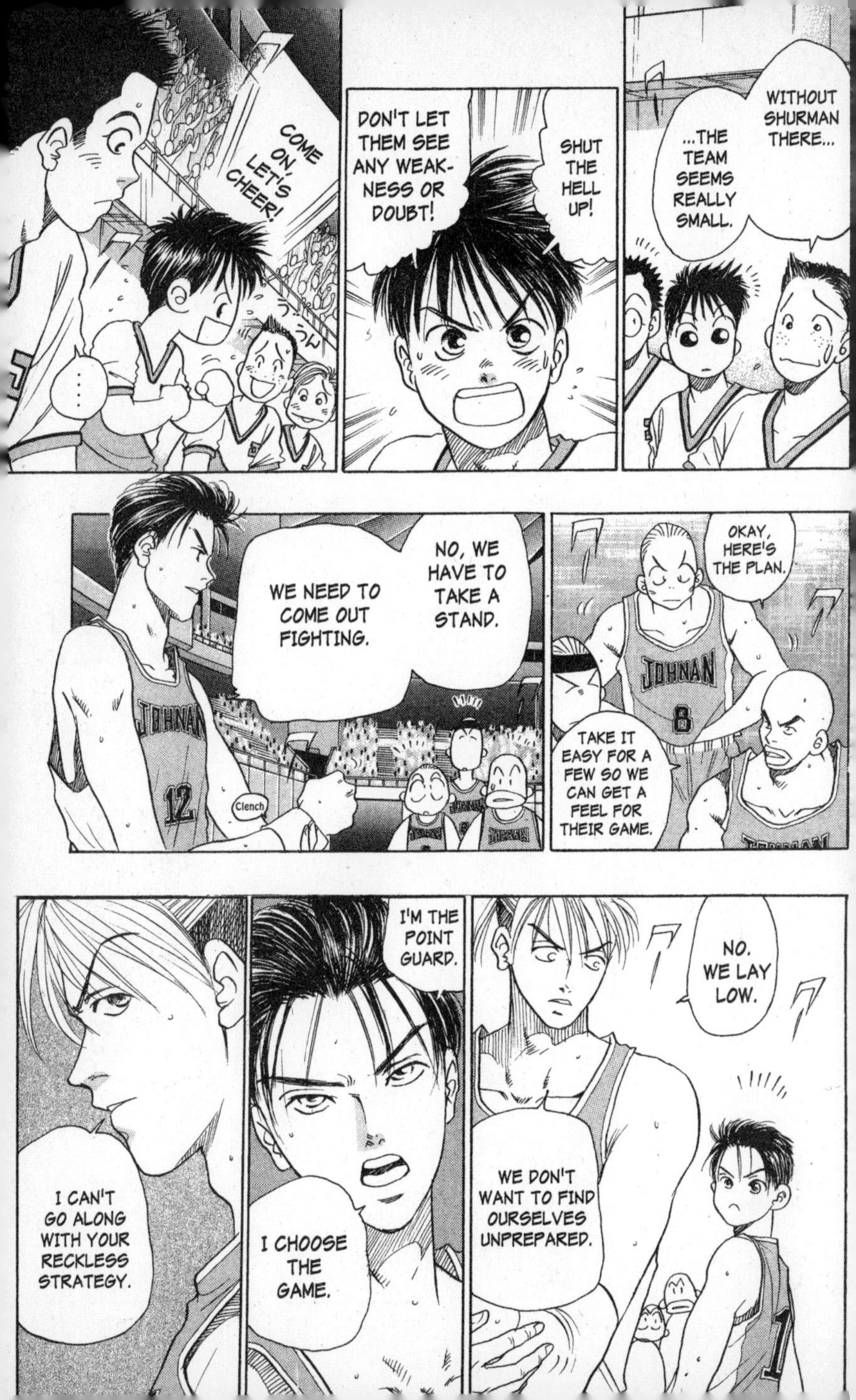
WITHOUT SHURMAN THERE...
...THE TEAM SEEMS REALLY SMALL.
SHUT THE HELL UP!
DON'T LET THEM SEE ANY WEAK-NESS OR DOUBT!
COME ON, LET'S CHEER!
......
OKAY, HERE'S THE PLAN.
TAKE IT EASY FOR A FEW SO WE CAN GET A FEEL FOR THEIR GAME.
NO, WE HAVE TO TAKE A STAND.
WE NEED TO COME OUT FIGHTING.
Clench
NO. WE LAY LOW.
WE DON'T WANT TO FIND OURSELVES UNPREPARED.
I'M THE POINT GUARD.
I CHOOSE THE GAME.
I CAN'T GO ALONG WITH YOUR RECKLESS STRATEGY.

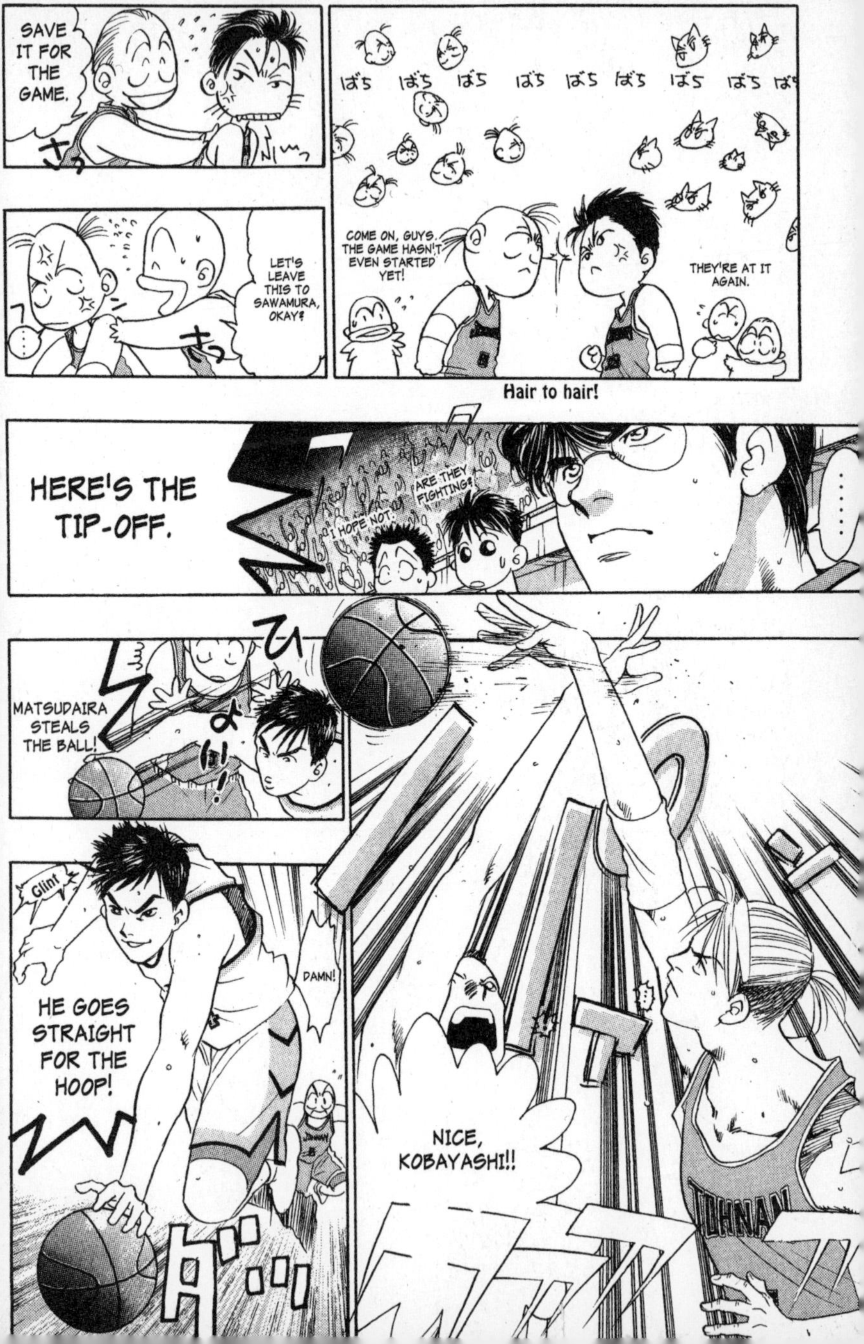
ばち ばち ばち ばち ばち ばち ばち ばち ばち
THEY'RE AT IT AGAIN.
COME ON, GUYS. THE GAME HASN'T EVEN STARTED YET!
Hair to hair!
SAVE IT FOR THE GAME.
さっ
LET'S LEAVE THIS TO SAWAMURA, OKAY?
...
さっ
......
ARE THEY FIGHTING?
I HOPE NOT.
HERE'S THE TIP-OFF.
NICE, KOBAYASHI!!
TOHNAN
ひょい
MATSUDAIRA STEALS THE BALL!
DAMN!
Glint
HE GOES STRAIGHT FOR THE HOOP!
ダッ

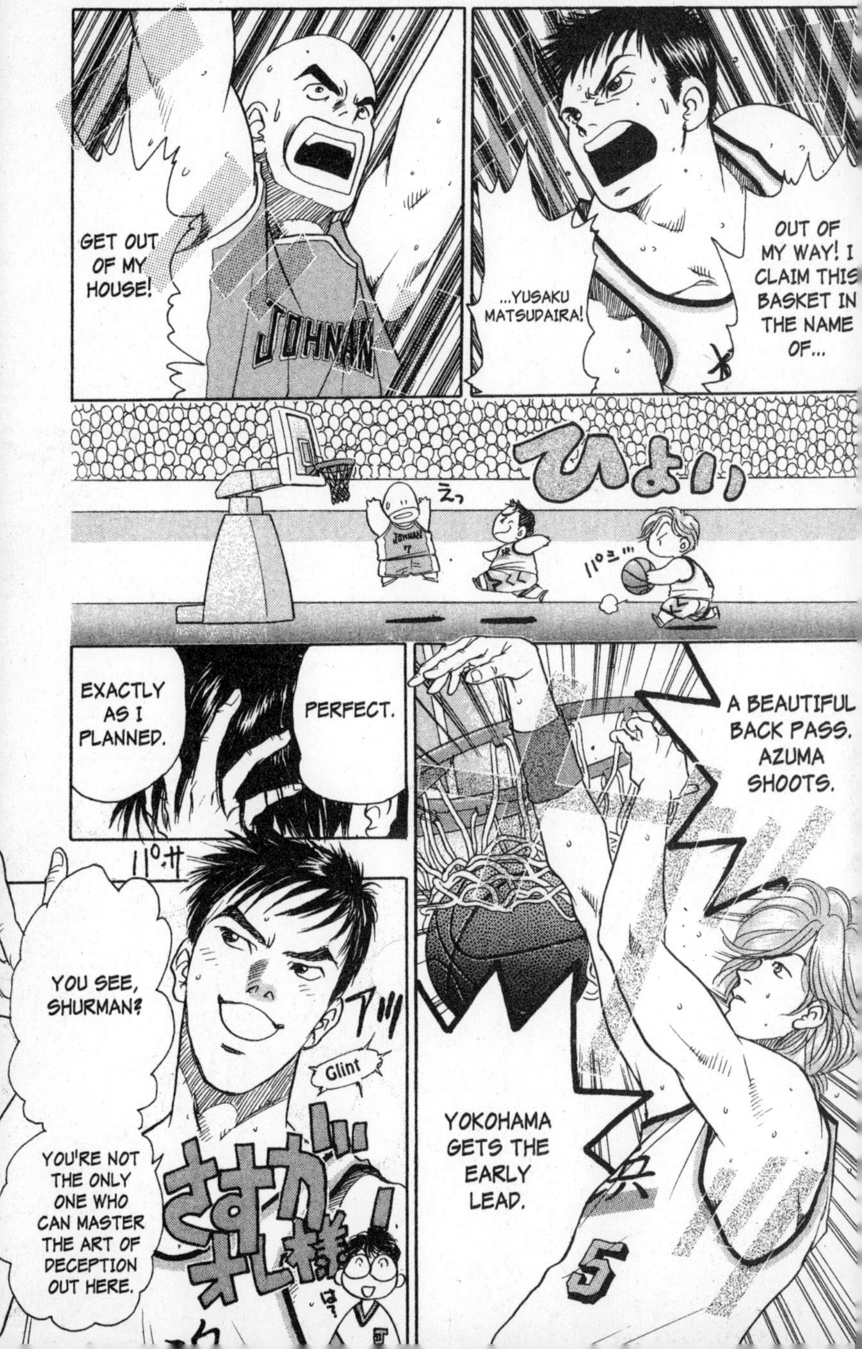
OUT OF MY WAY! I CLAIM THIS BASKET IN THE NAME OF...
...YUSAKU MATSUDAIRA!
GET OUT OF MY HOUSE!
JOHNAN
ひょい
A BEAUTIFUL BACK PASS. AZUMA SHOOTS.
YOKOHAMA GETS THE EARLY LEAD.
PERFECT.
EXACTLY AS I PLANNED.
YOU SEE, SHURMAN?
Glint
YOU'RE NOT THE ONLY ONE WHO CAN MASTER THE ART OF DECEPTION OUT HERE.
さすがオレ様

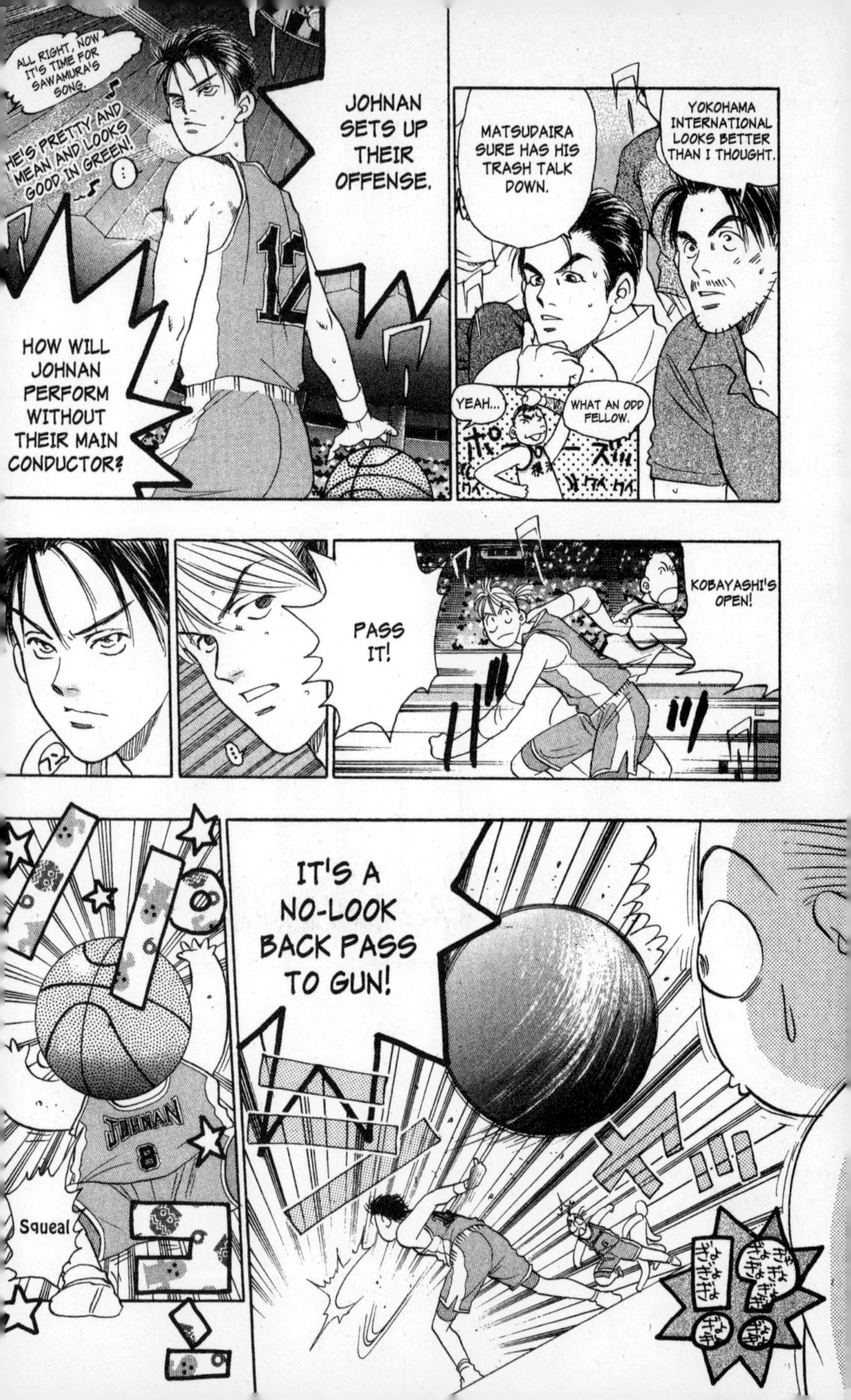
YOKOHAMA INTERNATIONAL LOOKS BETTER THAN I THOUGHT.
MATSUDAIRA SURE HAS HIS TRASH TALK DOWN.
WHAT AN ODD FELLOW.
YEAH...
JOHNAN SETS UP THEIR OFFENSE.
ALL RIGHT, NOW IT'S TIME FOR SAWAMURA'S SONG.
HE'S PRETTY AND MEAN AND LOOKS GOOD IN GREEN!
...
HOW WILL JOHNAN PERFORM WITHOUT THEIR MAIN CONDUCTOR?
KOBAYASHI'S OPEN!
PASS IT!
...
IT'S A NO-LOOK BACK PASS TO GUN!
JOHNAN
8
Squeal

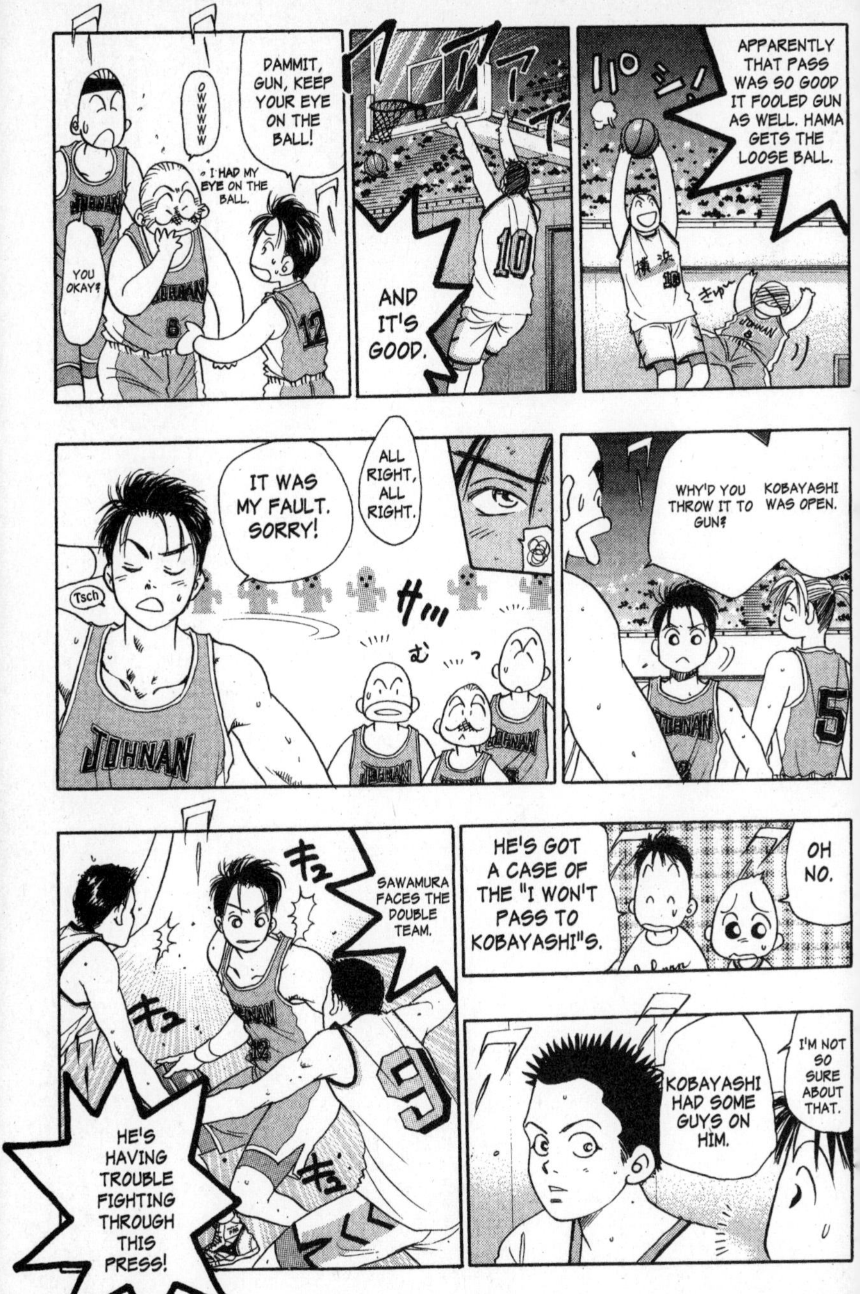

APPARENTLY THAT PASS WAS SO GOOD IT FOOLED GUN AS WELL. HAMA GETS THE LOOSE BALL.
AND IT'S GOOD.
DAMMIT, GUN, KEEP YOUR EYE ON THE BALL!
OWWWWW
I HAD MY EYE ON THE BALL.
YOU OKAY?
WHY'D YOU THROW IT TO GUN? KOBAYASHI WAS OPEN.
ALL RIGHT, ALL RIGHT.
IT WAS MY FAULT. SORRY!
Tsch
OH NO.
HE'S GOT A CASE OF THE "I WON'T PASS TO KOBAYASHI"S.
I'M NOT SO SURE ABOUT THAT.
KOBAYASHI HAD SOME GUYS ON HIM.
SAWAMURA FACES THE DOUBLE TEAM.
HE'S HAVING TROUBLE FIGHTING THROUGH THIS PRESS!

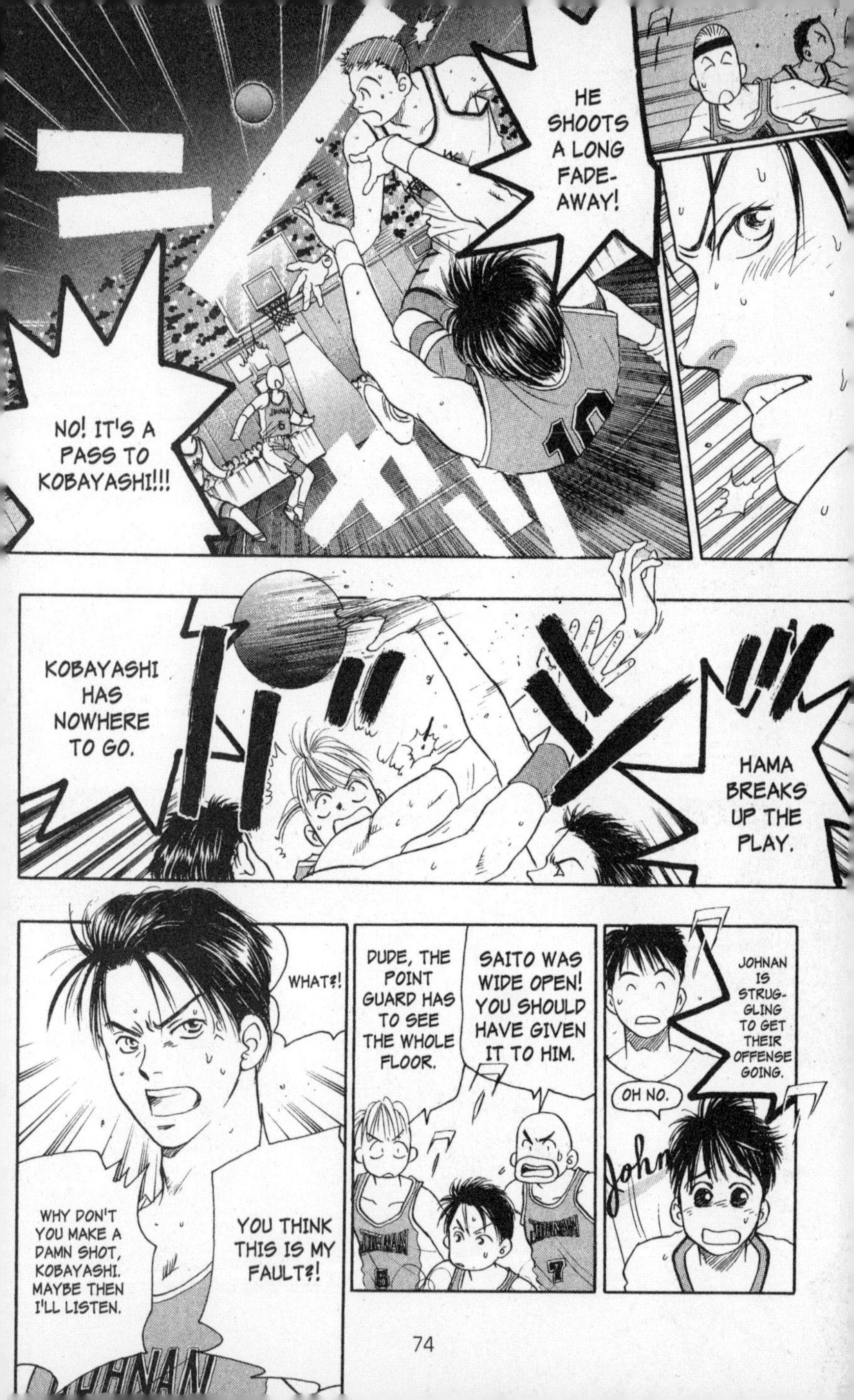
HE SHOOTS A LONG FADE-AWAY!
NO! IT'S A PASS TO KOBAYASHI!!!
KOBAYASHI HAS NOWHERE TO GO.
HAMA BREAKS UP THE PLAY.
JOHNAN IS STRUG-GLING TO GET THEIR OFFENSE GOING.
OH NO.
SAITO WAS WIDE OPEN! YOU SHOULD HAVE GIVEN IT TO HIM.
DUDE, THE POINT GUARD HAS TO SEE THE WHOLE FLOOR.
WHAT?!
YOU THINK THIS IS MY FAULT?!
WHY DON'T YOU MAKE A DAMN SHOT, KOBAYASHI. MAYBE THEN I'LL LISTEN.

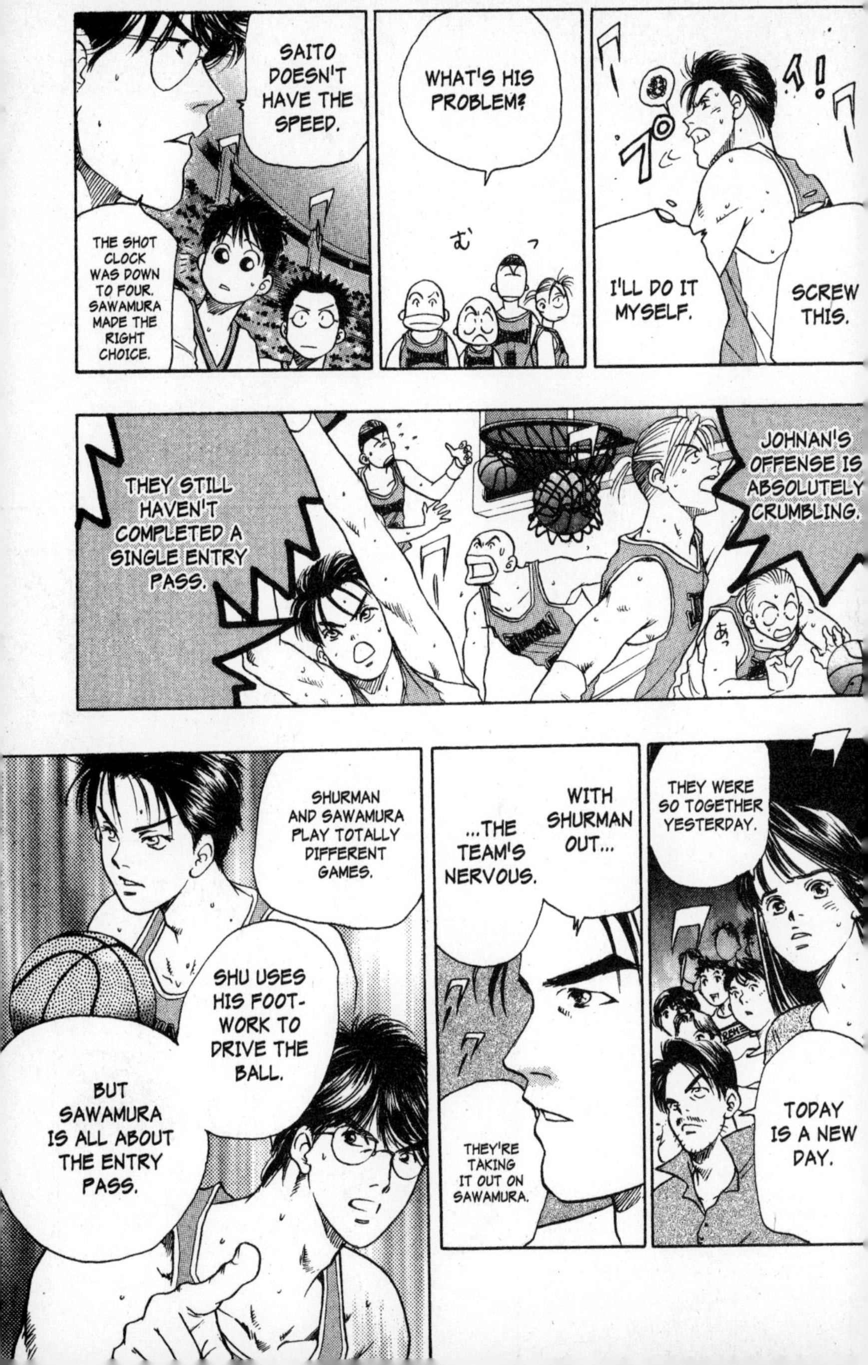
SCREW THIS.
I'LL DO IT MYSELF.
WHAT'S HIS PROBLEM?
SAITO DOESN'T HAVE THE SPEED.
THE SHOT CLOCK WAS DOWN TO FOUR. SAWAMURA MADE THE RIGHT CHOICE.
JOHNAN'S OFFENSE IS ABSOLUTELY CRUMBLING.
THEY STILL HAVEN'T COMPLETED A SINGLE ENTRY PASS.
THEY WERE SO TOGETHER YESTERDAY.
TODAY IS A NEW DAY.
WITH SHURMAN OUT...
...THE TEAM'S NERVOUS.
THEY'RE TAKING IT OUT ON SAWAMURA.
SHURMAN AND SAWAMURA PLAY TOTALLY DIFFERENT GAMES.
SHU USES HIS FOOT-WORK TO DRIVE THE BALL.
BUT SAWAMURA IS ALL ABOUT THE ENTRY PASS.

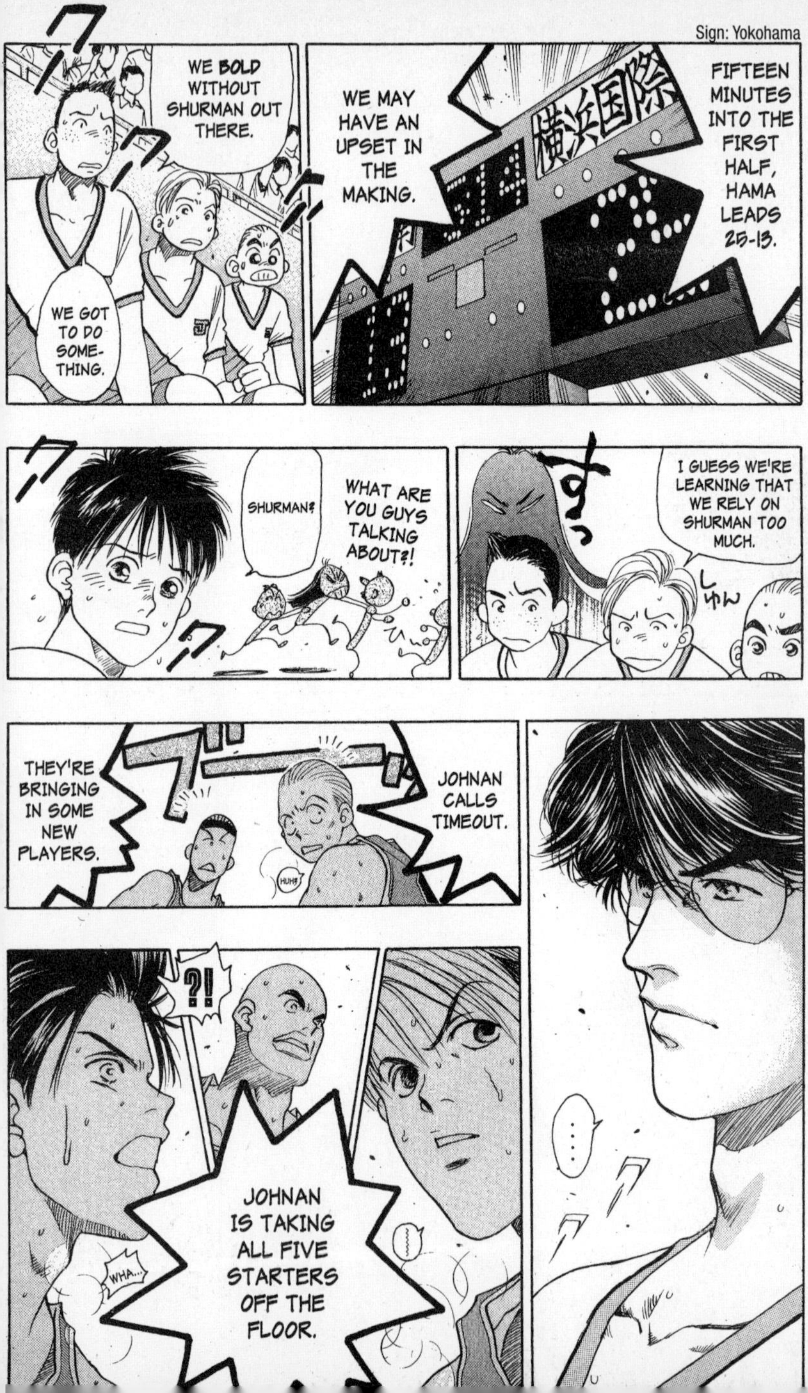
Sign: Yokohama
横浜国際
FIFTEEN MINUTES INTO THE FIRST HALF, HAMA LEADS 25-13.
WE MAY HAVE AN UPSET IN THE MAKING.
WE BOLD WITHOUT SHURMAN OUT THERE.
WE GOT TO DO SOME-THING.
すっ
I GUESS WE'RE LEARNING THAT WE RELY ON SHURMAN TOO MUCH.
しゅん
SHURMAN?
WHAT ARE YOU GUYS TALKING ABOUT?!
......
JOHNAN CALLS TIMEOUT.
THEY'RE BRINGING IN SOME NEW PLAYERS.
HUH?
?!
WHA...
JOHNAN IS TAKING ALL FIVE STARTERS OFF THE FLOOR.

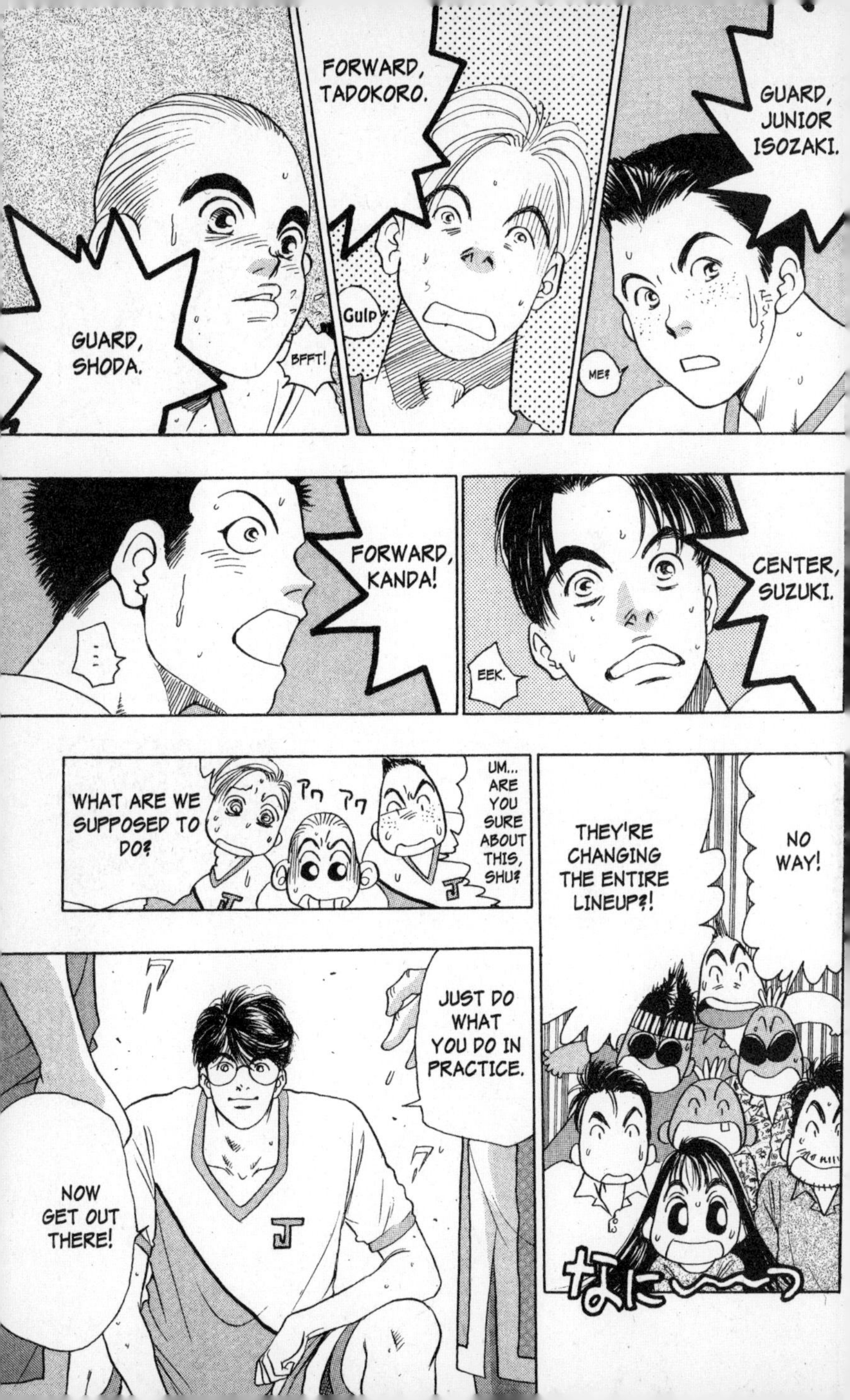
GUARD, JUNIOR ISOZAKI.
ME?
FORWARD, TADOKORO.
Gulp
GUARD, SHODA.
BFFT!
CENTER, SUZUKI.
EEK.
FORWARD, KANDA!
...
NO WAY!
THEY'RE CHANGING THE ENTIRE LINEUP?!
なに〜〜っ
UM... ARE YOU SURE ABOUT THIS, SHU?
アワ アワ
WHAT ARE WE SUPPOSED TO DO?
JUST DO WHAT YOU DO IN PRACTICE.
NOW GET OUT THERE!

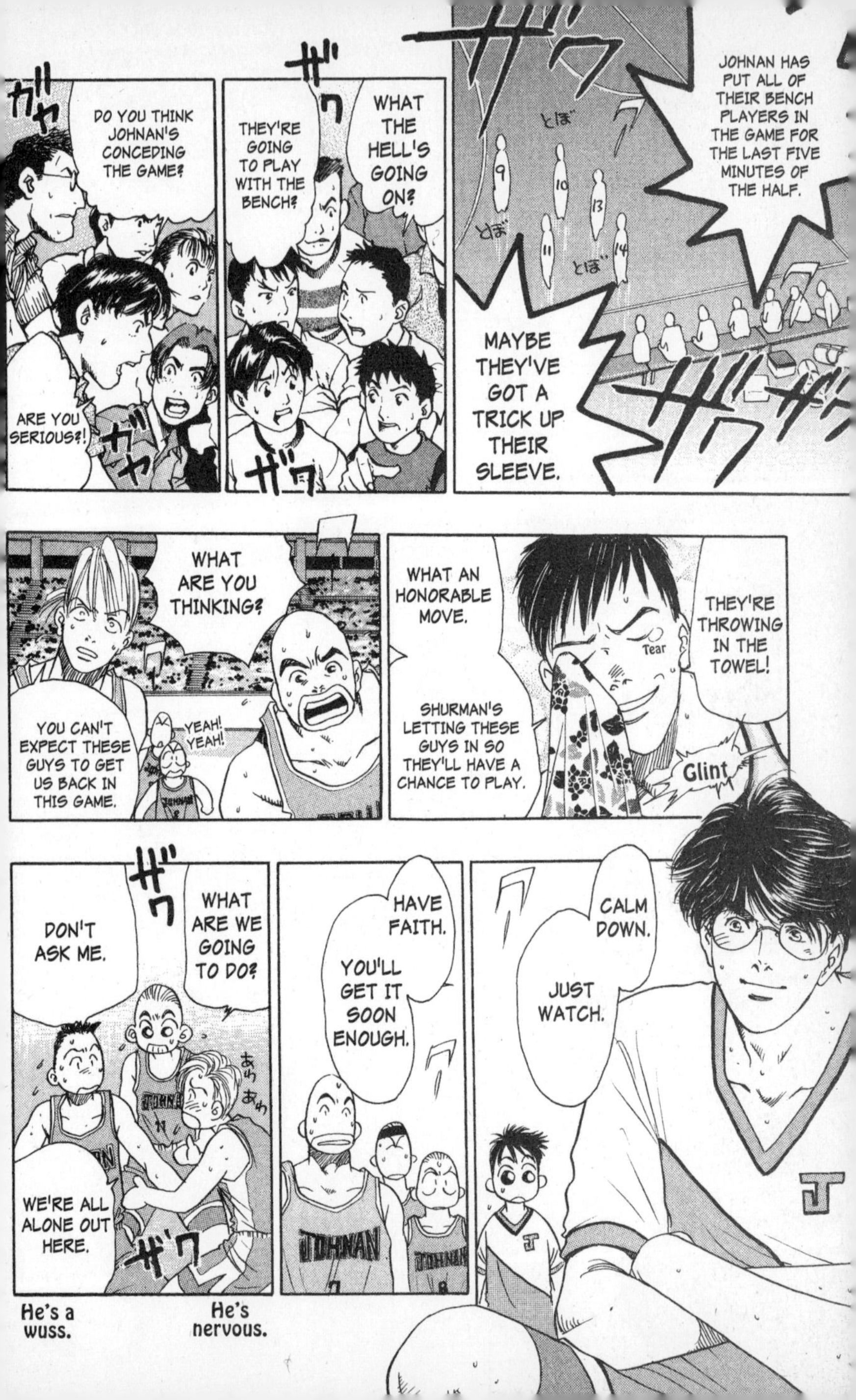
ザワ
JOHNAN HAS PUT ALL OF THEIR BENCH PLAYERS IN THE GAME FOR THE LAST FIVE MINUTES OF THE HALF.
とぼ
MAYBE THEY'VE GOT A TRICK UP THEIR SLEEVE.
ザワザワ
ザワ
WHAT THE HELL'S GOING ON?
THEY'RE GOING TO PLAY WITH THE BENCH?
ガヤ
DO YOU THINK JOHNAN'S CONCEDING THE GAME?
ARE YOU SERIOUS?!
THEY'RE THROWING IN THE TOWEL!
WHAT AN HONORABLE MOVE.
Tear
SHURMAN'S LETTING THESE GUYS IN SO THEY'LL HAVE A CHANCE TO PLAY.
Glint
WHAT ARE YOU THINKING?
YOU CAN'T EXPECT THESE GUYS TO GET US BACK IN THIS GAME.
YEAH! YEAH!
CALM DOWN.
JUST WATCH.
HAVE FAITH.
YOU'LL GET IT SOON ENOUGH.
ザワ
WHAT ARE WE GOING TO DO?
DON'T ASK ME.
あわあわ
WE'RE ALL ALONE OUT HERE.
He's nervous.
He's a wuss.

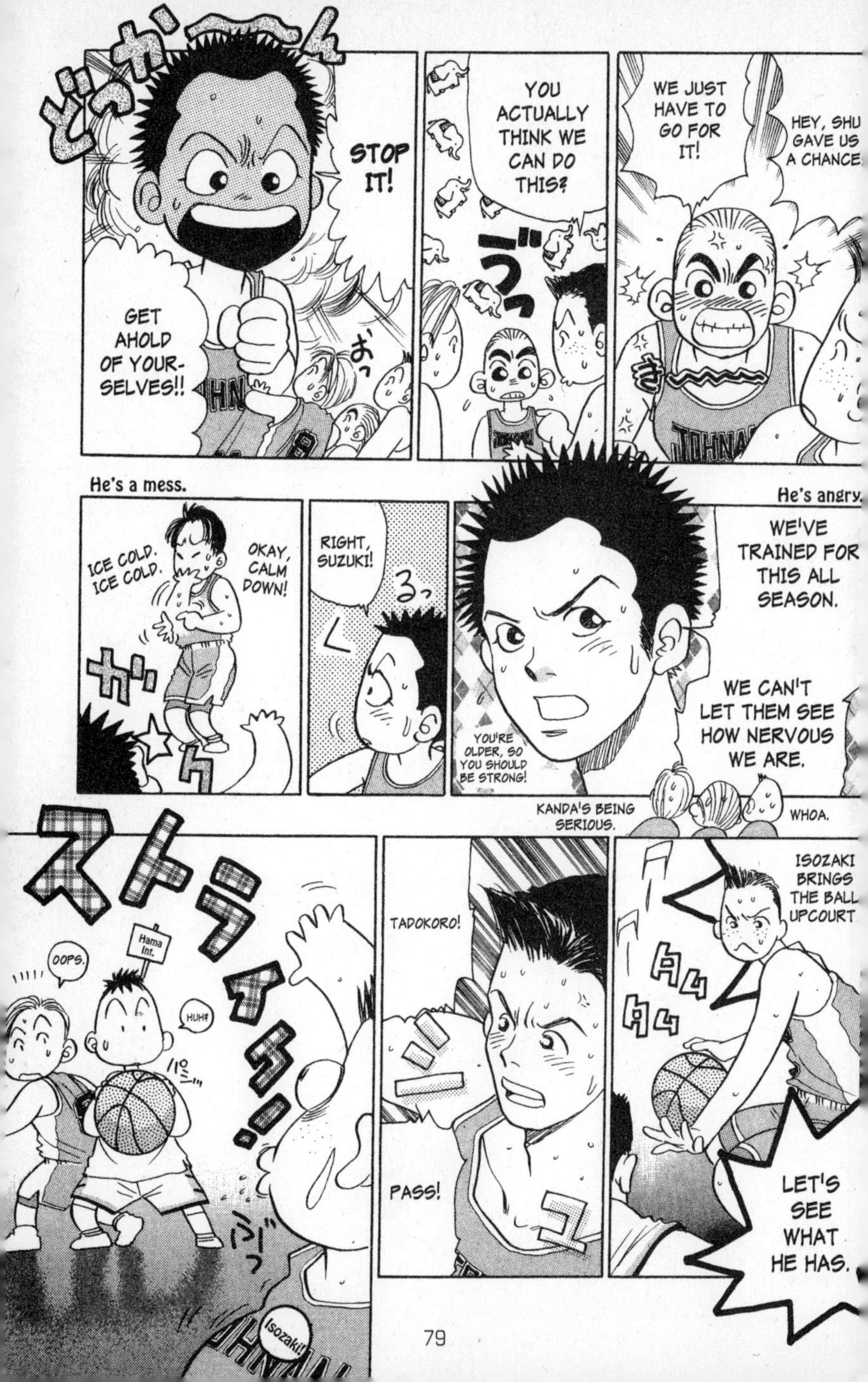
HEY, SHU GAVE US A CHANCE!
WE JUST HAVE TO GO FOR IT!
YOU ACTUALLY THINK WE CAN DO THIS?
どっかーーん
STOP IT!
GET AHOLD OF YOUR-SELVES!!
He's angry.
He's a mess.
WE'VE TRAINED FOR THIS ALL SEASON.
WE CAN'T LET THEM SEE HOW NERVOUS WE ARE.
YOU'RE OLDER, SO YOU SHOULD BE STRONG!
WHOA.
KANDA'S BEING SERIOUS.
RIGHT, SUZUKI!
OKAY, CALM DOWN!
ICE COLD. ICE COLD.
ISOZAKI BRINGS THE BALL UPCOURT
LET'S SEE WHAT HE HAS.
TADOKORO!
PASS!
ストライク!!
Hama Int.
OOPS.
HUH?
Isozaki!

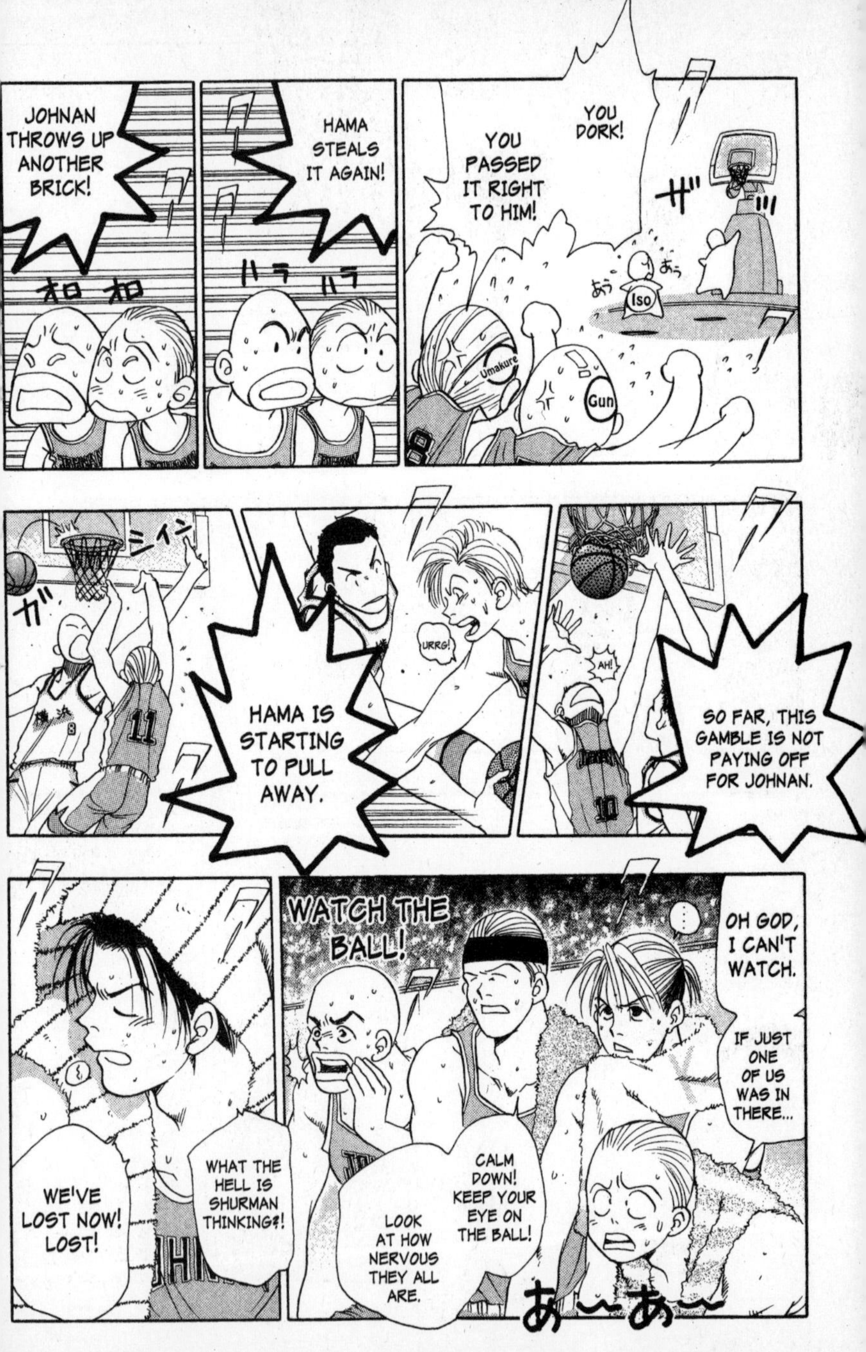
YOU DORK!
YOU PASSED IT RIGHT TO HIM!
あう
あう
Iso
Umakure
Gun
HAMA STEALS IT AGAIN!
ハラ ハラ
JOHNAN THROWS UP ANOTHER BRICK!
オロ オロ
AH!
SO FAR, THIS GAMBLE IS NOT PAYING OFF FOR JOHNAN.
URRG!
HAMA IS STARTING TO PULL AWAY.
シイン
ガ
...
OH GOD, I CAN'T WATCH.
IF JUST ONE OF US WAS IN THERE...
WATCH THE BALL!
CALM DOWN! KEEP YOUR EYE ON THE BALL!
LOOK AT HOW NERVOUS THEY ALL ARE.
あ〜あ〜
WHAT THE HELL IS SHURMAN THINKING?!
WE'VE LOST NOW! LOST!

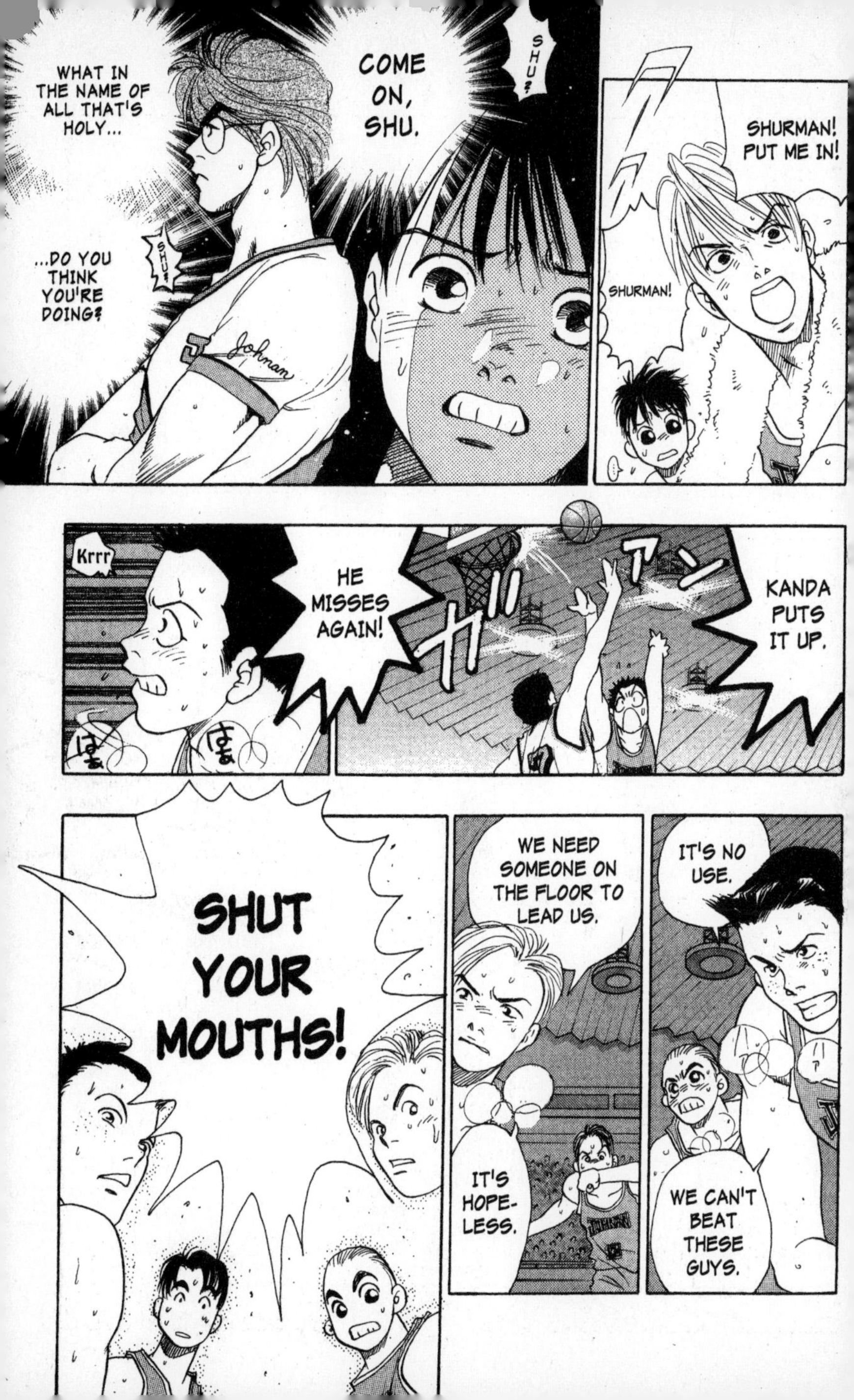
SHURMAN! PUT ME IN!
SHURMAN!
SHU?
COME ON, SHU.
WHAT IN THE NAME OF ALL THAT'S HOLY...
SHU?
...DO YOU THINK YOU'RE DOING?
KANDA PUTS IT UP.
HE MISSES AGAIN!
Krrr
IT'S NO USE.
WE CAN'T BEAT THESE GUYS.
WE NEED SOMEONE ON THE FLOOR TO LEAD US.
IT'S HOPE-LESS.
SHUT YOUR MOUTHS!

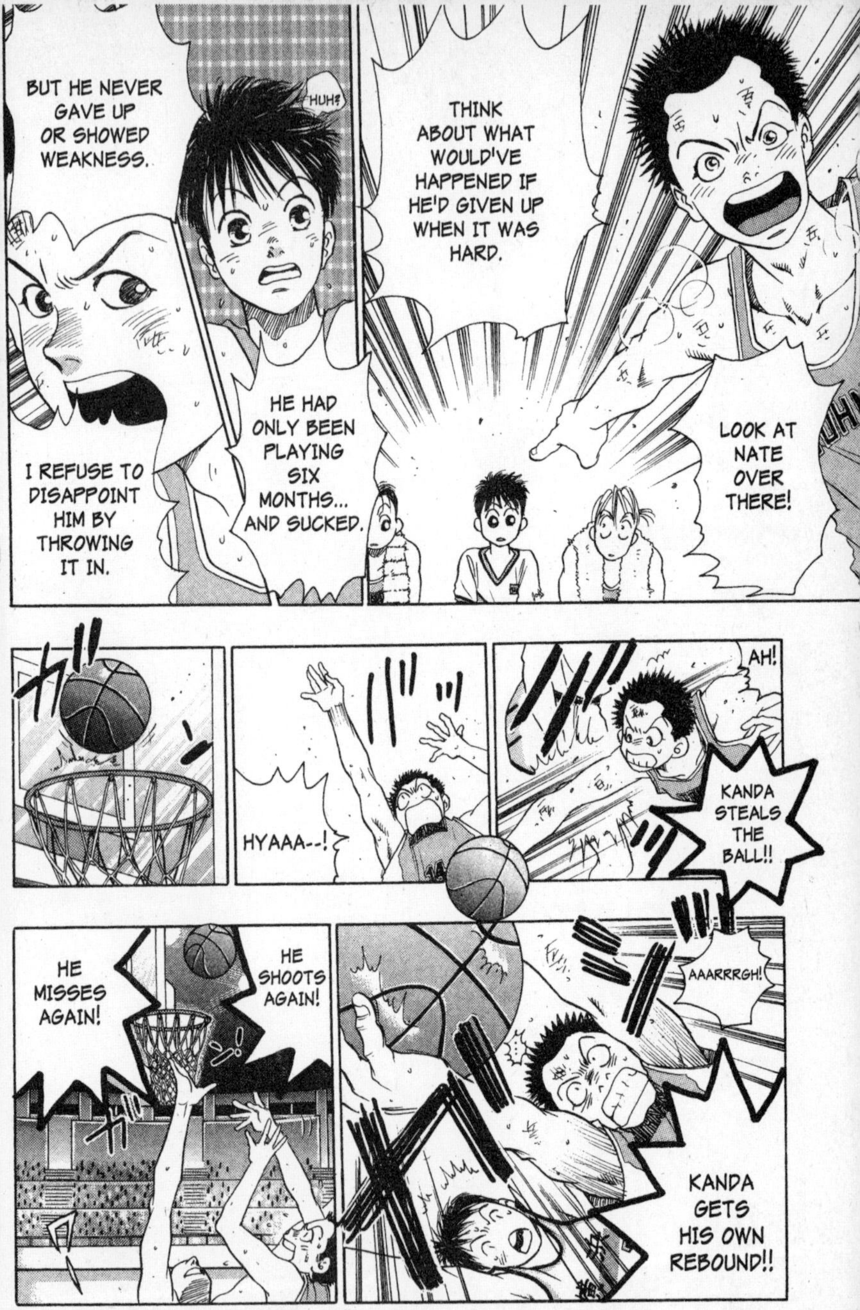
THINK ABOUT WHAT WOULD'VE HAPPENED IF HE'D GIVEN UP WHEN IT WAS HARD.
LOOK AT NATE OVER THERE!
HUH?
HE HAD ONLY BEEN PLAYING SIX MONTHS... AND SUCKED.
BUT HE NEVER GAVE UP OR SHOWED WEAKNESS.
I REFUSE TO DISAPPOINT HIM BY THROWING IT IN.
AH!
KANDA STEALS THE BALL!!
HYAAA--!
AAARRRGH!
KANDA GETS HIS OWN REBOUND!!
HE SHOOTS AGAIN!
HE MISSES AGAIN!

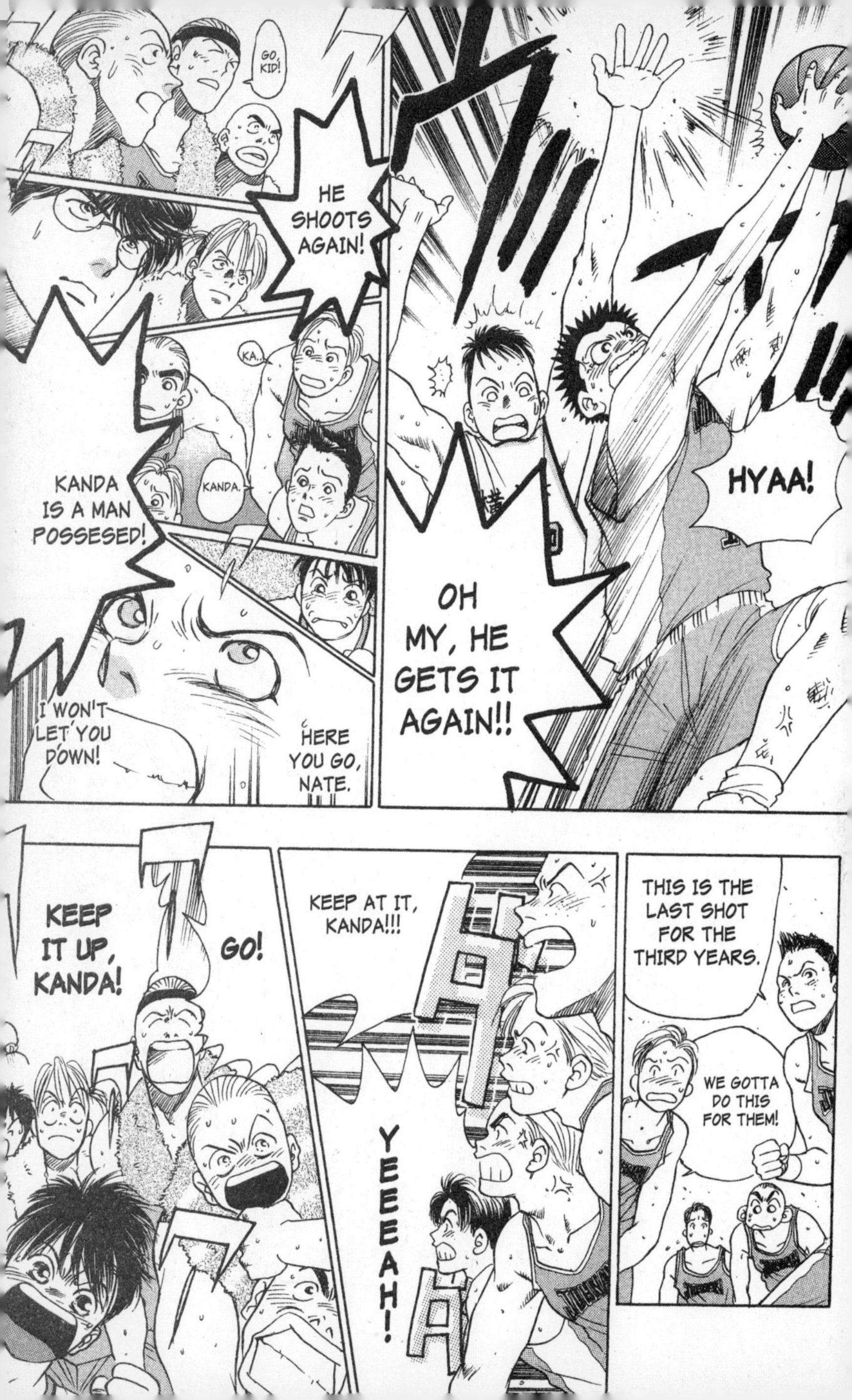
HYAA!
OH MY, HE GETS IT AGAIN!!
GO, KID!
HE SHOOTS AGAIN!
KA..
KANDA.
KANDA IS A MAN POSSESSED!
HERE YOU GO, NATE.
I WON'T LET YOU DOWN!
THIS IS THE LAST SHOT FOR THE THIRD YEARS.
WE GOTTA DO THIS FOR THEM!
KEEP AT IT, KANDA!!!
YEEEAH!
GO!
KEEP IT UP, KANDA!

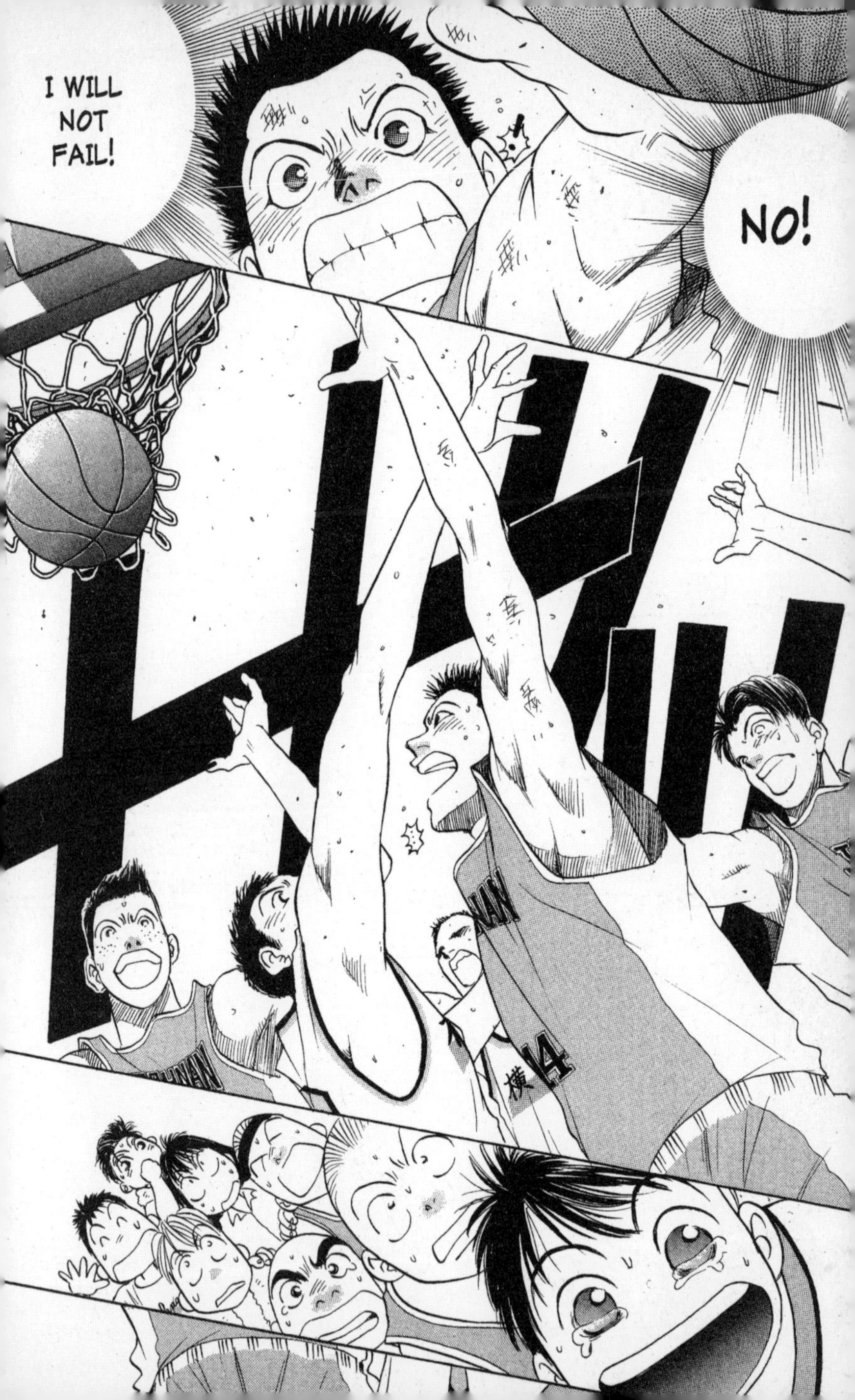

NO!
I WILL NOT FAIL!

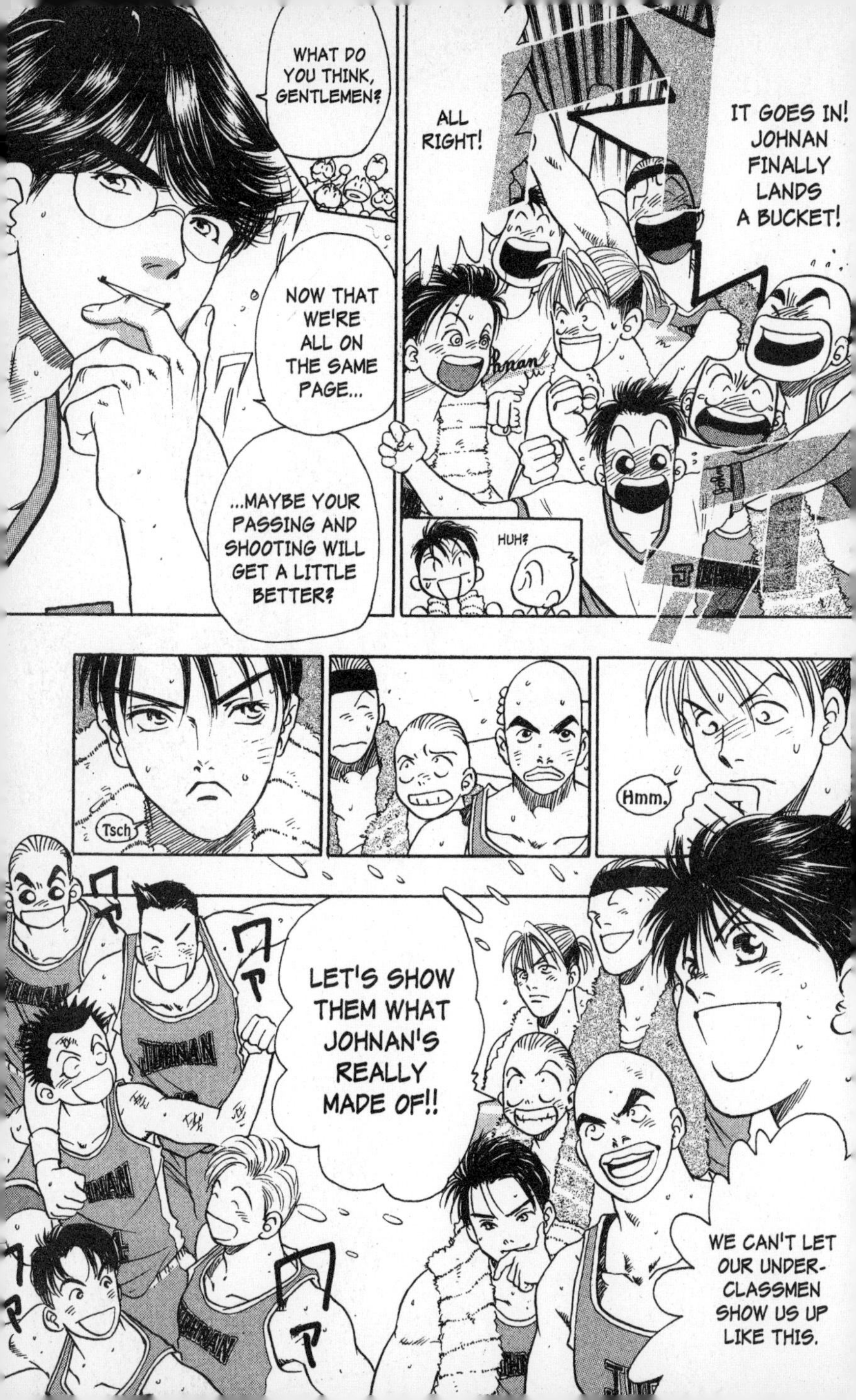
IT GOES IN! JOHNAN FINALLY LANDS A BUCKET!
ALL RIGHT!
HUH?
WHAT DO YOU THINK, GENTLEMEN?
NOW THAT WE'RE ALL ON THE SAME PAGE...
...MAYBE YOUR PASSING AND SHOOTING WILL GET A LITTLE BETTER?
Hmm.
Tsch
WE CAN'T LET OUR UNDER-CLASSMEN SHOW US UP LIKE THIS.
LET'S SHOW THEM WHAT JOHNAN'S REALLY MADE OF!!

You're Reading...

REBOUND

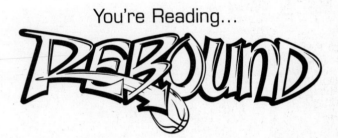

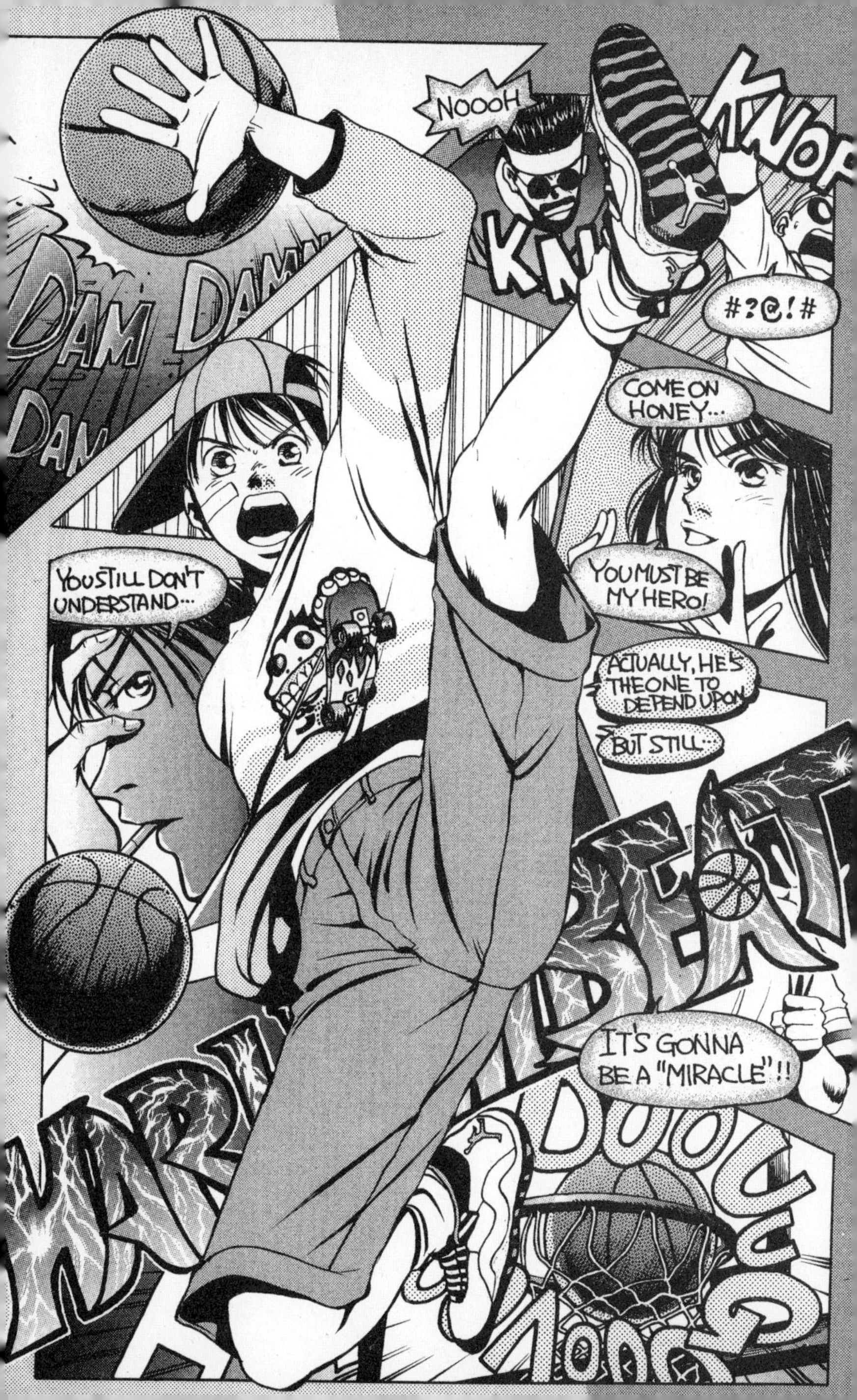
NOOOH
#?@!#
COME ON HONEY...
YOU MUST BE MY HERO!
ACTUALLY, HE'S THE ONE TO DEPEND UPON
BUT STILL...
IT'S GONNA BE A "MIRACLE"!!
DAM
YOU STILL DON'T UNDERSTAND...

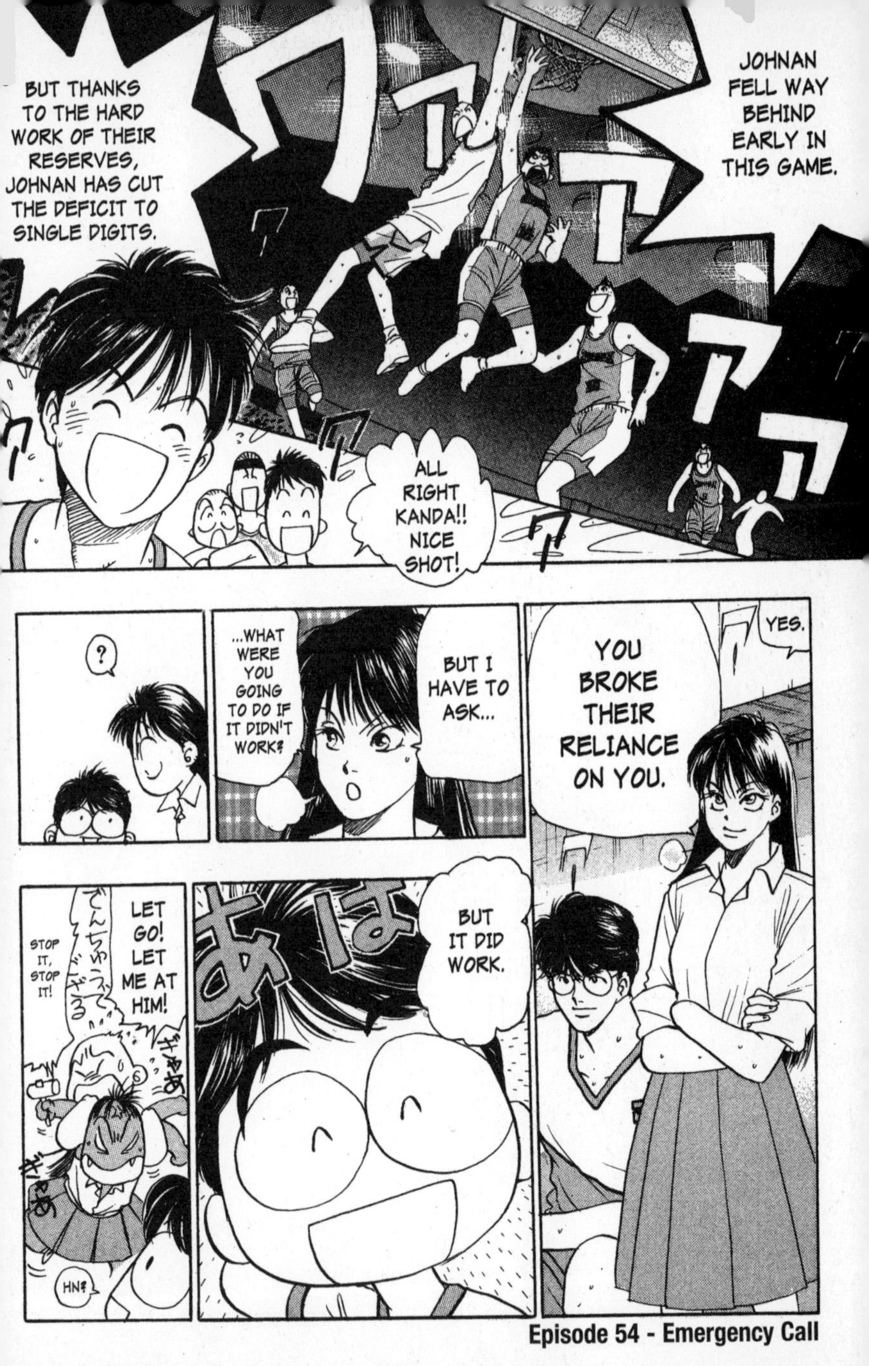
JOHNAN FELL WAY BEHIND EARLY IN THIS GAME.
BUT THANKS TO THE HARD WORK OF THEIR RESERVES, JOHNAN HAS CUT THE DEFICIT TO SINGLE DIGITS.
ALL RIGHT KANDA!! NICE SHOT!
YES.
YOU BROKE THEIR RELIANCE ON YOU.
BUT I HAVE TO ASK...
...WHAT WERE YOU GOING TO DO IF IT DIDN'T WORK?
?
BUT IT DID WORK.
LET GO! LET ME AT HIM!
STOP IT, STOP IT!
HN?

Episode 54 - Emergency Call

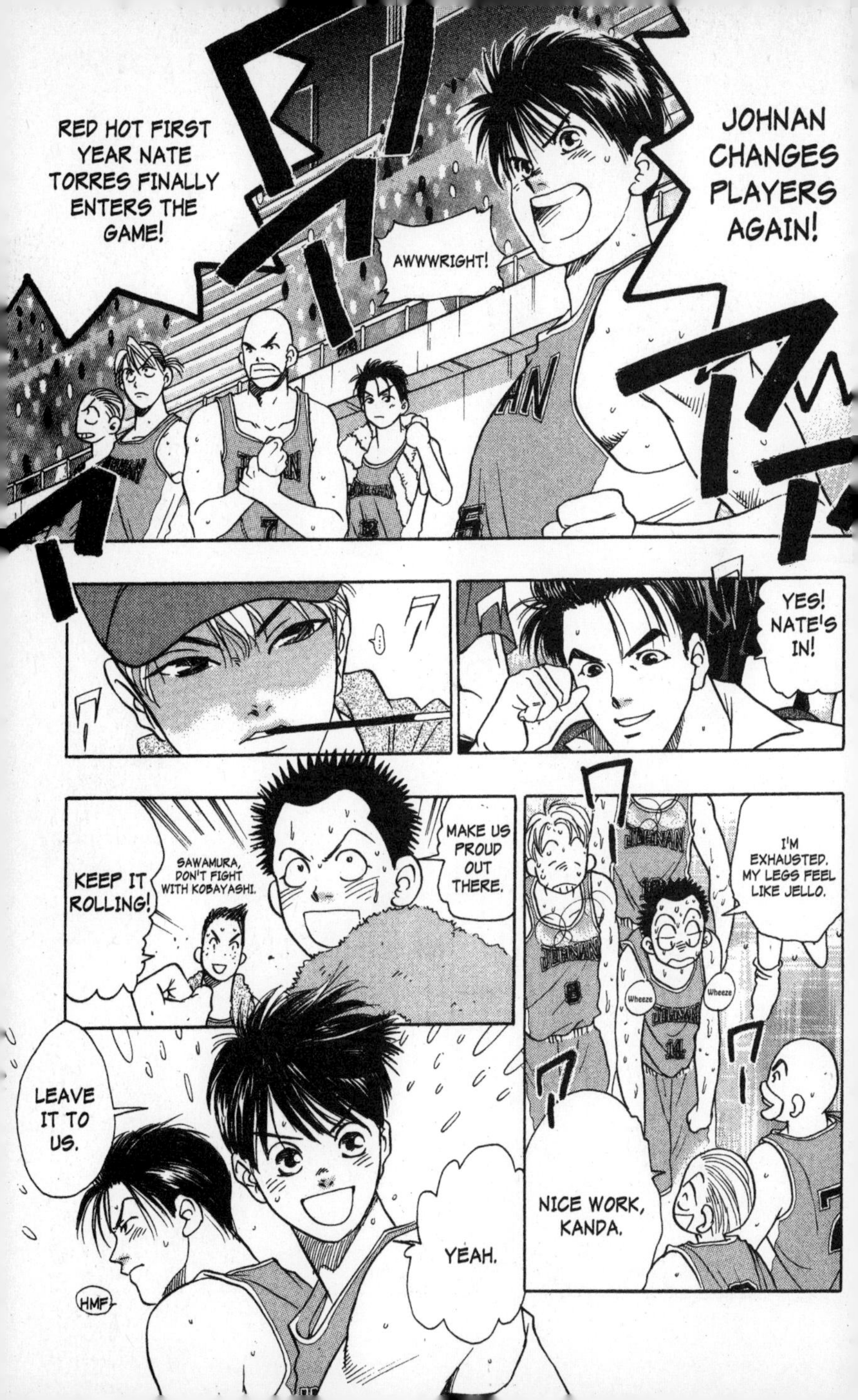
JOHNAN CHANGES PLAYERS AGAIN!
RED HOT FIRST YEAR NATE TORRES FINALLY ENTERS THE GAME!
AWWWRIGHT!
YES! NATE'S IN!
...
I'M EXHAUSTED. MY LEGS FEEL LIKE JELLO.
Wheeze
Wheeze
NICE WORK, KANDA.
MAKE US PROUD OUT THERE.
SAWAMURA, DON'T FIGHT WITH KOBAYASHI.
KEEP IT ROLLING!
YEAH.
LEAVE IT TO US.
HMF

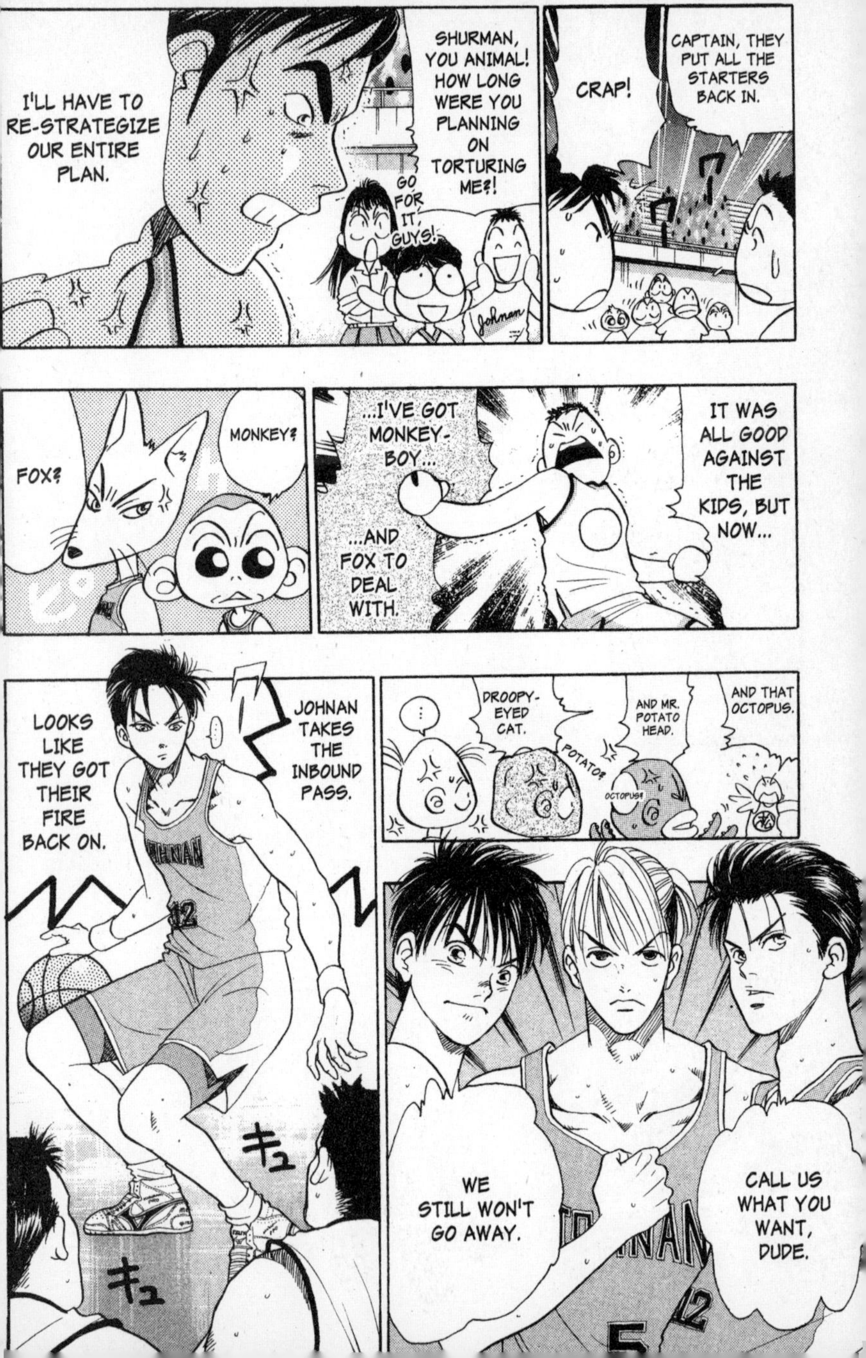
CAPTAIN, THEY PUT ALL THE STARTERS BACK IN.
CRAP!
SHURMAN, YOU ANIMAL! HOW LONG WERE YOU PLANNING ON TORTURING ME?!
GO FOR IT, GUYS!
I'LL HAVE TO RE-STRATEGIZE OUR ENTIRE PLAN.
IT WAS ALL GOOD AGAINST THE KIDS, BUT NOW...
...I'VE GOT MONKEY-BOY...
...AND FOX TO DEAL WITH.
MONKEY?
FOX?
AND THAT OCTOPUS.
AND MR. POTATO HEAD.
OCTOPUS?
DROOPY-EYED CAT.
POTATO?
...
CALL US WHAT YOU WANT, DUDE.
WE STILL WON'T GO AWAY.
JOHNAN TAKES THE INBOUND PASS.
...
LOOKS LIKE THEY GOT THEIR FIRE BACK ON.
キュ
キュ

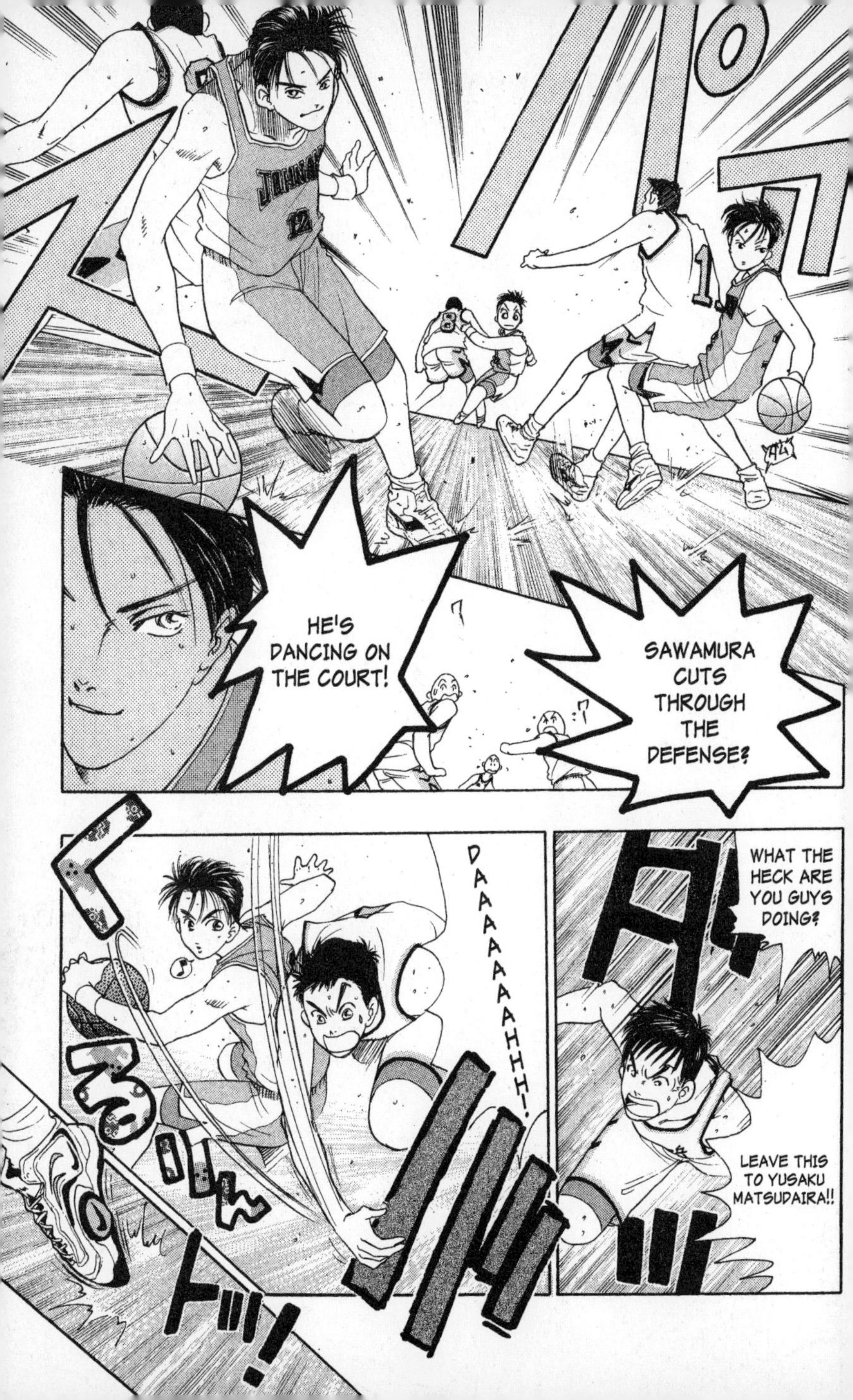
SAWAMURA CUTS THROUGH THE DEFENSE?
HE'S DANCING ON THE COURT!
WHAT THE HECK ARE YOU GUYS DOING?
LEAVE THIS TO YUSAKU MATSUDAIRA!!
DAAAAAAAAHHH!

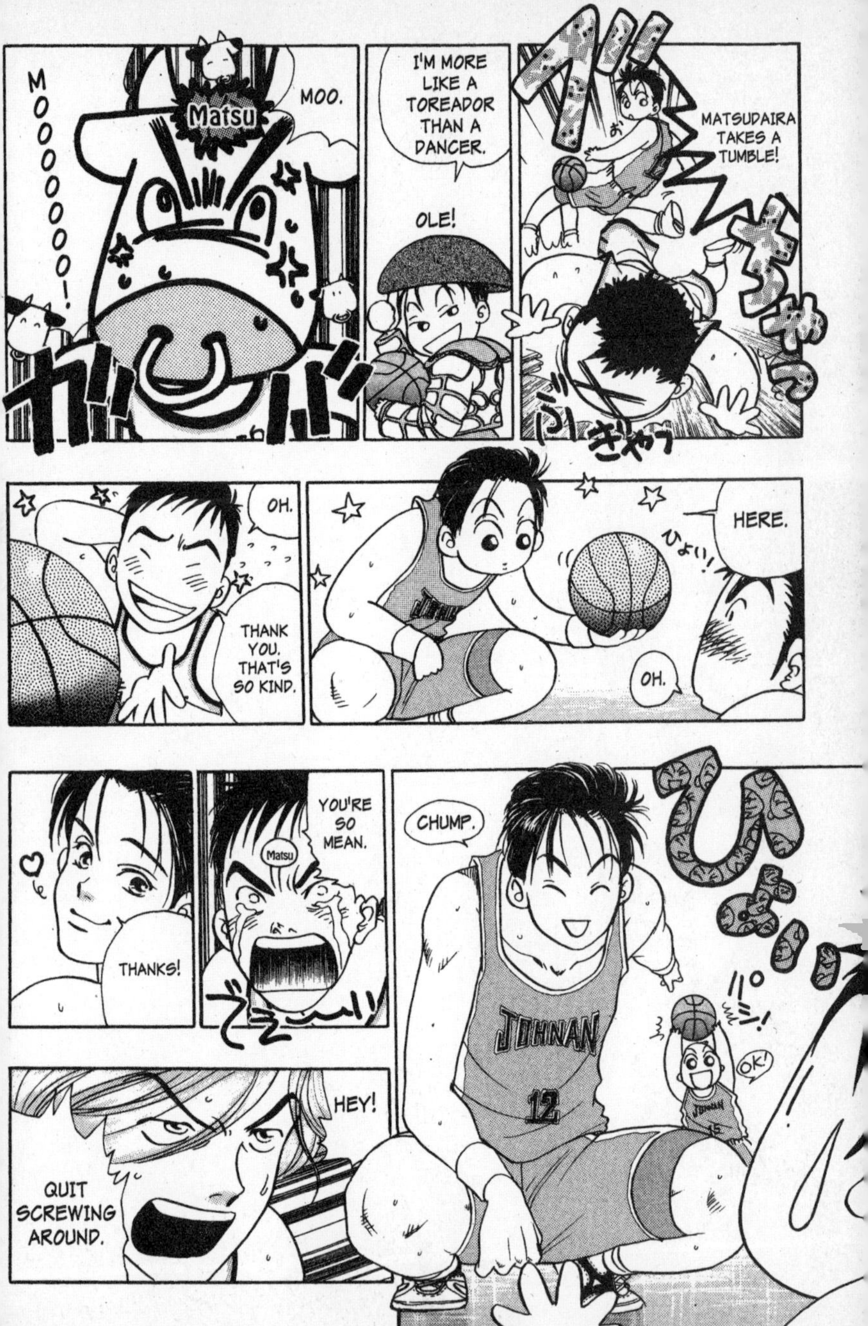
MATSUDAIRA TAKES A TUMBLE!
I'M MORE LIKE A TOREADOR THAN A DANCER.
OLE!
MOO.
Matsu
MOOOOOOOOOO!
HERE.
OH.
OH.
THANK YOU. THAT'S SO KIND.
CHUMP.
OK!
YOU'RE SO MEAN.
Matsu
THANKS!
HEY!
QUIT SCREWING AROUND.

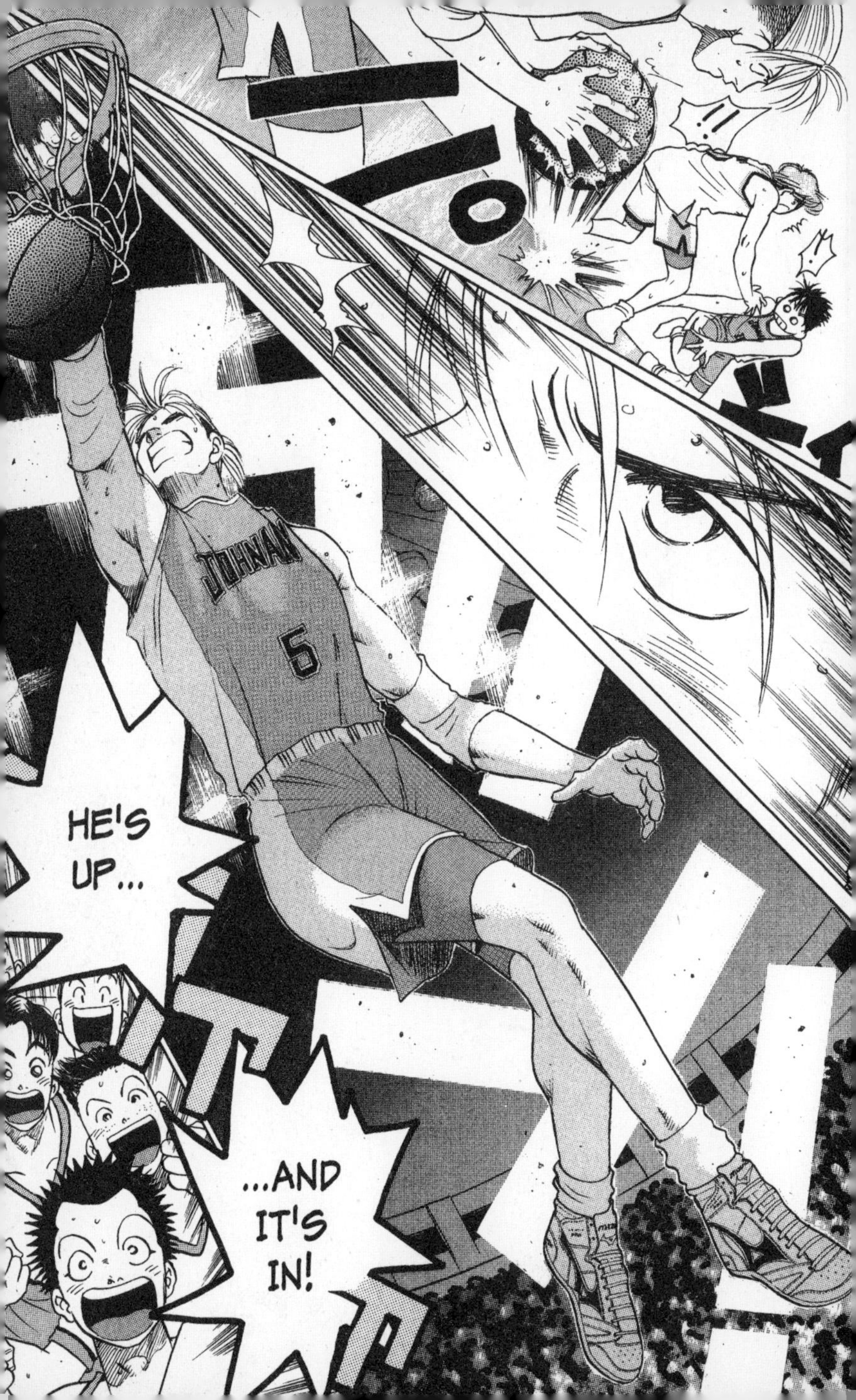
HE'S UP...
...AND IT'S IN!

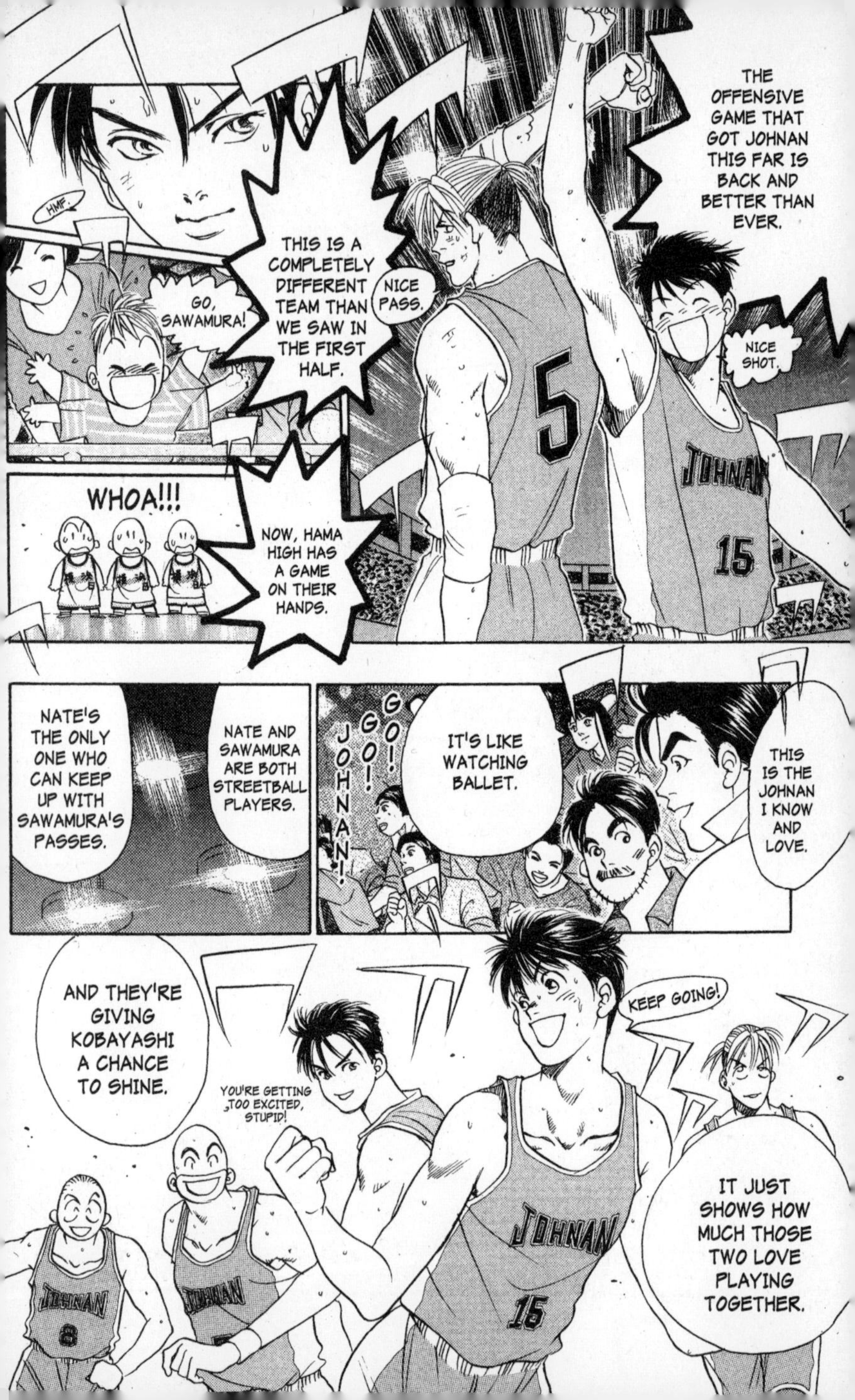
THE OFFENSIVE GAME THAT GOT JOHNAN THIS FAR IS BACK AND BETTER THAN EVER.
NICE SHOT.
NICE PASS.
THIS IS A COMPLETELY DIFFERENT TEAM THAN WE SAW IN THE FIRST HALF.
HMF.
GO, SAWAMURA!
NOW, HAMA HIGH HAS A GAME ON THEIR HANDS.
WHOA!!!
THIS IS THE JOHNAN I KNOW AND LOVE.
IT'S LIKE WATCHING BALLET.
GO! GO! JOHNAN!
NATE AND SAWAMURA ARE BOTH STREETBALL PLAYERS.
NATE'S THE ONLY ONE WHO CAN KEEP UP WITH SAWAMURA'S PASSES.
IT JUST SHOWS HOW MUCH THOSE TWO LOVE PLAYING TOGETHER.
KEEP GOING!
YOU'RE GETTING TOO EXCITED, STUPID!
AND THEY'RE GIVING KOBAYASHI A CHANCE TO SHINE.

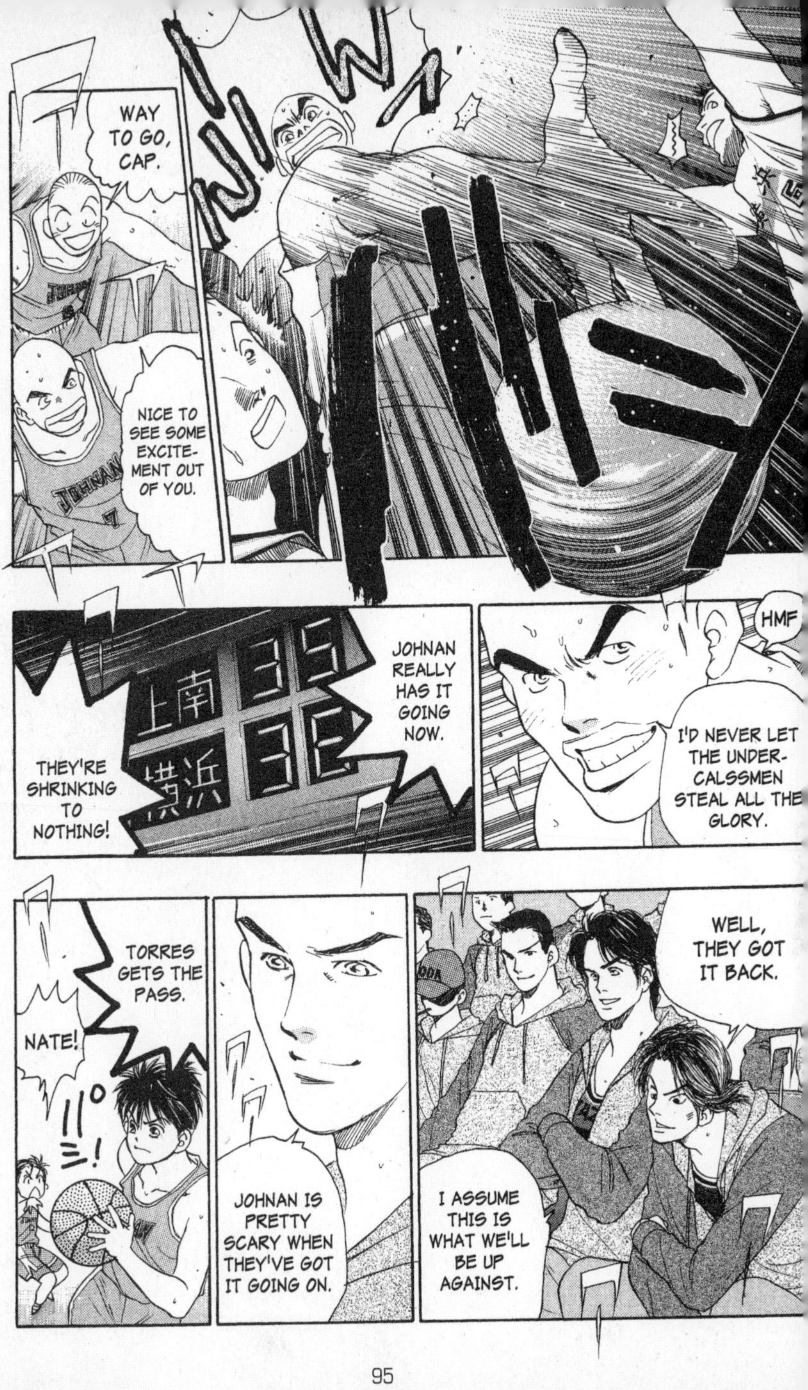
WAY TO GO, CAP.
NICE TO SEE SOME EXCITEMENT OUT OF YOU.
HMF
I'D NEVER LET THE UNDER-CALSSMEN STEAL ALL THE GLORY.
JOHNAN REALLY HAS IT GOING NOW.
THEY'RE SHRINKING TO NOTHING!
WELL, THEY GOT IT BACK.
I ASSUME THIS IS WHAT WE'LL BE UP AGAINST.
JOHNAN IS PRETTY SCARY WHEN THEY'VE GOT IT GOING ON.
TORRES GETS THE PASS.
NATE!

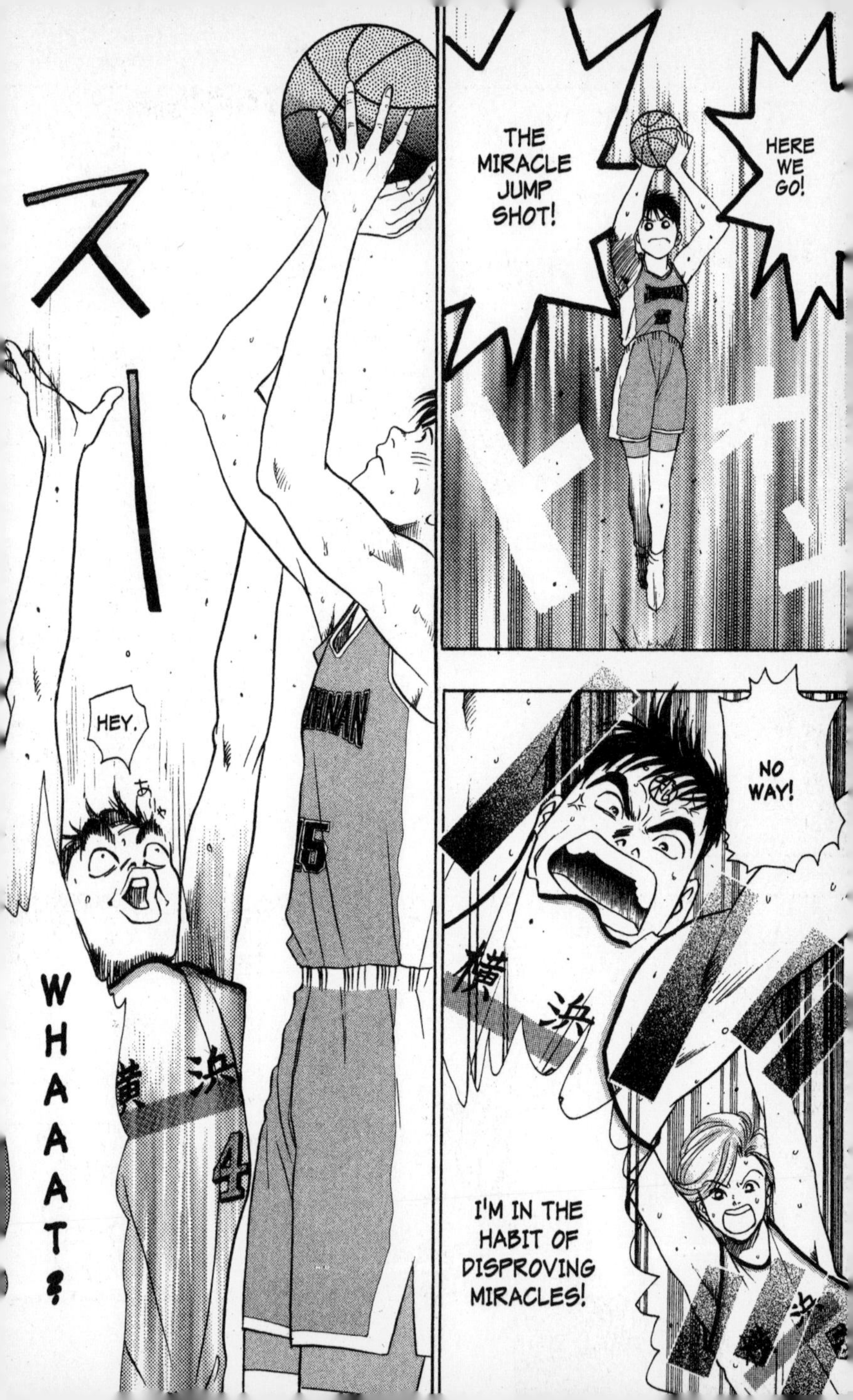
HERE WE GO!
THE MIRACLE JUMP SHOT!
NO WAY!
I'M IN THE HABIT OF DISPROVING MIRACLES!
HEY.
WHAAAAT?!

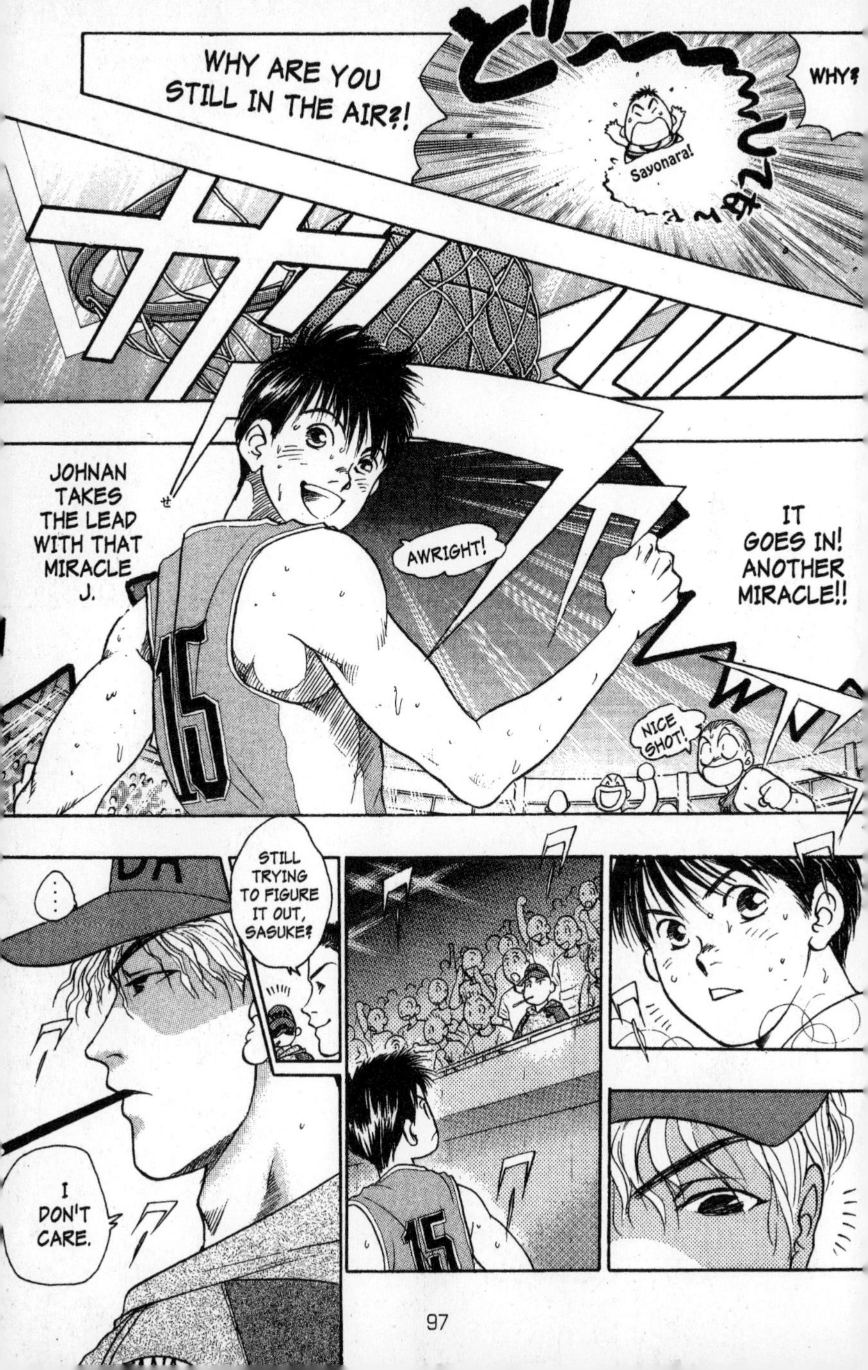
WHY?
Sayonara!
WHY ARE YOU STILL IN THE AIR?!
IT GOES IN! ANOTHER MIRACLE!!
NICE SHOT!
AWRIGHT!
JOHNAN TAKES THE LEAD WITH THAT MIRACLE J.
STILL TRYING TO FIGURE IT OUT, SASUKE?
...
I DON'T CARE.

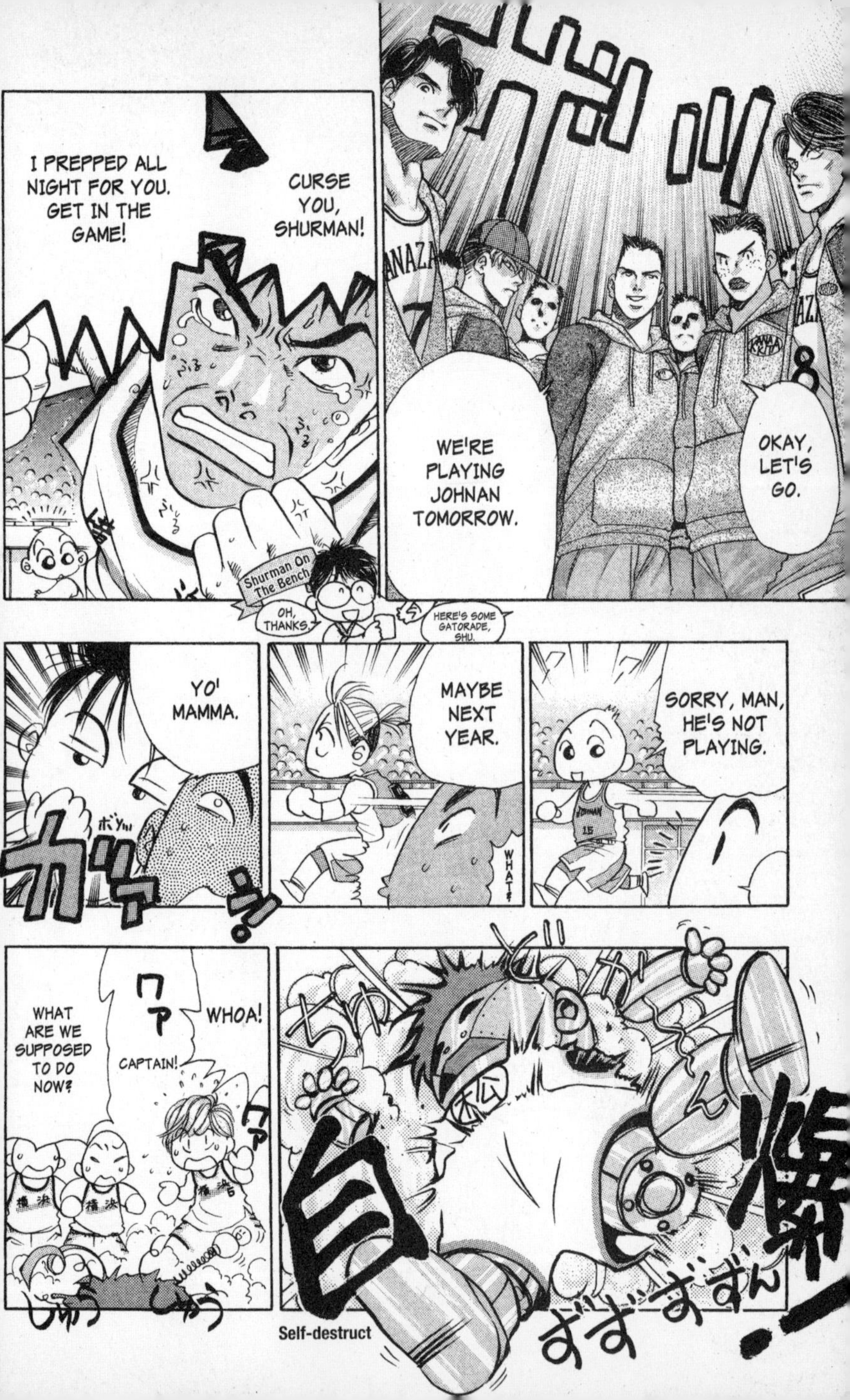
OKAY, LET'S GO.
WE'RE PLAYING JOHNAN TOMORROW.
CURSE YOU, SHURMAN!
I PREPPED ALL NIGHT FOR YOU. GET IN THE GAME!
Shurman On The Bench
HERE'S SOME GATORADE, SHU.
OH, THANKS.
SORRY, MAN, HE'S NOT PLAYING.
MAYBE NEXT YEAR.
WHAT!?
YO' MAMMA.
WHOA!
CAPTAIN!
WHAT ARE WE SUPPOSED TO DO NOW?
Self-destruct

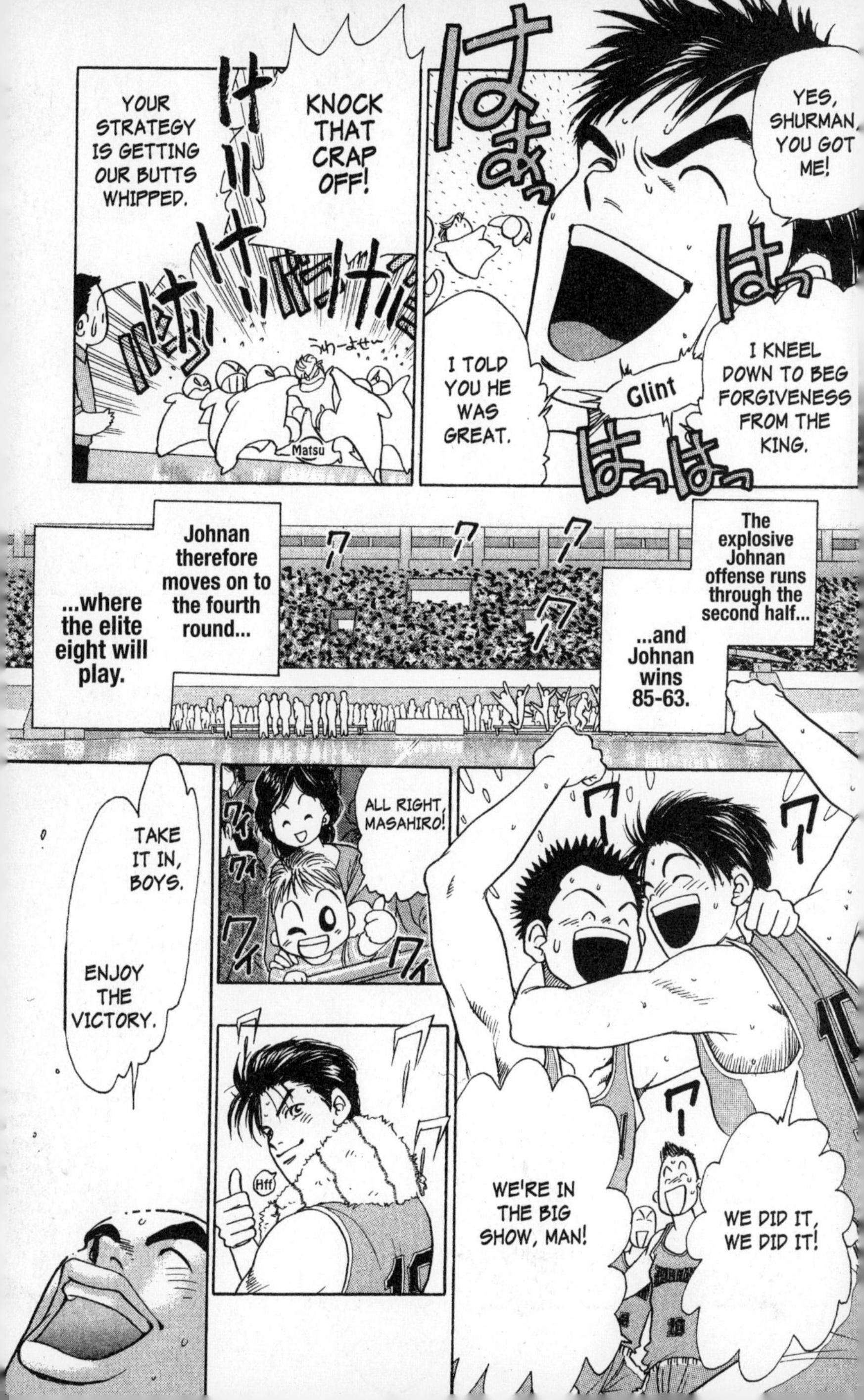

YES, SHURMAN, YOU GOT ME!
はぁっ
はっ
I KNEEL DOWN TO BEG FORGIVENESS FROM THE KING.
Glint
はっはっ
I TOLD YOU HE WAS GREAT.
KNOCK THAT CRAP OFF!
YOUR STRATEGY IS GETTING OUR BUTTS WHIPPED.
Matsu
The explosive Johnan offense runs through the second half...
...and Johnan wins 85-63.
Johnan therefore moves on to the fourth round...
...where the elite eight will play.
WE DID IT, WE DID IT!
WE'RE IN THE BIG SHOW, MAN!
ALL RIGHT, MASAHIRO!
Hff
TAKE IT IN, BOYS.
ENJOY THE VICTORY.

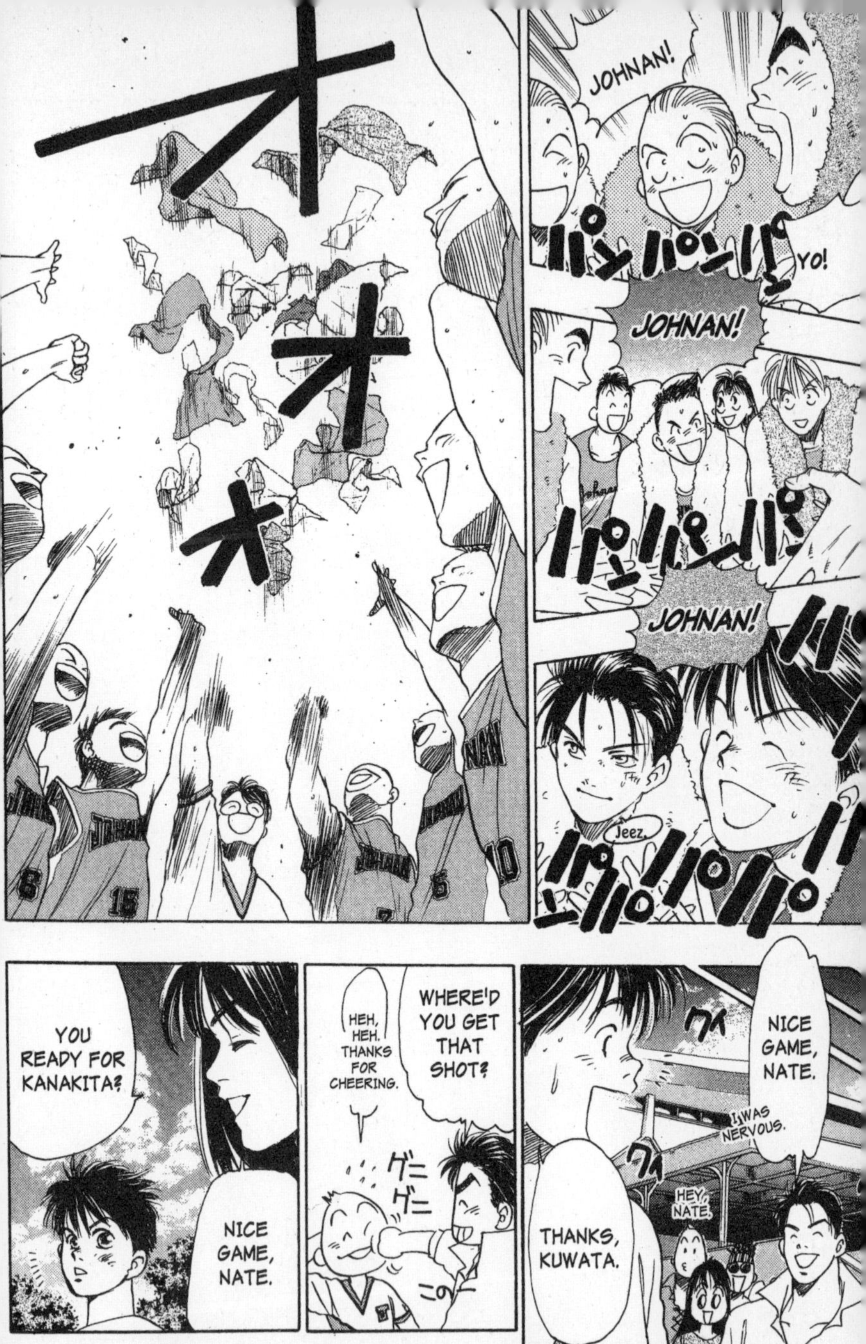
JOHNAN!
YO!
JOHNAN!
JOHNAN!
Jeez.
NICE GAME, NATE.
I WAS NERVOUS.
HEY, NATE.
THANKS, KUWATA.
WHERE'D YOU GET THAT SHOT?
HEH, HEH. THANKS FOR CHEERING.
YOU READY FOR KANAKITA?
NICE GAME, NATE.

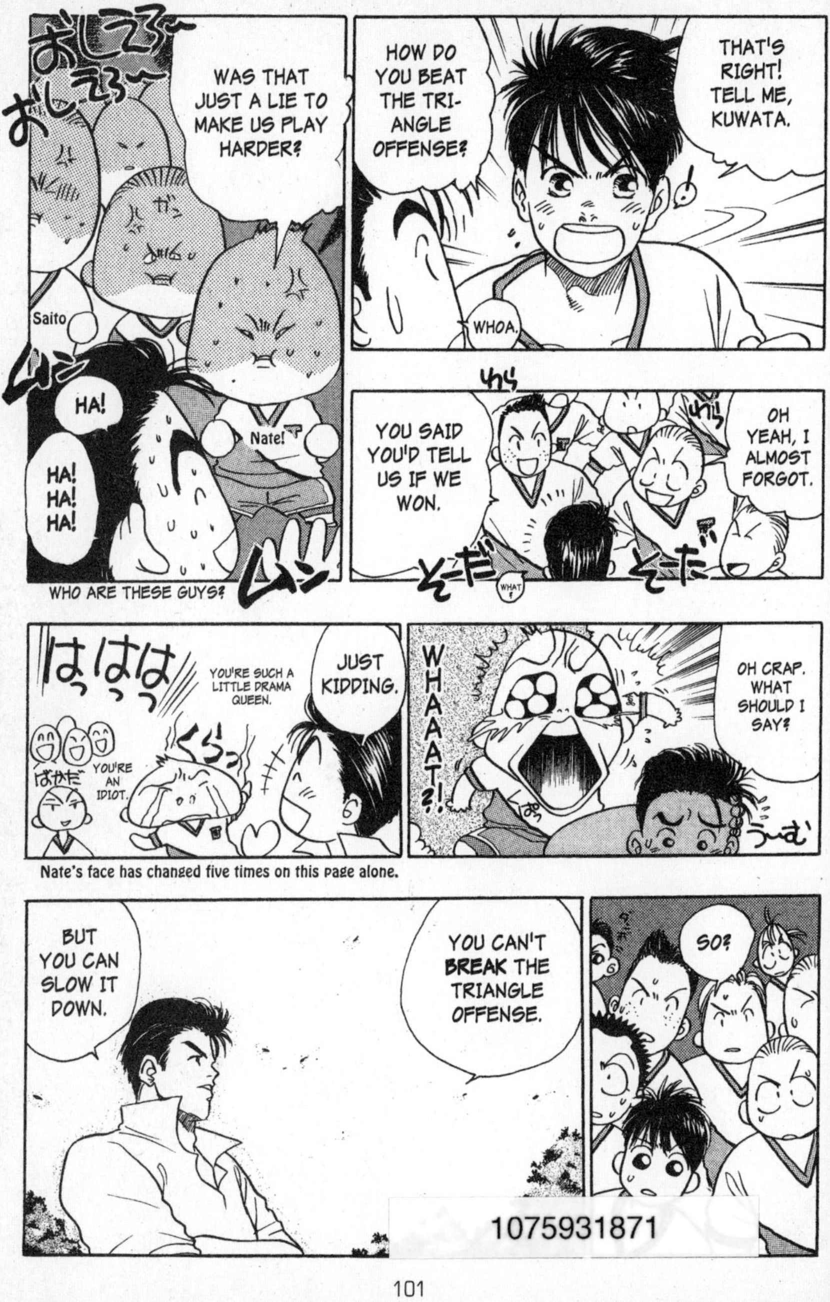
THAT'S RIGHT! TELL ME, KUWATA.
HOW DO YOU BEAT THE TRI-ANGLE OFFENSE?
WHOA.
わら
わら
OH YEAH, I ALMOST FORGOT.
YOU SAID YOU'D TELL US IF WE WON.
そーだ
そーだ
WHAT?
おしえろ〜
おしえろ〜
WAS THAT JUST A LIE TO MAKE US PLAY HARDER?
Saito
Nate!
ムン
HA!
HA! HA! HA!
ムン
WHO ARE THESE GUYS?
OH CRAP. WHAT SHOULD I SAY?
WHAAAT?!
うーむ
JUST KIDDING.
YOU'RE SUCH A LITTLE DRAMA QUEEN.
ははは
くらっ
YOU'RE AN IDIOT.
ばかだ
Nate's face has changed five times on this page alone.
SO?
YOU CAN'T BREAK THE TRIANGLE OFFENSE.
BUT YOU CAN SLOW IT DOWN.

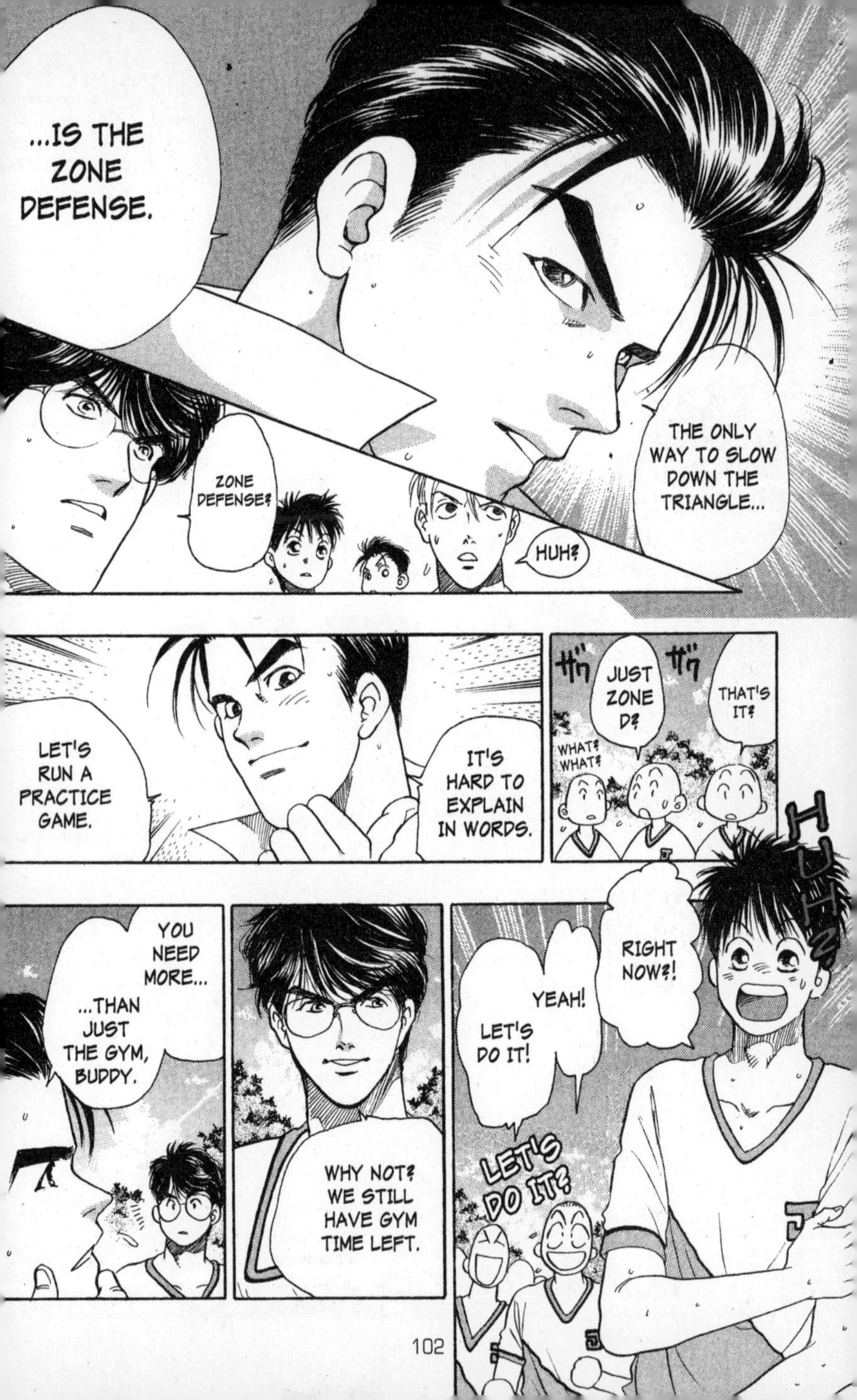
THE ONLY WAY TO SLOW DOWN THE TRIANGLE...
...IS THE ZONE DEFENSE.
HUH?
ZONE DEFENSE?
ザワ
ザワ
THAT'S IT?
JUST ZONE D?
WHAT? WHAT?
IT'S HARD TO EXPLAIN IN WORDS.
LET'S RUN A PRACTICE GAME.
HUH?
RIGHT NOW?!
YEAH!
LET'S DO IT!
LET'S DO IT?
WHY NOT? WE STILL HAVE GYM TIME LEFT.
YOU NEED MORE...
...THAN JUST THE GYM, BUDDY.

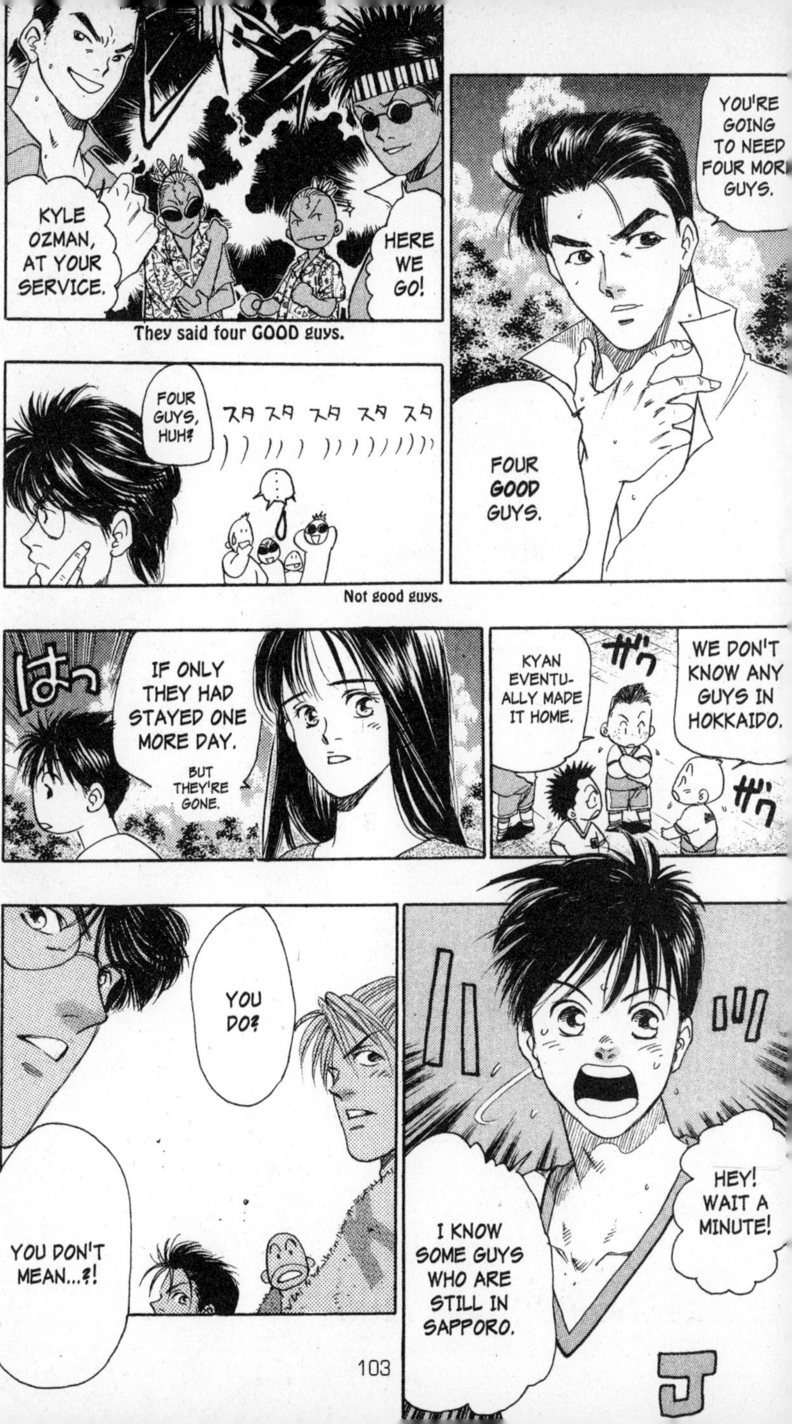
YOU'RE GOING TO NEED FOUR MOR GUYS.
FOUR GOOD GUYS.
HERE WE GO!
KYLE OZMAN, AT YOUR SERVICE.
They said four GOOD guys.
FOUR GUYS, HUH?
スタ スタ スタ スタ スタ
Not good guys.
WE DON'T KNOW ANY GUYS IN HOKKAIDO.
ザク
KYAN EVENTU-ALLY MADE IT HOME.
ザク
はっ
IF ONLY THEY HAD STAYED ONE MORE DAY.
BUT THEY'RE GONE.
HEY! WAIT A MINUTE!
I KNOW SOME GUYS WHO ARE STILL IN SAPPORO.
J
YOU DO?
YOU DON'T MEAN...?!

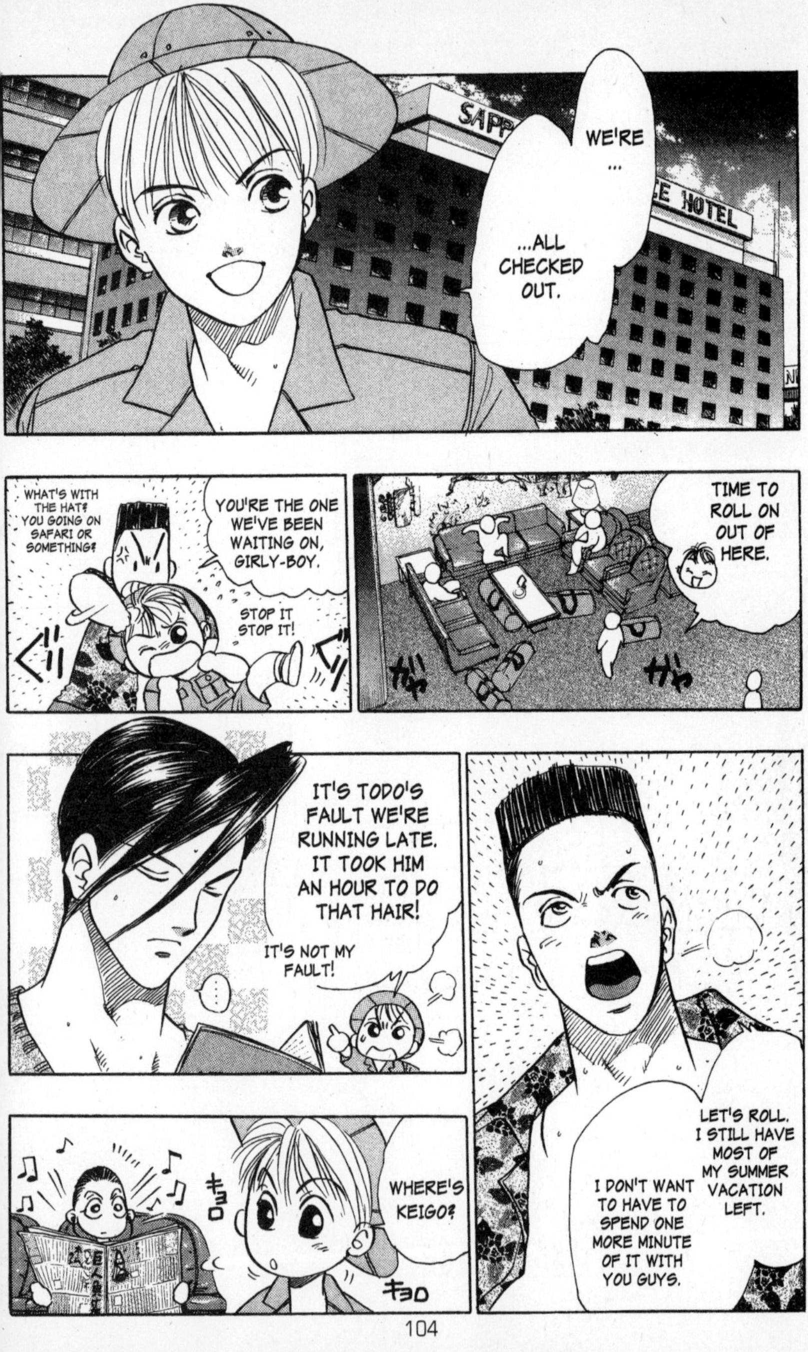
WE'RE ...
...ALL CHECKED OUT.
TIME TO ROLL ON OUT OF HERE.
がや
がや
YOU'RE THE ONE WE'VE BEEN WAITING ON, GIRLY-BOY.
WHAT'S WITH THE HAT? YOU GOING ON SAFARI OR SOMETHING?
STOP IT STOP IT!
LET'S ROLL. I STILL HAVE MOST OF MY SUMMER VACATION LEFT.
I DON'T WANT TO HAVE TO SPEND ONE MORE MINUTE OF IT WITH YOU GUYS.
IT'S TODO'S FAULT WE'RE RUNNING LATE. IT TOOK HIM AN HOUR TO DO THAT HAIR!
IT'S NOT MY FAULT!
...
WHERE'S KEIGO?
キョロ
キョロ

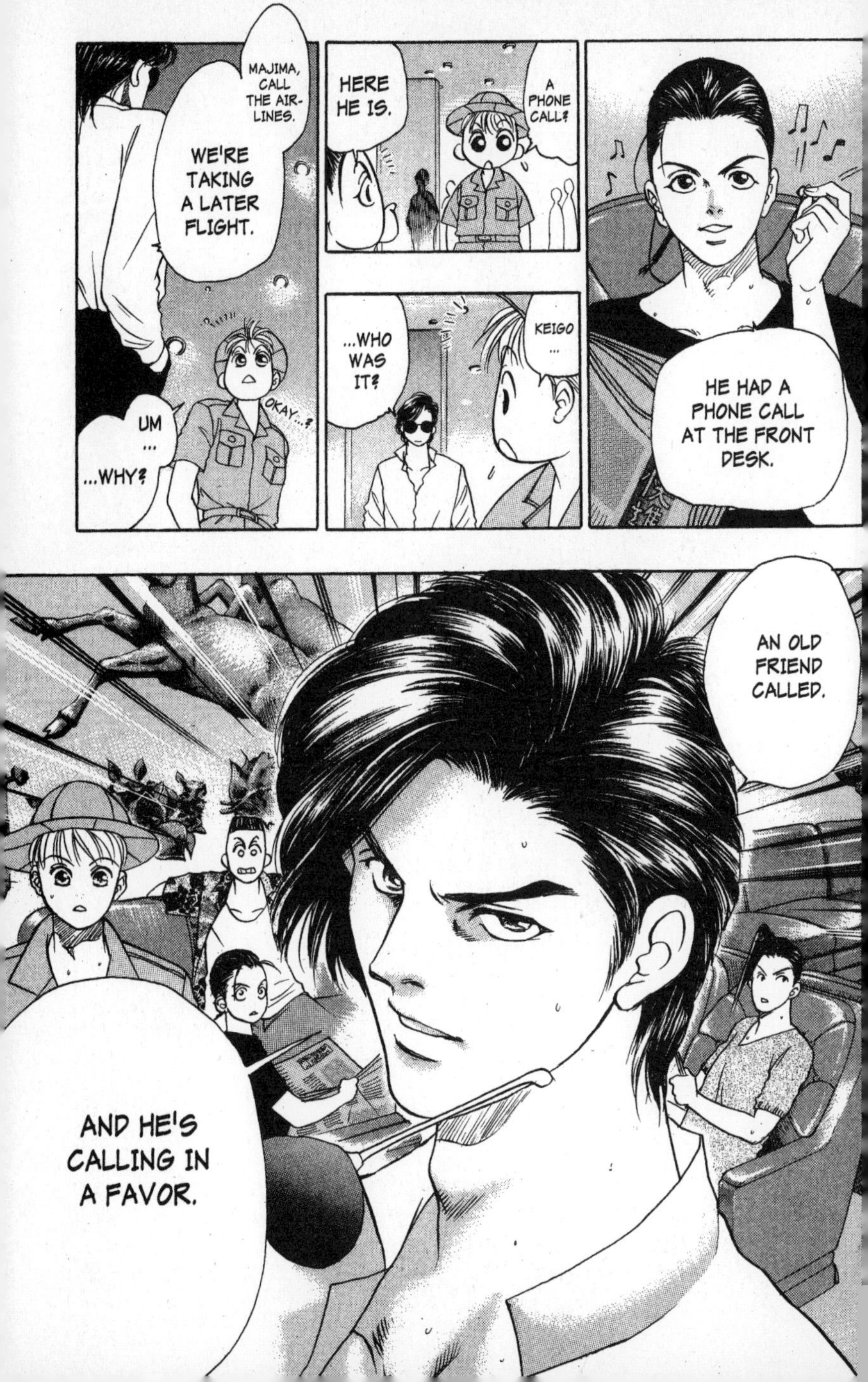
HE HAD A PHONE CALL AT THE FRONT DESK.
A PHONE CALL?
HERE HE IS.
KEIGO ...
...WHO WAS IT?
MAJIMA, CALL THE AIR-LINES.
WE'RE TAKING A LATER FLIGHT.
OKAY...?
UM ... ...WHY?
AN OLD FRIEND CALLED.
AND HE'S CALLING IN A FAVOR.

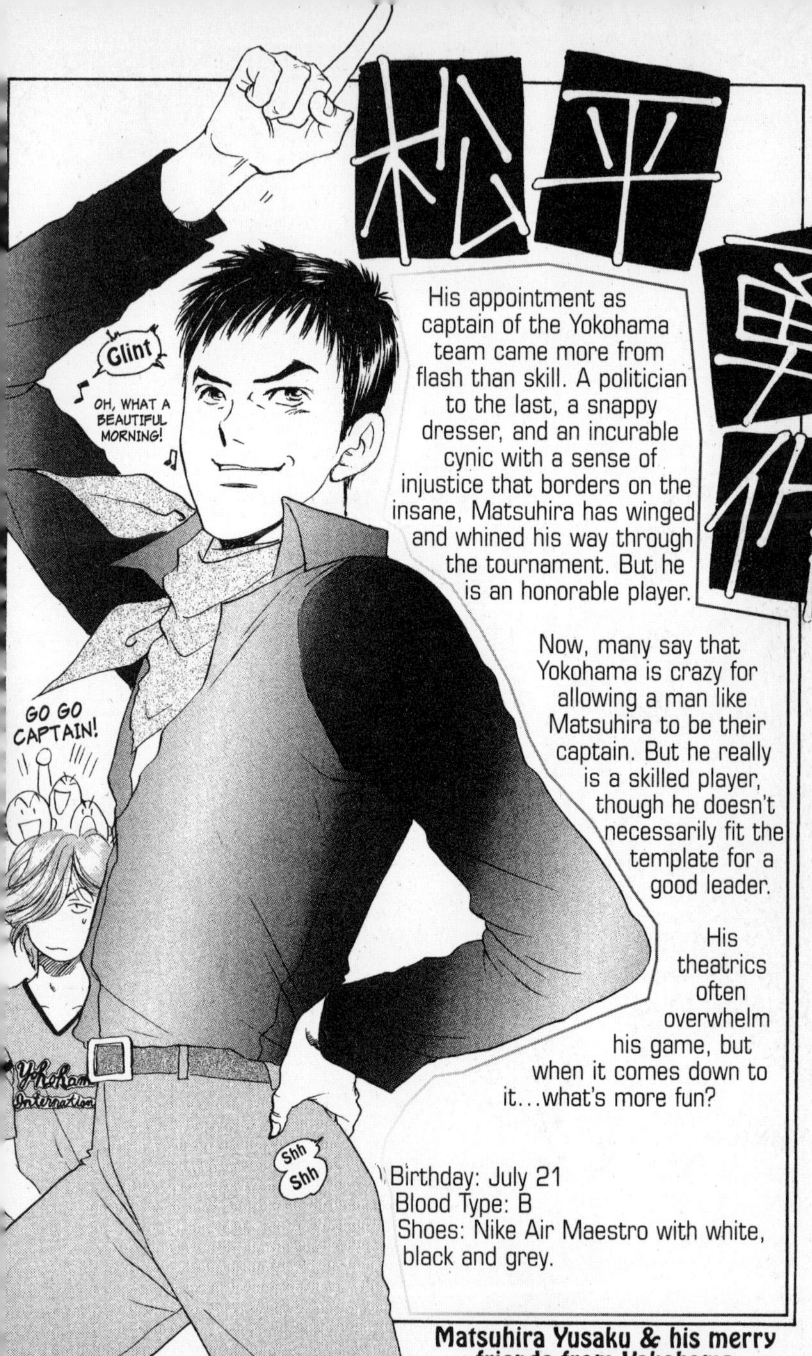
Glint
OH, WHAT A BEAUTIFUL MORNING!
GO GO CAPTAIN!
Shh Shh

松平勇作

His appointment as captain of the Yokohama team came more from flash than skill. A politician to the last, a snappy dresser, and an incurable cynic with a sense of injustice that borders on the insane, Matsuhira has winged and whined his way through the tournament. But he is an honorable player.

Now, many say that Yokohama is crazy for allowing a man like Matsuhira to be their captain. But he really is a skilled player, though he doesn't necessarily fit the template for a good leader.

His theatrics often overwhelm his game, but when it comes down to it…what's more fun?

Birthday: July 21
Blood Type: B
Shoes: Nike Air Maestro with white, black and grey.

Matsuhira Yusaku & his merry friends from Yokohama

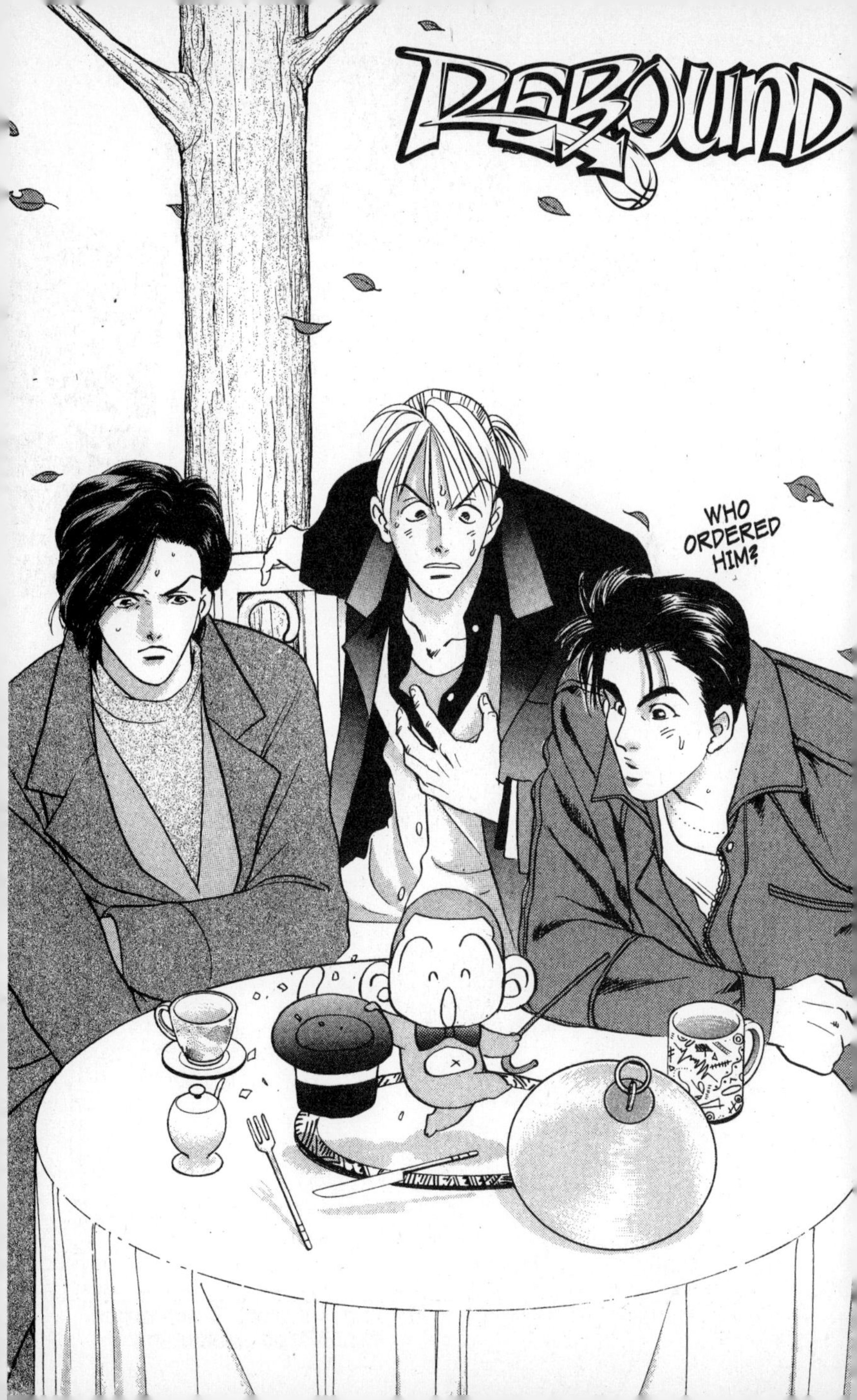
REBOUND
WHO ORDERED HIM?

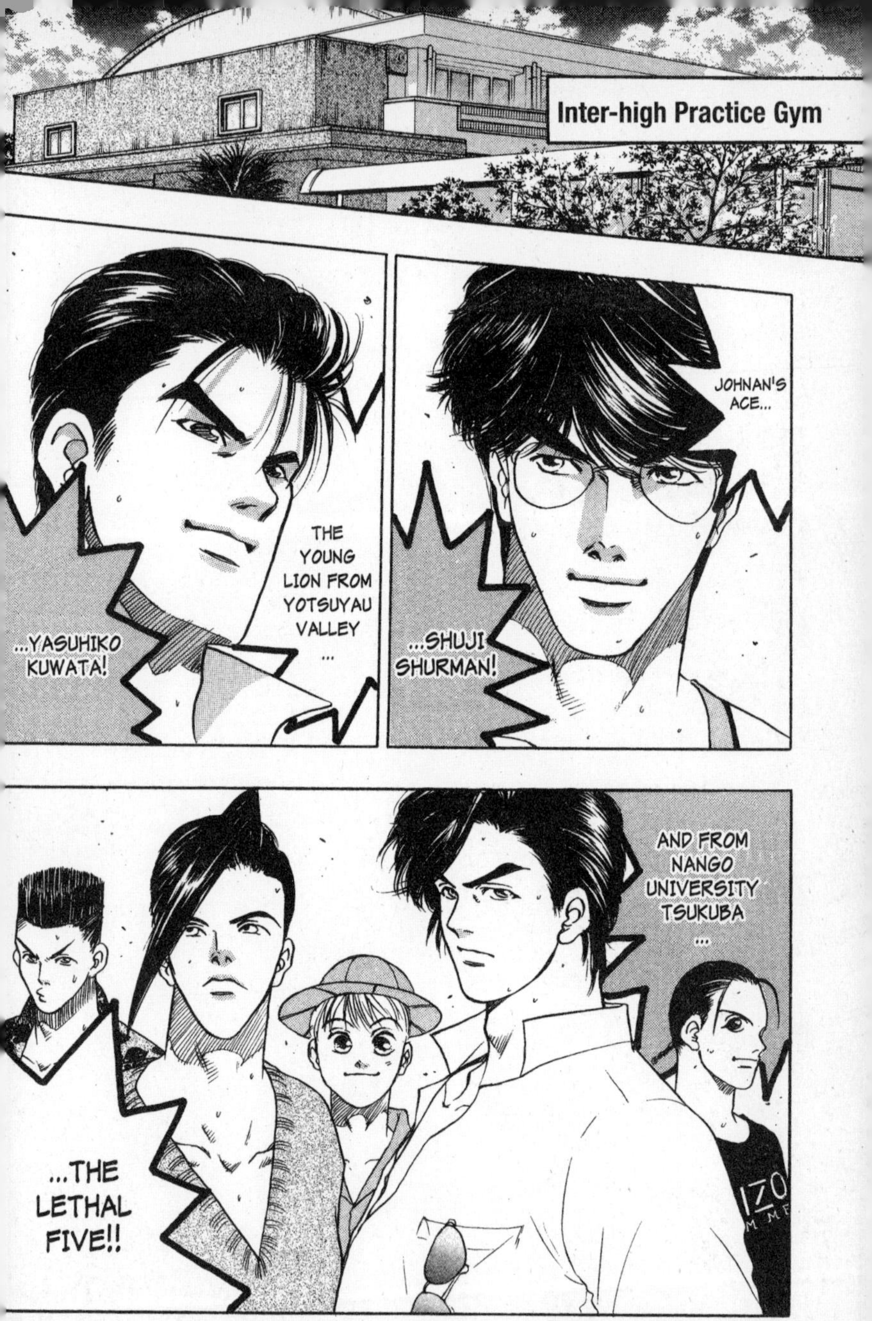
Inter-high Practice Gym
JOHNAN'S ACE...
...SHUJI SHURMAN!
THE YOUNG LION FROM YOTSUYAU VALLEY ...
...YASUHIKO KUWATA!
AND FROM NANGO UNIVERSITY TSUKUBA ...
...THE LETHAL FIVE!!

Episode 55 Triangle Offense Countermeasure

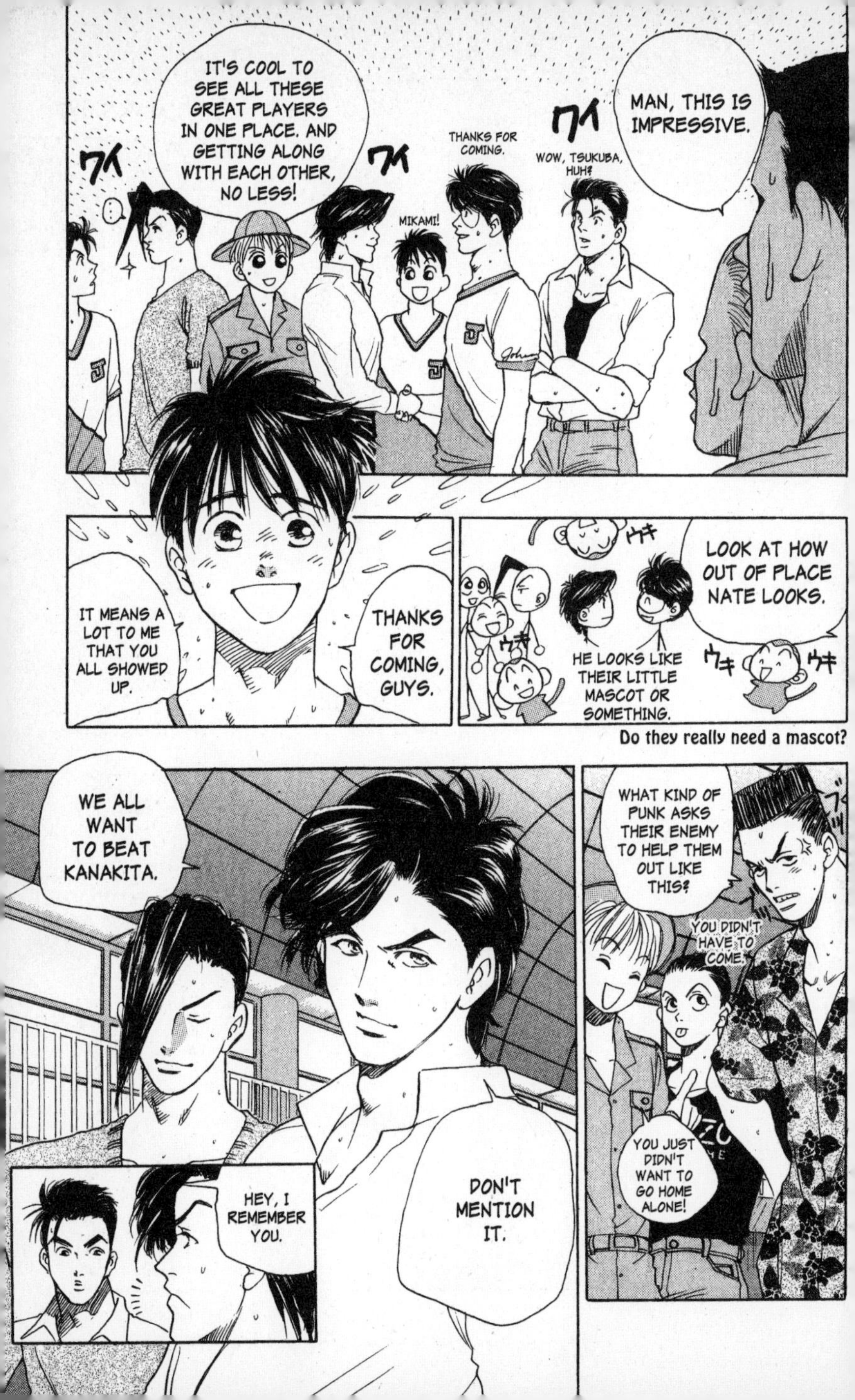
MAN, THIS IS IMPRESSIVE.
ワイ
WOW, TSUKUBA, HUH?
THANKS FOR COMING.
MIKAMI!
ワイ
IT'S COOL TO SEE ALL THESE GREAT PLAYERS IN ONE PLACE. AND GETTING ALONG WITH EACH OTHER, NO LESS!
ワイ
ウキ
LOOK AT HOW OUT OF PLACE NATE LOOKS.
ウキ
ウキ
HE LOOKS LIKE THEIR LITTLE MASCOT OR SOMETHING.
ウキ
THANKS FOR COMING, GUYS.
IT MEANS A LOT TO ME THAT YOU ALL SHOWED UP.
WHAT KIND OF PUNK ASKS THEIR ENEMY TO HELP THEM OUT LIKE THIS?
YOU DIDN'T HAVE TO COME.
YOU JUST DIDN'T WANT TO GO HOME ALONE!
WE ALL WANT TO BEAT KANAKITA.
DON'T MENTION IT.
HEY, I REMEMBER YOU.
Do they really need a mascot?

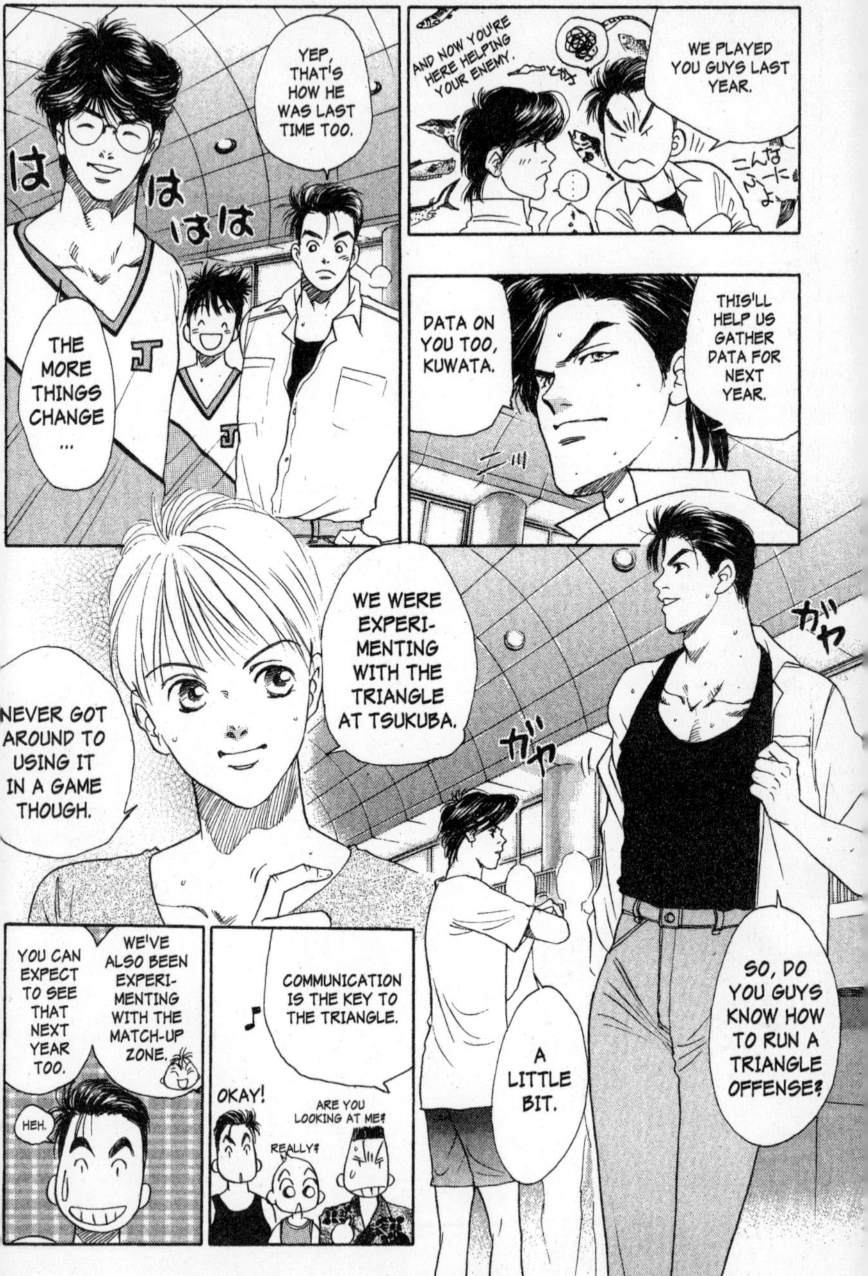
WE PLAYED YOU GUYS LAST YEAR.
AND NOW YOU'RE HERE HELPING YOUR ENEMY.
...
THIS'LL HELP US GATHER DATA FOR NEXT YEAR.
DATA ON YOU TOO, KUWATA.
YEP, THAT'S HOW HE WAS LAST TIME TOO.
は
は
はは
THE MORE THINGS CHANGE ...
ガヤ
SO, DO YOU GUYS KNOW HOW TO RUN A TRIANGLE OFFENSE?
A LITTLE BIT.
ガヤ
WE WERE EXPERIMENTING WITH THE TRIANGLE AT TSUKUBA.
NEVER GOT AROUND TO USING IT IN A GAME THOUGH.
COMMUNICATION IS THE KEY TO THE TRIANGLE.
OKAY!
ARE YOU LOOKING AT ME?
REALLY?
WE'VE ALSO BEEN EXPERIMENTING WITH THE MATCH-UP ZONE.
YOU CAN EXPECT TO SEE THAT NEXT YEAR TOO.
HEH.

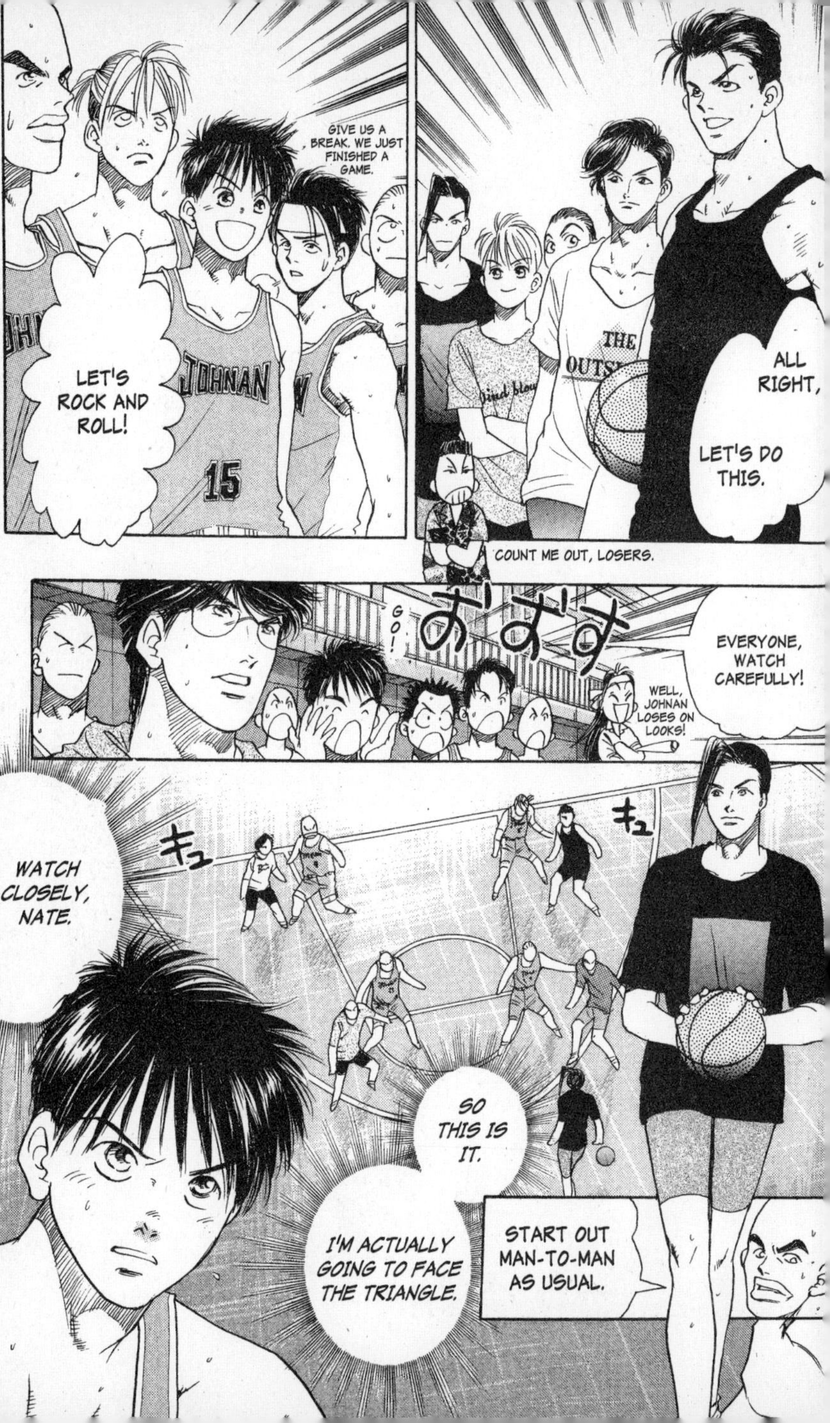
ALL RIGHT,
LET'S DO THIS.
COUNT ME OUT, LOSERS.
GIVE US A BREAK. WE JUST FINISHED A GAME.
LET'S ROCK AND ROLL!
EVERYONE, WATCH CAREFULLY!
WELL, JOHNAN LOSES ON LOOKS!
おおす
GO!
キュ
キュ
WATCH CLOSELY, NATE.
SO THIS IS IT.
START OUT MAN-TO-MAN AS USUAL.
I'M ACTUALLY GOING TO FACE THE TRIANGLE.

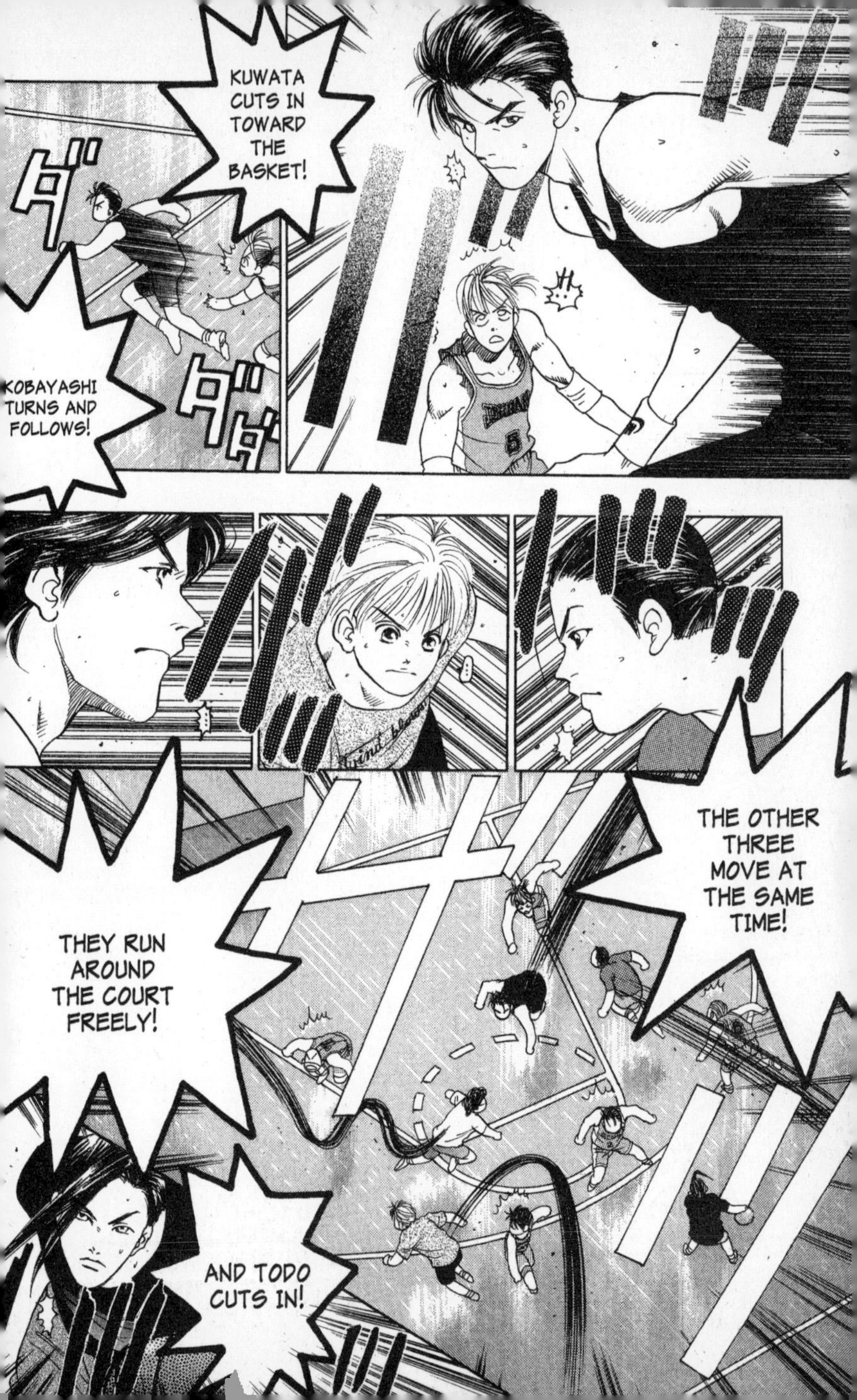
KUWATA CUTS IN TOWARD THE BASKET!
KOBAYASHI TURNS AND FOLLOWS!
THE OTHER THREE MOVE AT THE SAME TIME!
THEY RUN AROUND THE COURT FREELY!
AND TODO CUTS IN!

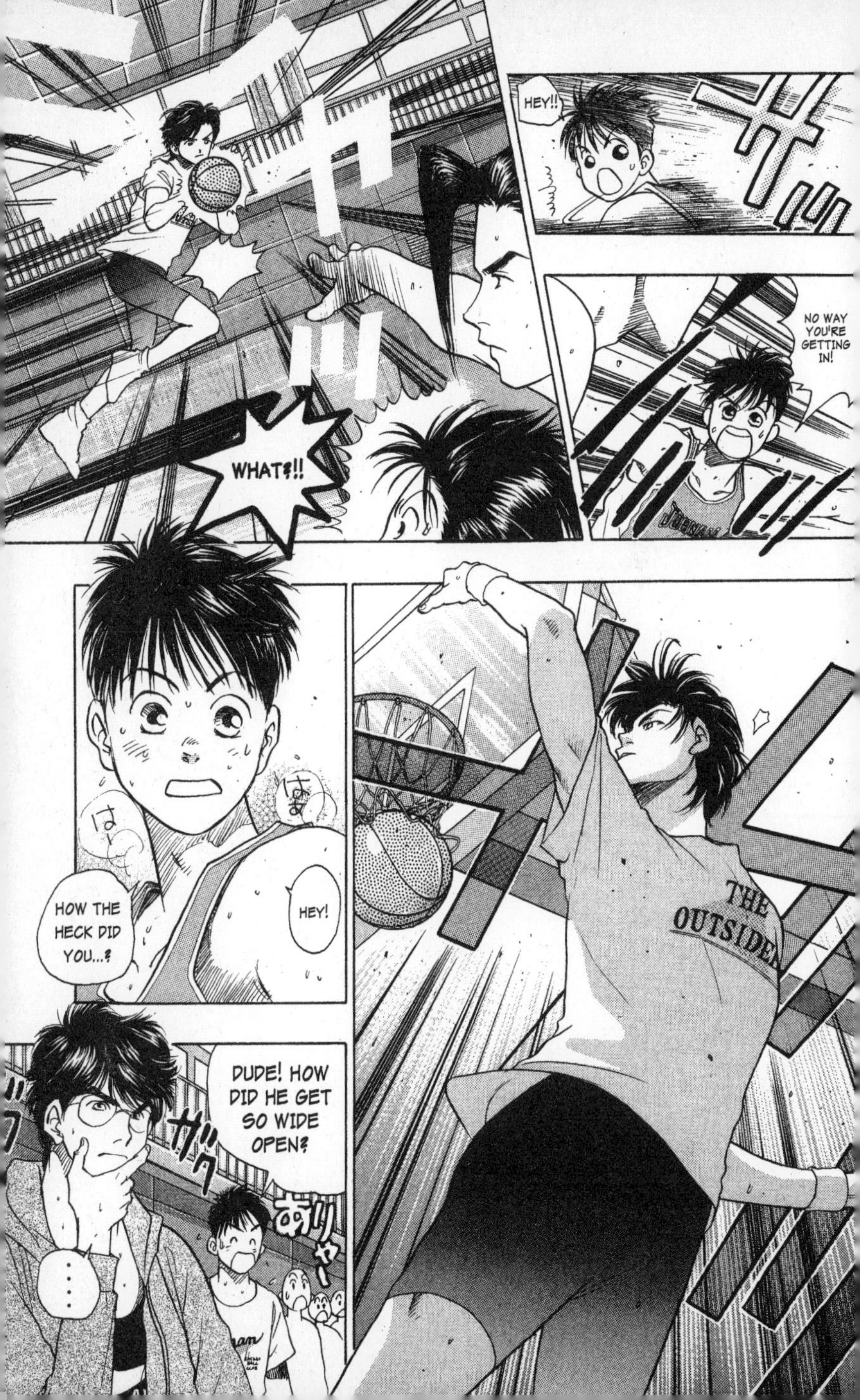
HEY!!
NO WAY YOU'RE GETTING IN!
WHAT?!!
HEY!
HOW THE HECK DID YOU...?
THE OUTSIDER
DUDE! HOW DID HE GET SO WIDE OPEN?
...

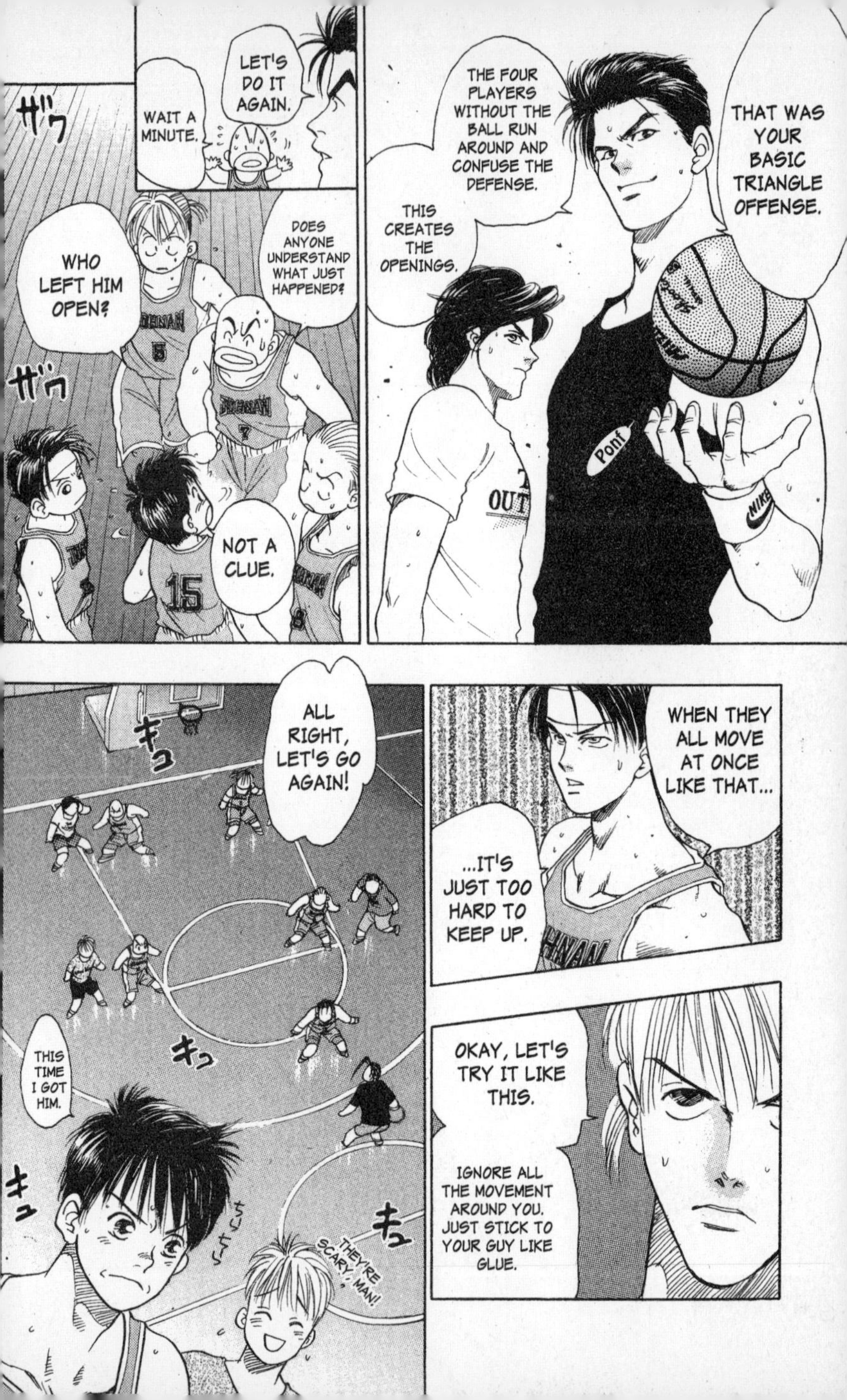
THAT WAS YOUR BASIC TRIANGLE OFFENSE.
THE FOUR PLAYERS WITHOUT THE BALL RUN AROUND AND CONFUSE THE DEFENSE.
THIS CREATES THE OPENINGS.
Ponf
LET'S DO IT AGAIN.
WAIT A MINUTE.
ザワ
DOES ANYONE UNDERSTAND WHAT JUST HAPPENED?
WHO LEFT HIM OPEN?
ザワ
NOT A CLUE.
WHEN THEY ALL MOVE AT ONCE LIKE THAT...
...IT'S JUST TOO HARD TO KEEP UP.
OKAY, LET'S TRY IT LIKE THIS.
IGNORE ALL THE MOVEMENT AROUND YOU. JUST STICK TO YOUR GUY LIKE GLUE.
ALL RIGHT, LET'S GO AGAIN!
キュ
キュ
THIS TIME I GOT HIM.
キュ
THEY'RE SCARY, MAN!
キュ

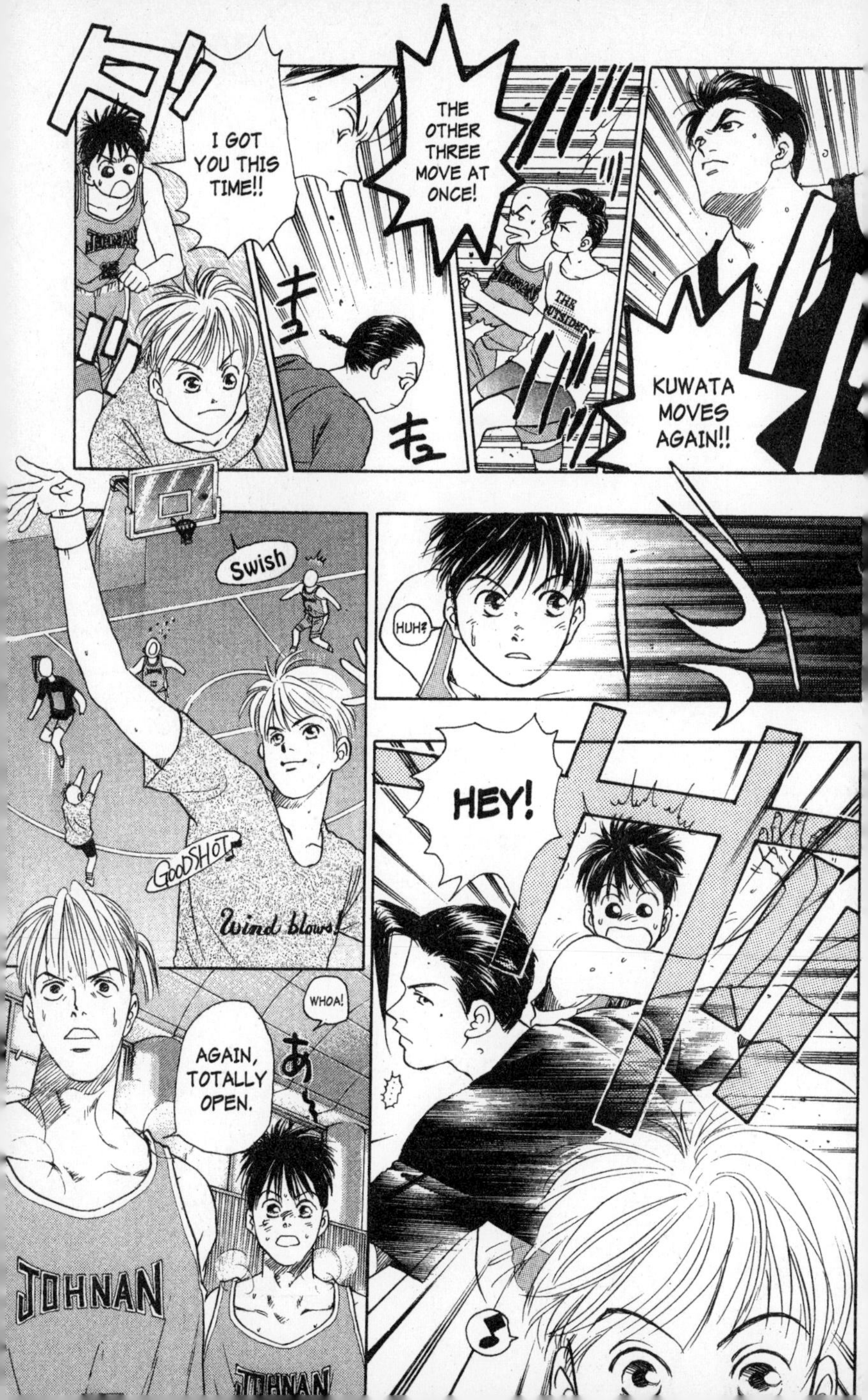
KUWATA MOVES AGAIN!!
THE OTHER THREE MOVE AT ONCE!
キュ
キュ
I GOT YOU THIS TIME!!
HUH?
HEY!
Swish
GOOD SHOT♪
Wind blows!
WHOA!
AGAIN, TOTALLY OPEN.
あ

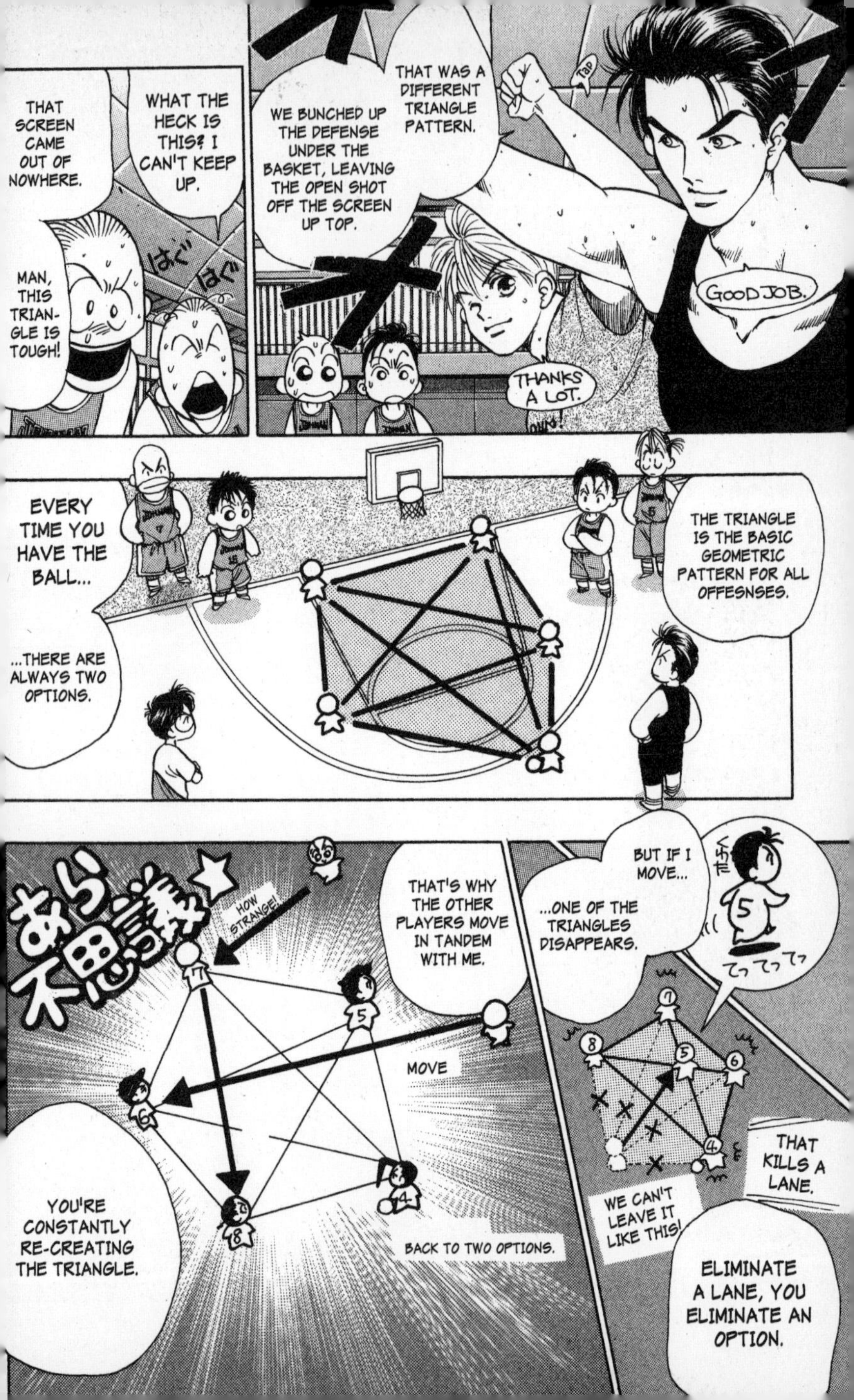
Tap
THAT WAS A DIFFERENT TRIANGLE PATTERN.
WE BUNCHED UP THE DEFENSE UNDER THE BASKET, LEAVING THE OPEN SHOT OFF THE SCREEN UP TOP.
GOOD JOB.
THANKS A LOT.
WHAT THE HECK IS THIS? I CAN'T KEEP UP.
THAT SCREEN CAME OUT OF NOWHERE.
はぐ はぐ
MAN, THIS TRIAN-GLE IS TOUGH!
THE TRIANGLE IS THE BASIC GEOMETRIC PATTERN FOR ALL OFFESNSES.
EVERY TIME YOU HAVE THE BALL...
...THERE ARE ALWAYS TWO OPTIONS.
BUT IF I MOVE...
...ONE OF THE TRIANGLES DISAPPEARS.
てってって
THAT KILLS A LANE.
WE CAN'T LEAVE IT LIKE THIS!
ELIMINATE A LANE, YOU ELIMINATE AN OPTION.
THAT'S WHY THE OTHER PLAYERS MOVE IN TANDEM WITH ME.
あら不思議★
HOW STRANGE!
MOVE
BACK TO TWO OPTIONS.
YOU'RE CONSTANTLY RE-CREATING THE TRIANGLE.

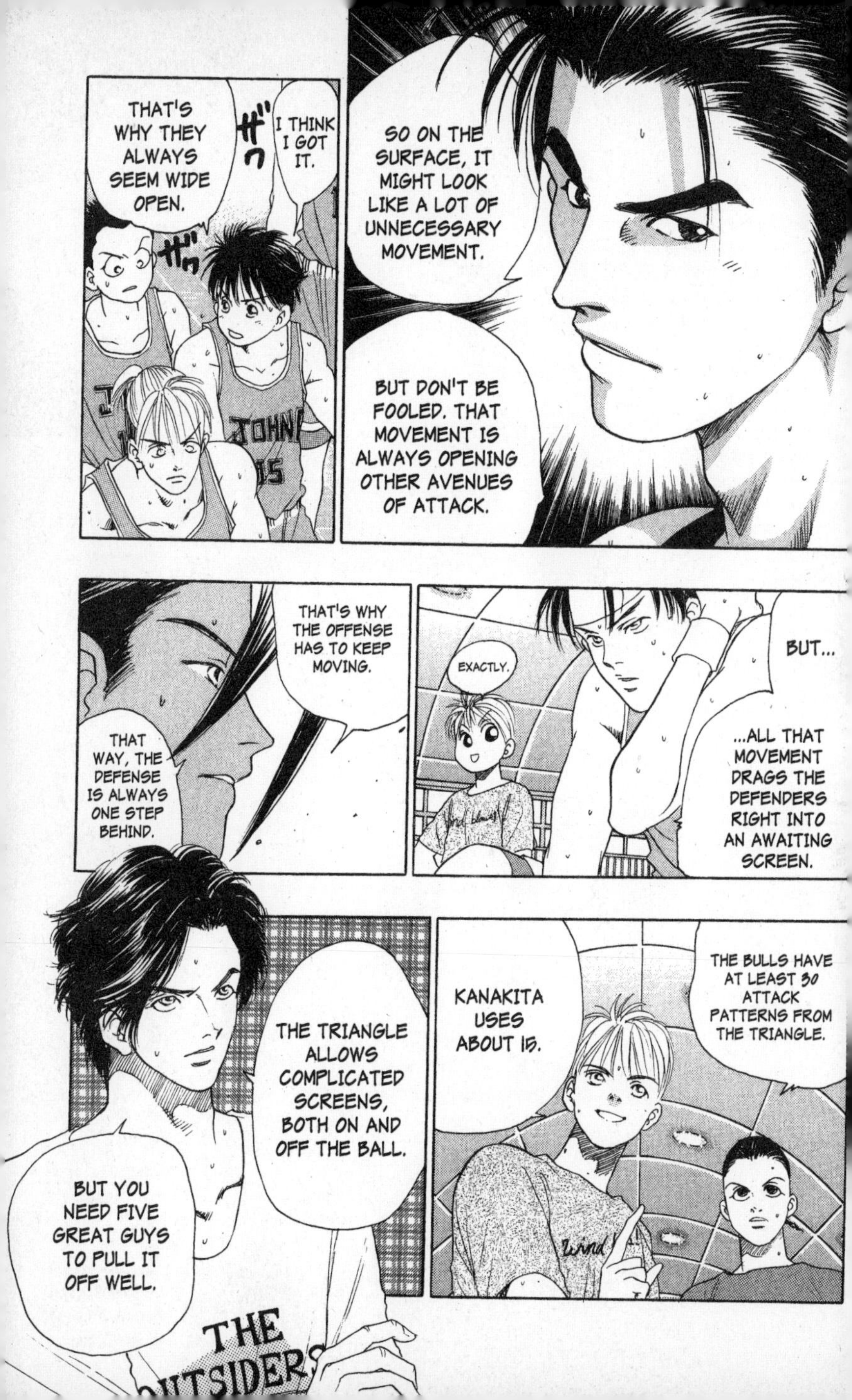
SO ON THE SURFACE, IT MIGHT LOOK LIKE A LOT OF UNNECESSARY MOVEMENT.
BUT DON'T BE FOOLED. THAT MOVEMENT IS ALWAYS OPENING OTHER AVENUES OF ATTACK.
I THINK I GOT IT.
ザワ
ザワ
THAT'S WHY THEY ALWAYS SEEM WIDE OPEN.
BUT...
...ALL THAT MOVEMENT DRAGS THE DEFENDERS RIGHT INTO AN AWAITING SCREEN.
EXACTLY.
THAT'S WHY THE OFFENSE HAS TO KEEP MOVING.
THAT WAY, THE DEFENSE IS ALWAYS ONE STEP BEHIND.
THE BULLS HAVE AT LEAST 30 ATTACK PATTERNS FROM THE TRIANGLE.
KANAKITA USES ABOUT 15.
THE TRIANGLE ALLOWS COMPLICATED SCREENS, BOTH ON AND OFF THE BALL.
BUT YOU NEED FIVE GREAT GUYS TO PULL IT OFF WELL.
THE
UTSIDERS

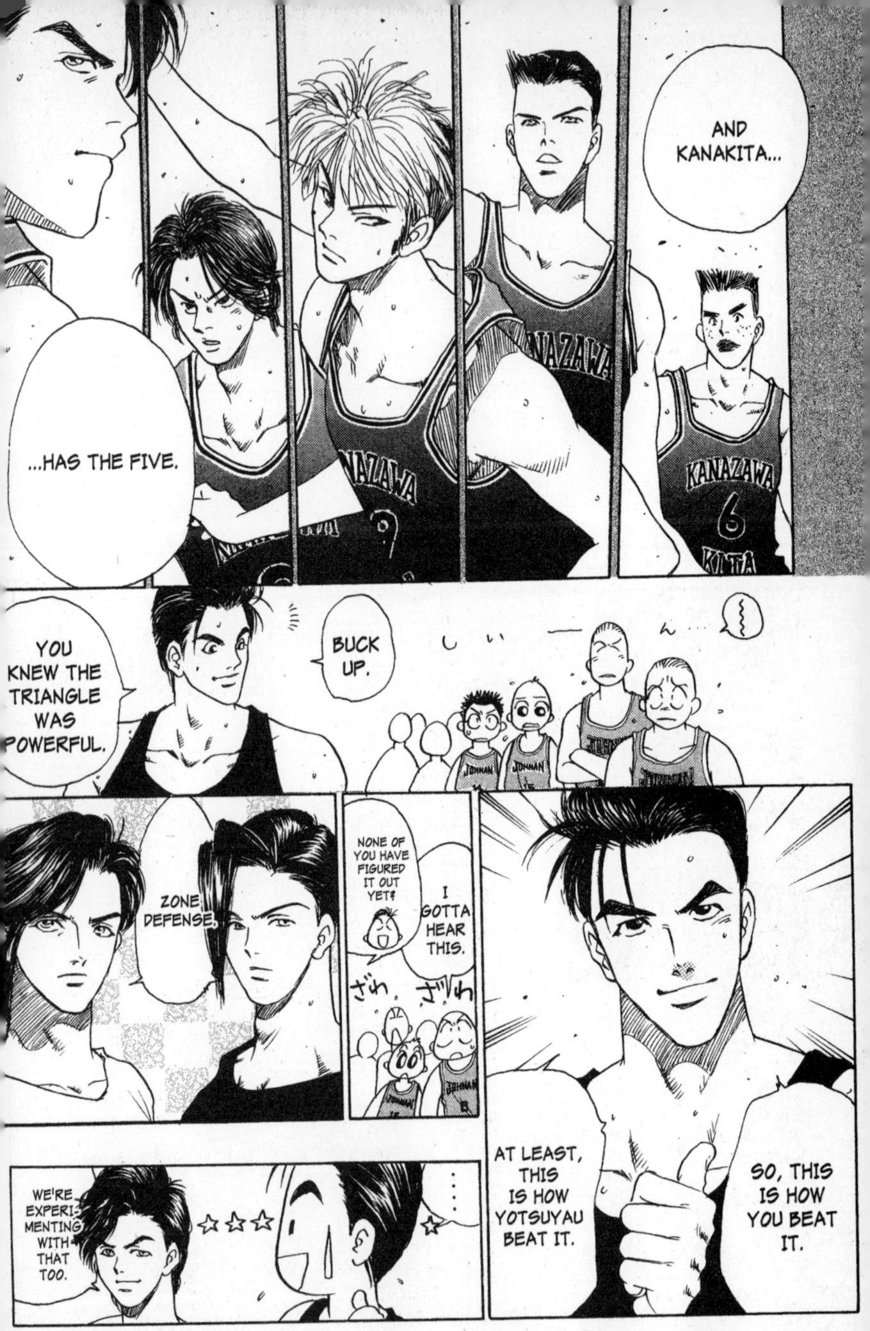
AND KANAKITA...
KANAZAWA
KANAZAWA 6 KITA
NAZAWA
NAZAWA
...HAS THE FIVE.
...
しいーーん…
BUCK UP.
YOU KNEW THE TRIANGLE WAS POWERFUL.
SO, THIS IS HOW YOU BEAT IT.
AT LEAST, THIS IS HOW YOTSUYAU BEAT IT.
I GOTTA HEAR THIS.
NONE OF YOU HAVE FIGURED IT OUT YET?
ざわ ざわ
ZONE DEFENSE.
....
☆☆☆☆
WE'RE EXPERIMENTING WITH THAT TOO.

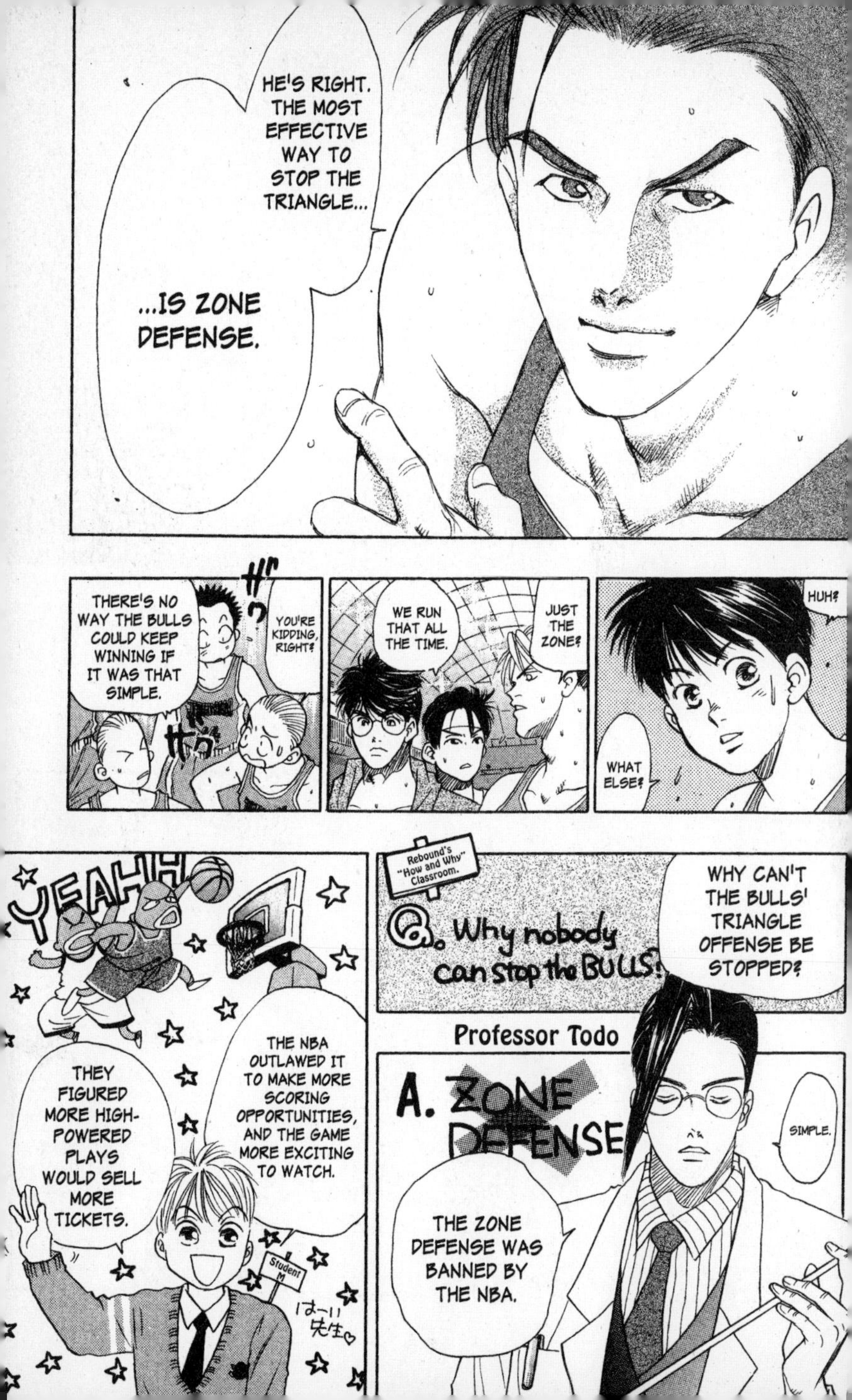

HE'S RIGHT. THE MOST EFFECTIVE WAY TO STOP THE TRIANGLE...
...IS ZONE DEFENSE.
HUH?
WHAT ELSE?
JUST THE ZONE?
WE RUN THAT ALL THE TIME.
YOU'RE KIDDING, RIGHT?
THERE'S NO WAY THE BULLS COULD KEEP WINNING IF IT WAS THAT SIMPLE.
Rebound's "How and Why" Classroom.
Q. Why nobody can stop the BULLS!
WHY CAN'T THE BULLS' TRIANGLE OFFENSE BE STOPPED?
Professor Todo
SIMPLE.
A. ZONE DEFENSE
THE ZONE DEFENSE WAS BANNED BY THE NBA.
YEAHH
THE NBA OUTLAWED IT TO MAKE MORE SCORING OPPORTUNITIES, AND THE GAME MORE EXCITING TO WATCH.
THEY FIGURED MORE HIGH-POWERED PLAYS WOULD SELL MORE TICKETS.
Student M
はーい先生♡

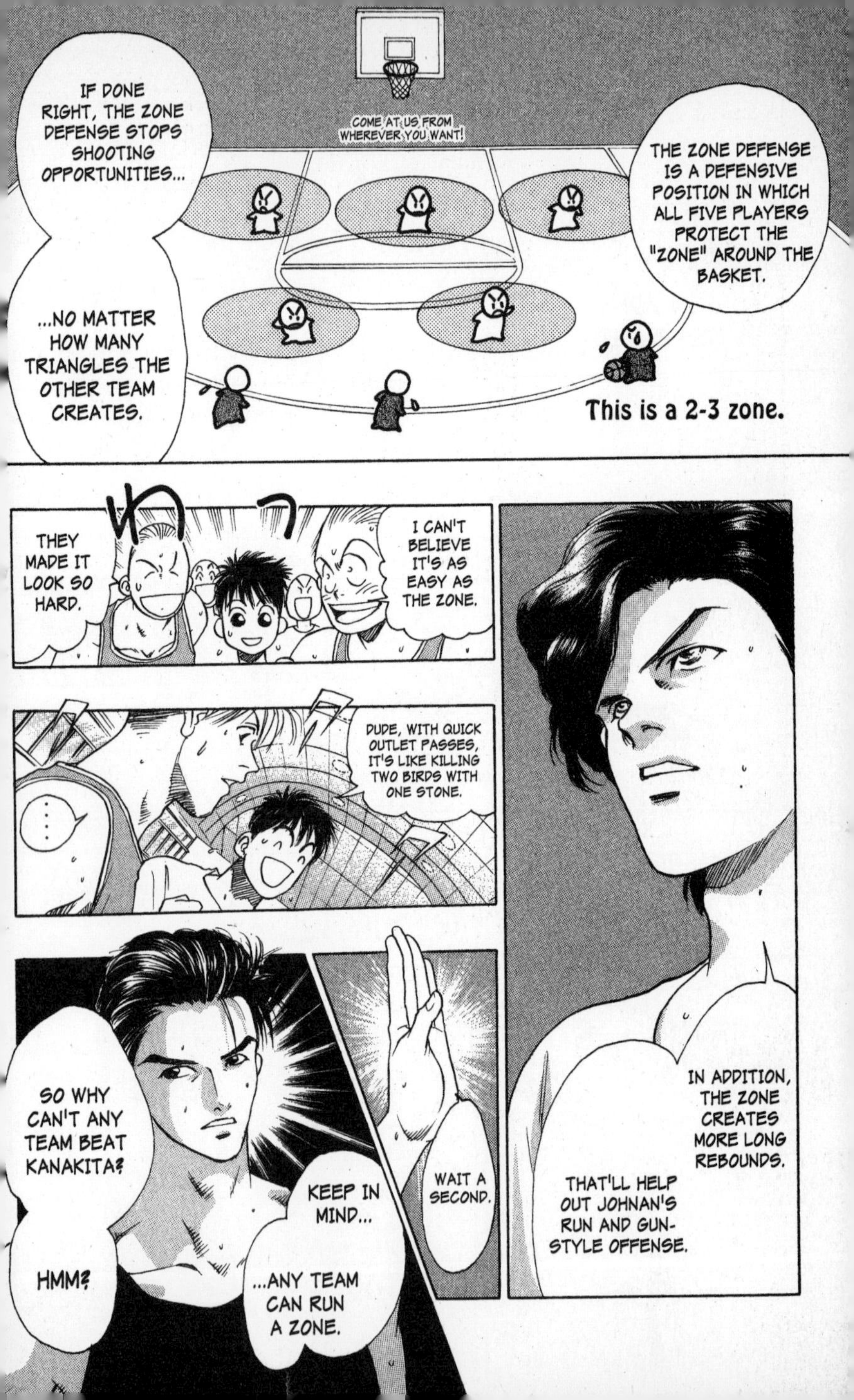
THE ZONE DEFENSE IS A DEFENSIVE POSITION IN WHICH ALL FIVE PLAYERS PROTECT THE "ZONE" AROUND THE BASKET.
COME AT US FROM WHEREVER YOU WANT!
IF DONE RIGHT, THE ZONE DEFENSE STOPS SHOOTING OPPORTUNITIES...
...NO MATTER HOW MANY TRIANGLES THE OTHER TEAM CREATES.
This is a 2-3 zone.
IN ADDITION, THE ZONE CREATES MORE LONG REBOUNDS.
THAT'LL HELP OUT JOHNAN'S RUN AND GUN-STYLE OFFENSE.
I CAN'T BELIEVE IT'S AS EASY AS THE ZONE.
THEY MADE IT LOOK SO HARD.
DUDE, WITH QUICK OUTLET PASSES, IT'S LIKE KILLING TWO BIRDS WITH ONE STONE.
......
WAIT A SECOND.
SO WHY CAN'T ANY TEAM BEAT KANAKITA?
HMM?
KEEP IN MIND...
...ANY TEAM CAN RUN A ZONE.

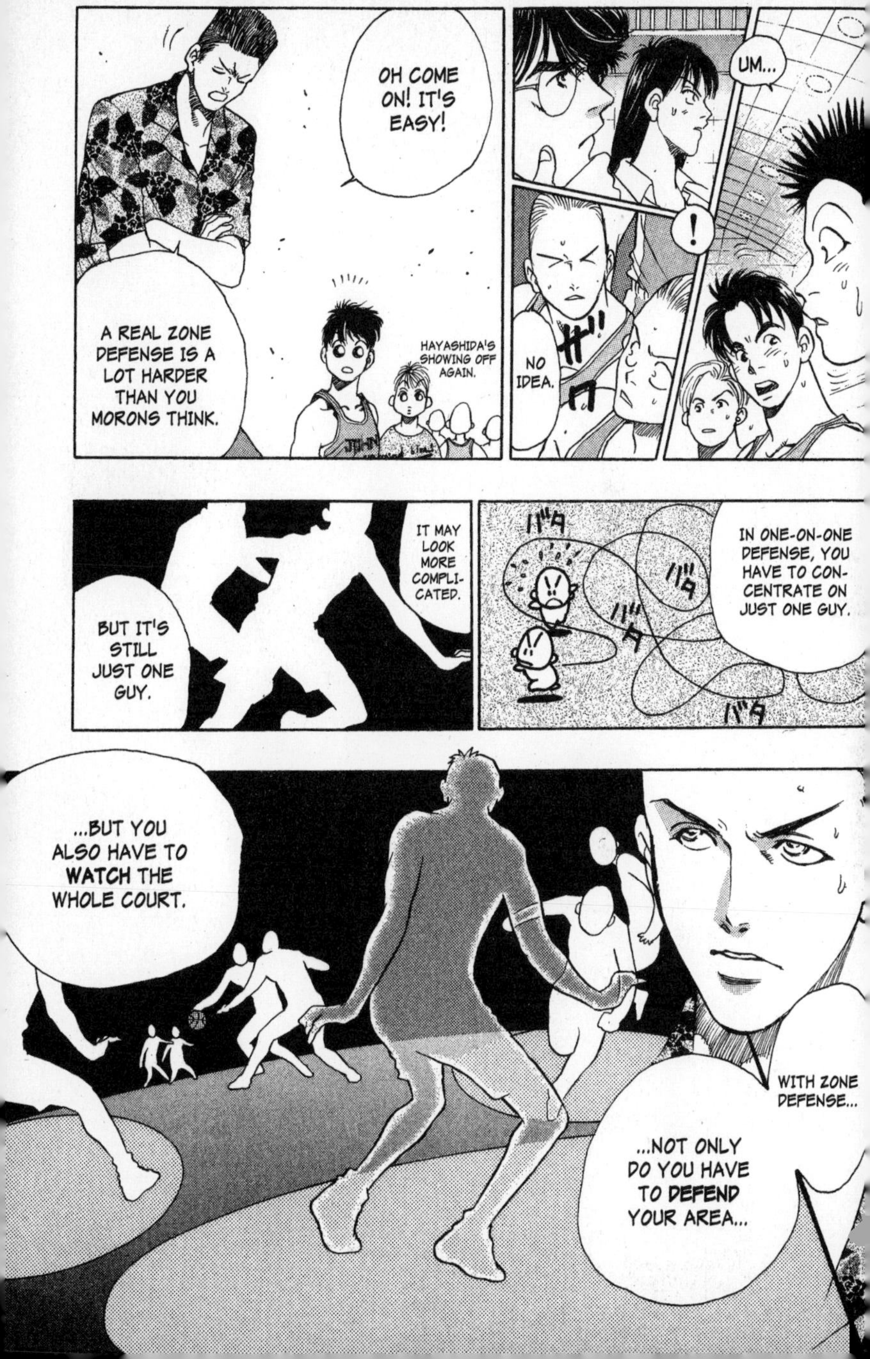
UM...
!
NO IDEA.
OH COME ON! IT'S EASY!
HAYASHIDA'S SHOWING OFF AGAIN.
A REAL ZONE DEFENSE IS A LOT HARDER THAN YOU MORONS THINK.
IN ONE-ON-ONE DEFENSE, YOU HAVE TO CONCENTRATE ON JUST ONE GUY.
IT MAY LOOK MORE COMPLICATED.
BUT IT'S STILL JUST ONE GUY.
WITH ZONE DEFENSE...
...NOT ONLY DO YOU HAVE TO **DEFEND** YOUR AREA...
...BUT YOU ALSO HAVE TO **WATCH** THE WHOLE COURT.

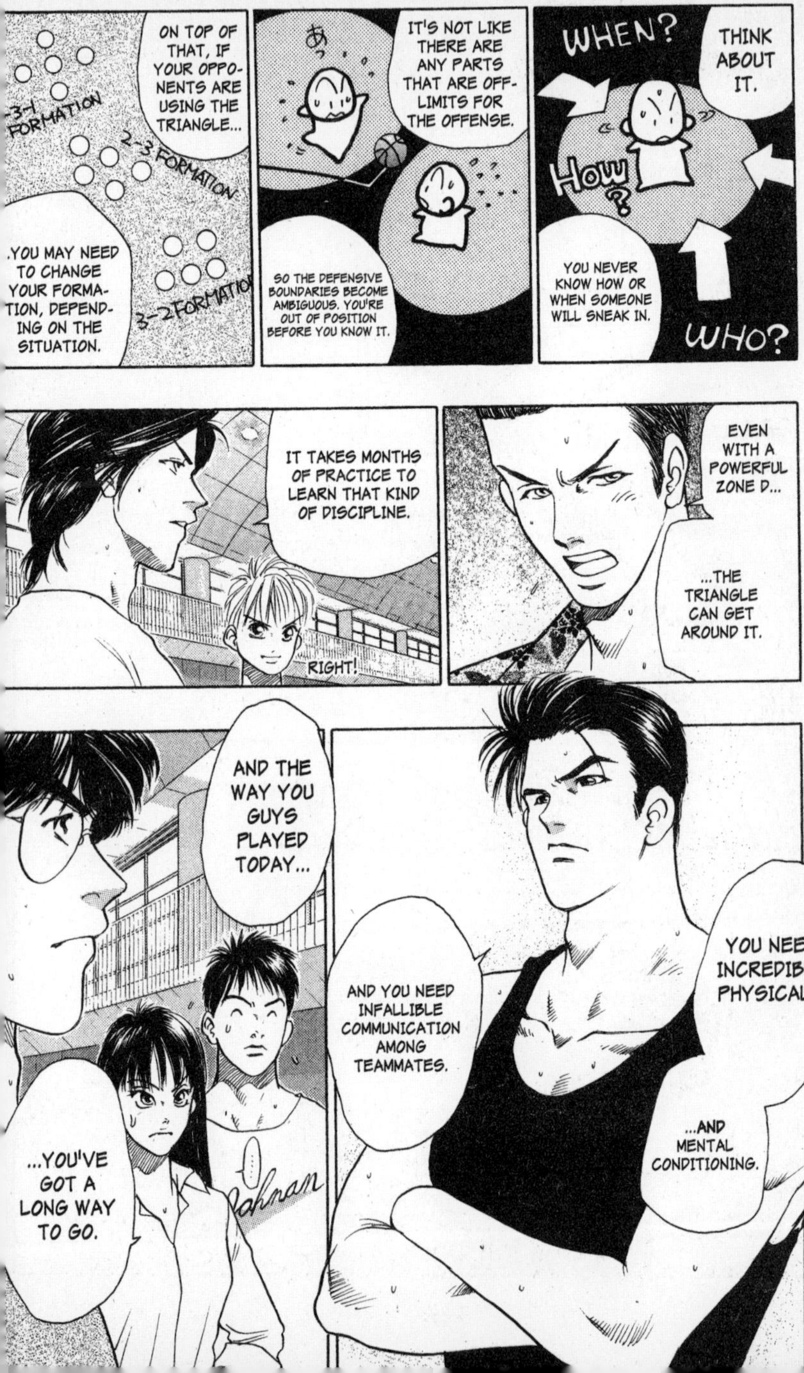
THINK ABOUT IT.
WHEN?
HOW?
WHO?
YOU NEVER KNOW HOW OR WHEN SOMEONE WILL SNEAK IN.
IT'S NOT LIKE THERE ARE ANY PARTS THAT ARE OFF-LIMITS FOR THE OFFENSE.
あ
SO THE DEFENSIVE BOUNDARIES BECOME AMBIGUOUS. YOU'RE OUT OF POSITION BEFORE YOU KNOW IT.
ON TOP OF THAT, IF YOUR OPPONENTS ARE USING THE TRIANGLE...
3-1 FORMATION
2-3 FORMATION
3-2 FORMATION
...YOU MAY NEED TO CHANGE YOUR FORMATION, DEPENDING ON THE SITUATION.
EVEN WITH A POWERFUL ZONE D...
...THE TRIANGLE CAN GET AROUND IT.
IT TAKES MONTHS OF PRACTICE TO LEARN THAT KIND OF DISCIPLINE.
RIGHT!
YOU NEED INCREDIBLE PHYSICAL...
...AND MENTAL CONDITIONING.
AND YOU NEED INFALLIBLE COMMUNICATION AMONG TEAMMATES.
AND THE WAY YOU GUYS PLAYED TODAY...
...YOU'VE GOT A LONG WAY TO GO.
...

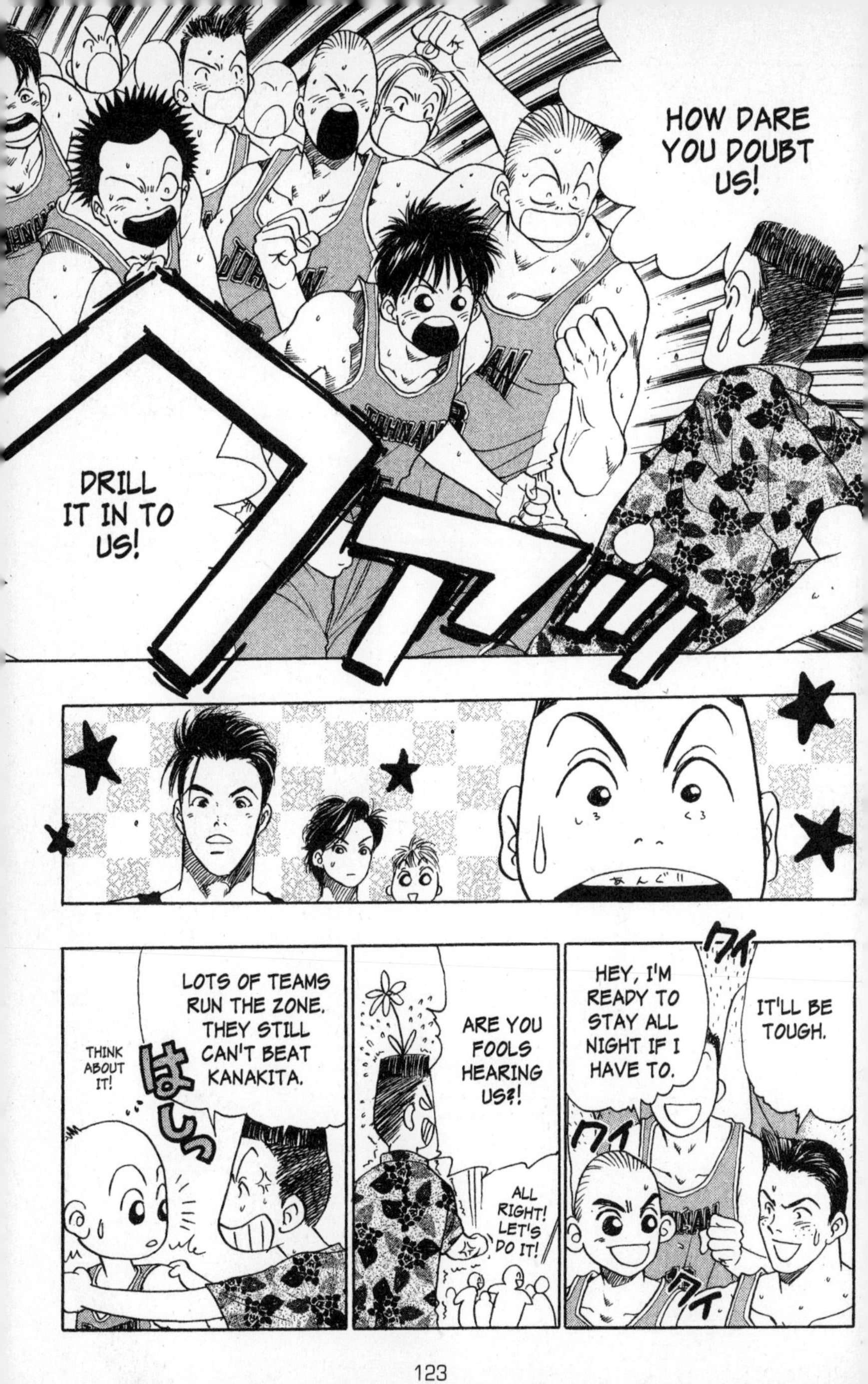
HOW DARE YOU DOUBT US!
DRILL IT IN TO US!
あんぐ!!
ワイ
IT'LL BE TOUGH.
HEY, I'M READY TO STAY ALL NIGHT IF I HAVE TO.
ワイ
ワイ
ARE YOU FOOLS HEARING US?!
ALL RIGHT! LET'S DO IT!
LOTS OF TEAMS RUN THE ZONE. THEY STILL CAN'T BEAT KANAKITA.
はしっ
THINK ABOUT IT!

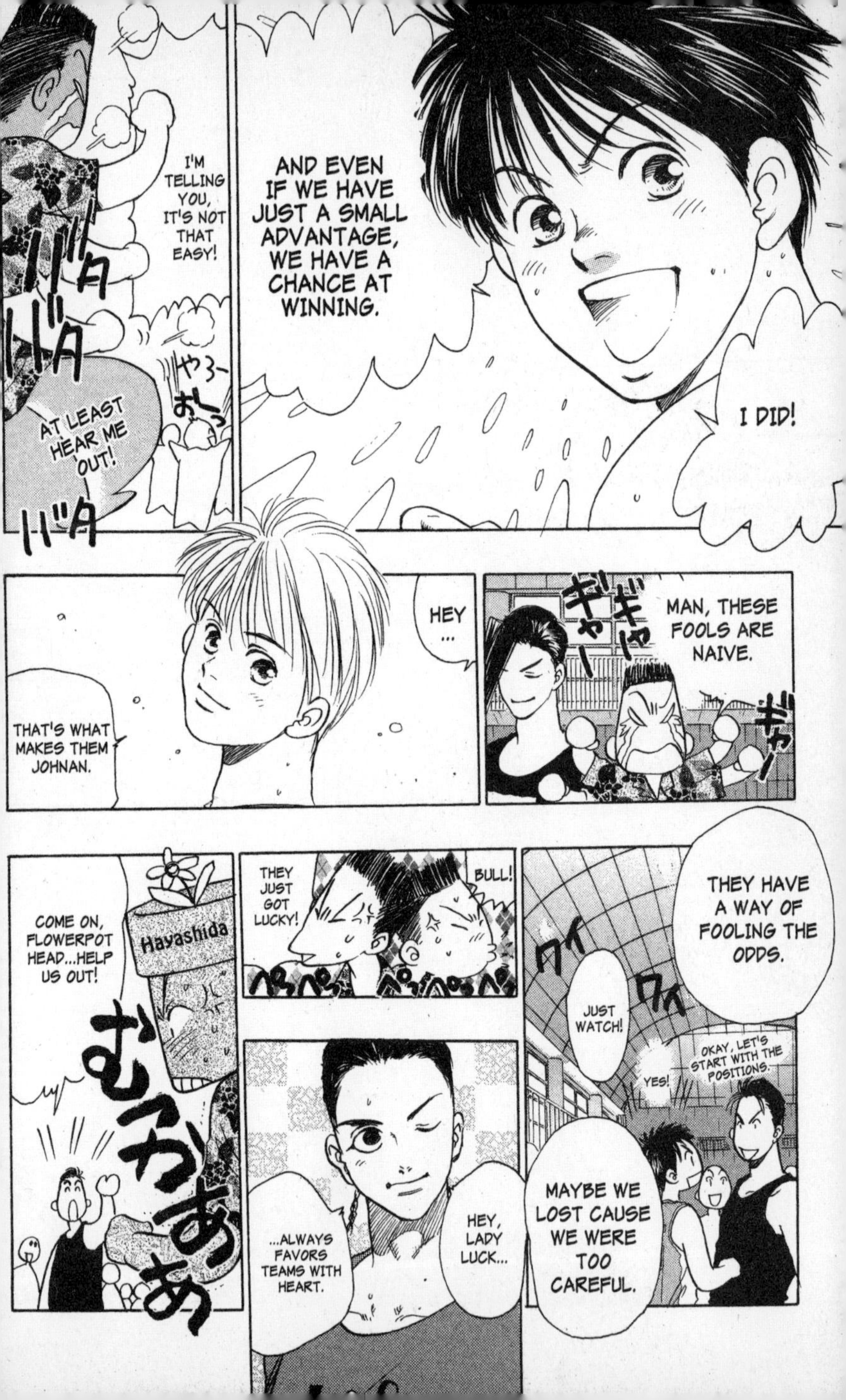
I DID!
AND EVEN IF WE HAVE JUST A SMALL ADVANTAGE, WE HAVE A CHANCE AT WINNING.
I'M TELLING YOU, IT'S NOT THAT EASY!
AT LEAST HEAR ME OUT!
MAN, THESE FOOLS ARE NAIVE.
HEY ...
THAT'S WHAT MAKES THEM JOHNAN.
THEY HAVE A WAY OF FOOLING THE ODDS.
JUST WATCH!
OKAY, LET'S START WITH THE POSITIONS.
YES!
MAYBE WE LOST CAUSE WE WERE TOO CAREFUL.
BULL!
THEY JUST GOT LUCKY!
HEY, LADY LUCK...
...ALWAYS FAVORS TEAMS WITH HEART.
COME ON, FLOWERPOT HEAD...HELP US OUT!
Hayashida

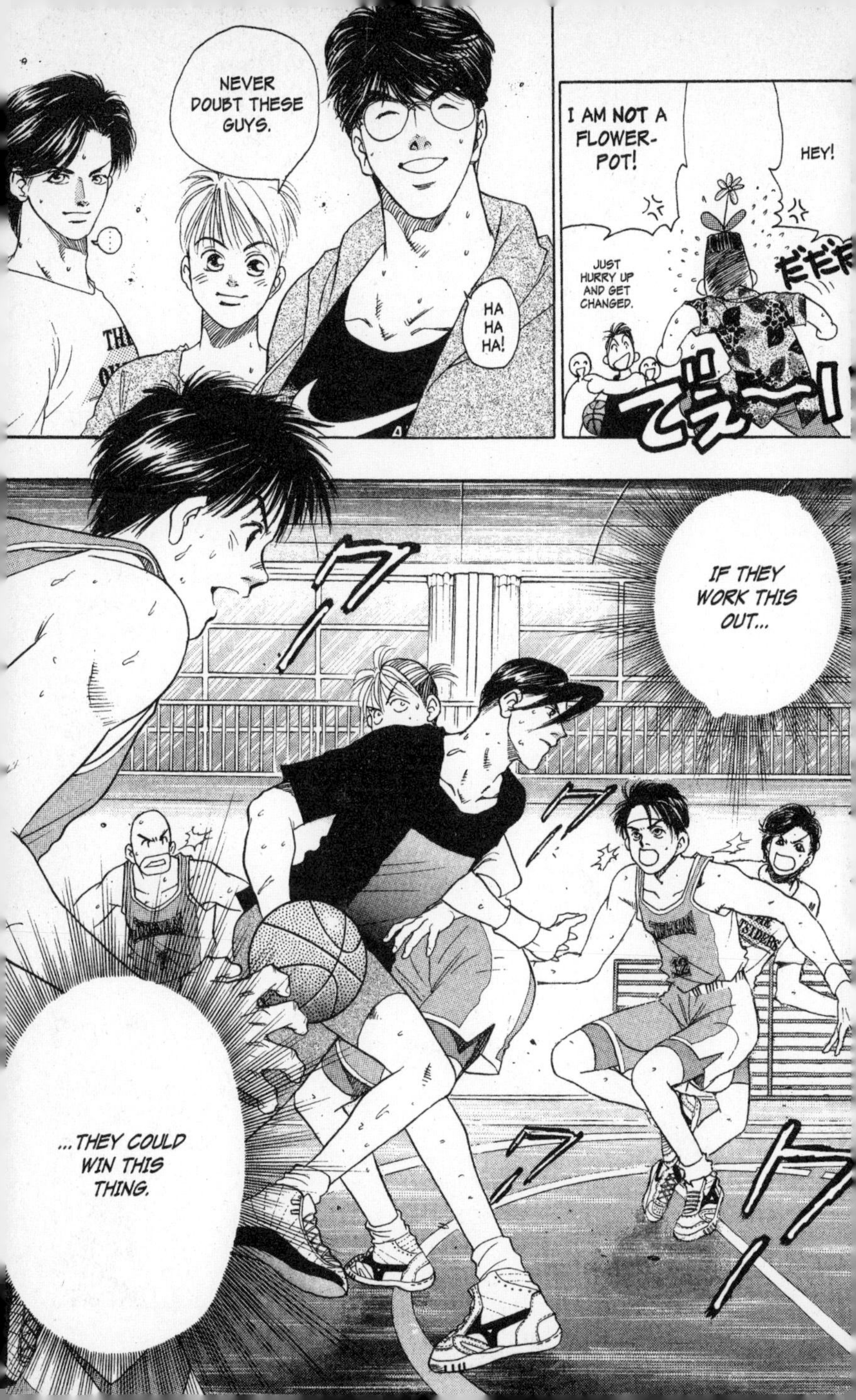
HEY!
I AM NOT A FLOWER-POT!
だだ
JUST HURRY UP AND GET CHANGED.
でぇーー!!
NEVER DOUBT THESE GUYS.
HA HA HA!
IF THEY WORK THIS OUT...
...THEY COULD WIN THIS THING.

You're Reading...

And now a time out to
enjoy the clean, refreshing
taste of TOKYOPOP Air.
Yes, stop, take a breath,
and feel the gaseous
goodness of TOKYOPOP
Air...you'll be glad you did.
Made with only the best
invisible gases on Earth.

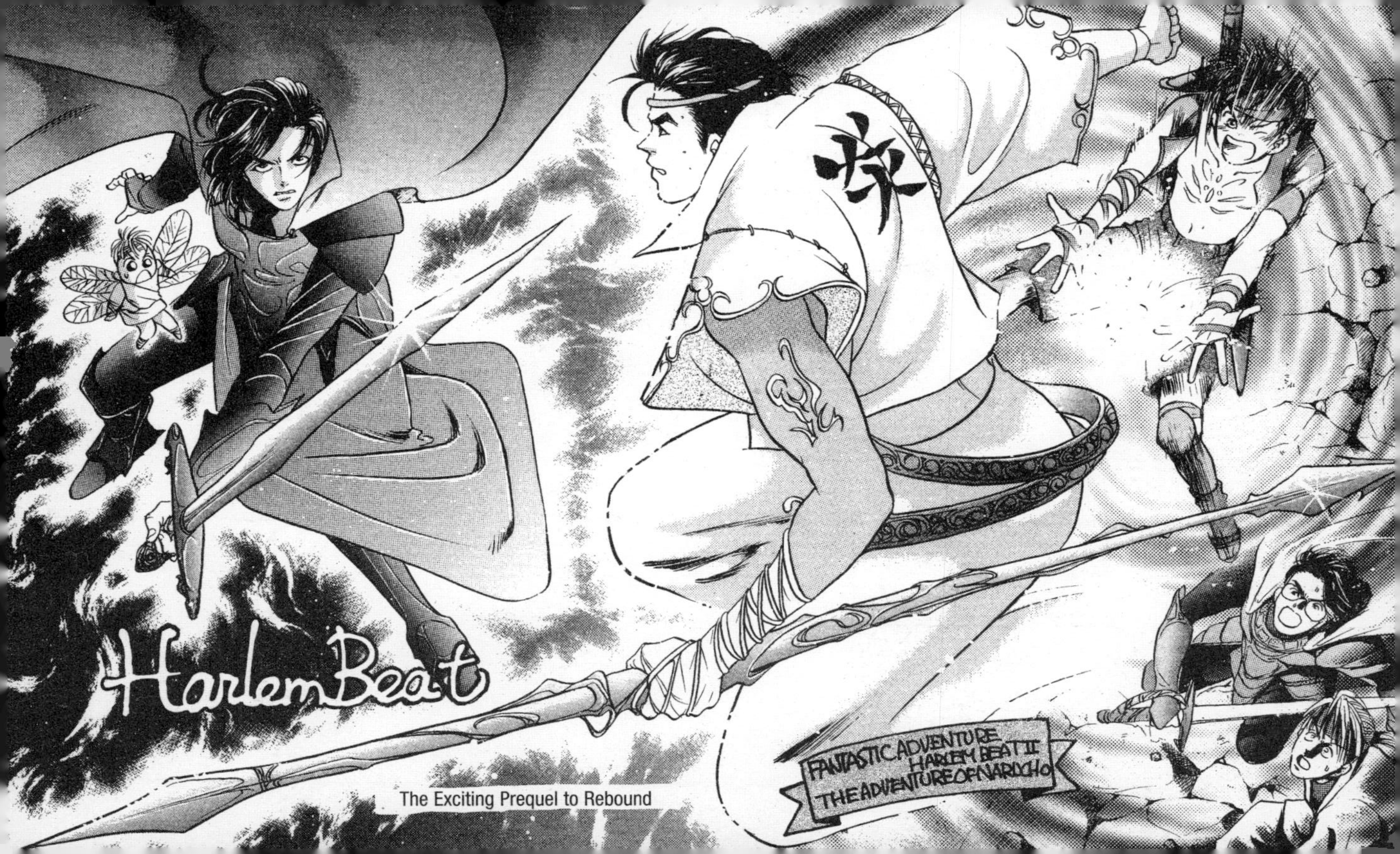
Harlem Beat
The Exciting Prequel to Rebound
FANTASTIC ADVENTURE
HARLEM BEAT II
THE ADVENTURE OF NARUCHO

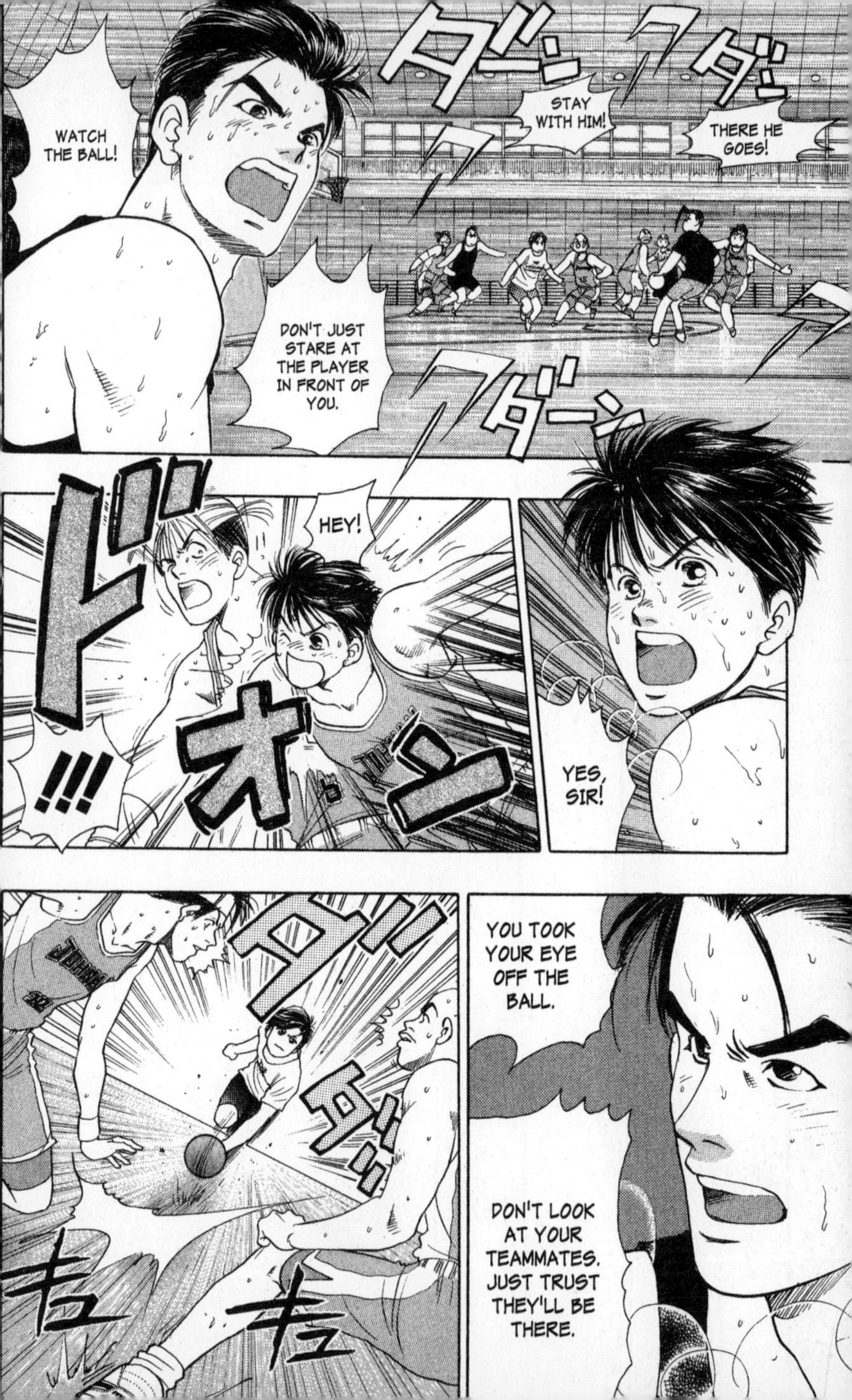
ダン
THERE HE GOES!
STAY WITH HIM!
ダーン
WATCH THE BALL!
DON'T JUST STARE AT THE PLAYER IN FRONT OF YOU.
ダーン
YES, SIR!
HEY!
ドオン
!!!
YOU TOOK YOUR EYE OFF THE BALL.
DON'T LOOK AT YOUR TEAMMATES. JUST TRUST THEY'LL BE THERE.
ダン
ダン
キュ
キュ

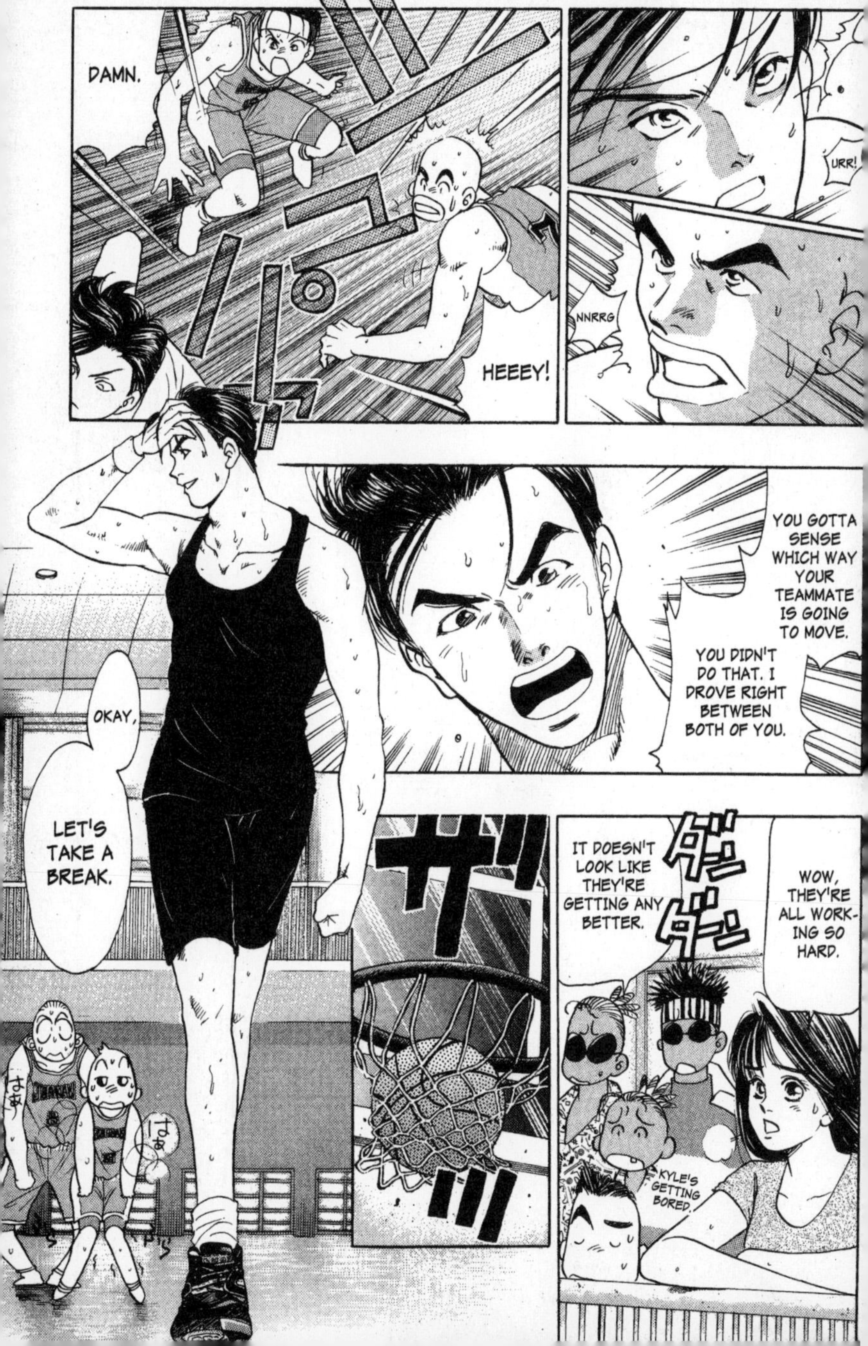
URR!
NNRRG
DAMN.
HEEEY!
YOU GOTTA SENSE WHICH WAY YOUR TEAMMATE IS GOING TO MOVE.
YOU DIDN'T DO THAT. I DROVE RIGHT BETWEEN BOTH OF YOU.
WOW, THEY'RE ALL WORK-ING SO HARD.
IT DOESN'T LOOK LIKE THEY'RE GETTING ANY BETTER.
KYLE'S GETTING BORED.
OKAY,
LET'S TAKE A BREAK.
はぁ
はぁ

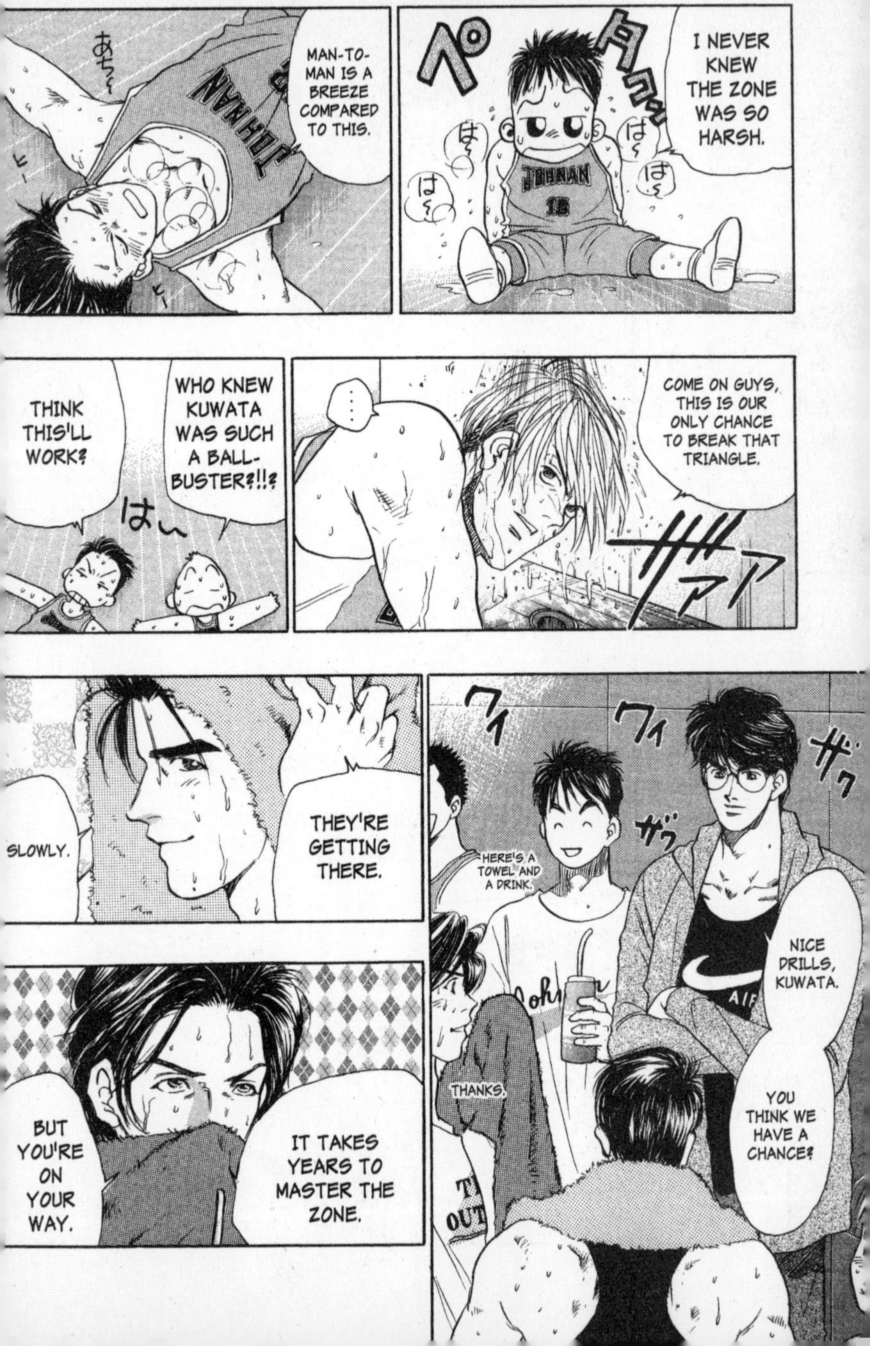
I NEVER KNEW THE ZONE WAS SO HARSH.
MAN-TO-MAN IS A BREEZE COMPARED TO THIS.
COME ON GUYS, THIS IS OUR ONLY CHANCE TO BREAK THAT TRIANGLE.
......
WHO KNEW KUWATA WAS SUCH A BALL-BUSTER?!!?
THINK THIS'LL WORK?
NICE DRILLS, KUWATA.
HERE'S A TOWEL AND A DRINK.
THANKS.
YOU THINK WE HAVE A CHANCE?
THEY'RE GETTING THERE.
SLOWLY.
IT TAKES YEARS TO MASTER THE ZONE.
BUT YOU'RE ON YOUR WAY.

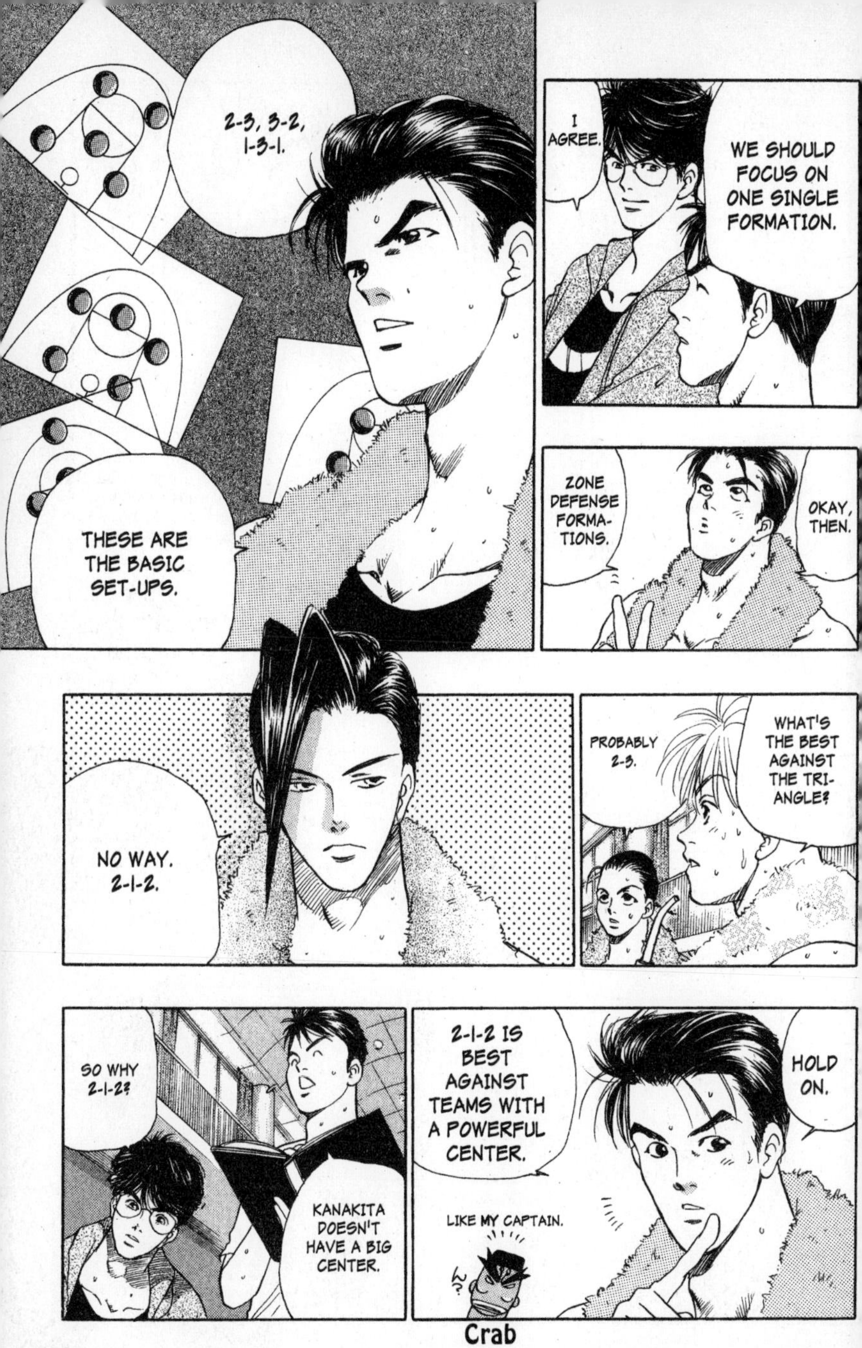
WE SHOULD FOCUS ON ONE SINGLE FORMATION.
I AGREE.
OKAY, THEN.
ZONE DEFENSE FORMATIONS.
2-3, 3-2, 1-3-1.
THESE ARE THE BASIC SET-UPS.
WHAT'S THE BEST AGAINST THE TRI-ANGLE?
PROBABLY 2-3.
NO WAY. 2-1-2.
HOLD ON.
2-1-2 IS BEST AGAINST TEAMS WITH A POWERFUL CENTER.
LIKE MY CAPTAIN.
SO WHY 2-1-2?
KANAKITA DOESN'T HAVE A BIG CENTER.

Crab

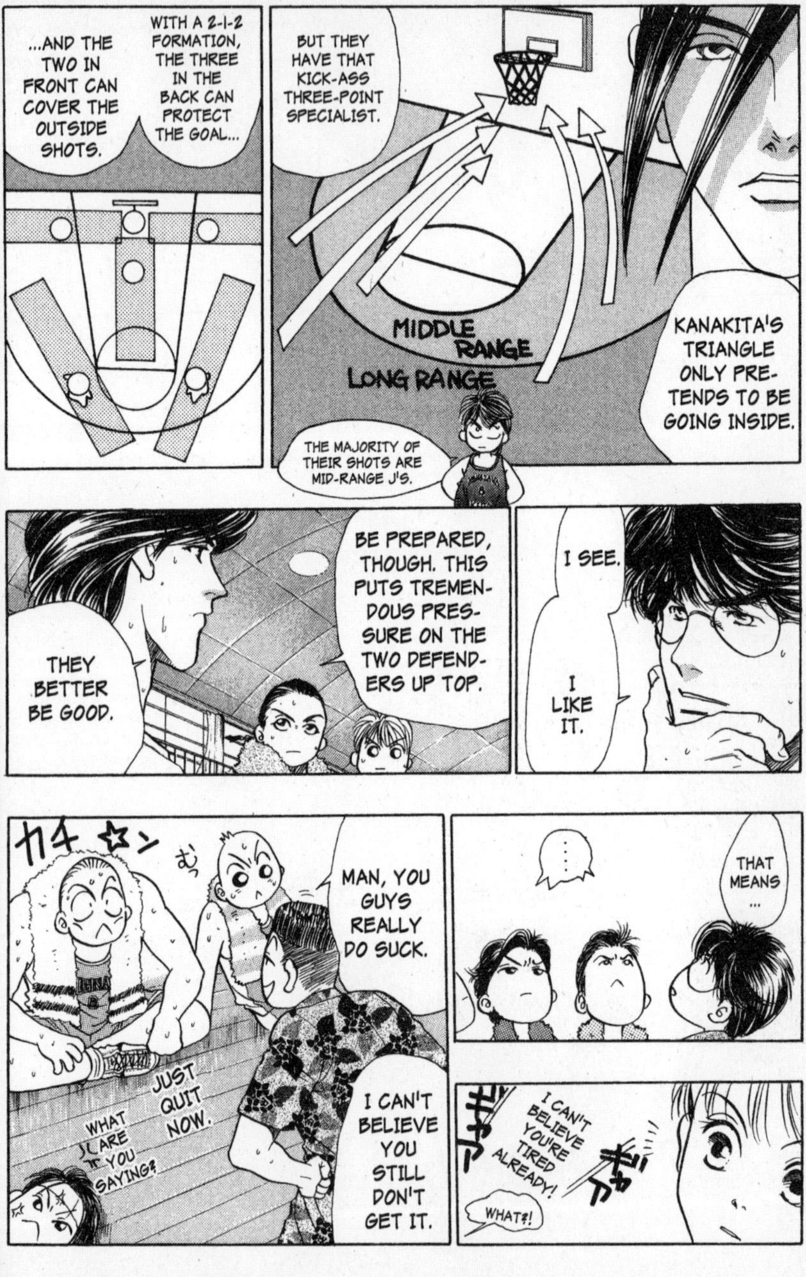
KANAKITA'S TRIANGLE ONLY PRETENDS TO BE GOING INSIDE.
MIDDLE RANGE
LONG RANGE
THE MAJORITY OF THEIR SHOTS ARE MID-RANGE J'S.
BUT THEY HAVE THAT KICK-ASS THREE-POINT SPECIALIST.
WITH A 2-1-2 FORMATION, THE THREE IN THE BACK CAN PROTECT THE GOAL...
...AND THE TWO IN FRONT CAN COVER THE OUTSIDE SHOTS.
I SEE.
I LIKE IT.
BE PREPARED, THOUGH. THIS PUTS TREMENDOUS PRESSURE ON THE TWO DEFENDERS UP TOP.
THEY BETTER BE GOOD.
THAT MEANS ...
...
I CAN'T BELIEVE YOU'RE TIRED ALREADY!
WHAT?!
カキ☆ン
むっ
MAN, YOU GUYS REALLY DO SUCK.
JUST QUIT NOW.
WHAT ARE YOU SAYING?
I CAN'T BELIEVE YOU STILL DON'T GET IT.

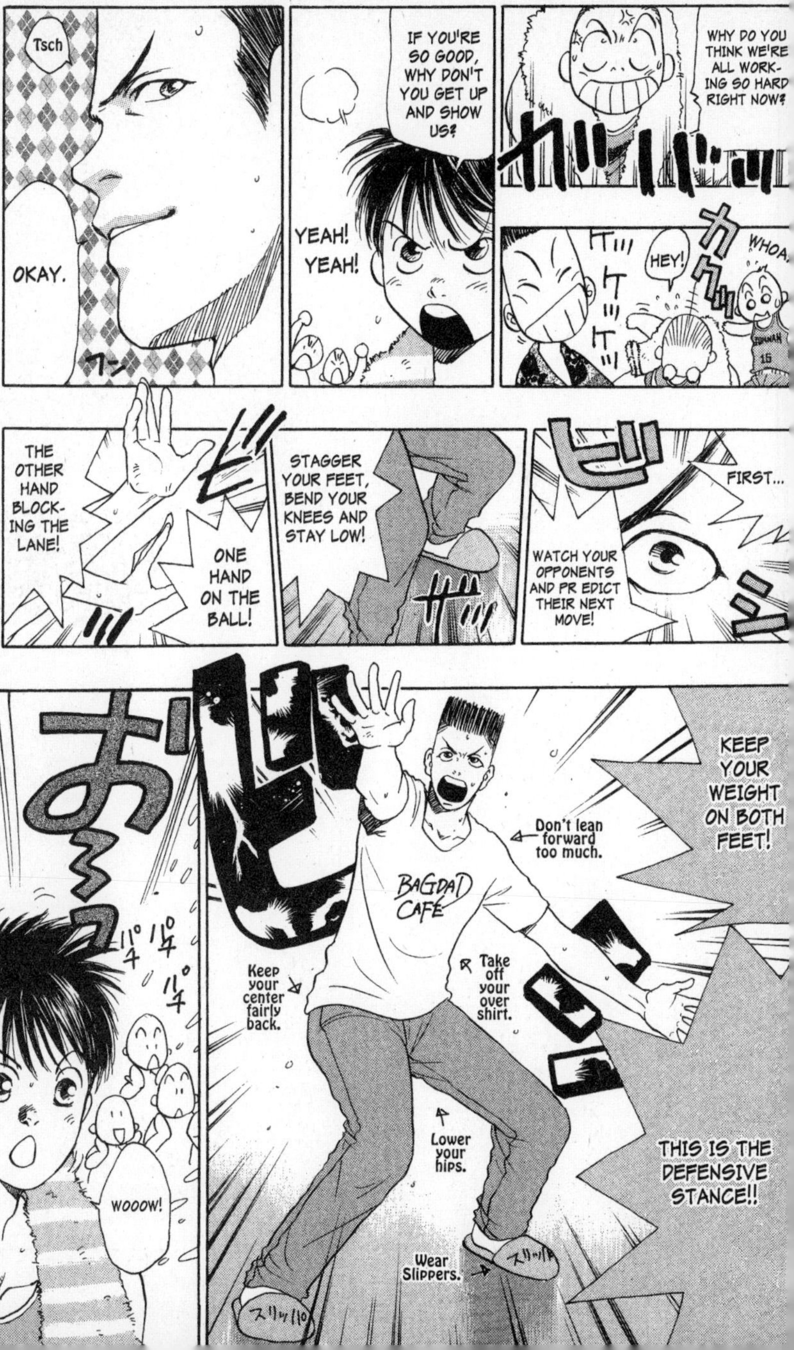
WHY DO YOU THINK WE'RE ALL WORKING SO HARD RIGHT NOW?
WHOA.
HEY!
IF YOU'RE SO GOOD, WHY DON'T YOU GET UP AND SHOW US?
YEAH! YEAH!
Tsch
OKAY.
FIRST...
WATCH YOUR OPPONENTS AND PR EDICT THEIR NEXT MOVE!
STAGGER YOUR FEET, BEND YOUR KNEES AND STAY LOW!
ONE HAND ON THE BALL!
THE OTHER HAND BLOCKING THE LANE!
KEEP YOUR WEIGHT ON BOTH FEET!
Don't lean forward too much.
Take off your over shirt.
Keep your center fairly back.
Lower your hips.
Wear Slippers.
THIS IS THE DEFENSIVE STANCE!!
WOOOW!

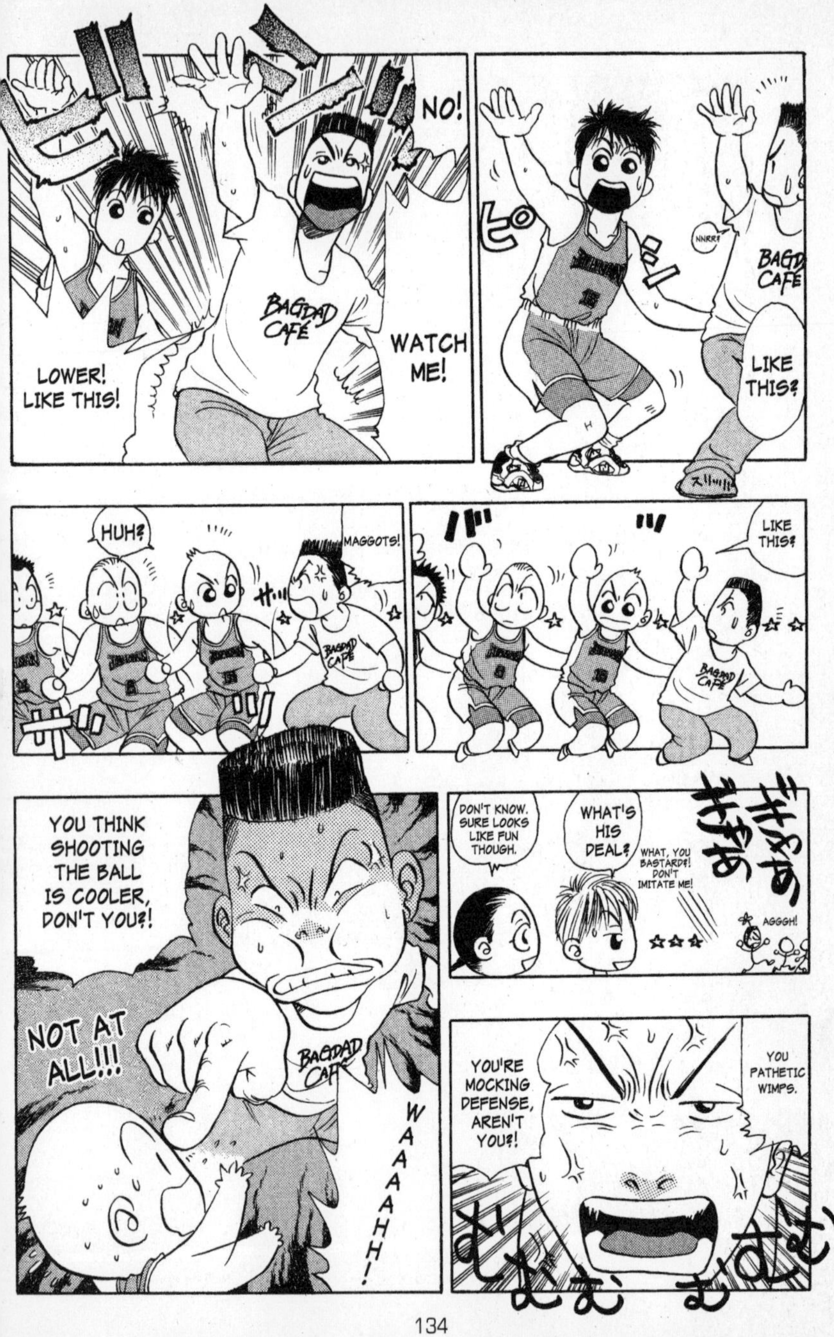
NNRR?
LIKE THIS?
NO!
WATCH ME!
LOWER! LIKE THIS!
LIKE THIS?
MAGGOTS!
HUH?
ぎゃあぎゃあ
WHAT, YOU BASTARDS?! DON'T IMITATE ME!
WHAT'S HIS DEAL?
DON'T KNOW. SURE LOOKS LIKE FUN THOUGH.
AGGGH!
YOU PATHETIC WIMPS.
YOU'RE MOCKING DEFENSE, AREN'T YOU?!
YOU THINK SHOOTING THE BALL IS COOLER, DON'T YOU?!
NOT AT ALL!!!
WAAAAAAHH!

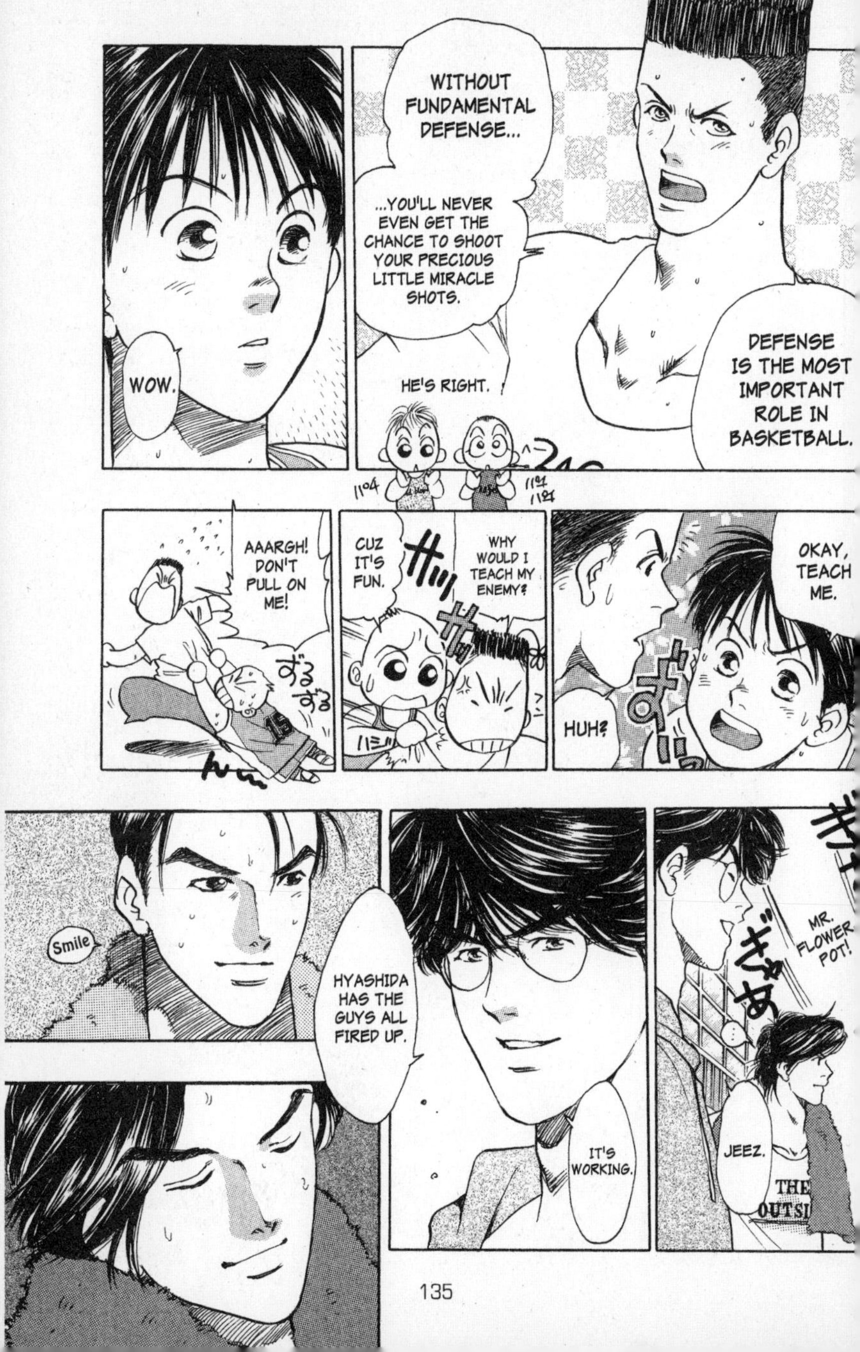
WITHOUT FUNDAMENTAL DEFENSE...
...YOU'LL NEVER EVEN GET THE CHANCE TO SHOOT YOUR PRECIOUS LITTLE MIRACLE SHOTS.
DEFENSE IS THE MOST IMPORTANT ROLE IN BASKETBALL.
HE'S RIGHT.
WOW.
OKAY, TEACH ME.
HUH?
WHY WOULD I TEACH MY ENEMY?
CUZ IT'S FUN.
AAARGH! DON'T PULL ON ME!
ずるずる
ぎゃあ
MR. FLOWER POT!
JEEZ.
HYASHIDA HAS THE GUYS ALL FIRED UP.
IT'S WORKING.
Smile

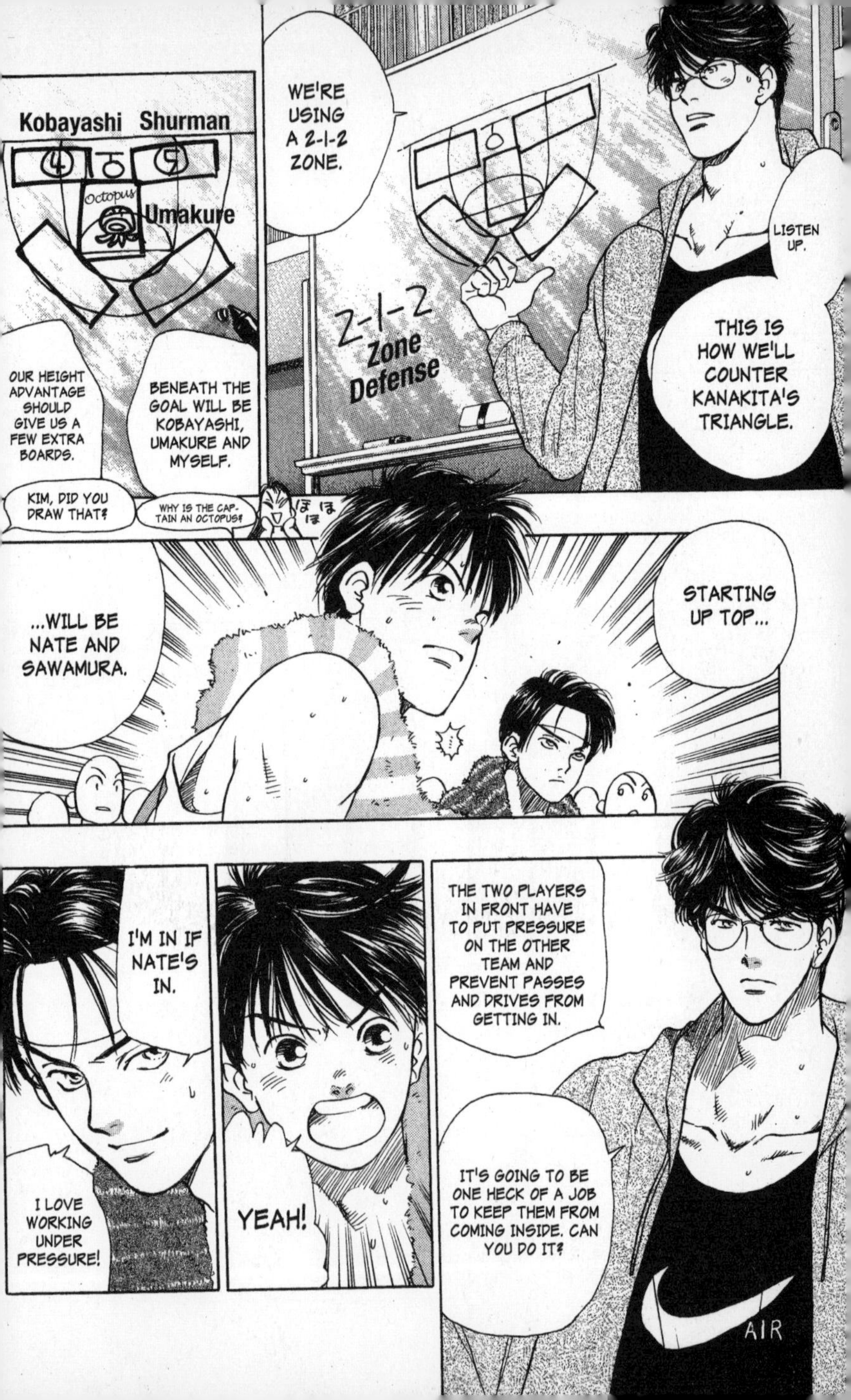
LISTEN UP.
THIS IS HOW WE'LL COUNTER KANAKITA'S TRIANGLE.
WE'RE USING A 2-1-2 ZONE.
2-1-2 Zone Defense
Kobayashi Shurman
4 5
Octopus
Umakure
BENEATH THE GOAL WILL BE KOBAYASHI, UMAKURE AND MYSELF.
OUR HEIGHT ADVANTAGE SHOULD GIVE US A FEW EXTRA BOARDS.
ほほほ
WHY IS THE CAPTAIN AN OCTOPUS?
KIM, DID YOU DRAW THAT?
STARTING UP TOP...
...WILL BE NATE AND SAWAMURA.
THE TWO PLAYERS IN FRONT HAVE TO PUT PRESSURE ON THE OTHER TEAM AND PREVENT PASSES AND DRIVES FROM GETTING IN.
IT'S GOING TO BE ONE HECK OF A JOB TO KEEP THEM FROM COMING INSIDE. CAN YOU DO IT?
AIR
YEAH!
I'M IN IF NATE'S IN.
I LOVE WORKING UNDER PRESSURE!

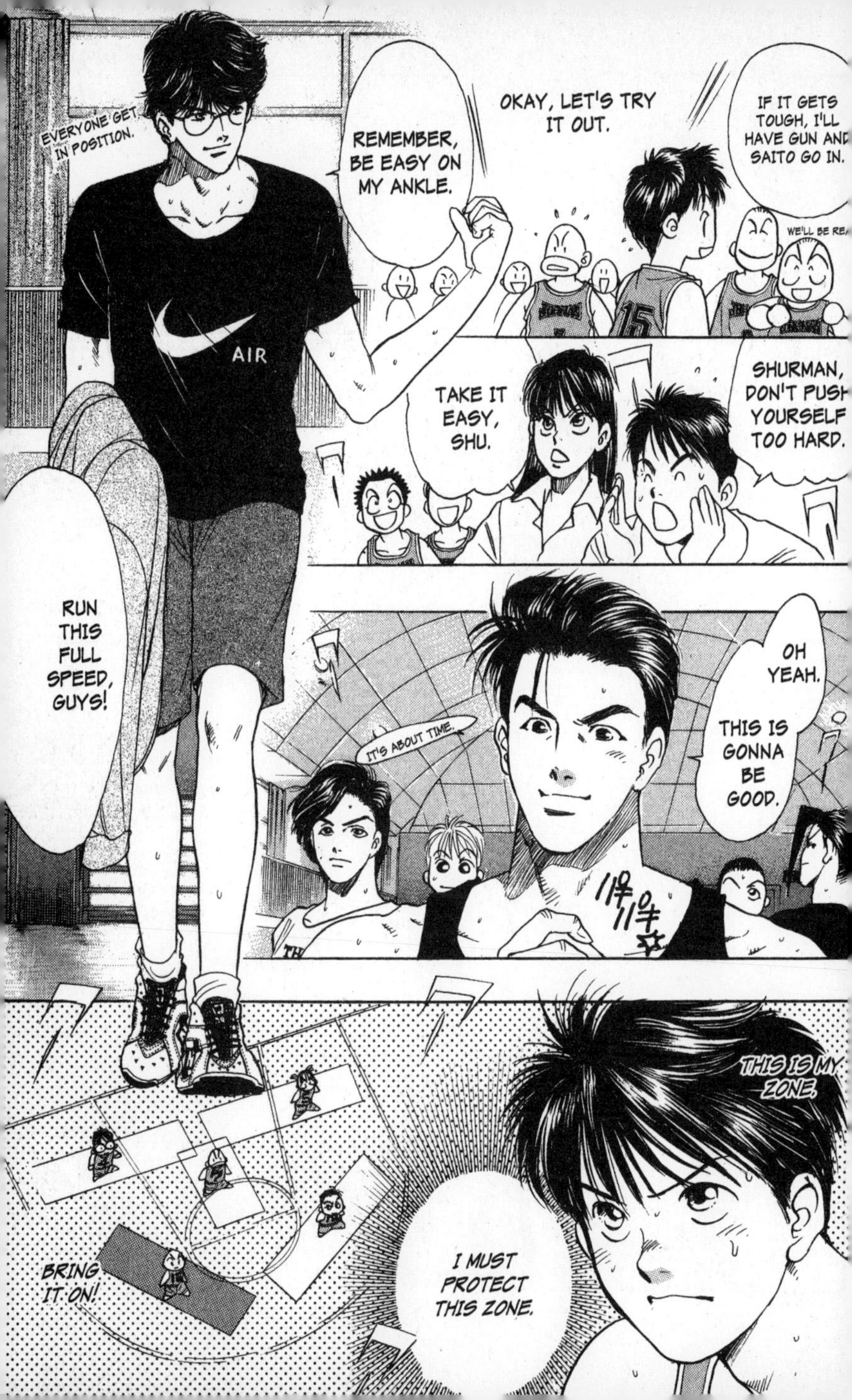

IF IT GETS TOUGH, I'LL HAVE GUN AND SAITO GO IN.
WE'LL BE RE
OKAY, LET'S TRY IT OUT.
REMEMBER, BE EASY ON MY ANKLE.
SHURMAN, DON'T PUSH YOURSELF TOO HARD.
TAKE IT EASY, SHU.
OH YEAH.
THIS IS GONNA BE GOOD.
IT'S ABOUT TIME.
EVERYONE GET IN POSITION.
RUN THIS FULL SPEED, GUYS!
THIS IS MY ZONE.
I MUST PROTECT THIS ZONE.
BRING IT ON!

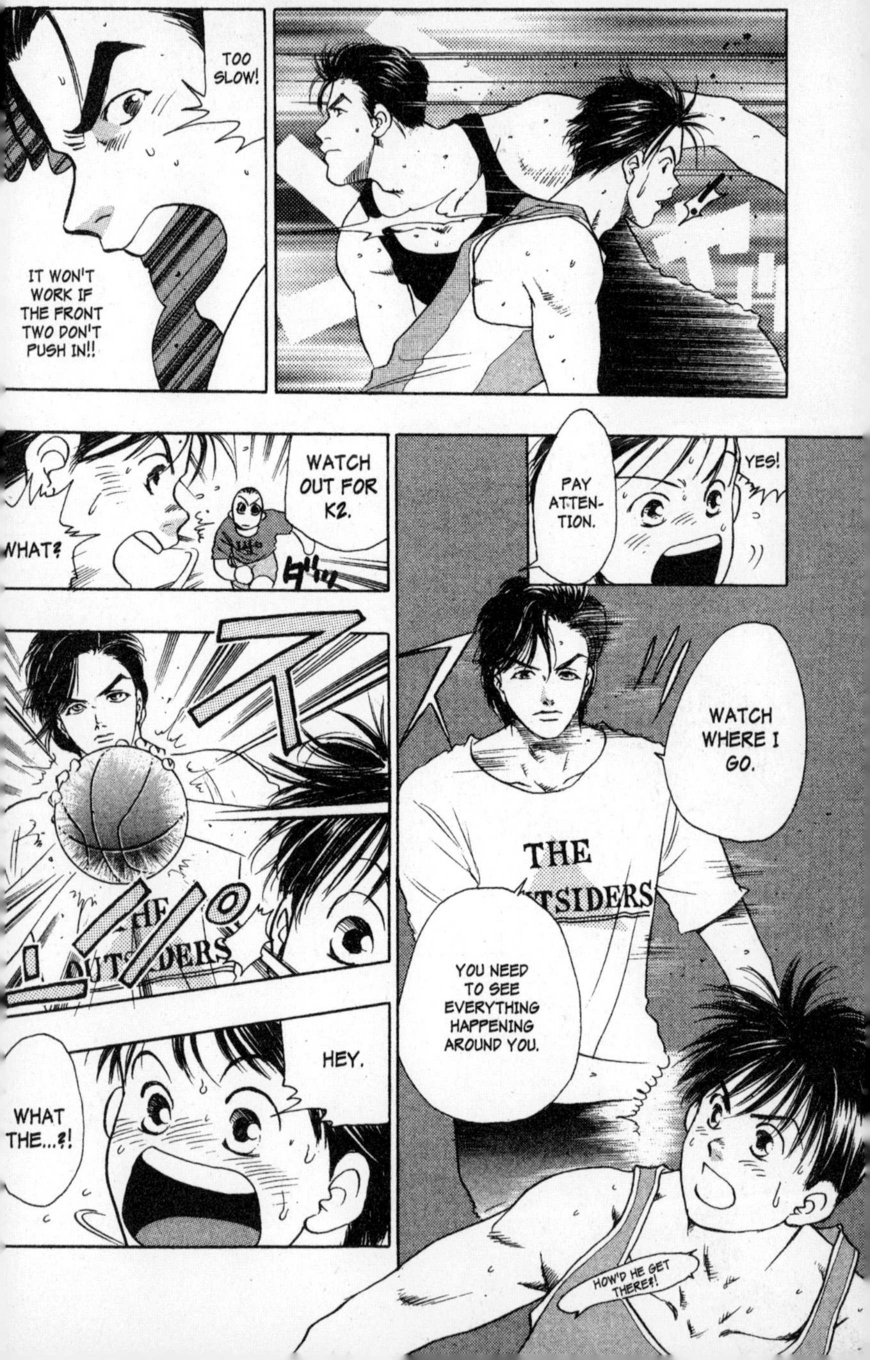
TOO SLOW!
IT WON'T WORK IF THE FRONT TWO DON'T PUSH IN!!
PAY ATTENTION.
YES!
WATCH WHERE I GO.
YOU NEED TO SEE EVERYTHING HAPPENING AROUND YOU.
HOW'D HE GET THERE?!
WATCH OUT FOR K2.
WHAT?
HEY.
WHAT THE...?!

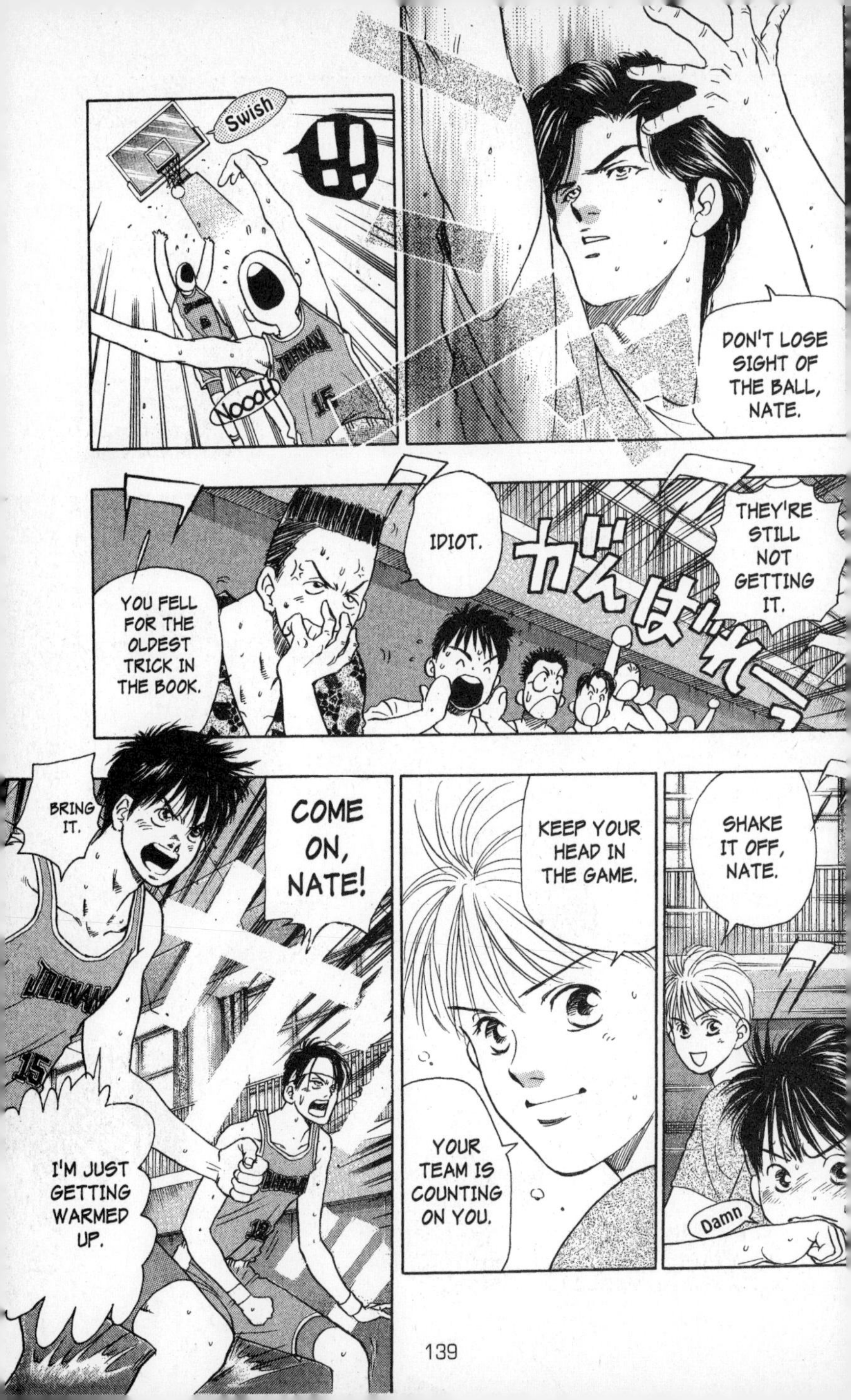
DON'T LOSE SIGHT OF THE BALL, NATE.
Swish
!!
NOOOH
THEY'RE STILL NOT GETTING IT.
がんばれー
IDIOT.
YOU FELL FOR THE OLDEST TRICK IN THE BOOK.
SHAKE IT OFF, NATE.
Damn
KEEP YOUR HEAD IN THE GAME.
YOUR TEAM IS COUNTING ON YOU.
COME ON, NATE!
BRING IT.
I'M JUST GETTING WARMED UP.

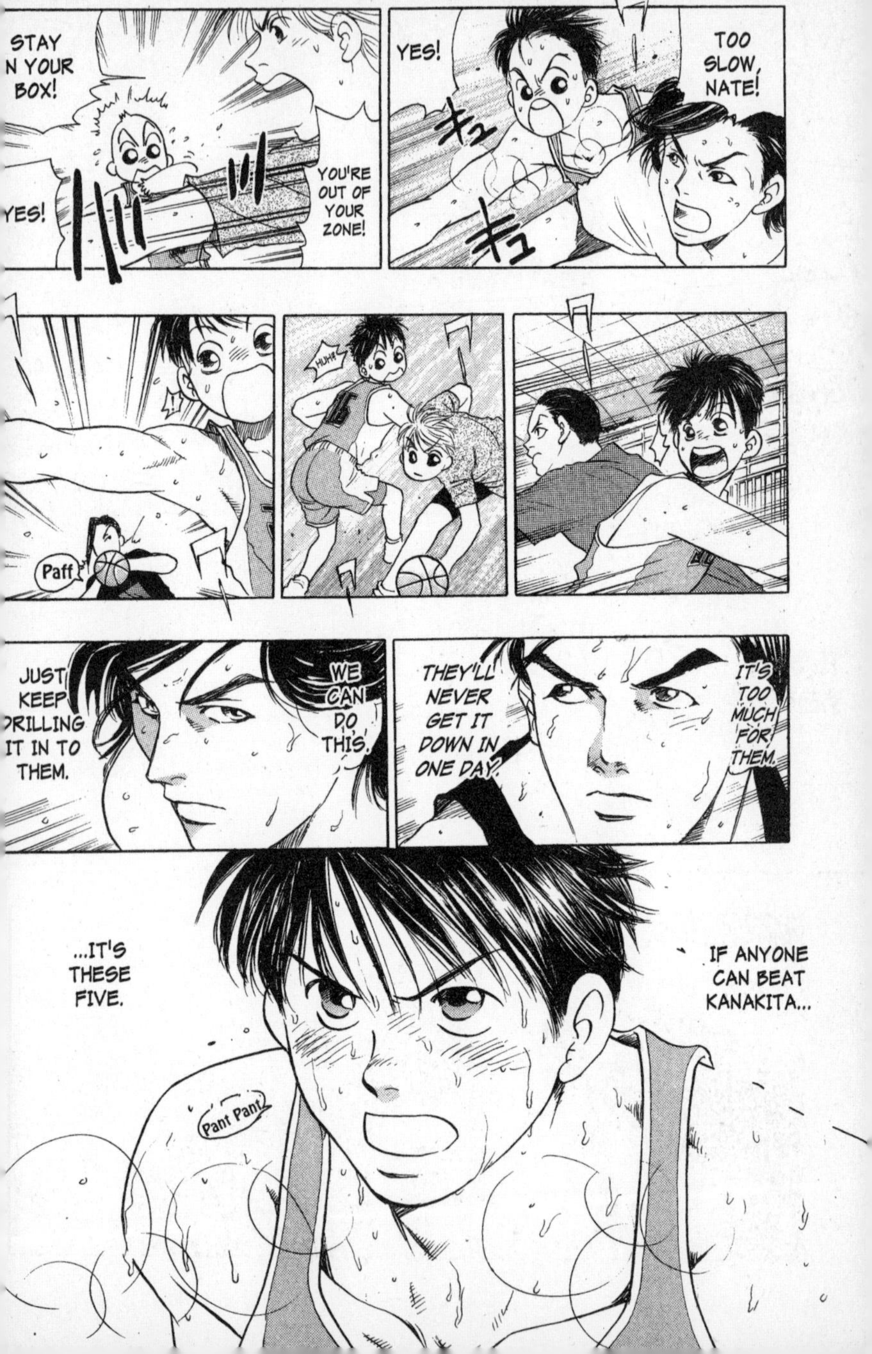
TOO SLOW, NATE!
YES!
キュ
キュ
STAY N YOUR BOX!
YOU'RE OUT OF YOUR ZONE!
YES!
HUH?
!!
Paff
IT'S TOO MUCH FOR THEM.
THEY'LL NEVER GET IT DOWN IN ONE DAY.
WE CAN DO THIS.
JUST KEEP RILLING IT IN TO THEM.
IF ANYONE CAN BEAT KANAKITA...
...IT'S THESE FIVE.
Pant Pant

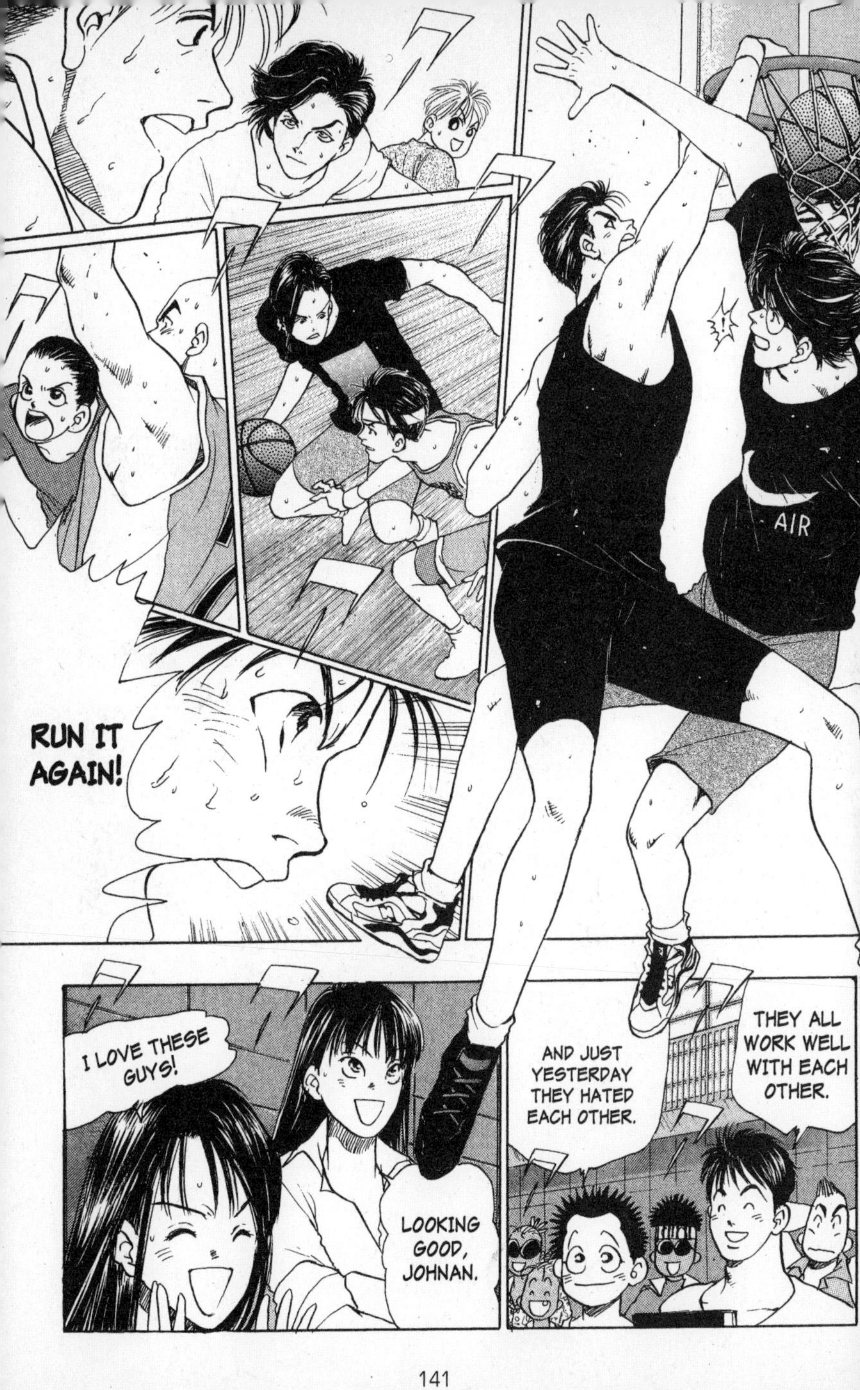
AIR
RUN IT AGAIN!
THEY ALL WORK WELL WITH EACH OTHER.
AND JUST YESTERDAY THEY HATED EACH OTHER.
I LOVE THESE GUYS!
LOOKING GOOD, JOHNAN.

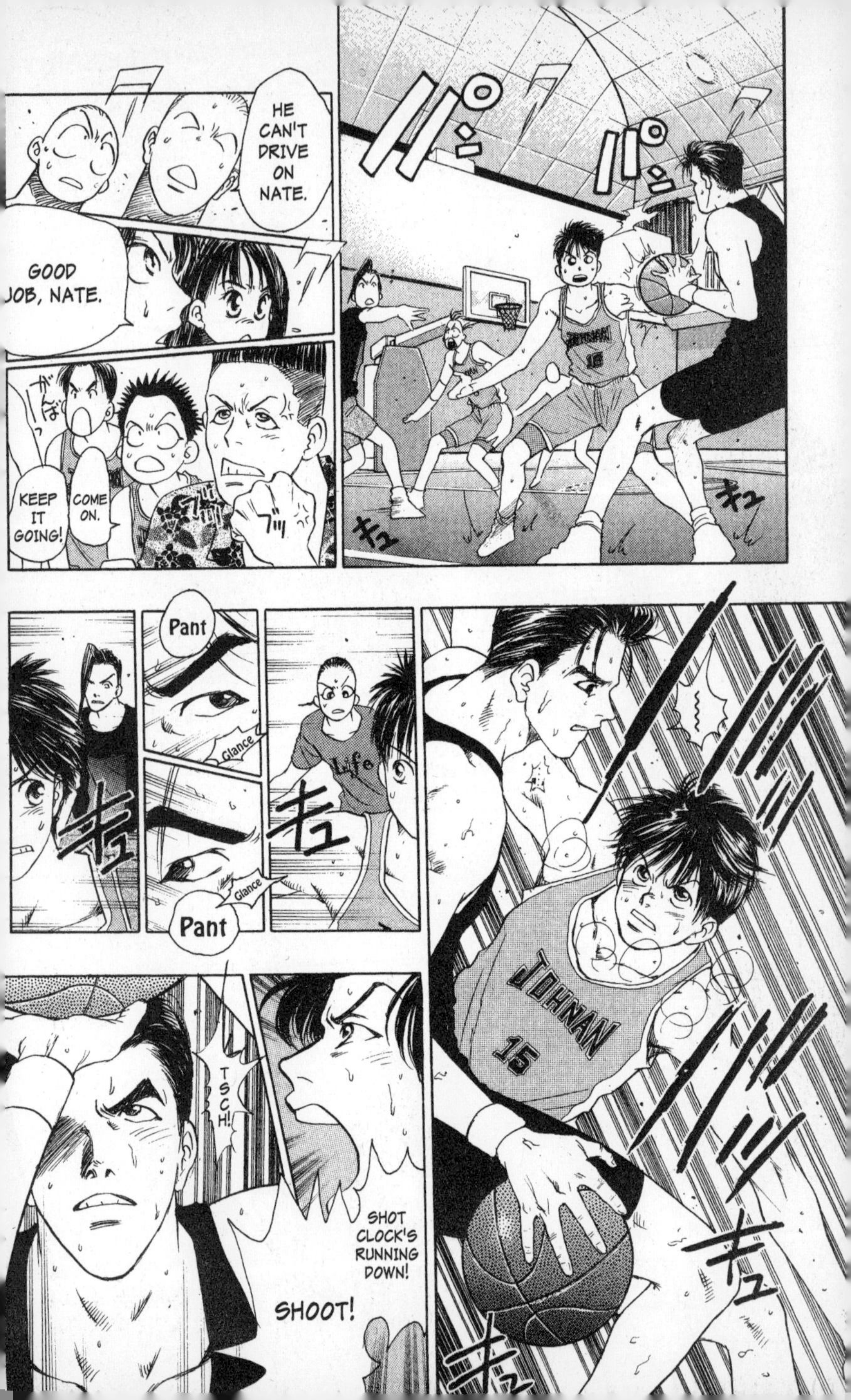
パ
パ
キュ
キュ
HE CAN'T DRIVE ON NATE.
GOOD JOB, NATE.
がんばっ
COME ON.
KEEP IT GOING!
ブッ
JOHNAN
15
キュ
キュ
Life
キュ
Pant
Glance
Glance
Pant
キュ
TSCH!
SHOT CLOCK'S RUNNING DOWN!
SHOOT!

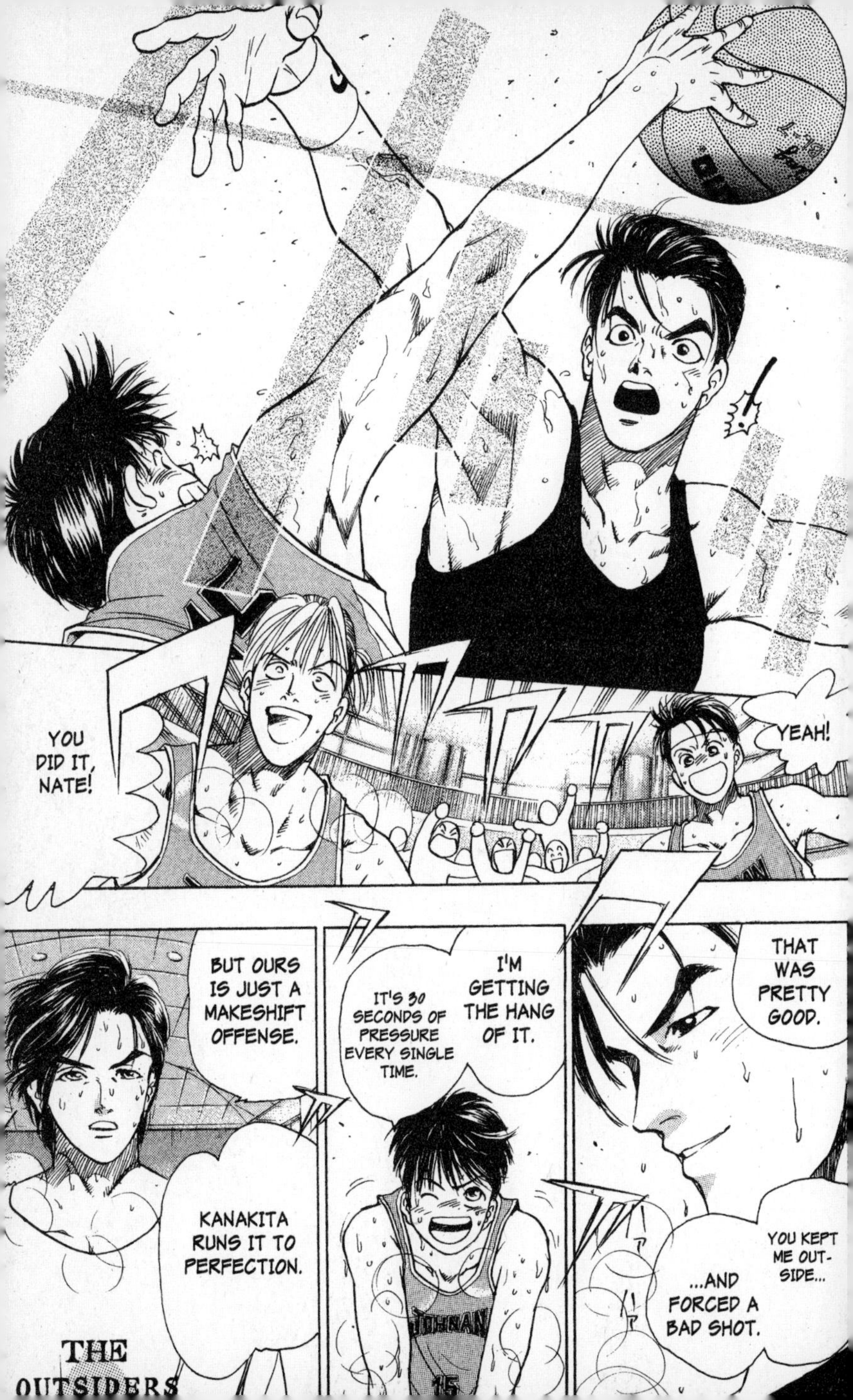
YEAH!
YOU DID IT, NATE!
THAT WAS PRETTY GOOD.
YOU KEPT ME OUTSIDE...
...AND FORCED A BAD SHOT.
I'M GETTING THE HANG OF IT.
IT'S 30 SECONDS OF PRESSURE EVERY SINGLE TIME.
BUT OURS IS JUST A MAKESHIFT OFFENSE.
KANAKITA RUNS IT TO PERFECTION.
THE OUTSIDERS

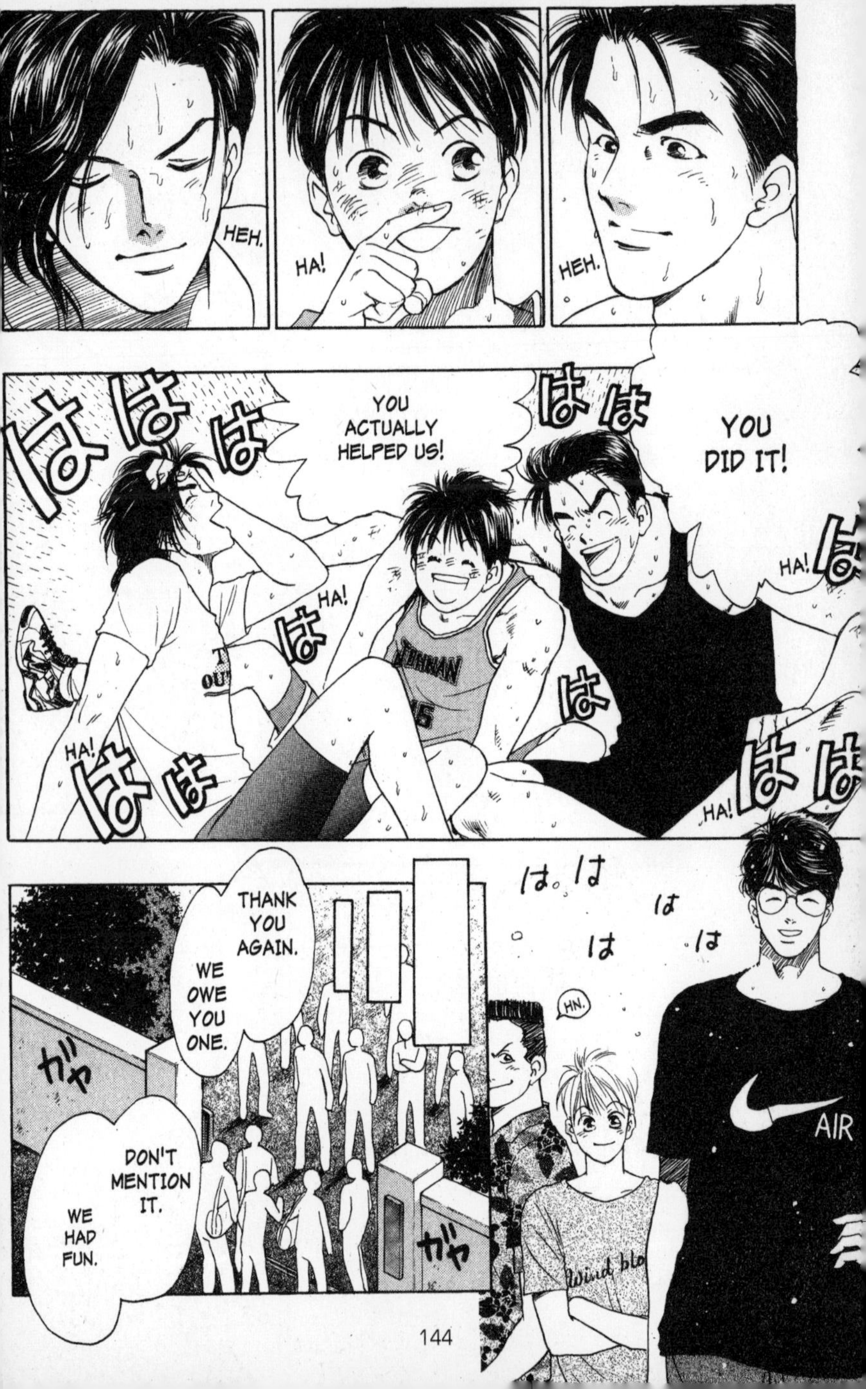
HEH.
HA!
HEH.
YOU DID IT!
HA!
は
YOU ACTUALLY HELPED US!
はは
はは
HA!
は
は
HA!
はは
HA!
はは
はは
はは
HN.
THANK YOU AGAIN.
WE OWE YOU ONE.
DON'T MENTION IT.
WE HAD FUN.
がや
がや

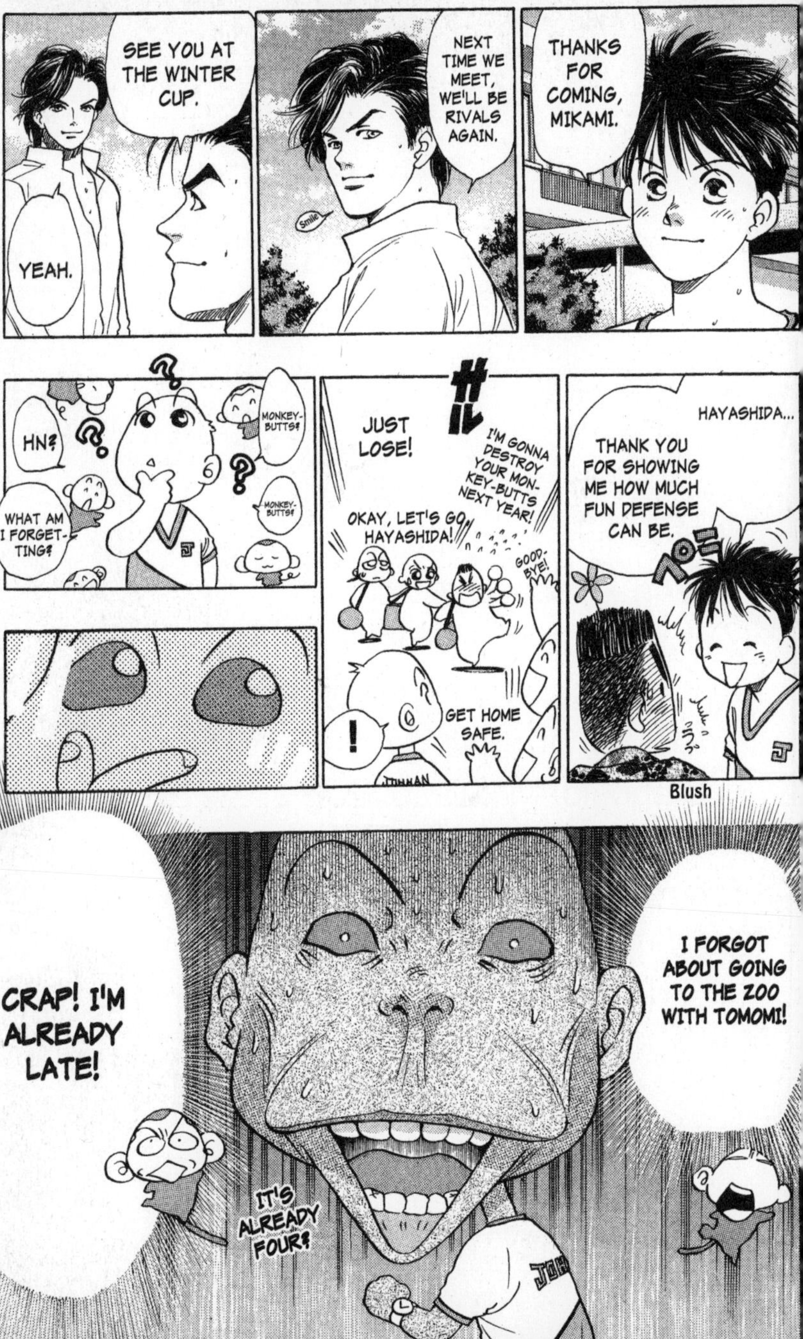
THANKS FOR COMING, MIKAMI.
NEXT TIME WE MEET, WE'LL BE RIVALS AGAIN.
Smile
SEE YOU AT THE WINTER CUP.
YEAH.
HAYASHIDA...
THANK YOU FOR SHOWING ME HOW MUCH FUN DEFENSE CAN BE.
Blush
JUST LOSE!
I'M GONNA DESTROY YOUR MON-KEY-BUTTS NEXT YEAR!
OKAY, LET'S GO, HAYASHIDA!
GOOD-BYE!
GET HOME SAFE.
!
HN?
WHAT AM I FORGET-TING?
MONKEY-BUTTS?
MONKEY-BUTTS?
I FORGOT ABOUT GOING TO THE ZOO WITH TOMOMI!
CRAP! I'M ALREADY LATE!
IT'S ALREADY FOUR?

You're Reading...

We're glad that you're
finding Rebound worth
sinking your teeth into...
but if that's proving to be
a little bit of a problem,
you should try TOKYOPOP's
new Dentoro, the dentures
for reading.

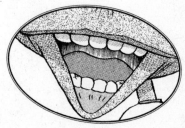

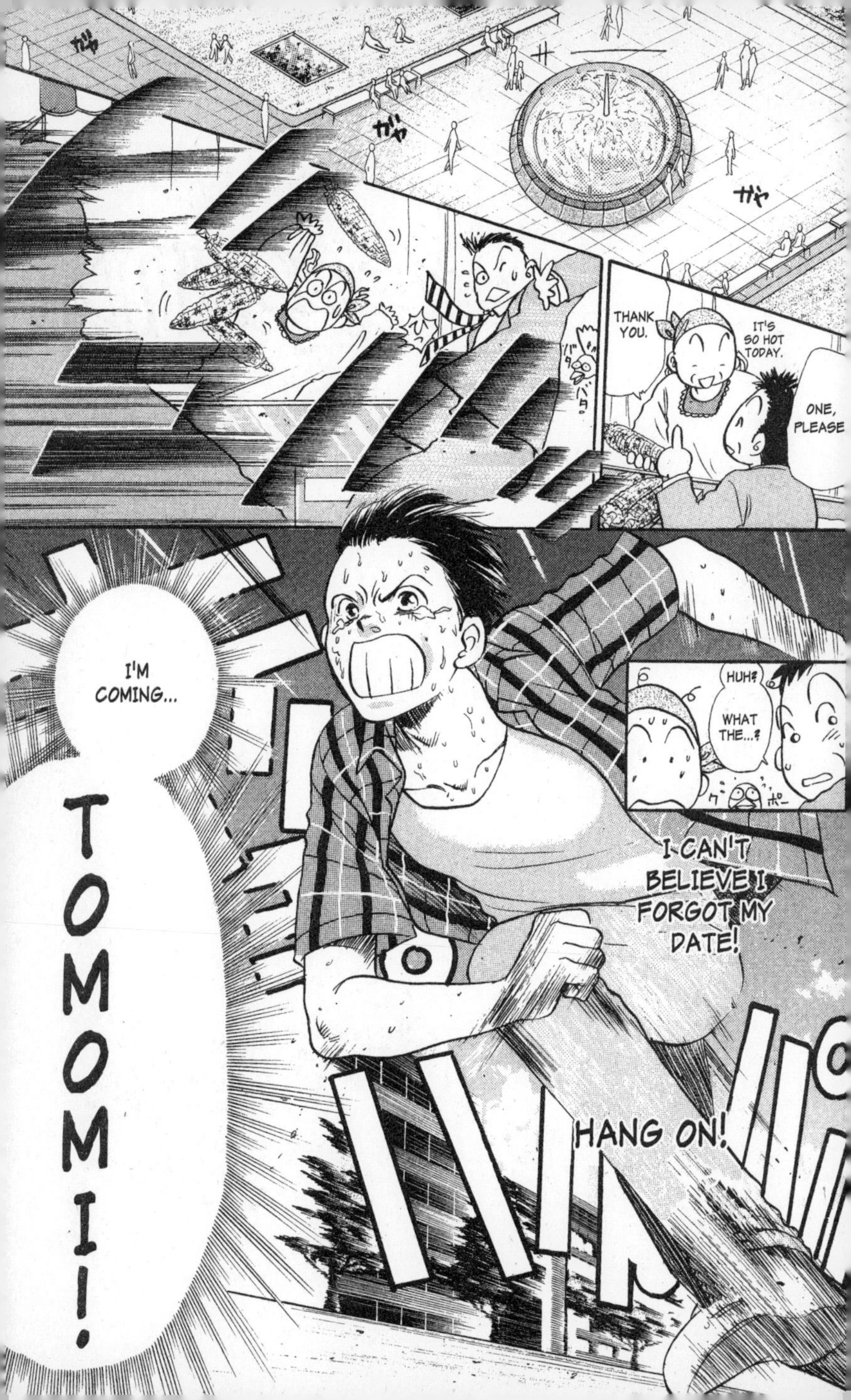
IT'S SO HOT TODAY.
THANK YOU.
ONE, PLEASE
HUH?
WHAT THE...?
I'M COMING...
TOMOMI!
I CAN'T BELIEVE I FORGOT MY DATE!
HANG ON!

Episode 57 Happy!

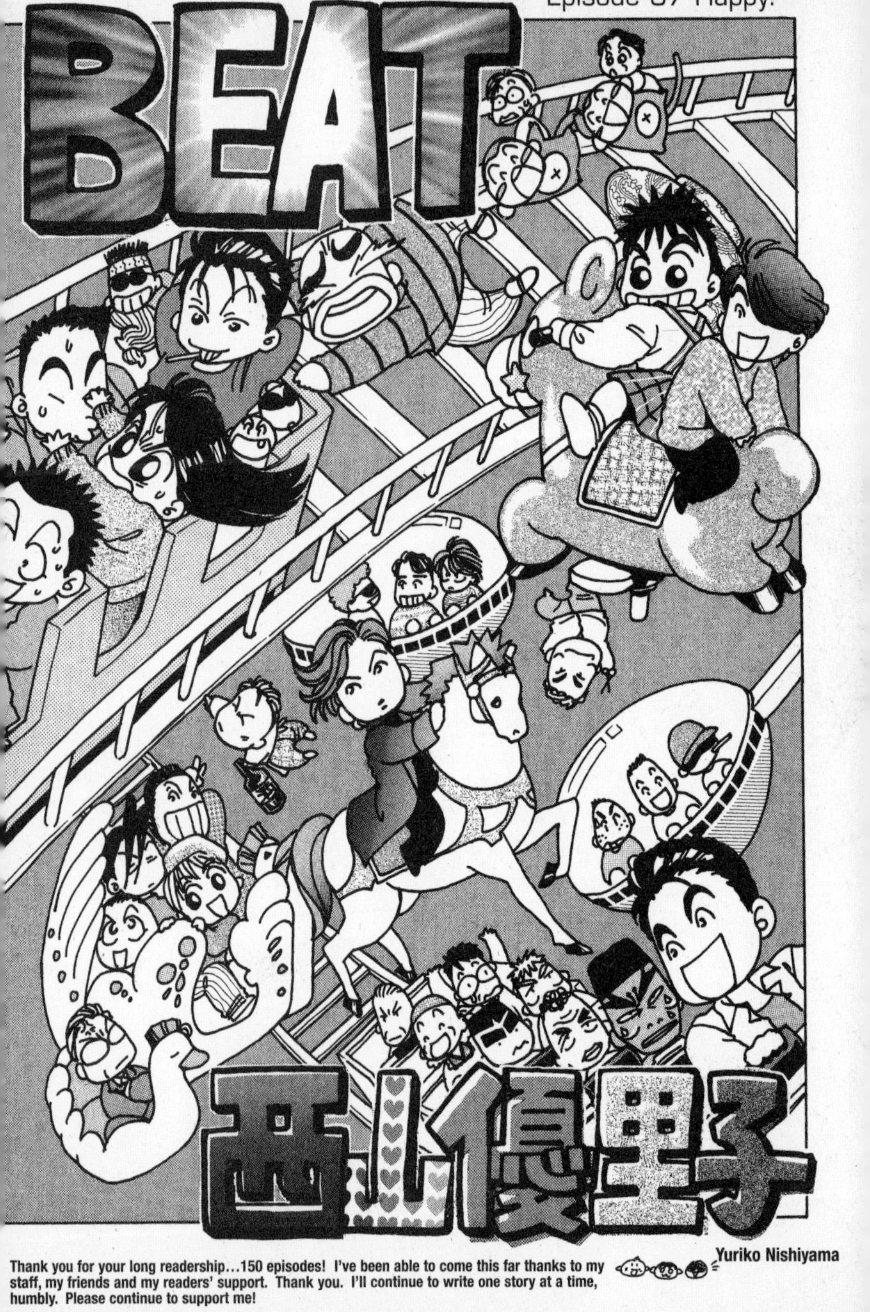
BEAT
西山優里子

Yuriko Nishiyama

Thank you for your long readership…150 episodes! I've been able to come this far thanks to my staff, my friends and my readers' support. Thank you. I'll continue to write one story at a time, humbly. Please continue to support me!

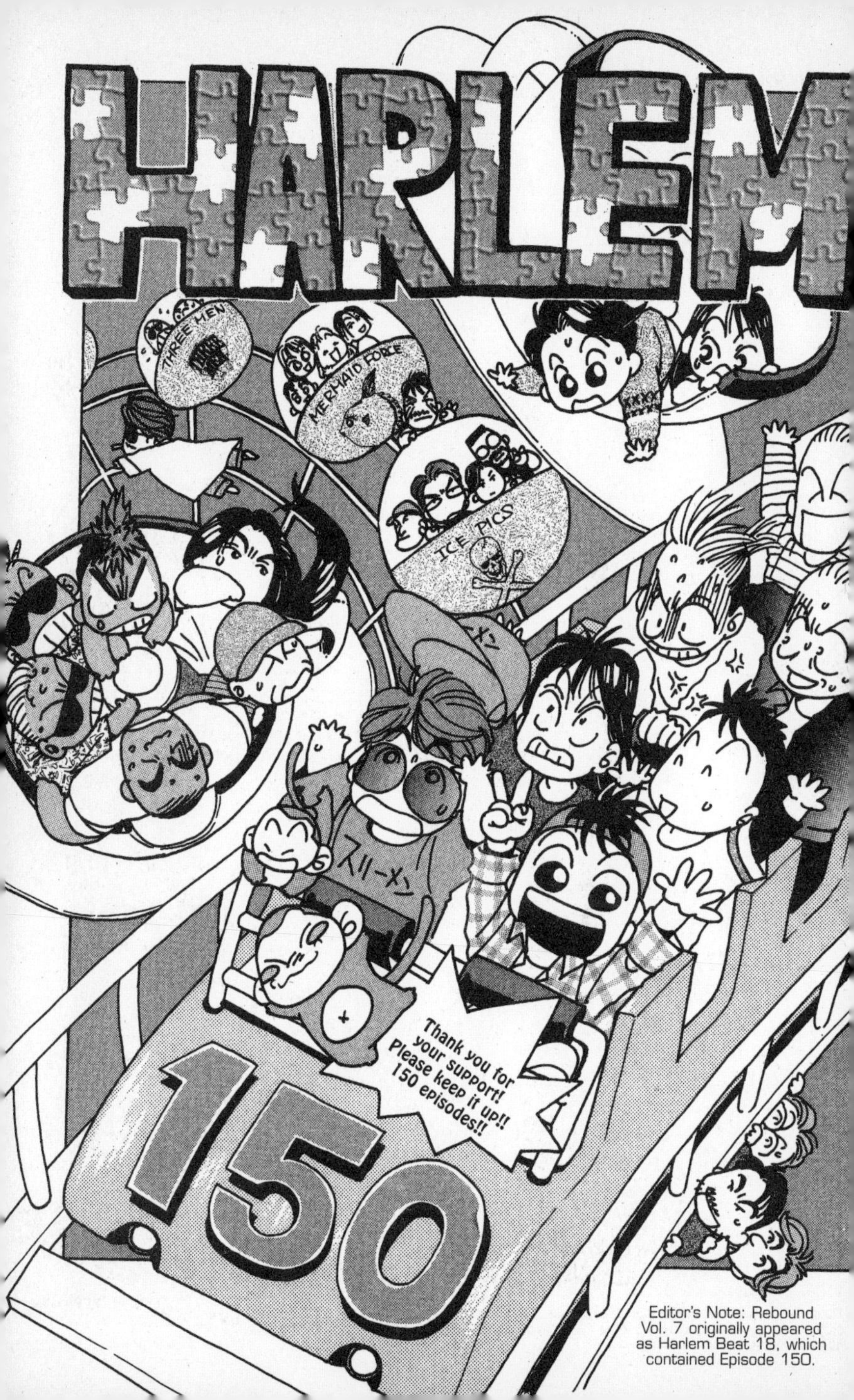
HARLEM
THREE MEN
MERMAID FORCE
ICE PICS
スリーメン
Thank you for your support! Please keep it up!! 150 episodes!!
150

Editor's Note: Rebound Vol. 7 originally appeared as Harlem Beat 18, which contained Episode 150.

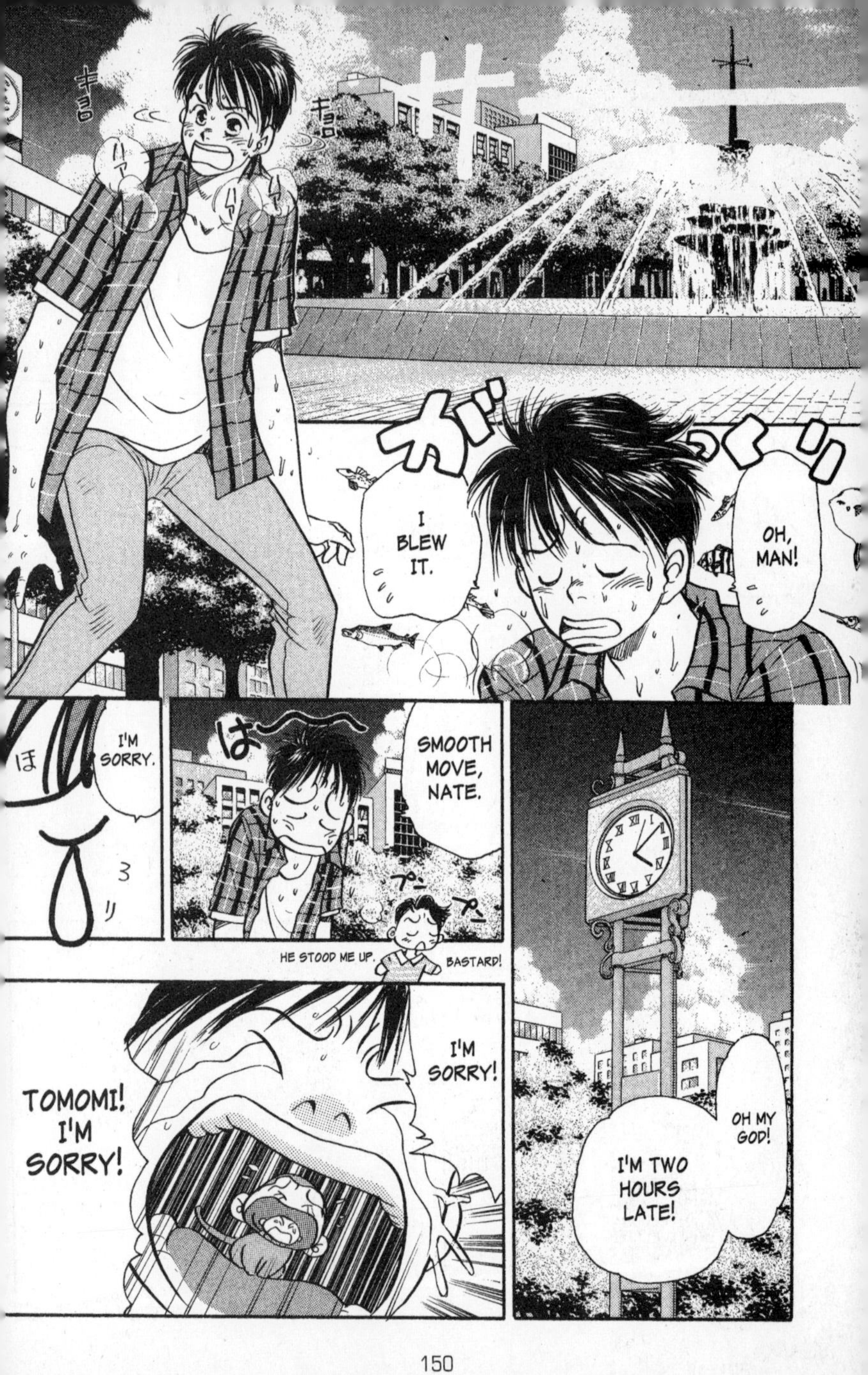
OH, MAN!
I BLEW IT.
OH MY GOD!
I'M TWO HOURS LATE!
SMOOTH MOVE, NATE.
HE STOOD ME UP.
BASTARD!
I'M SORRY.
I'M SORRY!
TOMOMI! I'M SORRY!

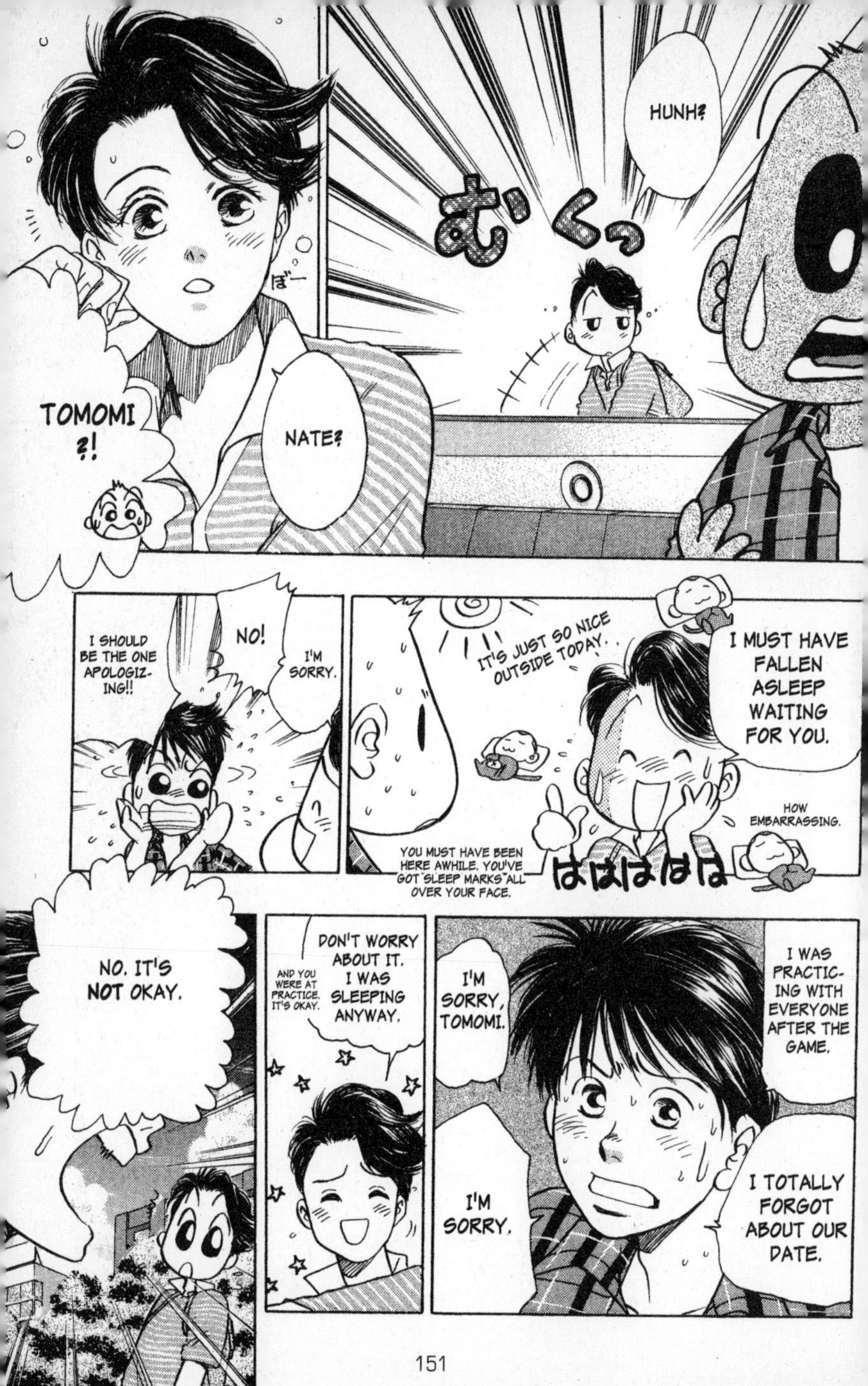
HUNH?
むくっ
ぼー
NATE?
TOMOMI ?!
I MUST HAVE FALLEN ASLEEP WAITING FOR YOU.
IT'S JUST SO NICE OUTSIDE TODAY.
HOW EMBARRASSING.
ははははは
YOU MUST HAVE BEEN HERE AWHILE. YOU'VE GOT SLEEP MARKS ALL OVER YOUR FACE.
I'M SORRY.
NO!
I SHOULD BE THE ONE APOLOGIZING!!
I WAS PRACTICING WITH EVERYONE AFTER THE GAME.
I'M SORRY, TOMOMI.
I TOTALLY FORGOT ABOUT OUR DATE.
I'M SORRY.
DON'T WORRY ABOUT IT. I WAS SLEEPING ANYWAY.
AND YOU WERE AT PRACTICE. IT'S OKAY.
NO. IT'S NOT OKAY.

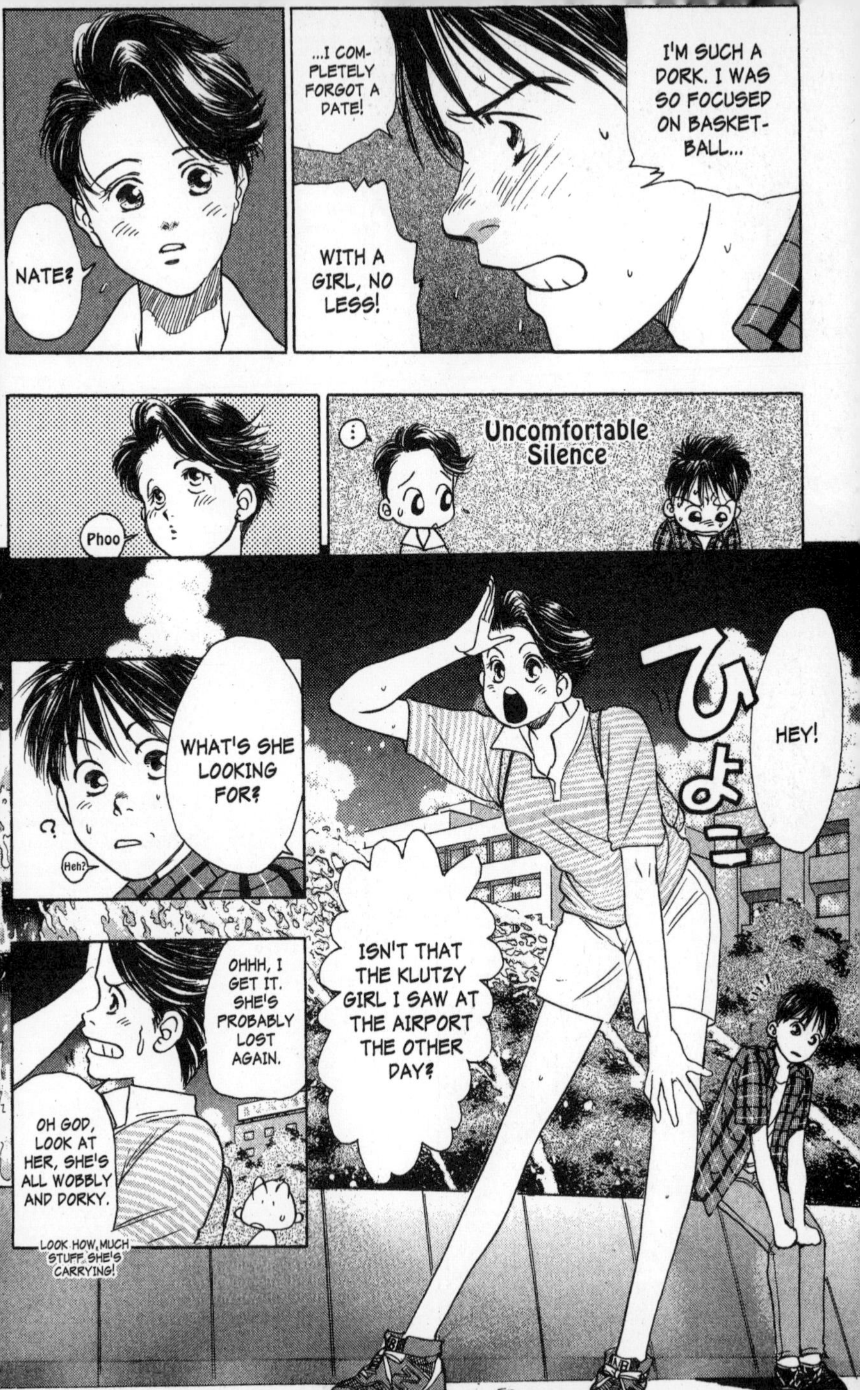
I'M SUCH A DORK. I WAS SO FOCUSED ON BASKET-BALL...
...I COM-PLETELY FORGOT A DATE!
WITH A GIRL, NO LESS!
NATE?
...
Uncomfortable Silence
Phoo
ひょこ
HEY!
ISN'T THAT THE KLUTZY GIRL I SAW AT THE AIRPORT THE OTHER DAY?
WHAT'S SHE LOOKING FOR?
?
Heh?
OHHH, I GET IT. SHE'S PROBABLY LOST AGAIN.
OH GOD, LOOK AT HER, SHE'S ALL WOBBLY AND DORKY.
LOOK HOW MUCH STUFF SHE'S CARRYING!

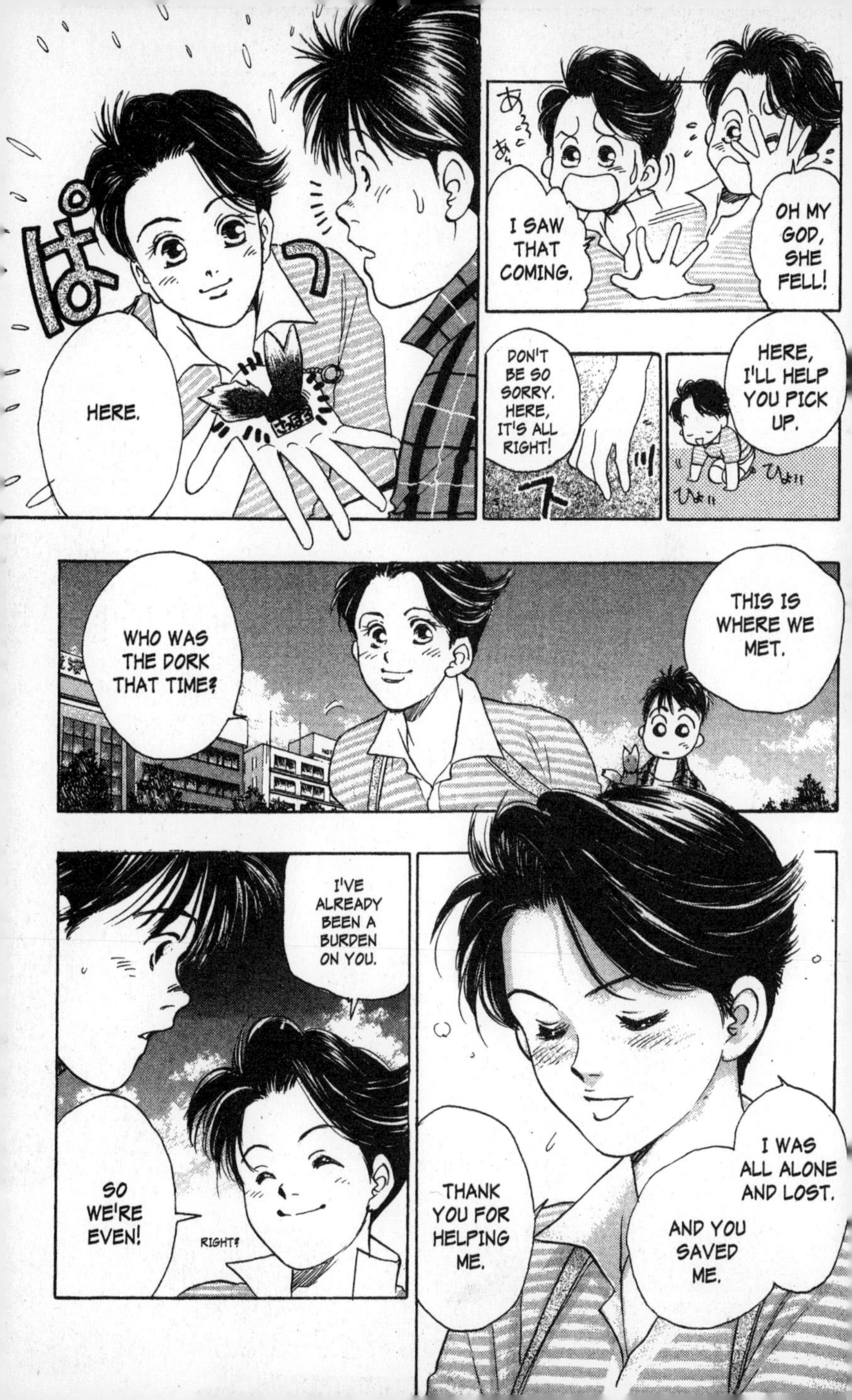
OH MY GOD, SHE FELL!
I SAW THAT COMING.
HERE, I'LL HELP YOU PICK UP.
DON'T BE SO SORRY. HERE, IT'S ALL RIGHT!
ぱっ
HERE.
THIS IS WHERE WE MET.
WHO WAS THE DORK THAT TIME?
I WAS ALL ALONE AND LOST.
AND YOU SAVED ME.
THANK YOU FOR HELPING ME.
I'VE ALREADY BEEN A BURDEN ON YOU.
SO WE'RE EVEN!
RIGHT?

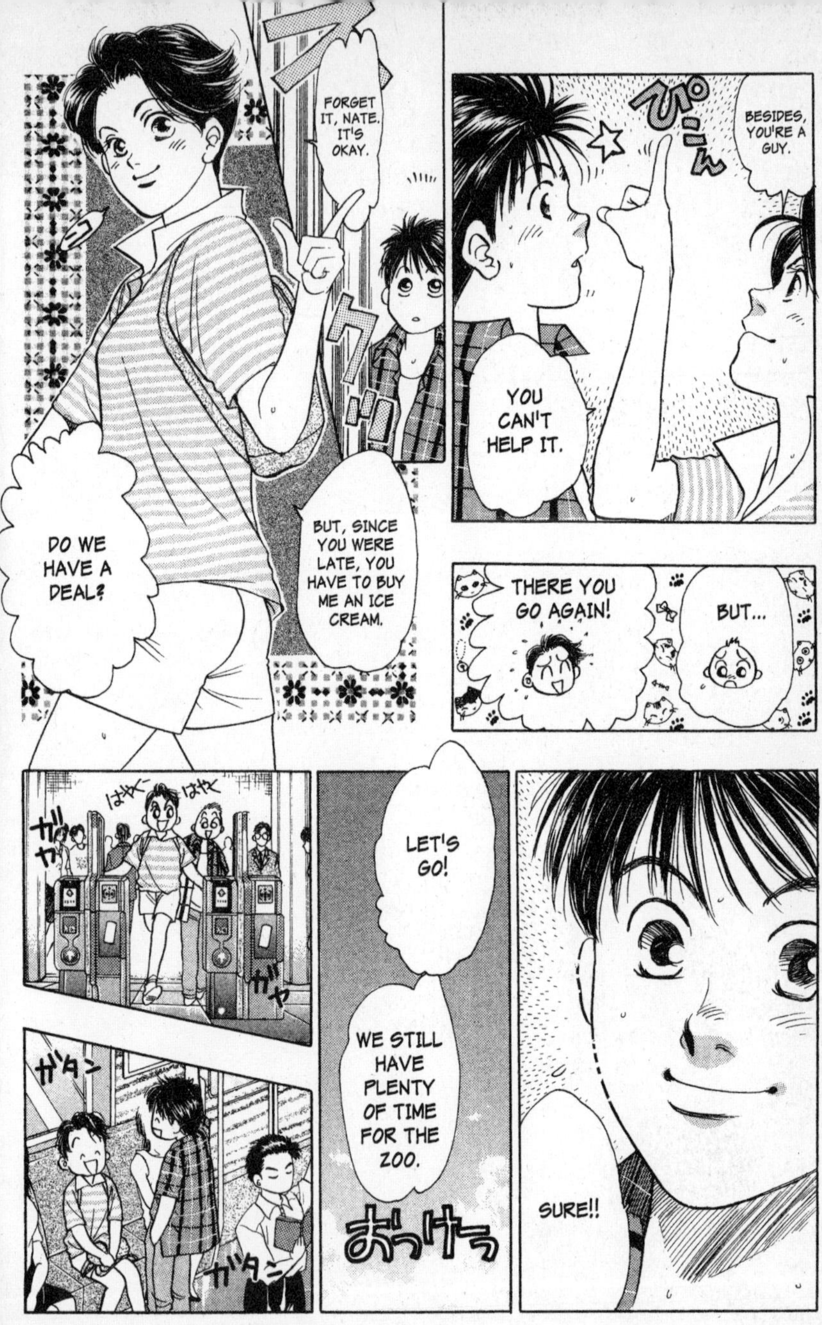
ぴこん
BESIDES, YOU'RE A GUY.
YOU CAN'T HELP IT.
BUT...
THERE YOU GO AGAIN!
FORGET IT, NATE. IT'S OKAY.
BUT, SINCE YOU WERE LATE, YOU HAVE TO BUY ME AN ICE CREAM.
DO WE HAVE A DEAL?
SURE!!
LET'S GO!
WE STILL HAVE PLENTY OF TIME FOR THE ZOO.
おっけー
はやく はやく
ガヤ
ガヤ
ガタン
ガタン

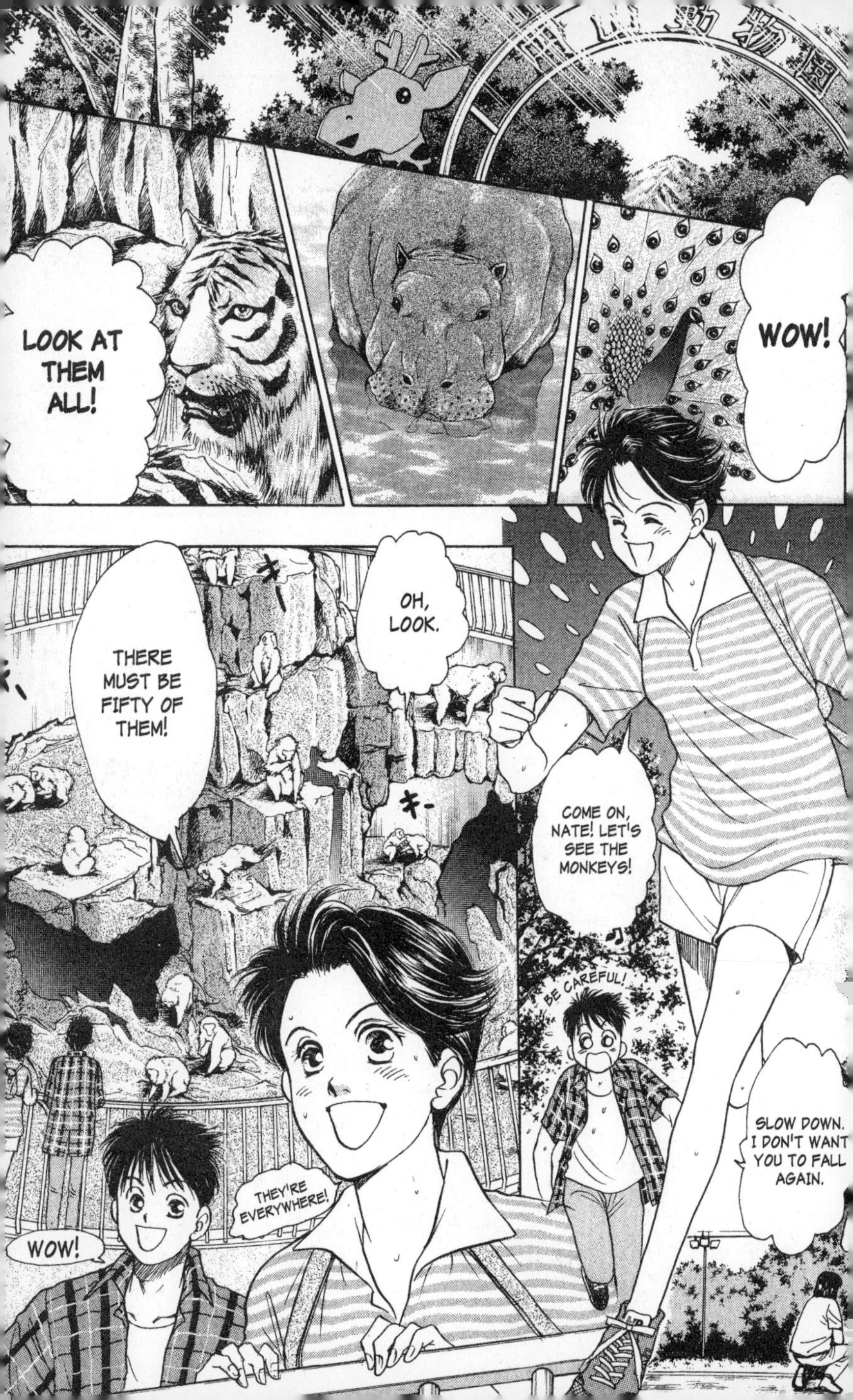
WOW!
LOOK AT THEM ALL!
COME ON, NATE! LET'S SEE THE MONKEYS!
BE CAREFUL!
SLOW DOWN. I DON'T WANT YOU TO FALL AGAIN.
OH, LOOK.
キ
THERE MUST BE FIFTY OF THEM!
キー
THEY'RE EVERYWHERE!
WOW!

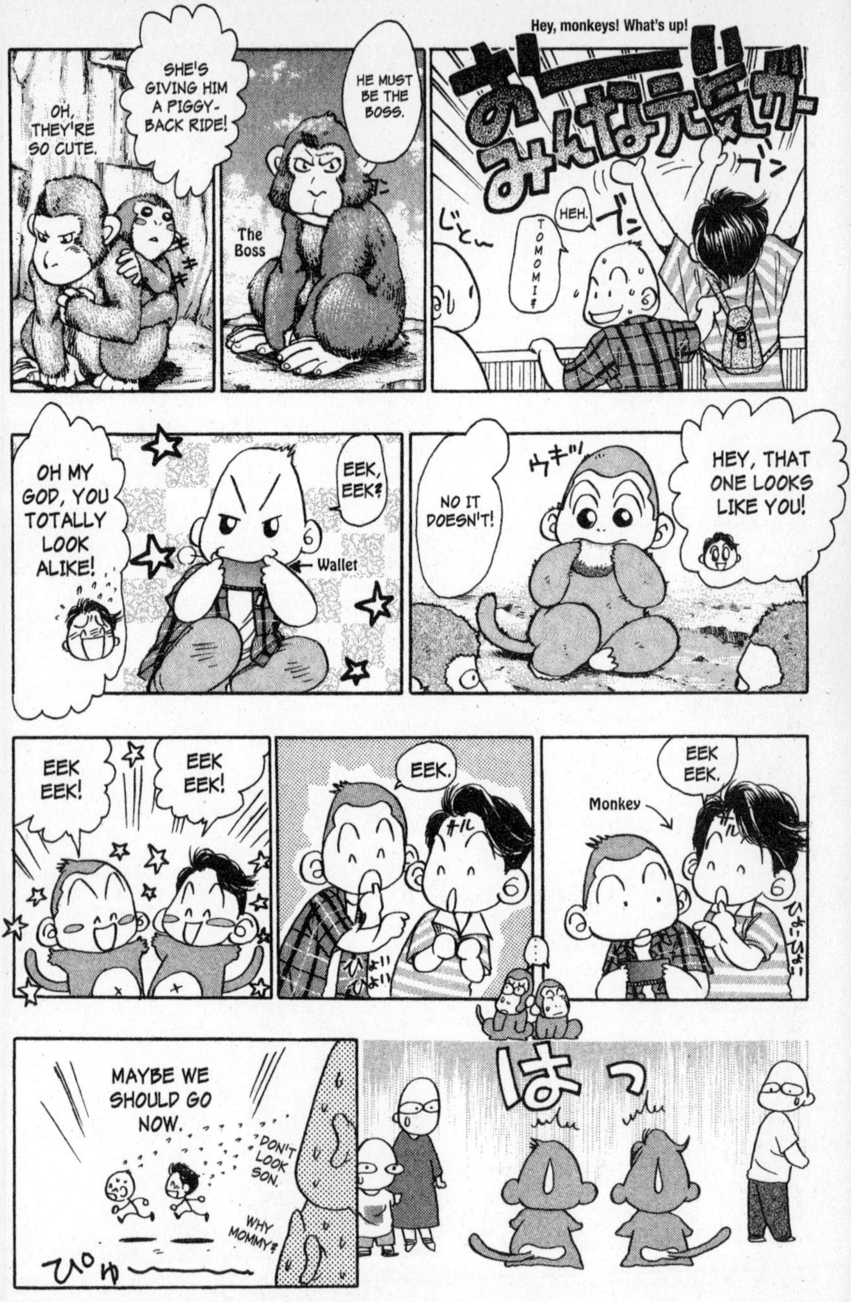
Hey, monkeys! What's up!
おーい みんな元気か
ブン
HEH.
TOMOMI?
ブン
じと~
HE MUST BE THE BOSS.
The Boss
SHE'S GIVING HIM A PIGGY-BACK RIDE!
OH, THEY'RE SO CUTE.
HEY, THAT ONE LOOKS LIKE YOU!
ウギッ
NO IT DOESN'T!
EEK, EEK?
Wallet
OH MY GOD, YOU TOTALLY LOOK ALIKE!
EEK EEK.
Monkey
ひょいひょい
EEK.
ひょいひょい
EEK EEK!
EEK EEK!
はっ
MAYBE WE SHOULD GO NOW.
DON'T LOOK SON.
WHY MOMMY?
ぴゅ~

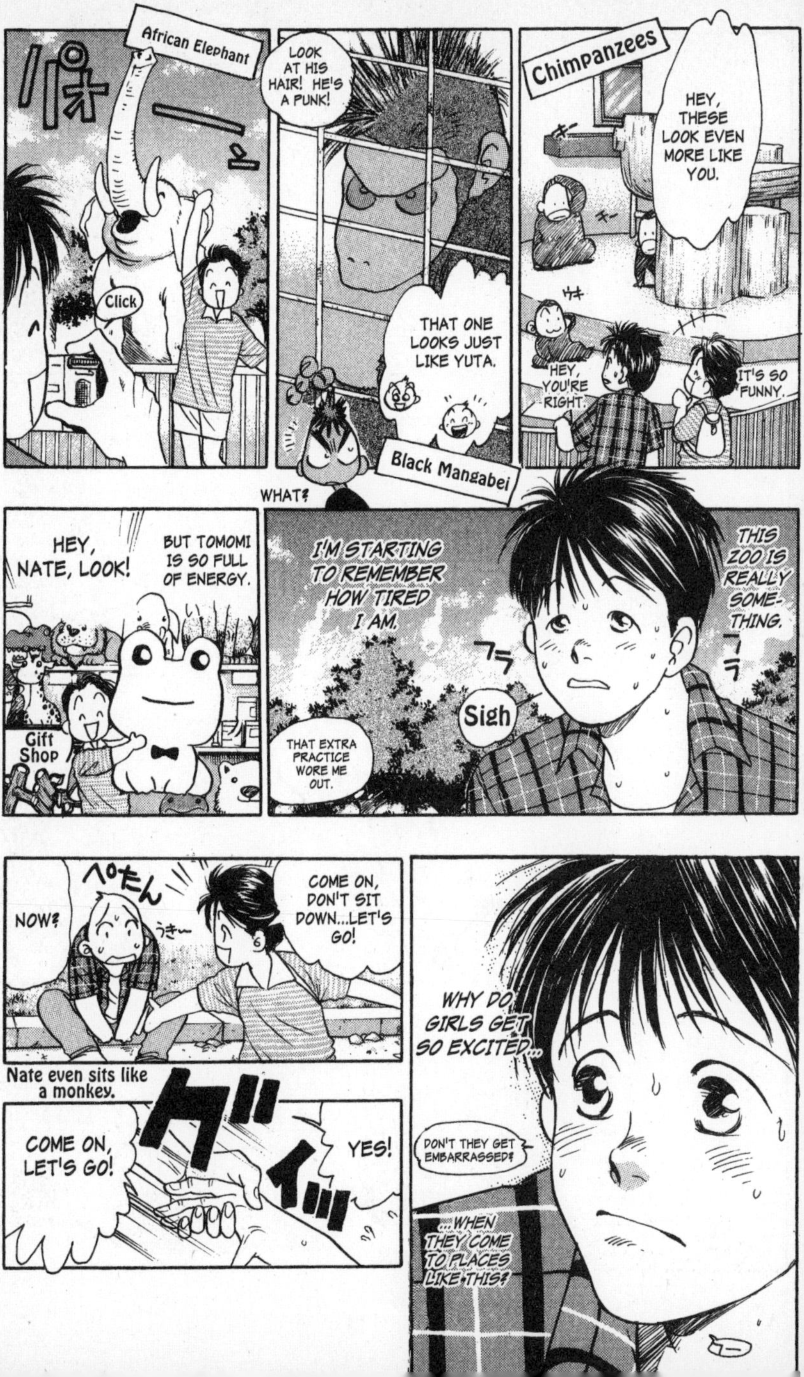
Chimpanzees
HEY, THESE LOOK EVEN MORE LIKE YOU.
IT'S SO FUNNY.
HEY, YOU'RE RIGHT.
LOOK AT HIS HAIR! HE'S A PUNK!
THAT ONE LOOKS JUST LIKE YUTA.
Black Mangabei
WHAT?
African Elephant
パオー
Click
THIS ZOO IS REALLY SOME-THING.
I'M STARTING TO REMEMBER HOW TIRED I AM.
Sigh
THAT EXTRA PRACTICE WORE ME OUT.
BUT TOMOMI IS SO FULL OF ENERGY.
HEY, NATE, LOOK!
Gift Shop
WHY DO GIRLS GET SO EXCITED...
DON'T THEY GET EMBARRASSED?
...WHEN THEY COME TO PLACES LIKE THIS?
COME ON, DON'T SIT DOWN...LET'S GO!
ぺたん
NOW?
Nate even sits like a monkey.
YES!
グイ
COME ON, LET'S GO!

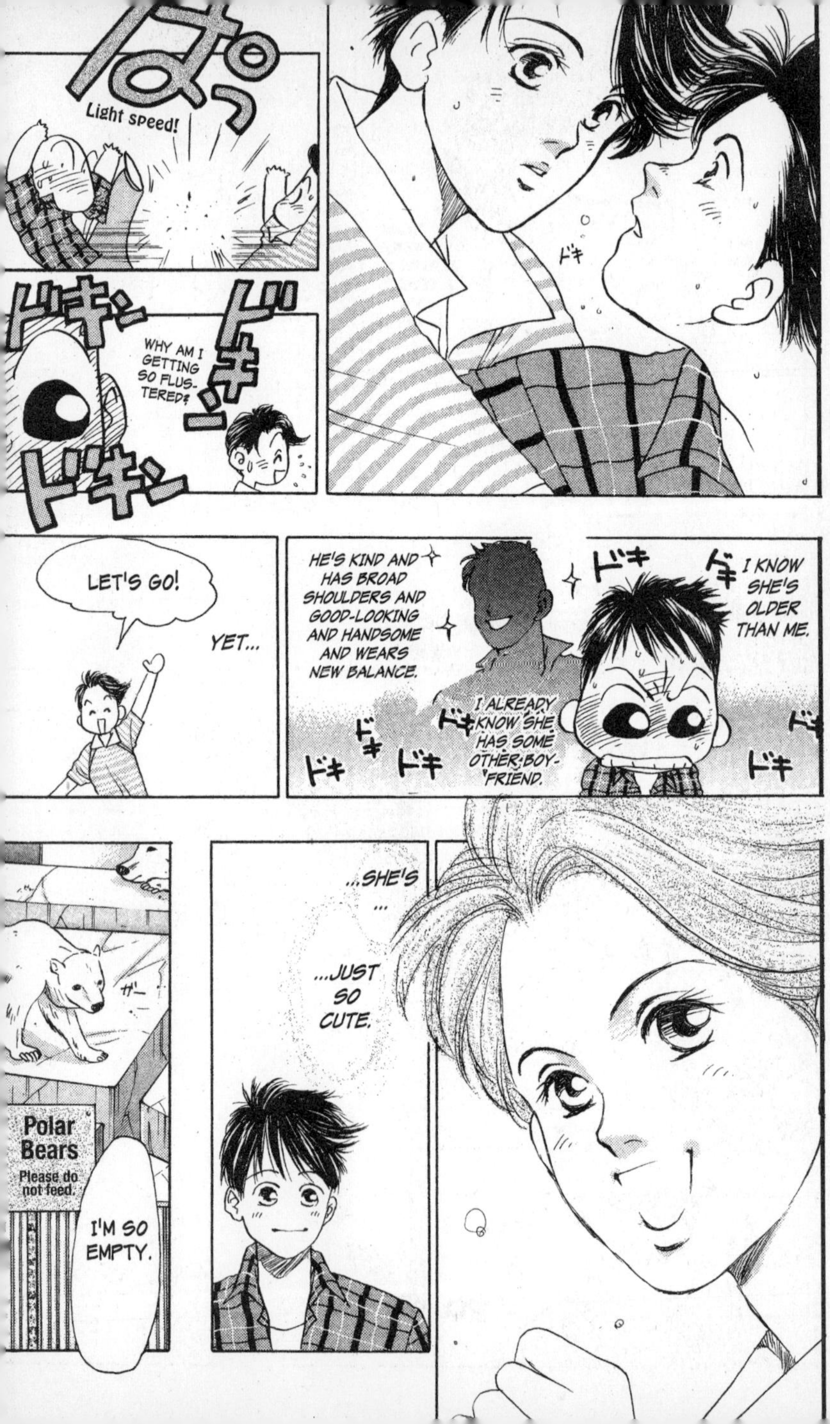

ドキ
ぱっ
Light speed!
ドキン
ドギュー
WHY AM I GETTING SO FLUS-TERED?
ドキン
I KNOW SHE'S OLDER THAN ME.
ドキ
ドキ
HE'S KIND AND HAS BROAD SHOULDERS AND GOOD-LOOKING AND HANDSOME AND WEARS NEW BALANCE.
I ALREADY KNOW SHE HAS SOME OTHER BOY-FRIEND.
ドキ
ドキ
ドキ
ドキ
ドキ
LET'S GO!
YET...
...SHE'S ...
...JUST SO CUTE.
Polar Bears
Please do not feed.
I'M SO EMPTY.

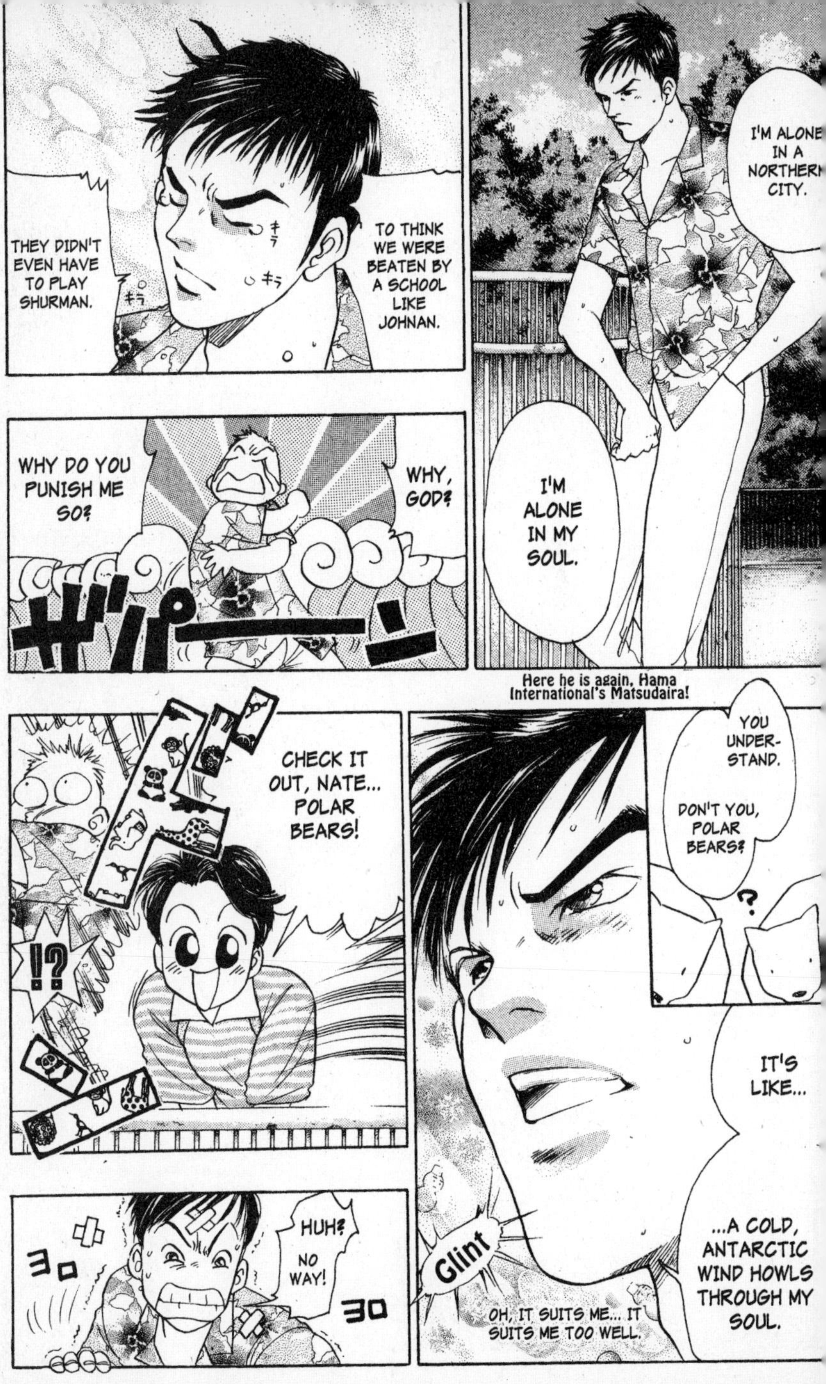
I'M ALONE IN A NORTHERN CITY.
I'M ALONE IN MY SOUL.
TO THINK WE WERE BEATEN BY A SCHOOL LIKE JOHNAN.
キラ
キラ
キラ
THEY DIDN'T EVEN HAVE TO PLAY SHURMAN.
WHY, GOD?
WHY DO YOU PUNISH ME SO?
ザパーーン
Here he is again, Hama International's Matsudaira!
YOU UNDERSTAND.
DON'T YOU, POLAR BEARS?
?
IT'S LIKE...
...A COLD, ANTARCTIC WIND HOWLS THROUGH MY SOUL.
Glint
OH, IT SUITS ME... IT SUITS ME TOO WELL.
CHECK IT OUT, NATE... POLAR BEARS!
!?
HUH?
NO WAY!
ヨロ
ヨロ

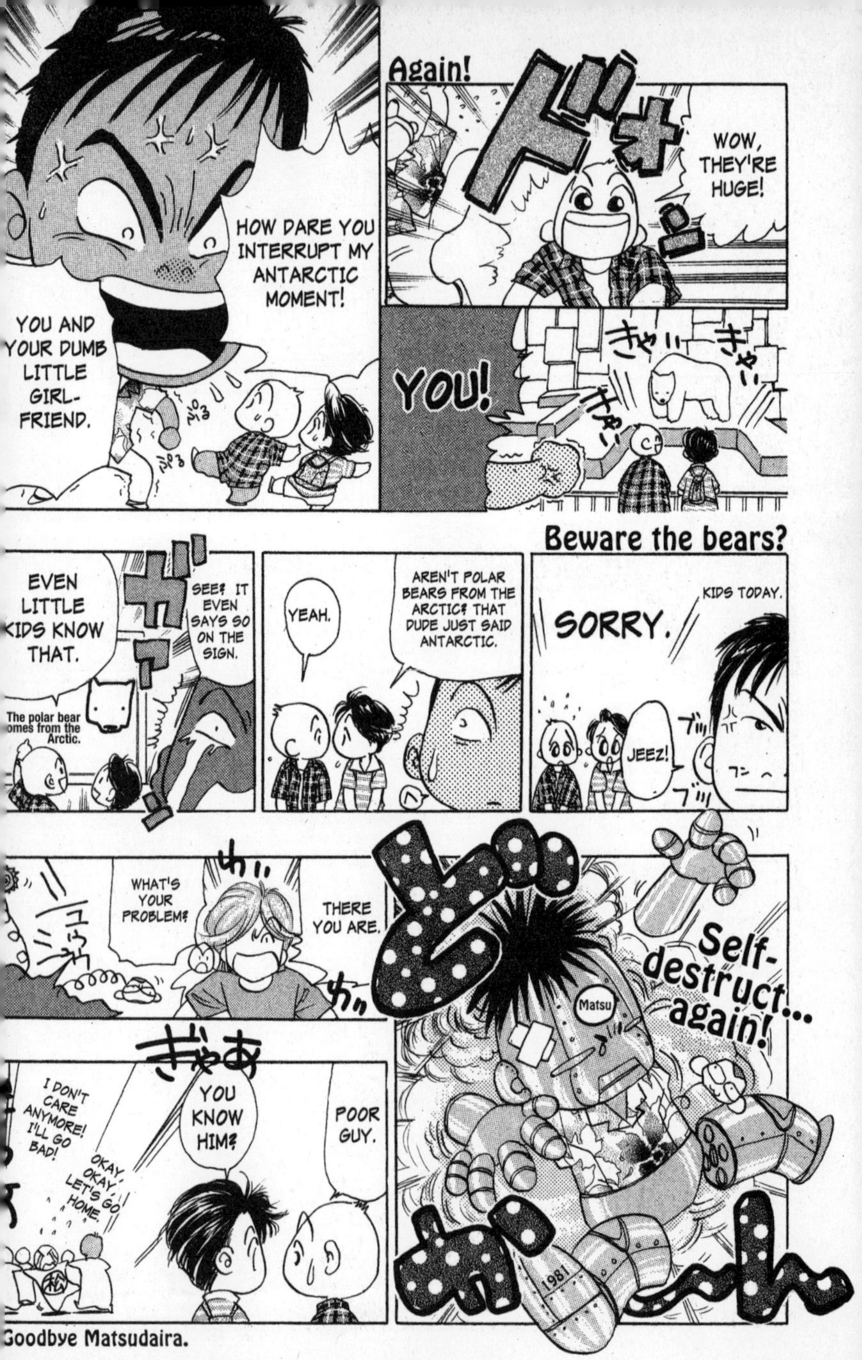
Again!
WOW, THEY'RE HUGE!
YOU!
HOW DARE YOU INTERRUPT MY ANTARCTIC MOMENT!
YOU AND YOUR DUMB LITTLE GIRL-FRIEND.
Beware the bears?
SORRY.
KIDS TODAY.
JEEZ!
AREN'T POLAR BEARS FROM THE ARCTIC? THAT DUDE JUST SAID ANTARCTIC.
YEAH.
SEE? IT EVEN SAYS SO ON THE SIGN.
EVEN LITTLE KIDS KNOW THAT.
The polar bear omes from the Arctic.
Self-destruct... again!
Matsu
1981
THERE YOU ARE.
WHAT'S YOUR PROBLEM?
POOR GUY.
YOU KNOW HIM?
I DON'T CARE ANYMORE! I'LL GO BAD!
OKAY, OKAY, LET'S GO HOME.
Goodbye Matsudaira.

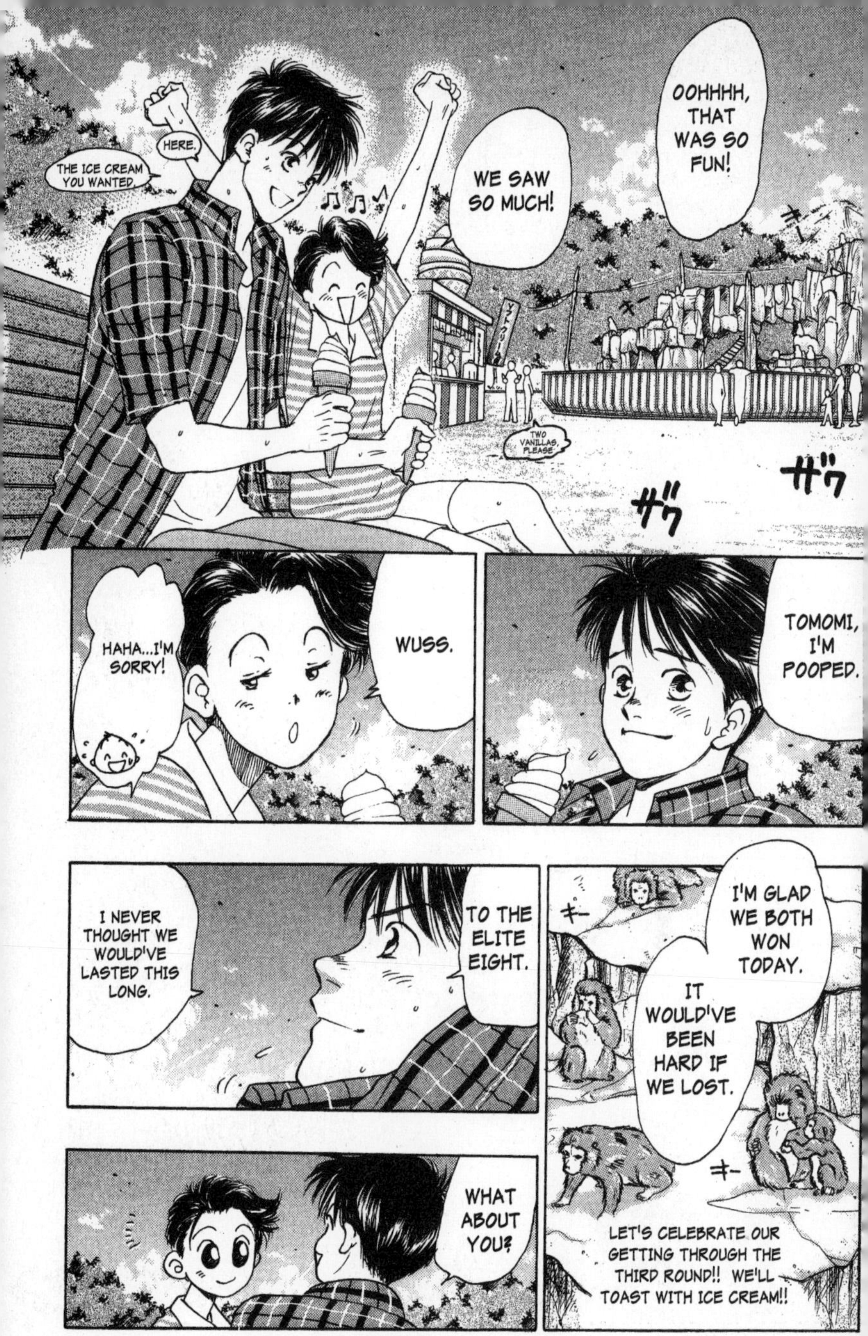
OOHHHH, THAT WAS SO FUN!
WE SAW SO MUCH!
HERE.
THE ICE CREAM YOU WANTED.
TWO VANILLAS, PLEASE.
ザワ
ザワ
TOMOMI, I'M POOPED.
WUSS.
HAHA...I'M SORRY!
キー
I'M GLAD WE BOTH WON TODAY.
IT WOULD'VE BEEN HARD IF WE LOST.
キー
LET'S CELEBRATE OUR GETTING THROUGH THE THIRD ROUND!! WE'LL TOAST WITH ICE CREAM!!
TO THE ELITE EIGHT.
I NEVER THOUGHT WE WOULD'VE LASTED THIS LONG.
WHAT ABOUT YOU?

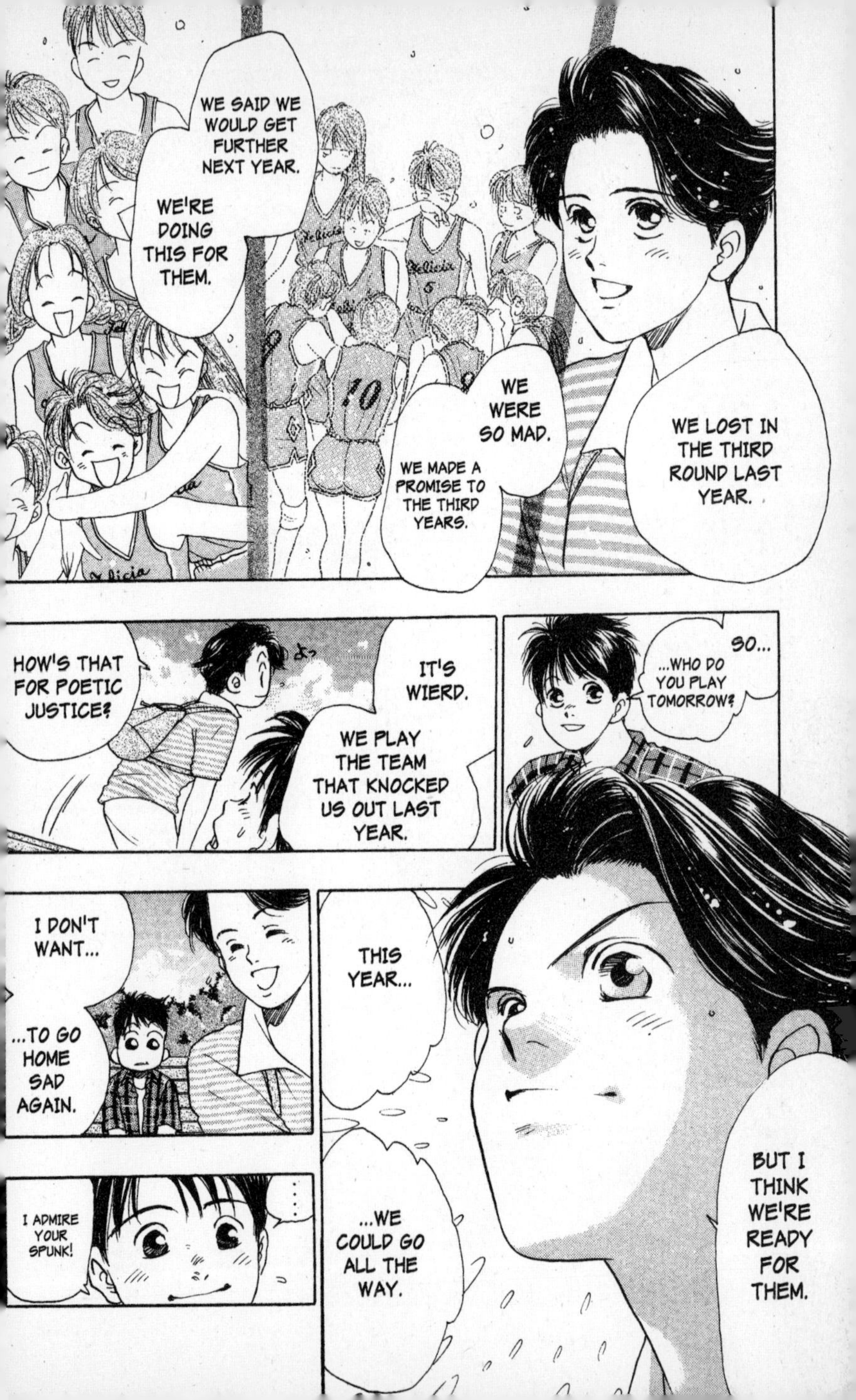
WE LOST IN THE THIRD ROUND LAST YEAR.
WE WERE SO MAD.
WE MADE A PROMISE TO THE THIRD YEARS.
WE SAID WE WOULD GET FURTHER NEXT YEAR.
WE'RE DOING THIS FOR THEM.
SO...
...WHO DO YOU PLAY TOMORROW?
IT'S WIERD.
WE PLAY THE TEAM THAT KNOCKED US OUT LAST YEAR.
HOW'S THAT FOR POETIC JUSTICE?
BUT I THINK WE'RE READY FOR THEM.
THIS YEAR...
...WE COULD GO ALL THE WAY.
I DON'T WANT...
...TO GO HOME SAD AGAIN.
.....
I ADMIRE YOUR SPUNK!

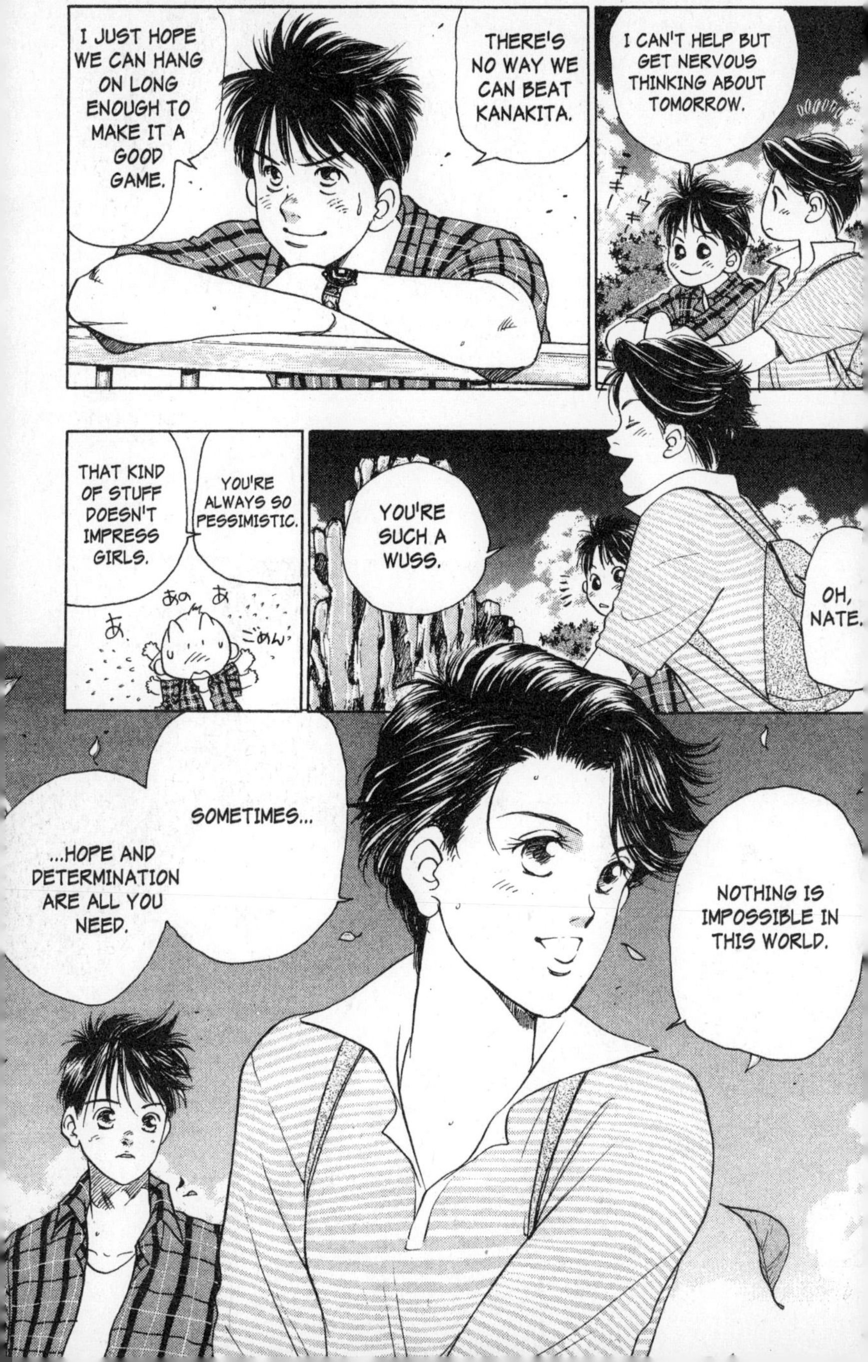
I CAN'T HELP BUT GET NERVOUS THINKING ABOUT TOMORROW.
THERE'S NO WAY WE CAN BEAT KANAKITA.
I JUST HOPE WE CAN HANG ON LONG ENOUGH TO MAKE IT A GOOD GAME.
OH, NATE.
YOU'RE SUCH A WUSS.
YOU'RE ALWAYS SO PESSIMISTIC.
THAT KIND OF STUFF DOESN'T IMPRESS GIRLS.
あの
あ
あ
ごめん
NOTHING IS IMPOSSIBLE IN THIS WORLD.
SOMETIMES...
...HOPE AND DETERMINATION ARE ALL YOU NEED.

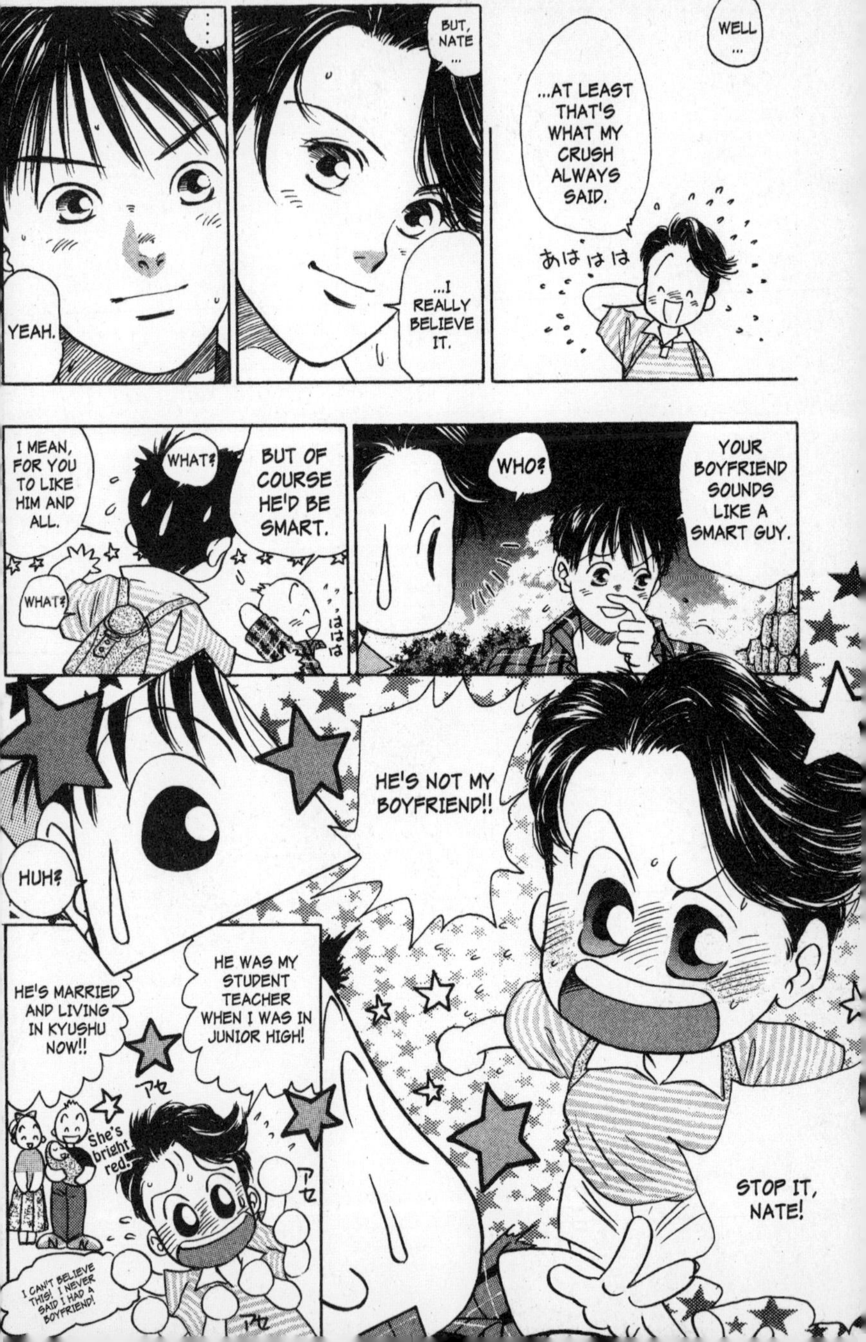
WELL ...
...AT LEAST THAT'S WHAT MY CRUSH ALWAYS SAID.
あははは
BUT, NATE ...
...I REALLY BELIEVE IT.
....
YEAH.
YOUR BOYFRIEND SOUNDS LIKE A SMART GUY.
WHO?
BUT OF COURSE HE'D BE SMART.
WHAT?
I MEAN, FOR YOU TO LIKE HIM AND ALL.
WHAT?
ははは
HE'S NOT MY BOYFRIEND!!
HUH?
STOP IT, NATE!
HE WAS MY STUDENT TEACHER WHEN I WAS IN JUNIOR HIGH!
HE'S MARRIED AND LIVING IN KYUSHU NOW!!
アセ
She's bright red.
アセ
I CAN'T BELIEVE THIS!! I NEVER SAID I HAD A BOYFRIEND!
アセ

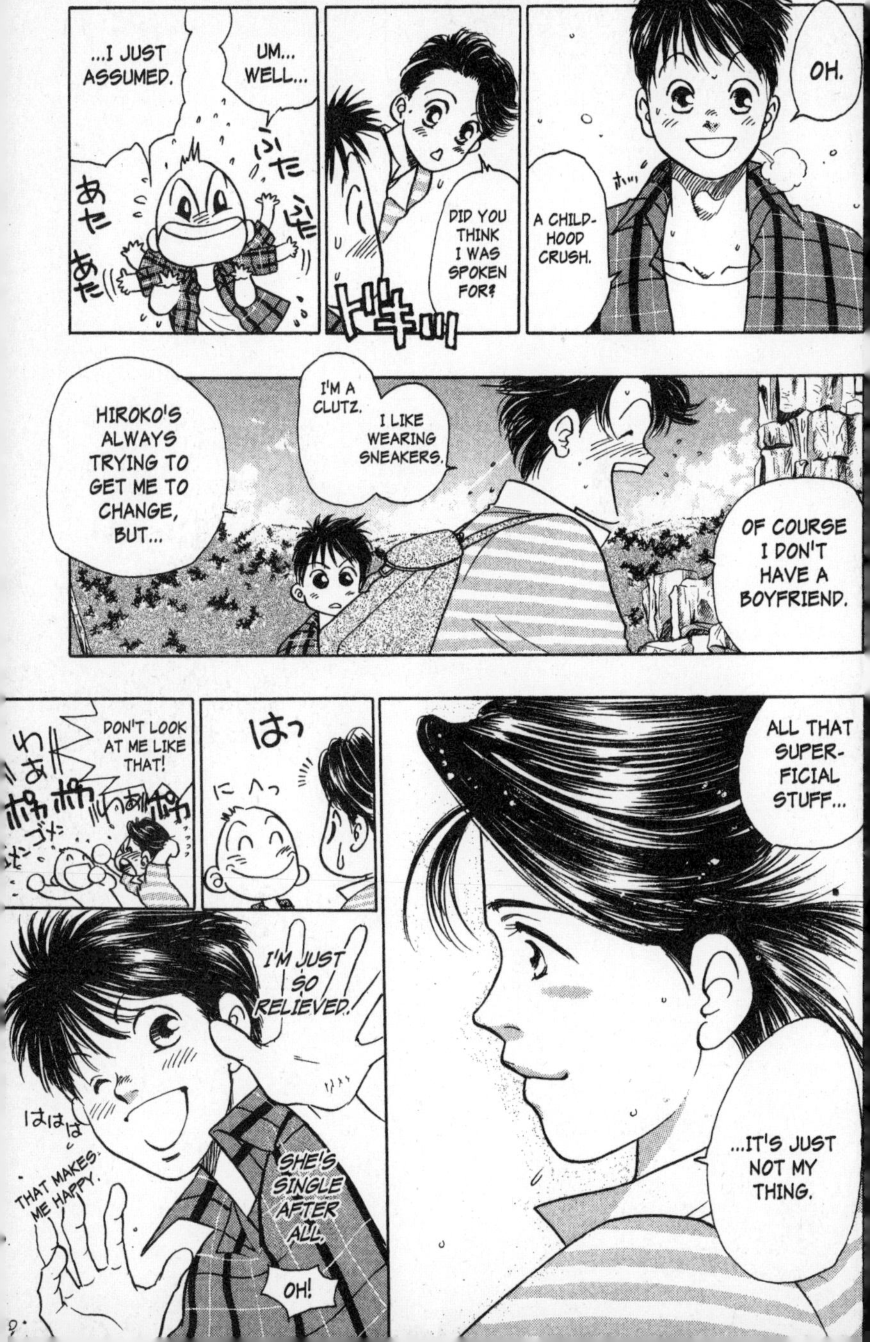
OH.
ホッ
A CHILD-HOOD CRUSH.
DID YOU THINK I WAS SPOKEN FOR?
ドキッ
UM... WELL...
...I JUST ASSUMED.
ふたふた
あたあた
OF COURSE I DON'T HAVE A BOYFRIEND.
I'M A CLUTZ.
I LIKE WEARING SNEAKERS.
HIROKO'S ALWAYS TRYING TO GET ME TO CHANGE, BUT...
ALL THAT SUPER-FICIAL STUFF...
...IT'S JUST NOT MY THING.
はっ
にへっ
DON'T LOOK AT ME LIKE THAT!
わあ
ポカポカ
ゴメン
I'M JUST SO RELIEVED.
SHE'S SINGLE AFTER ALL.
OH!
ははは
THAT MAKES ME HAPPY.

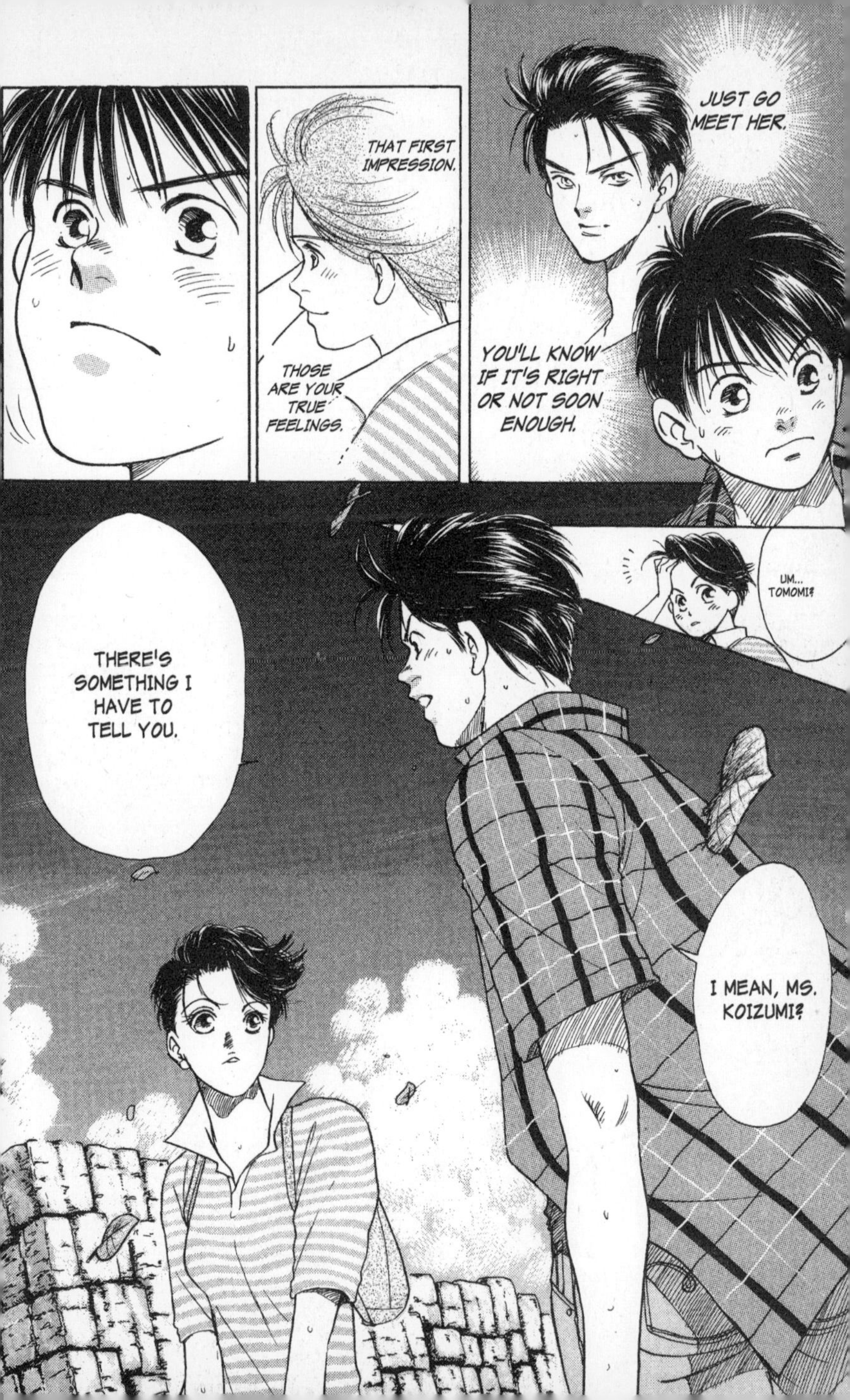
JUST GO MEET HER.
YOU'LL KNOW IF IT'S RIGHT OR NOT SOON ENOUGH.
THAT FIRST IMPRESSION.
THOSE ARE YOUR TRUE FEELINGS.
UM... TOMOMI?
I MEAN, MS. KOIZUMI?
THERE'S SOMETHING I HAVE TO TELL YOU.

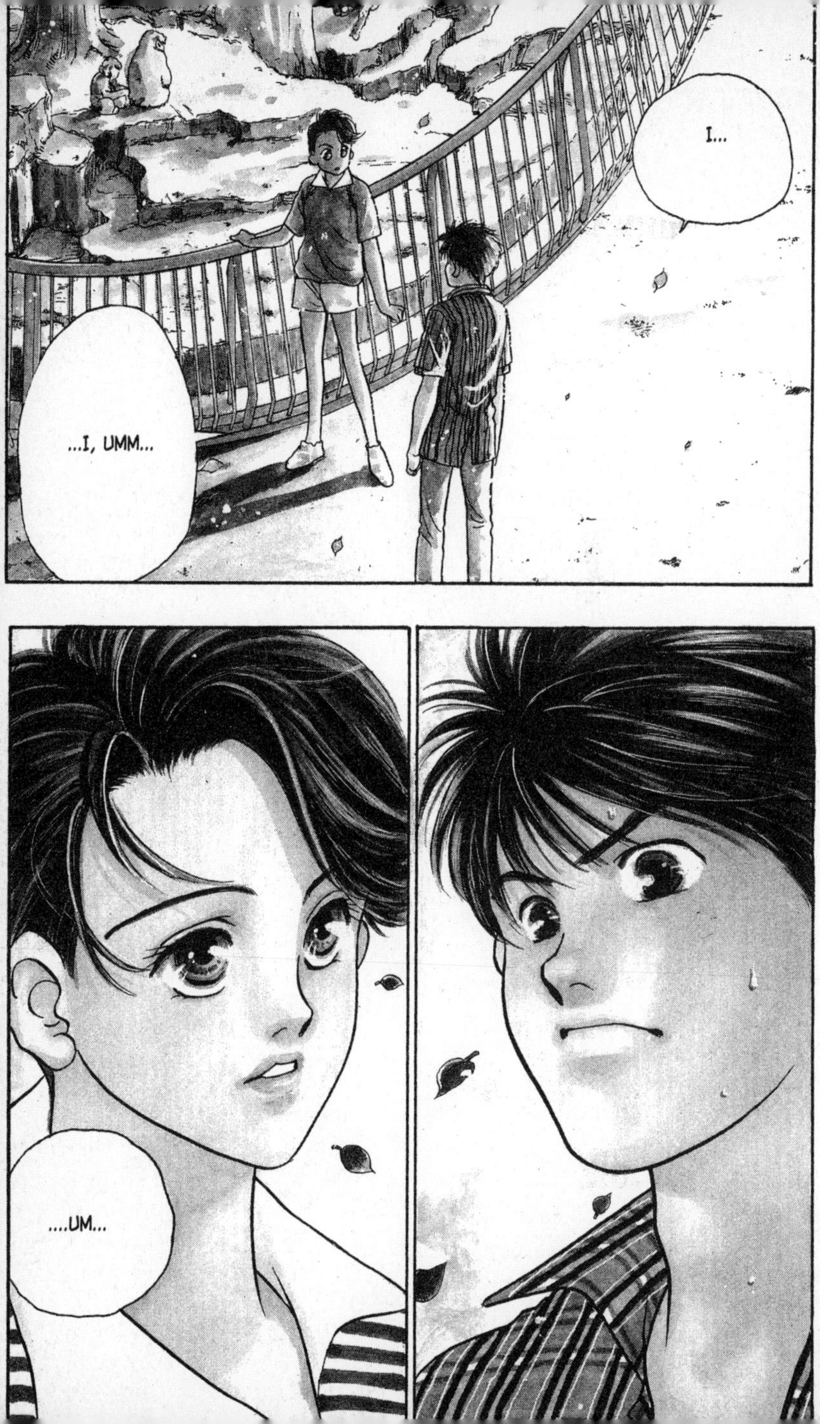
I...
...I, UMM...
....UM...

Episode 58 Angel Voice

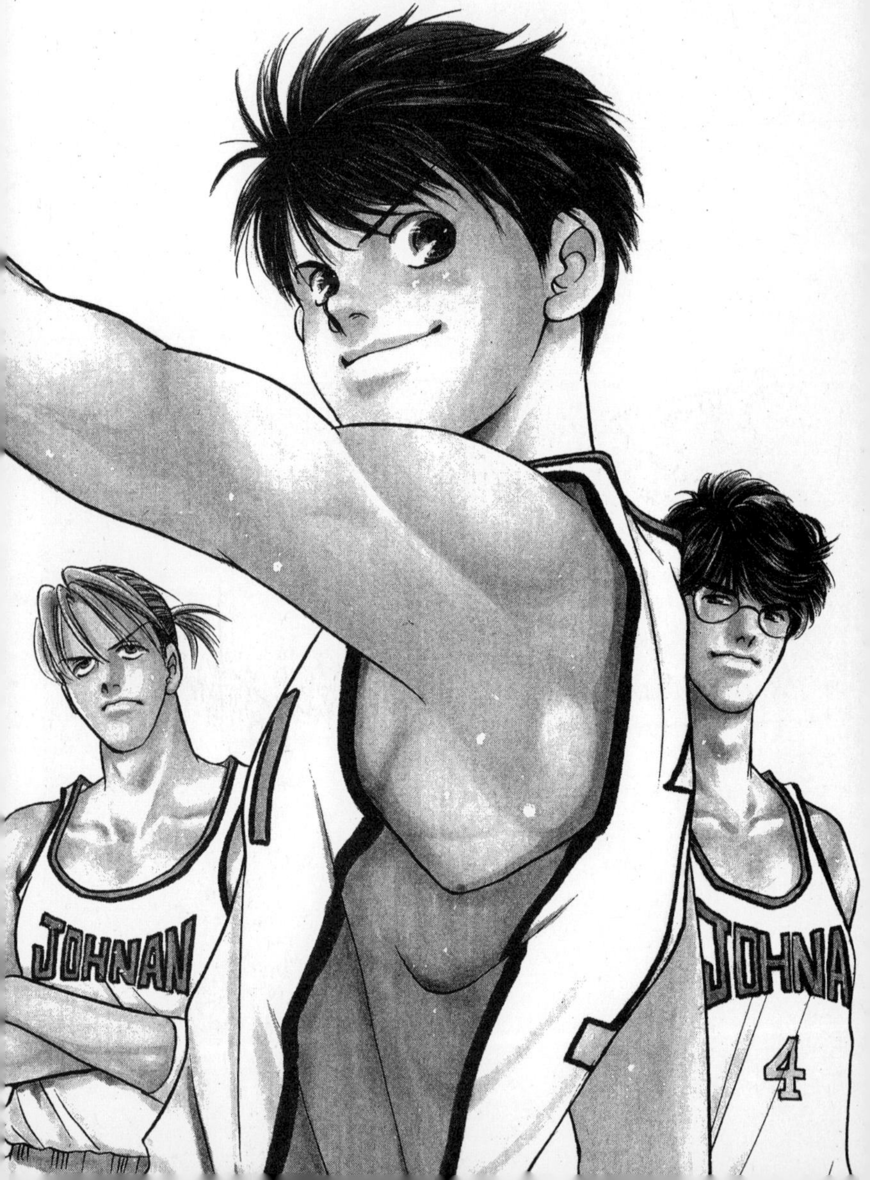
JOHNAN
JOHNA
4

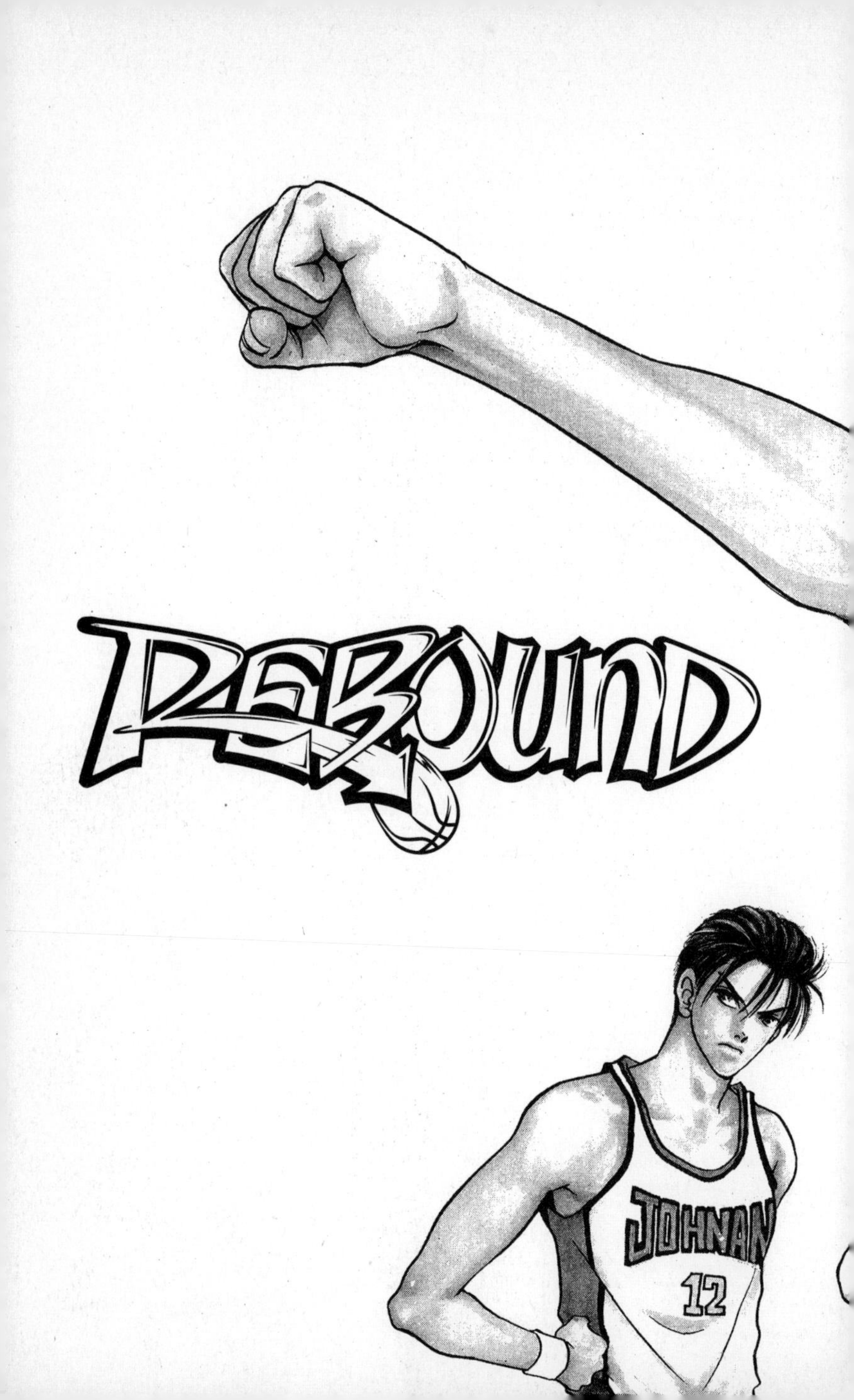
REBOUND
JOHNAN
12

Nate Torres In A TOKYOPOP Service Announcement.

Continuous exposure to Kim, the manager of the Johnan High School basketball team, can result in the infestation of Kim bacteria, a horrible parasite that results in cuts and burises to the head region!

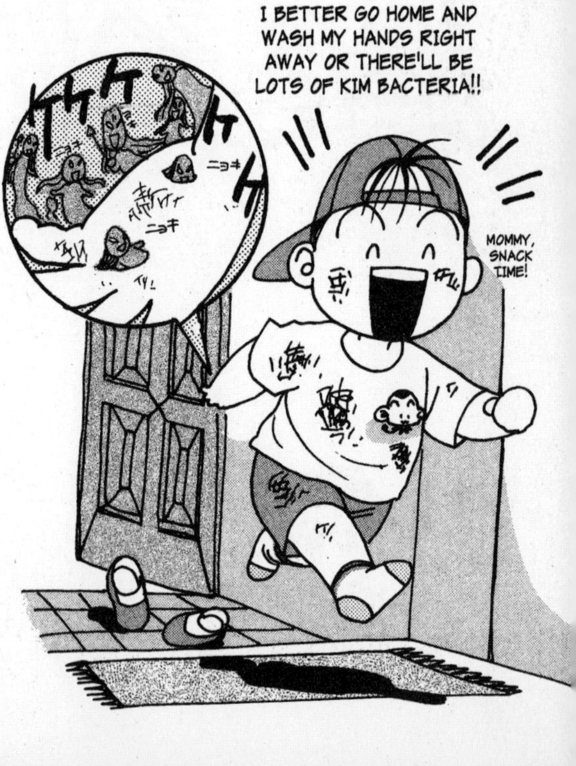
I BETTER GO HOME AND WASH MY HANDS RIGHT AWAY OR THERE'LL BE LOTS OF KIM BACTERIA!!
MOMMY, SNACK TIME!
ニョキ
ニョキ
ニョキ

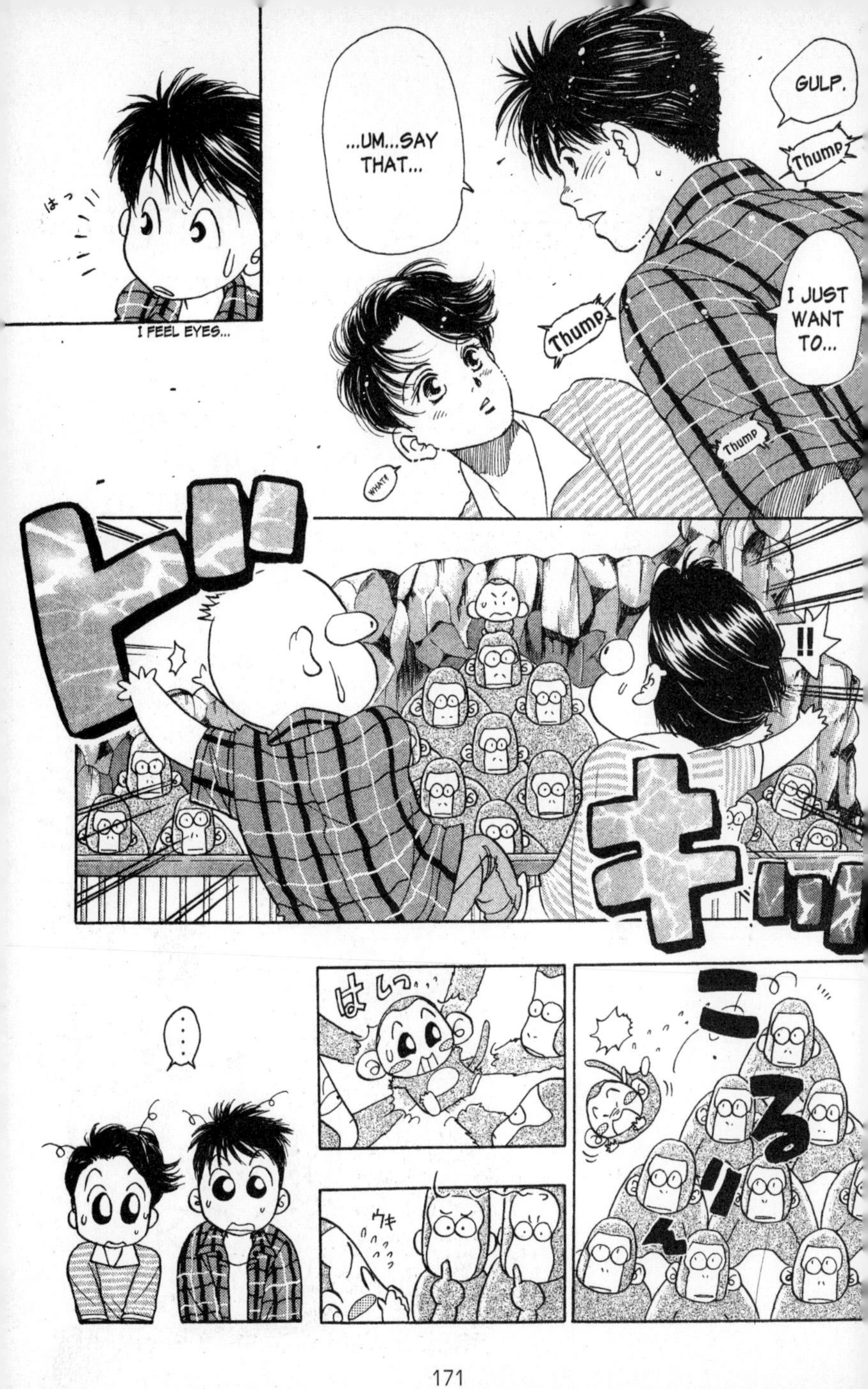
GULP.
Thump
...UM...SAY THAT...
I JUST WANT TO...
Thump
Thump
WHAT?
はっ
I FEEL EYES...
ドッ
!!
キ
ころりん
はっ
ウキ
...

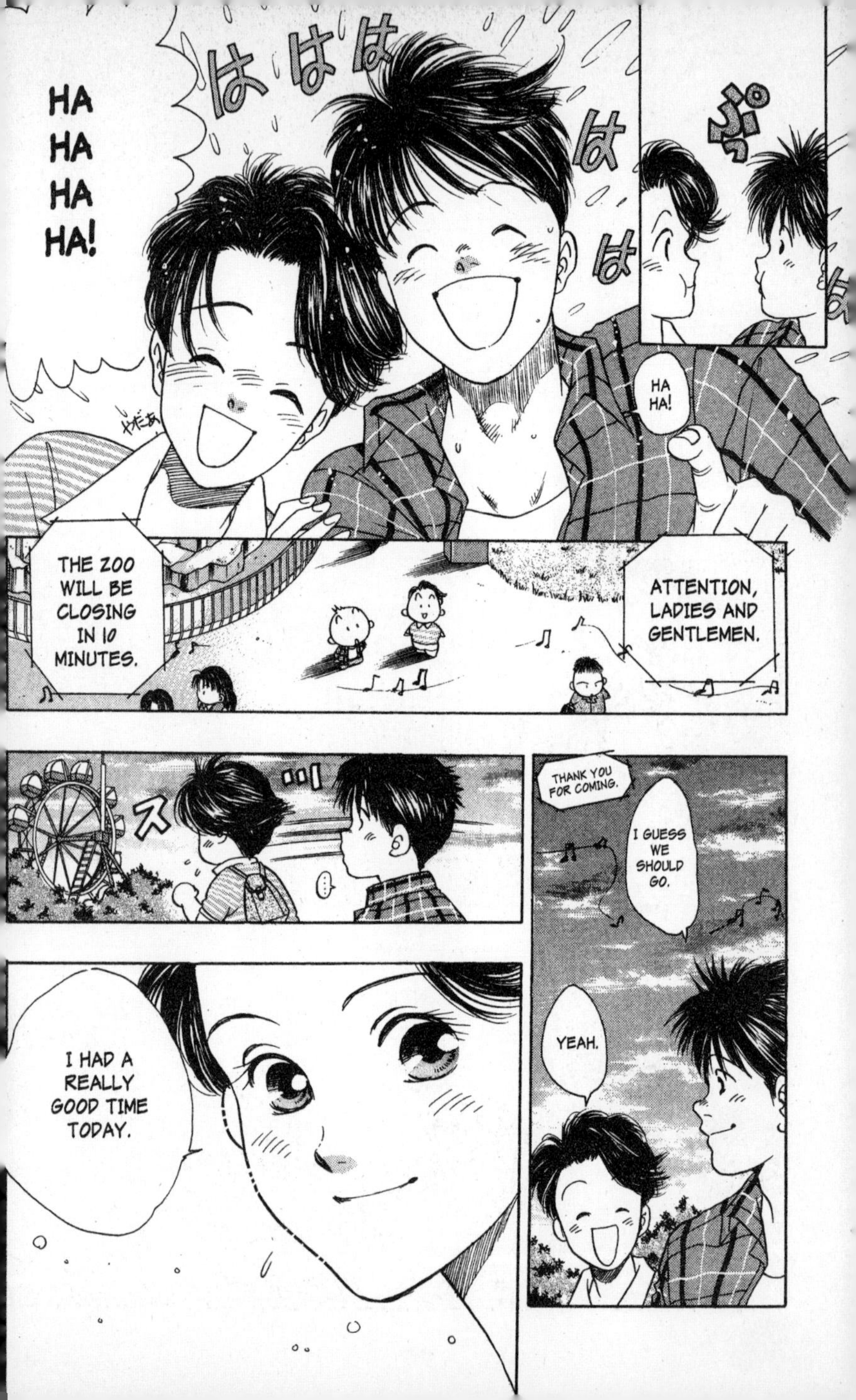
ぷっ
はは
HA HA!
ははは
HA HA HA HA!
やだぁ
ATTENTION, LADIES AND GENTLEMEN.
THE ZOO WILL BE CLOSING IN 10 MINUTES.
THANK YOU FOR COMING.
I GUESS WE SHOULD GO.
YEAH.
ス
...
I HAD A REALLY GOOD TIME TODAY.

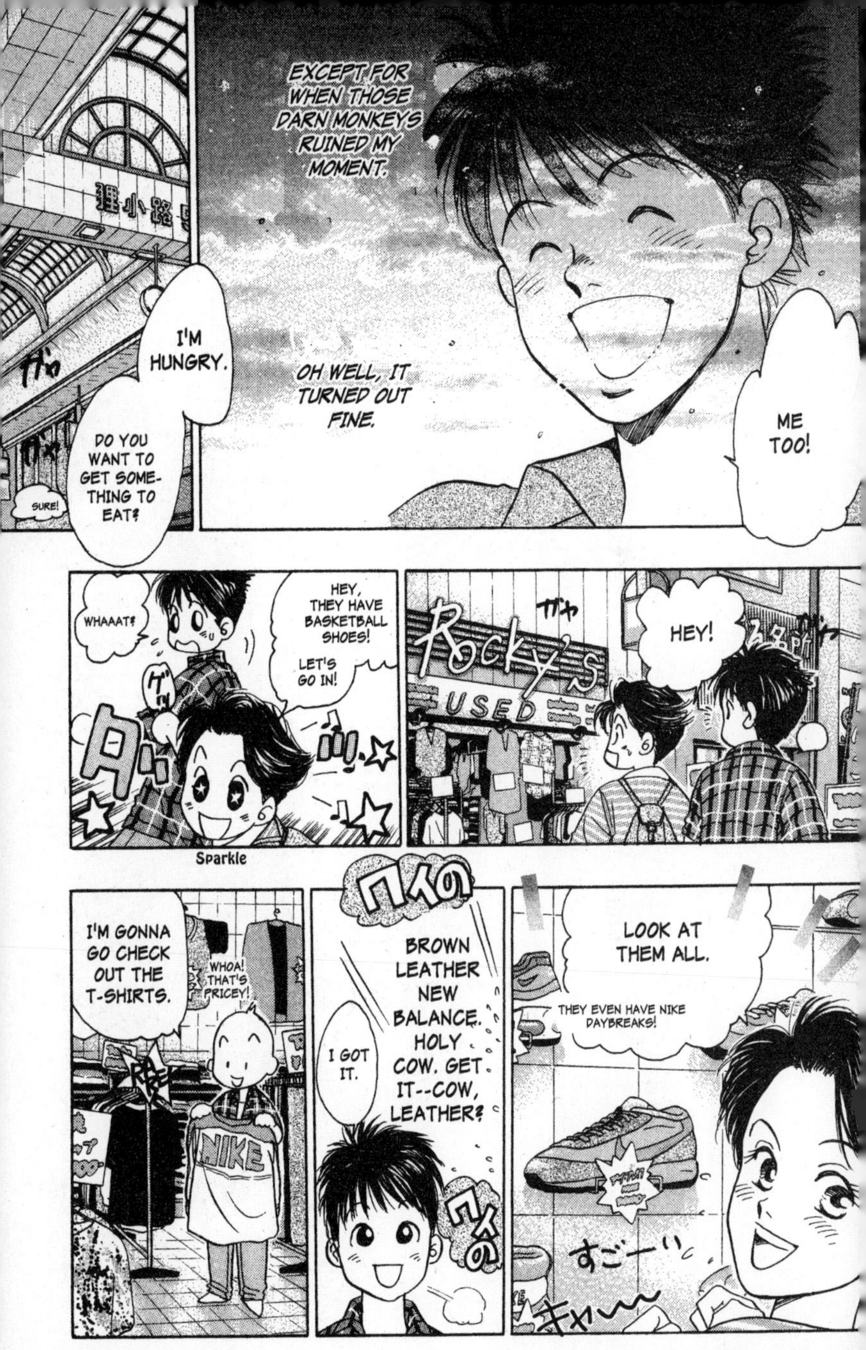
EXCEPT FOR WHEN THOSE DARN MONKEYS RUINED MY MOMENT.
OH WELL, IT TURNED OUT FINE.
I'M HUNGRY.
ME TOO!
DO YOU WANT TO GET SOME-THING TO EAT?
SURE!
Rocky's
USED
HEY!
HEY, THEY HAVE BASKETBALL SHOES!
LET'S GO IN!
WHAAAT?
Sparkle
LOOK AT THEM ALL.
THEY EVEN HAVE NIKE DAYBREAKS!
すごーい
BROWN LEATHER NEW BALANCE. HOLY COW. GET IT--COW, LEATHER?
I GOT IT.
I'M GONNA GO CHECK OUT THE T-SHIRTS.
WHOA! THAT'S PRICEY!
NIKE

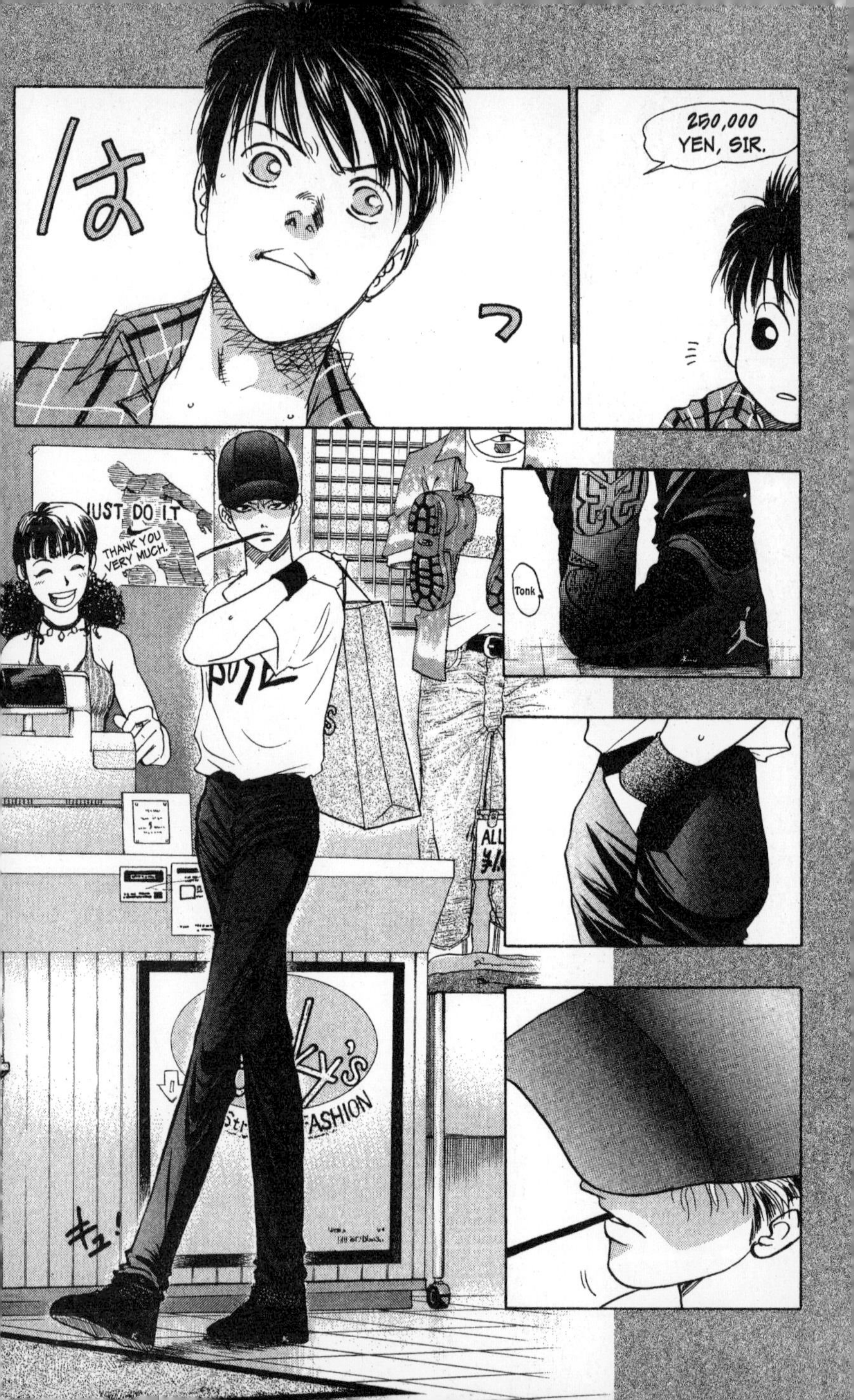
250,000 YEN, SIR.
はっ
Tonk
JUST DO IT
THANK YOU VERY MUCH.
キュ
FASHION

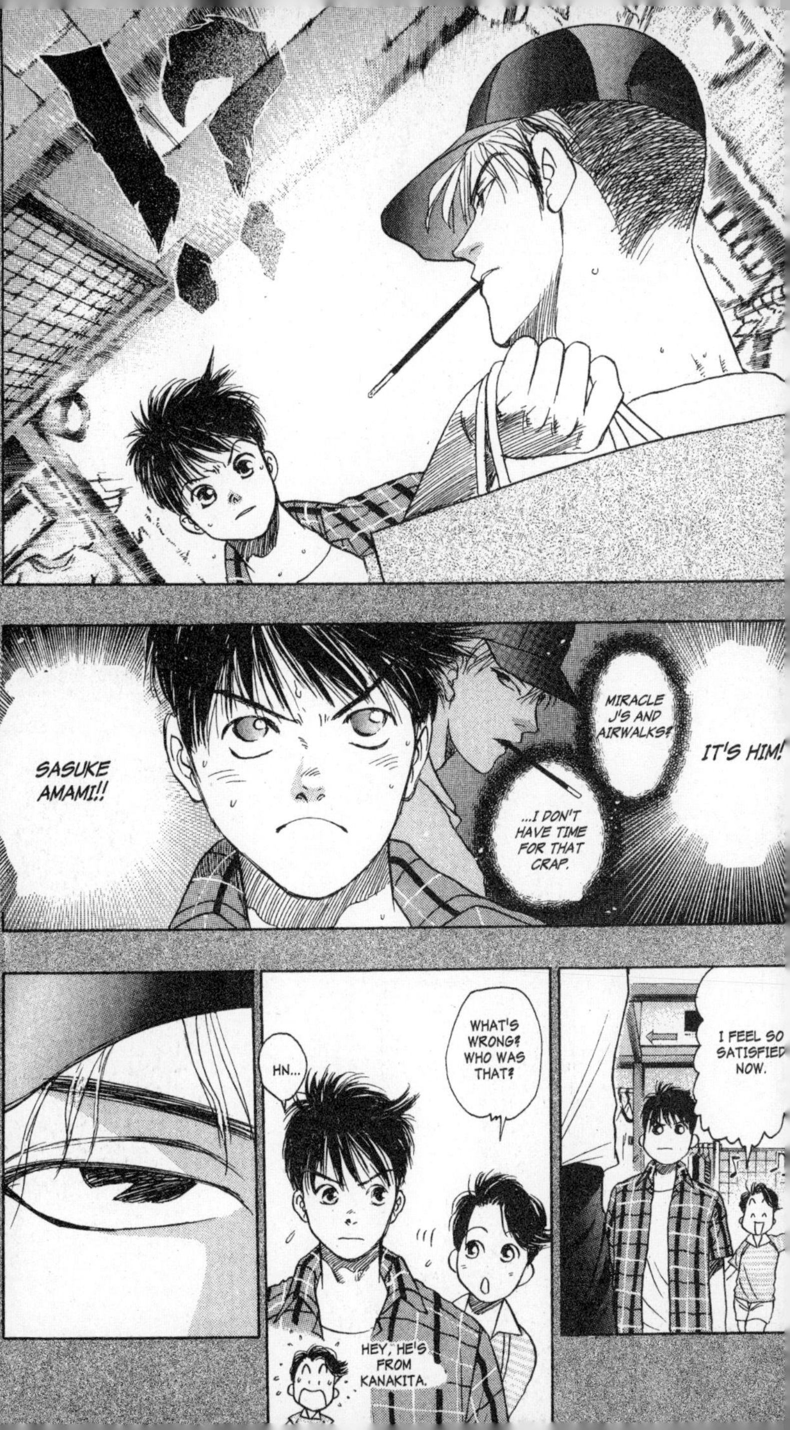
IT'S HIM!
MIRACLE J'S AND AIRWALKS?
...I DON'T HAVE TIME FOR THAT CRAP.
SASUKE AMAMI!!
I FEEL SO SATISFIED NOW.
WHAT'S WRONG? WHO WAS THAT?
HN...
HEY, HE'S FROM KANAKITA.

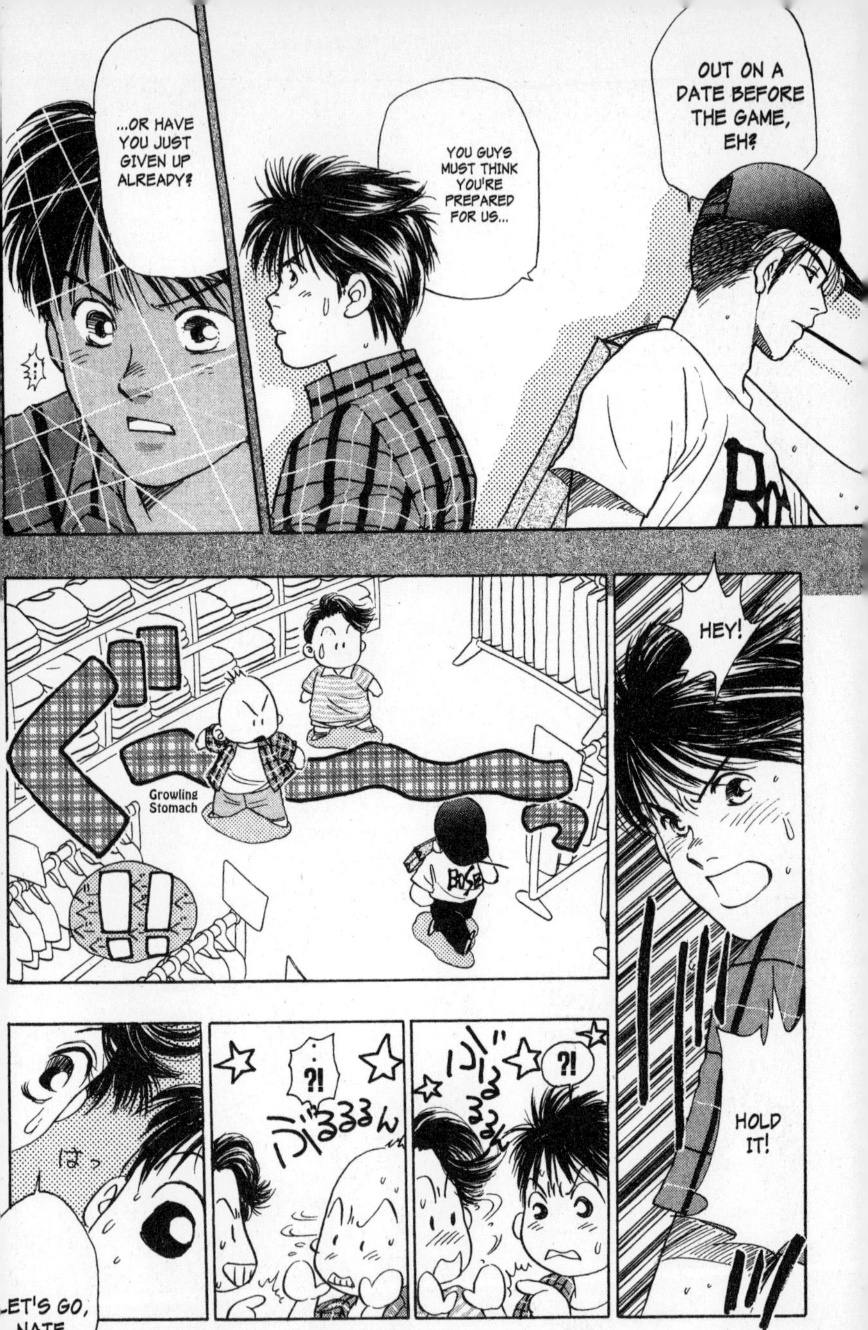
OUT ON A DATE BEFORE THE GAME, EH?
YOU GUYS MUST THINK YOU'RE PREPARED FOR US...
...OR HAVE YOU JUST GIVEN UP ALREADY?
HEY!
HOLD IT!
Growling Stomach
?!
ぶるるるん
?!
ぶるるるん
はっ
ET'S GO, NATE.

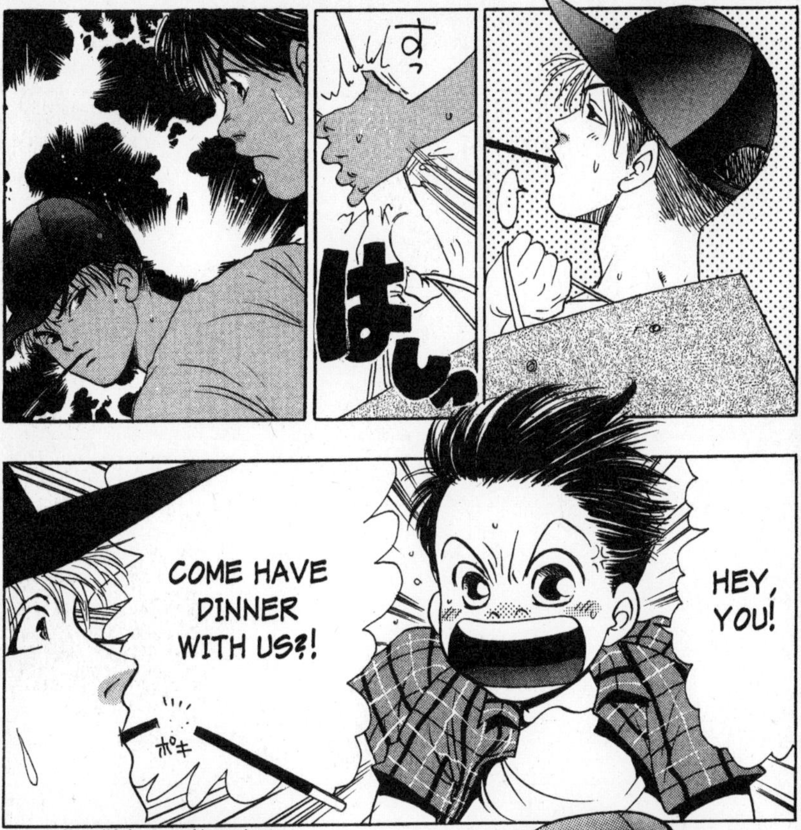
すっ
はしっ
HEY, YOU!
COME HAVE DINNER WITH US?!
ポキ

Nate did the same thing trying to apologize to Yuta (Rebound #1).

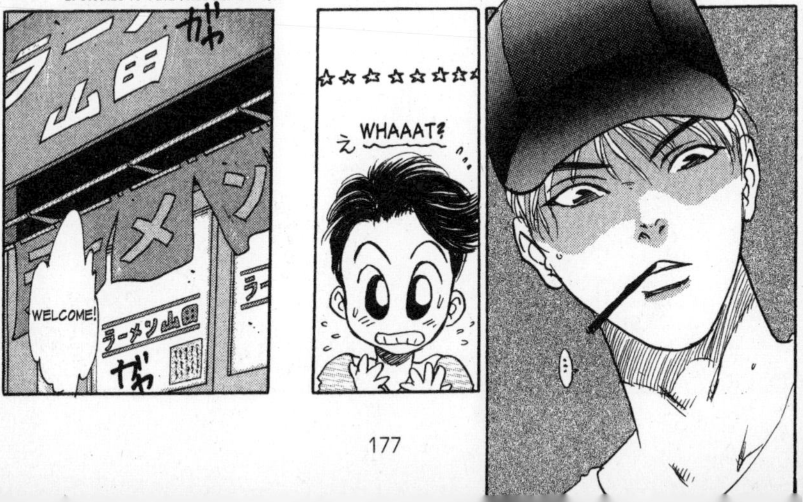
え
WHAAAT?
ガヤ
WELCOME!
ラーメン山田
ガヤ

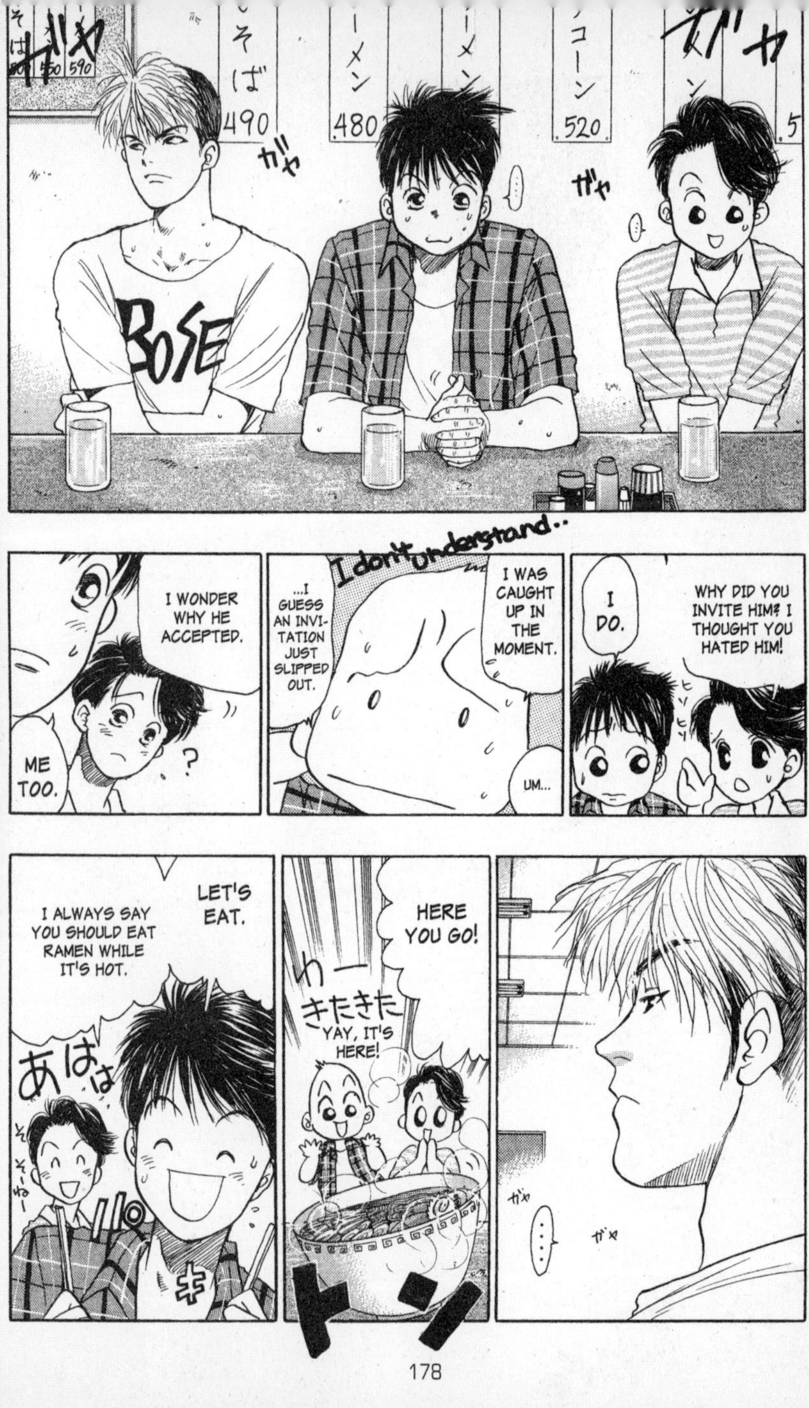

ガヤ
そば 490
480
520
…
…
ガヤ
ガヤ
ガヤ
WHY DID YOU INVITE HIM? I THOUGHT YOU HATED HIM!
ヒソヒソ
I DO.
I WAS CAUGHT UP IN THE MOMENT.
...I GUESS AN INVITATION JUST SLIPPED OUT.
UM...
I don't understand..
I WONDER WHY HE ACCEPTED.
ME TOO.
ガヤ
....
ガヤ
HERE YOU GO!
わーきたきた
YAY, IT'S HERE!
トン
LET'S EAT.
I ALWAYS SAY YOU SHOULD EAT RAMEN WHILE IT'S HOT.
あはは

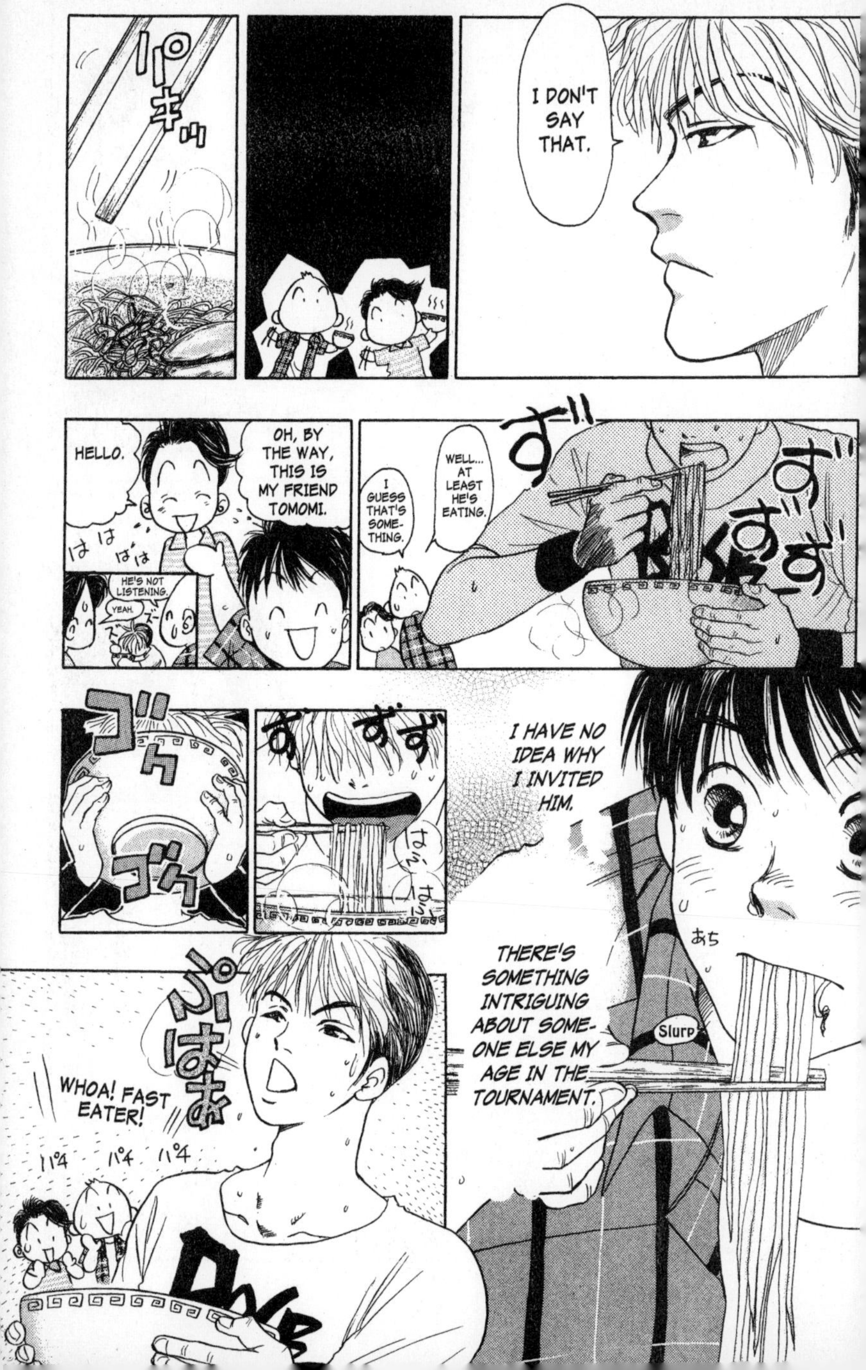
I DON'T SAY THAT.
WELL... AT LEAST HE'S EATING.
I GUESS THAT'S SOME-THING.
OH, BY THE WAY, THIS IS MY FRIEND TOMOMI.
HELLO.
HE'S NOT LISTENING.
YEAH.
I HAVE NO IDEA WHY I INVITED HIM.
あち
Slurp
THERE'S SOMETHING INTRIGUING ABOUT SOME-ONE ELSE MY AGE IN THE TOURNAMENT.
WHOA! FAST EATER!

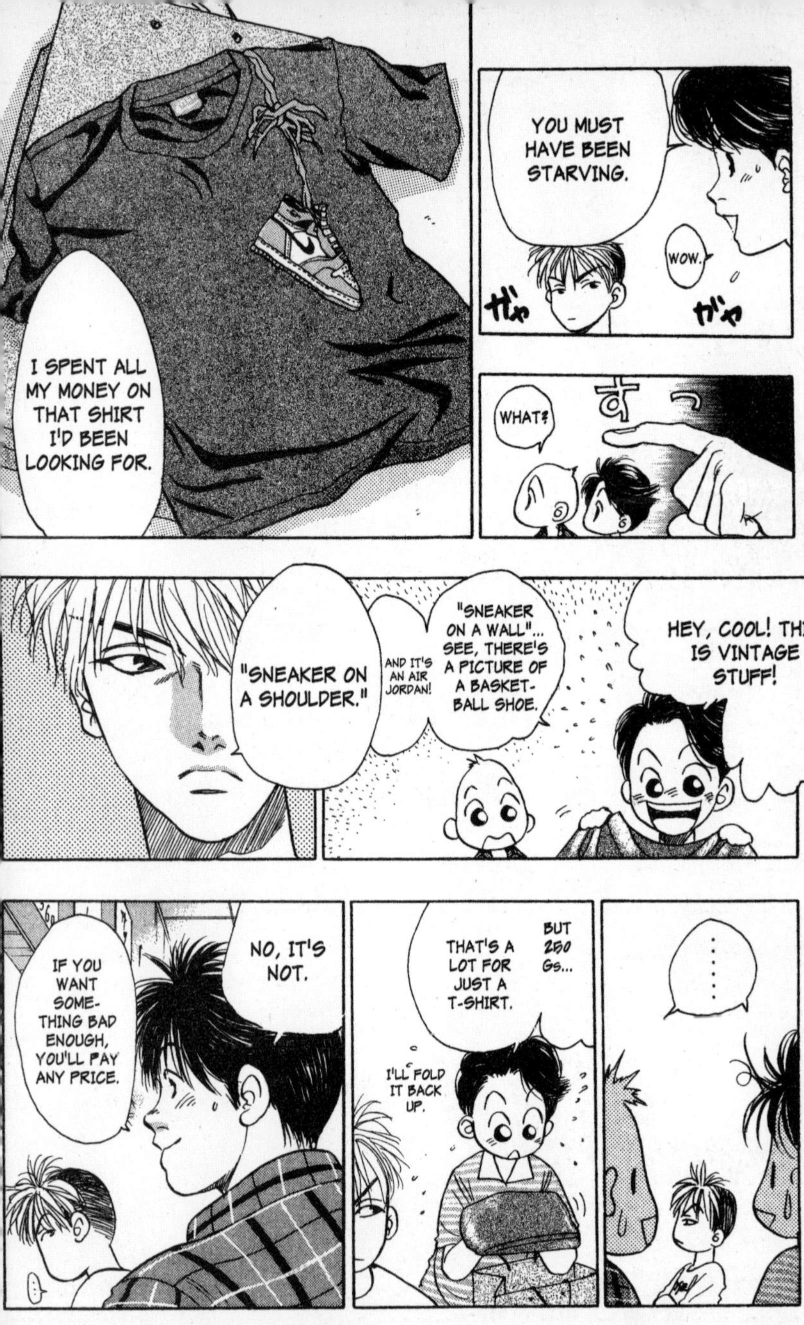

YOU MUST HAVE BEEN STARVING.
WOW.
ガャ
ガャ
WHAT?
すっ
I SPENT ALL MY MONEY ON THAT SHIRT I'D BEEN LOOKING FOR.
HEY, COOL! THIS IS VINTAGE STUFF!
"SNEAKER ON A WALL"... SEE, THERE'S A PICTURE OF A BASKET-BALL SHOE.
AND IT'S AN AIR JORDAN!
"SNEAKER ON A SHOULDER."
......
BUT 250 Gs...
THAT'S A LOT FOR JUST A T-SHIRT.
I'LL FOLD IT BACK UP.
NO, IT'S NOT.
IF YOU WANT SOME-THING BAD ENOUGH, YOU'LL PAY ANY PRICE.
...

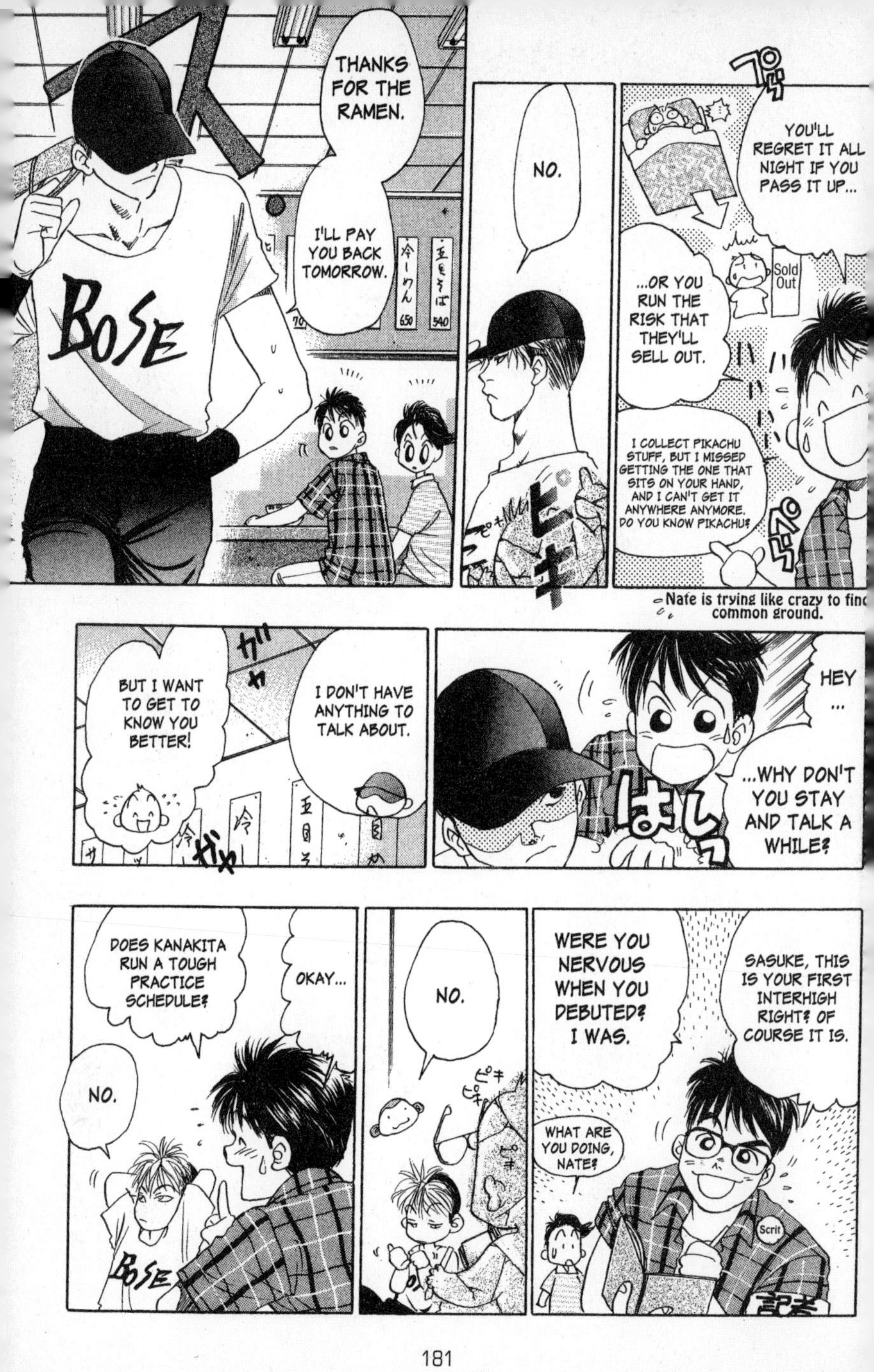
YOU'LL REGRET IT ALL NIGHT IF YOU PASS IT UP...
...OR YOU RUN THE RISK THAT THEY'LL SELL OUT.
Sold Out
I COLLECT PIKACHU STUFF, BUT I MISSED GETTING THE ONE THAT SITS ON YOUR HAND, AND I CAN'T GET IT ANYWHERE ANYMORE. DO YOU KNOW PIKACHU?
NO.
THANKS FOR THE RAMEN.
I'LL PAY YOU BACK TOMORROW.
Nate is trying like crazy to fin
common ground.
HEY ...
...WHY DON'T YOU STAY AND TALK A WHILE?
はしっ
I DON'T HAVE ANYTHING TO TALK ABOUT.
BUT I WANT TO GET TO KNOW YOU BETTER!
SASUKE, THIS IS YOUR FIRST INTERHIGH RIGHT? OF COURSE IT IS.
WERE YOU NERVOUS WHEN YOU DEBUTED? I WAS.
WHAT ARE YOU DOING, NATE?
Scrit
NO.
OKAY...
DOES KANAKITA RUN A TOUGH PRACTICE SCHEDULE?
NO.

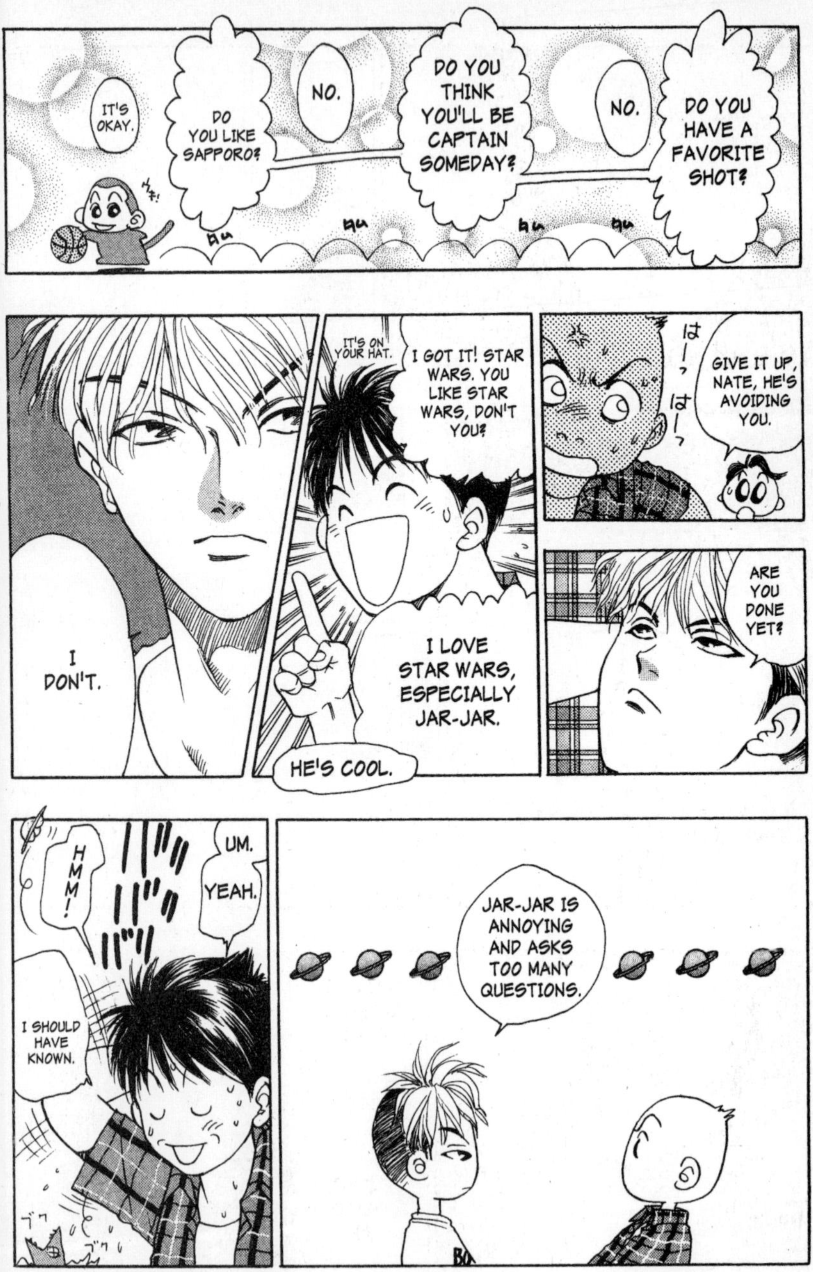
DO YOU HAVE A FAVORITE SHOT?
NO.
DO YOU THINK YOU'LL BE CAPTAIN SOMEDAY?
NO.
DO YOU LIKE SAPPORO?
IT'S OKAY.
GIVE IT UP, NATE, HE'S AVOIDING YOU.
はーっ はーっ
ARE YOU DONE YET?
I GOT IT! STAR WARS. YOU LIKE STAR WARS, DON'T YOU?
IT'S ON YOUR HAT.
I LOVE STAR WARS, ESPECIALLY JAR-JAR.
HE'S COOL.
I DON'T.
JAR-JAR IS ANNOYING AND ASKS TOO MANY QUESTIONS.
UM.
YEAH.
HMM!
I SHOULD HAVE KNOWN.

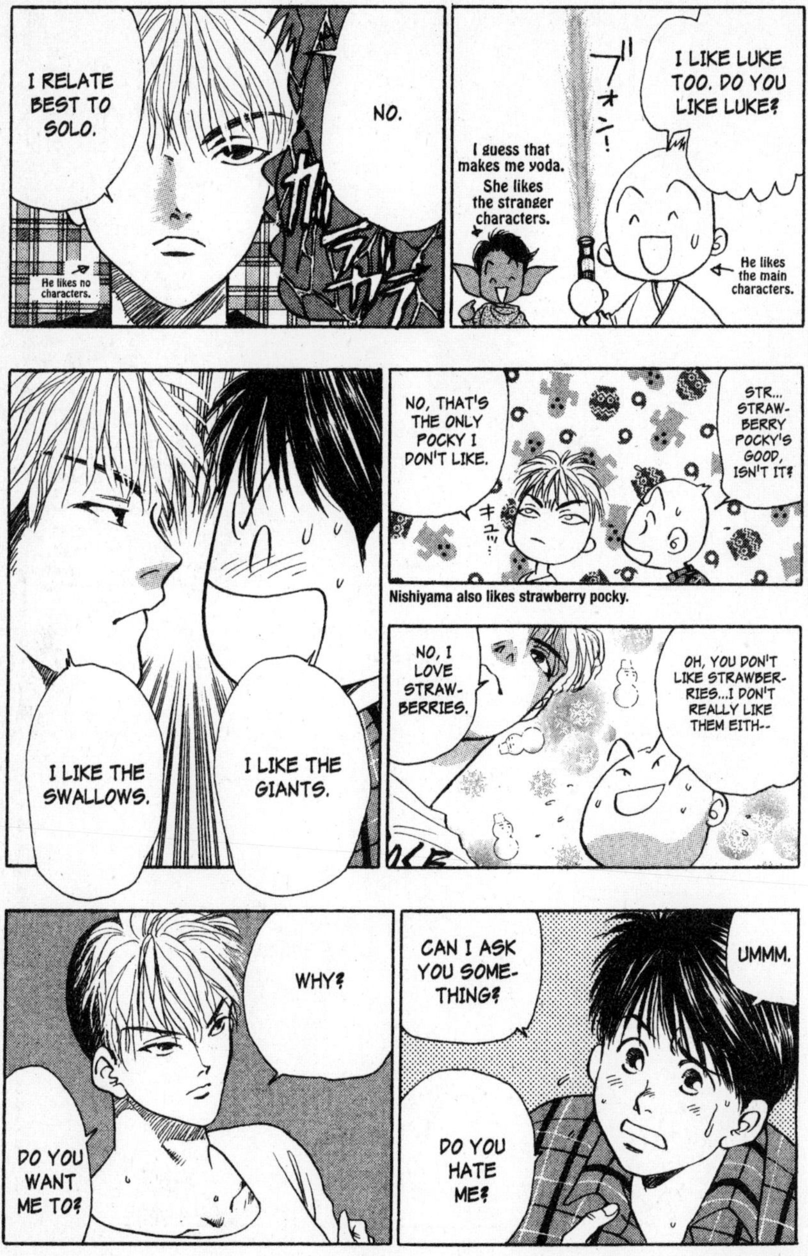
I LIKE LUKE TOO. DO YOU LIKE LUKE?
ブオン!
He likes the main characters.
I guess that makes me yoda.
She likes the stranger characters.
NO.
I RELATE BEST TO SOLO.
He likes no characters.
STR... STRAWBERRY POCKY'S GOOD, ISN'T IT?
NO, THAT'S THE ONLY POCKY I DON'T LIKE.
キュッ…
Nishiyama also likes strawberry pocky.
OH, YOU DON'T LIKE STRAWBERRIES...I DON'T REALLY LIKE THEM EITH--
NO, I LOVE STRAWBERRIES.
I LIKE THE GIANTS.
I LIKE THE SWALLOWS.
UMMM.
CAN I ASK YOU SOMETHING?
DO YOU HATE ME?
WHY?
DO YOU WANT ME TO?

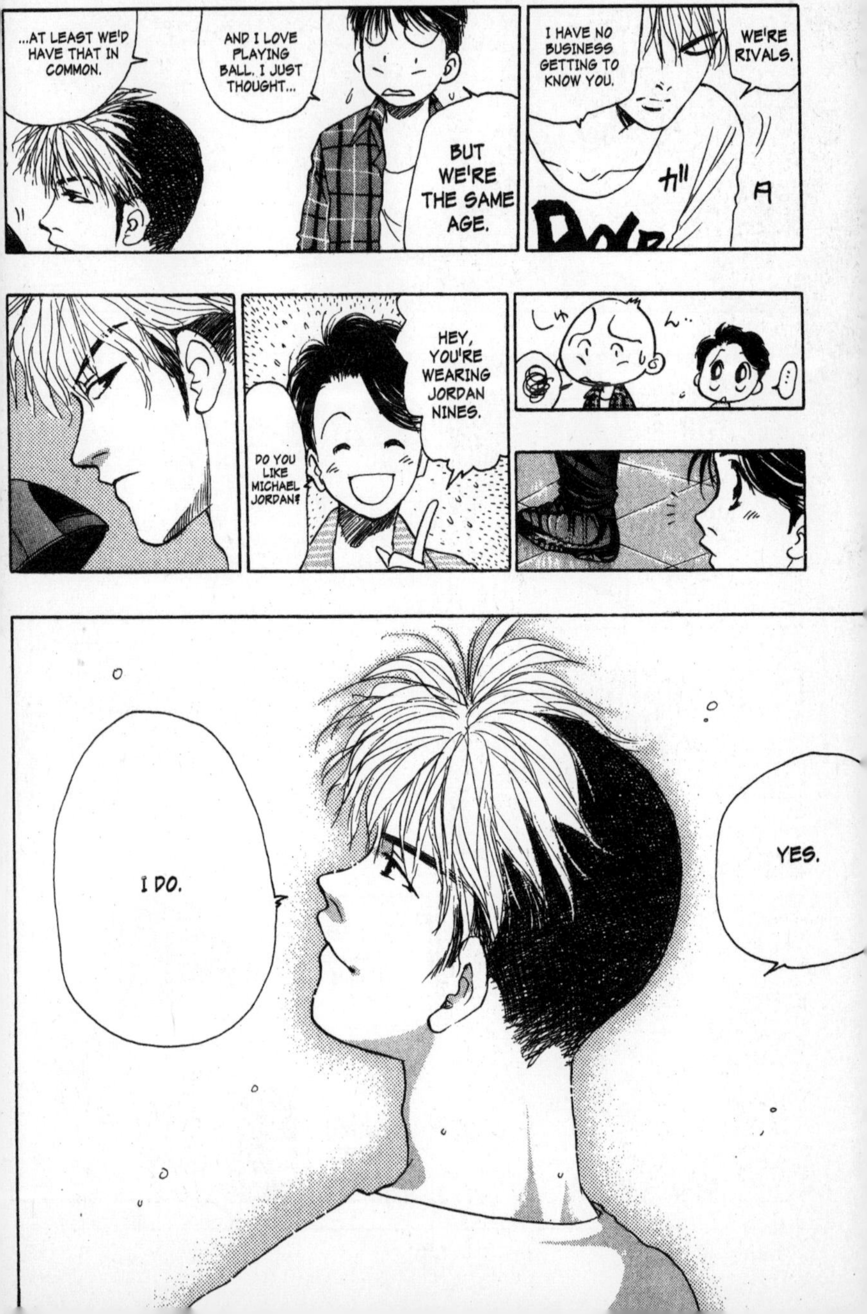
WE'RE RIVALS.
I HAVE NO BUSINESS GETTING TO KNOW YOU.
BUT WE'RE THE SAME AGE.
AND I LOVE PLAYING BALL. I JUST THOUGHT...
...AT LEAST WE'D HAVE THAT IN COMMON.
しゅん..
HEY, YOU'RE WEARING JORDAN NINES.
DO YOU LIKE MICHAEL JORDAN?
YES.
I DO.

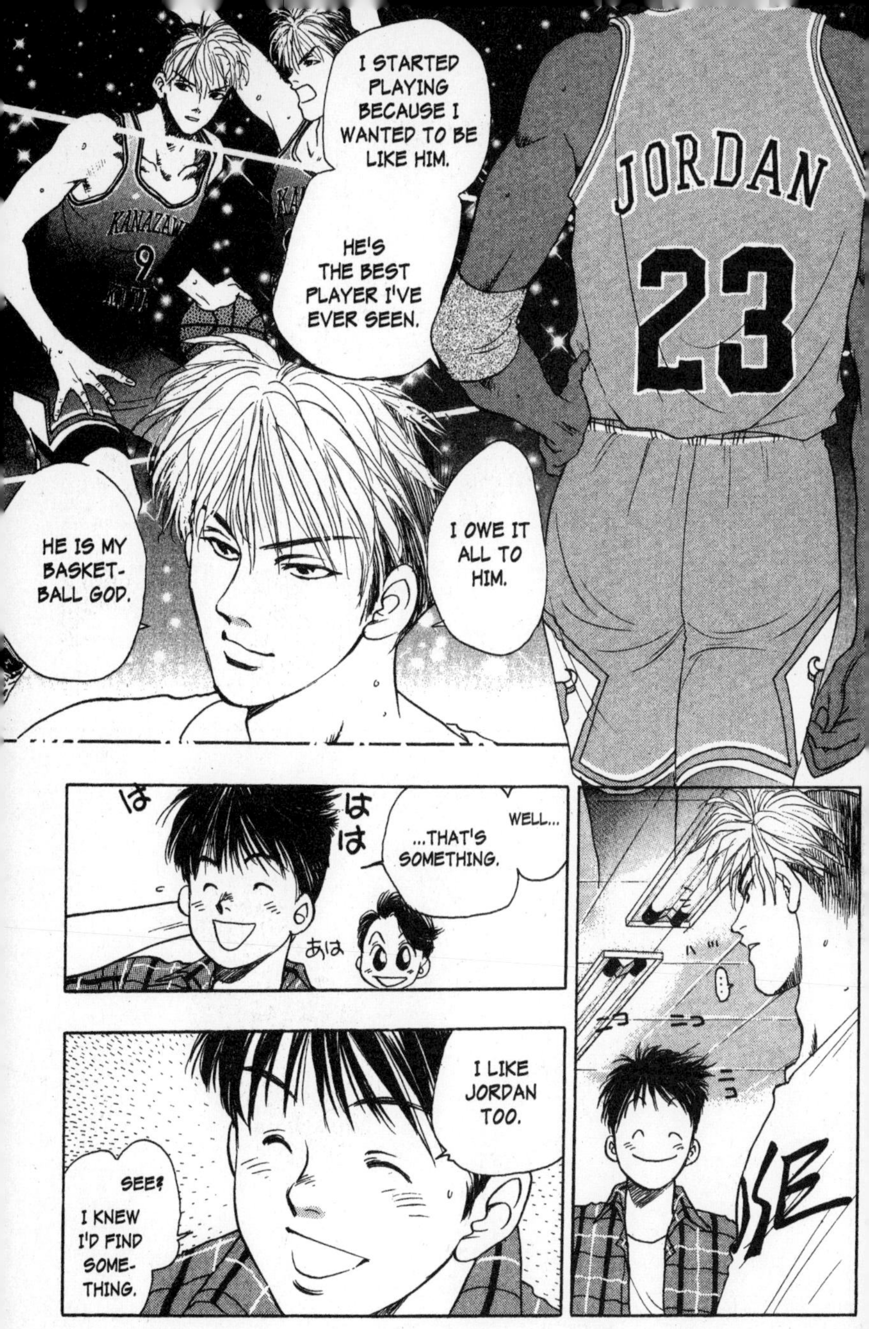

JORDAN
23
KANAZAWA
9
I STARTED PLAYING BECAUSE I WANTED TO BE LIKE HIM.
HE'S THE BEST PLAYER I'VE EVER SEEN.
I OWE IT ALL TO HIM.
HE IS MY BASKET-BALL GOD.
...
WELL...
...THAT'S SOMETHING.
はは
ぱ
あは
I LIKE JORDAN TOO.
SEE? I KNEW I'D FIND SOME-THING.

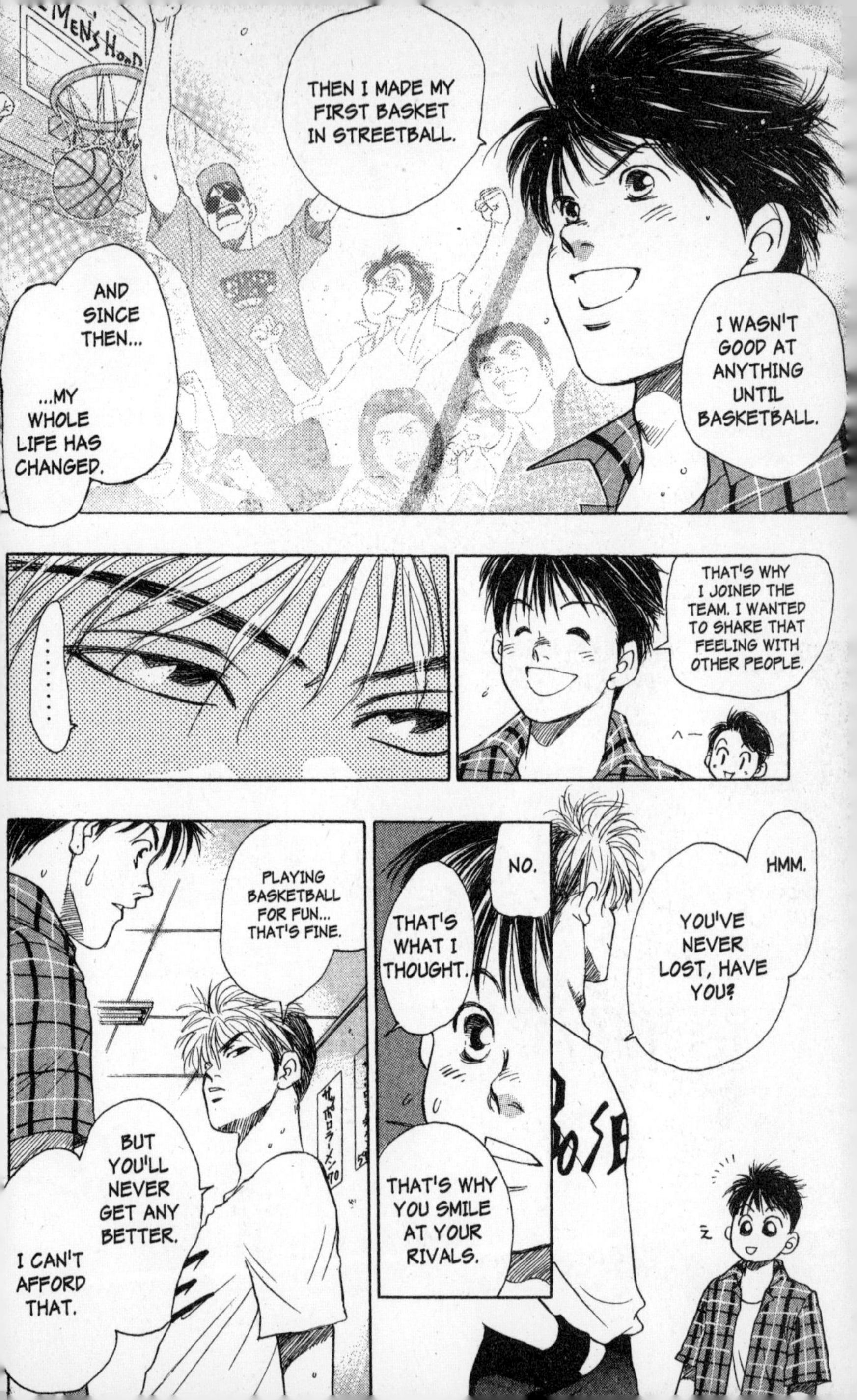
I WASN'T GOOD AT ANYTHING UNTIL BASKETBALL.
THEN I MADE MY FIRST BASKET IN STREETBALL.
AND SINCE THEN...
...MY WHOLE LIFE HAS CHANGED.
THAT'S WHY I JOINED THE TEAM. I WANTED TO SHARE THAT FEELING WITH OTHER PEOPLE.
ヘー
......
HMM.
YOU'VE NEVER LOST, HAVE YOU?
NO.
THAT'S WHAT I THOUGHT.
THAT'S WHY YOU SMILE AT YOUR RIVALS.
え
PLAYING BASKETBALL FOR FUN... THAT'S FINE.
BUT YOU'LL NEVER GET ANY BETTER.
I CAN'T AFFORD THAT.

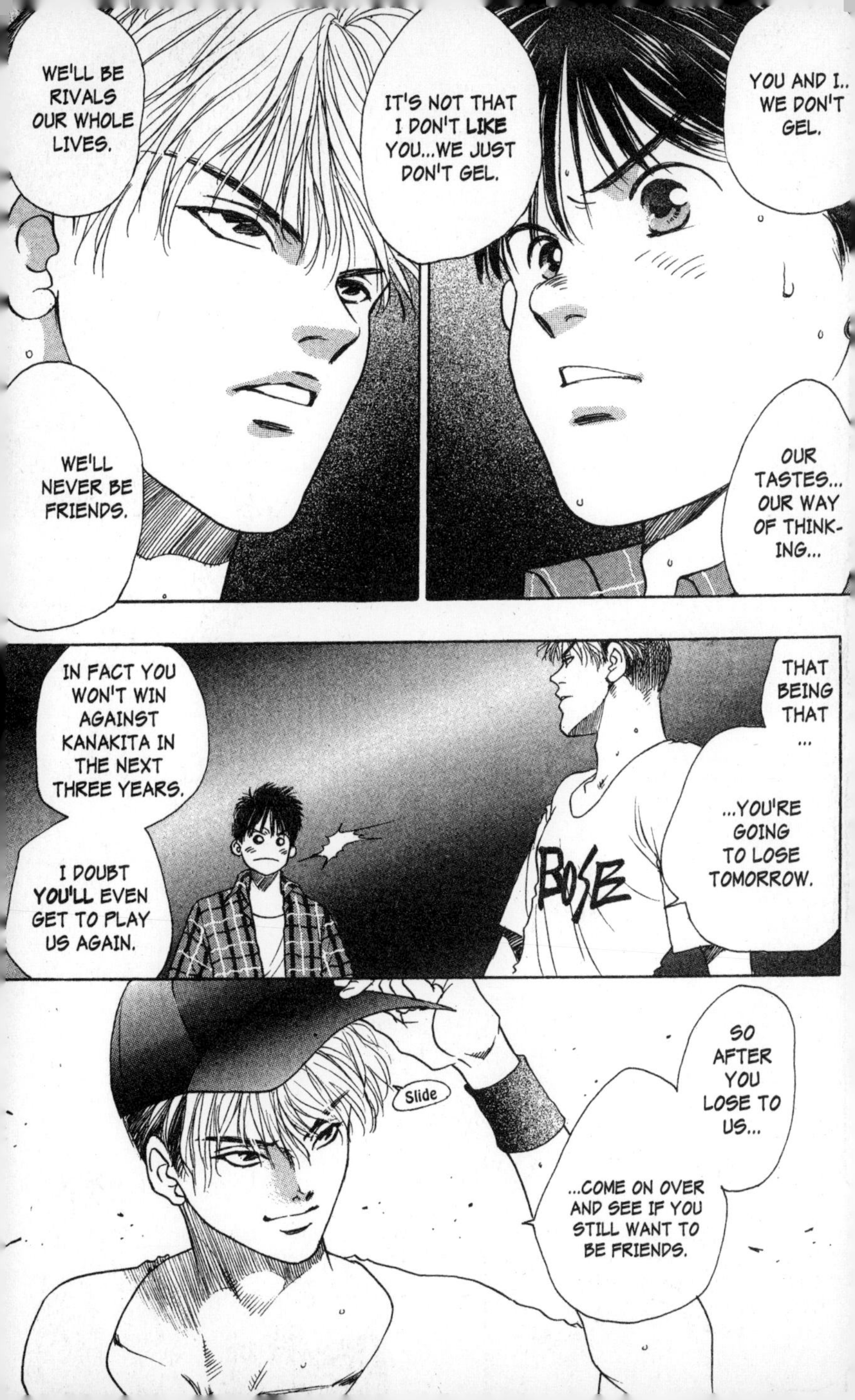

YOU AND I.. WE DON'T GEL.
IT'S NOT THAT I DON'T LIKE YOU...WE JUST DON'T GEL.
OUR TASTES... OUR WAY OF THINK-ING...
WE'LL BE RIVALS OUR WHOLE LIVES.
WE'LL NEVER BE FRIENDS.
THAT BEING THAT ...
...YOU'RE GOING TO LOSE TOMORROW.
IN FACT YOU WON'T WIN AGAINST KANAKITA IN THE NEXT THREE YEARS.
I DOUBT YOU'LL EVEN GET TO PLAY US AGAIN.
SO AFTER YOU LOSE TO US...
Slide
...COME ON OVER AND SEE IF YOU STILL WANT TO BE FRIENDS.

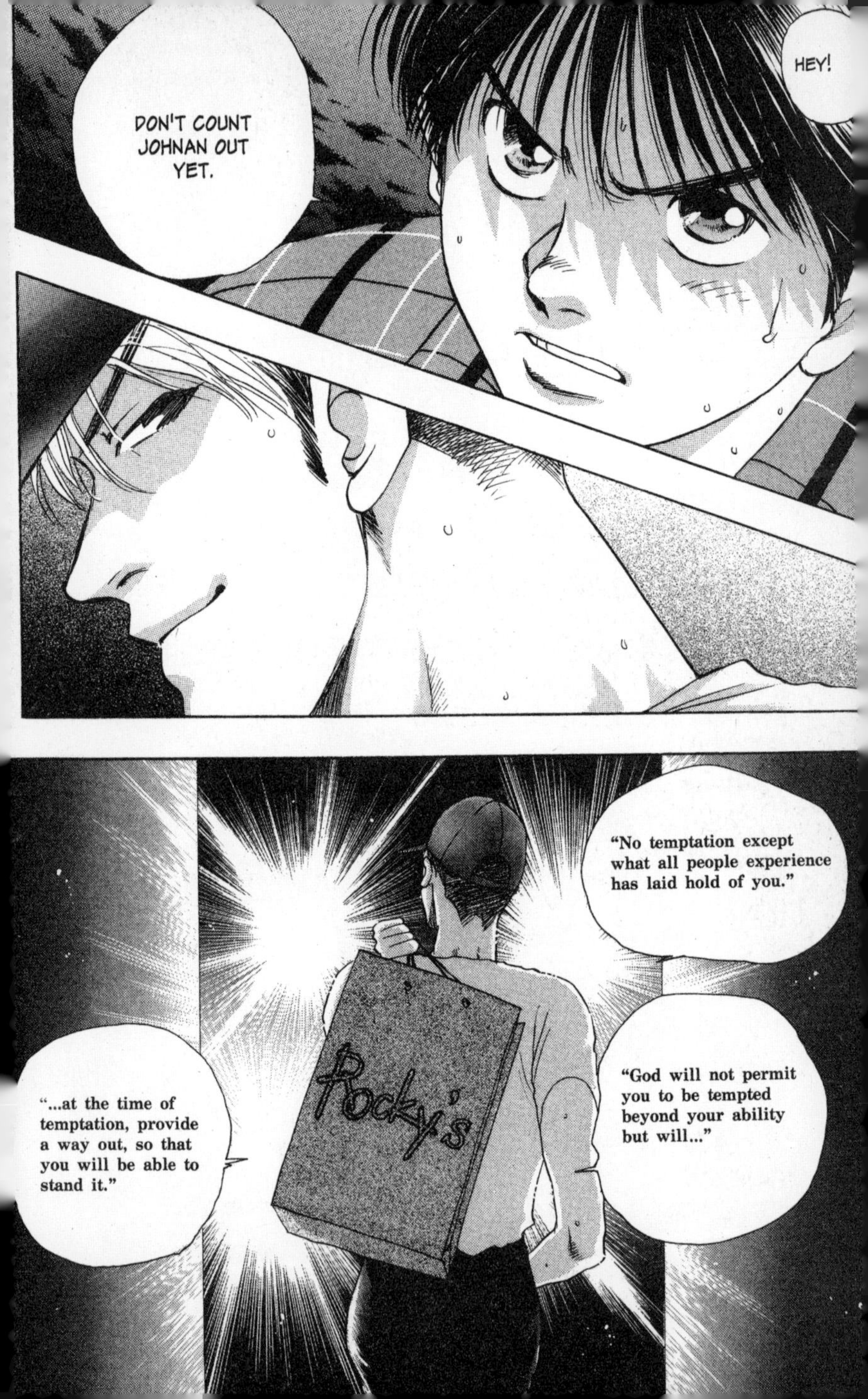
HEY!
DON'T COUNT JOHNAN OUT YET.
"No temptation except what all people experience has laid hold of you."
"God will not permit you to be tempted beyond your ability but will..."
"...at the time of temptation, provide a way out, so that you will be able to stand it."
Rocky's

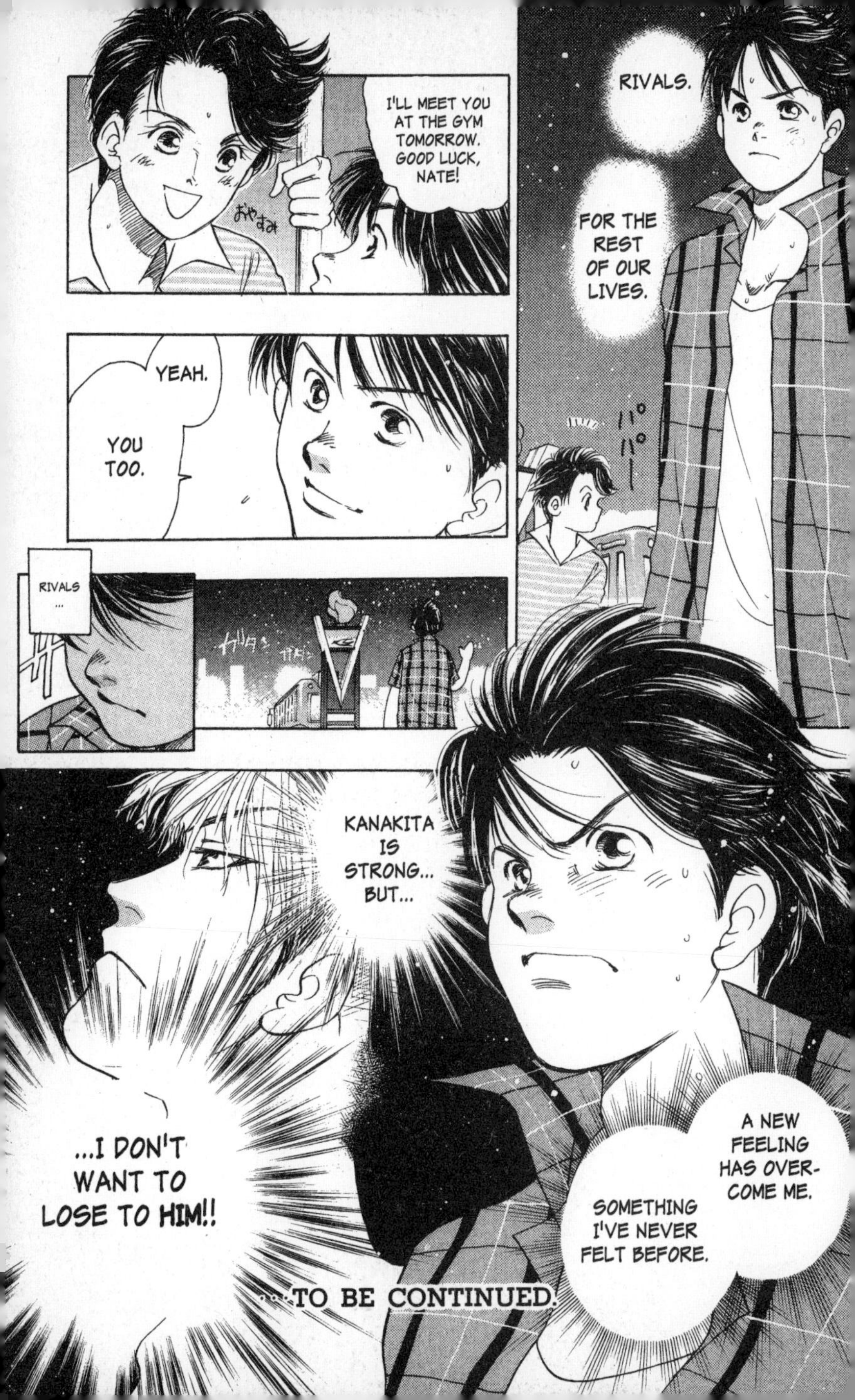
RIVALS.
FOR THE REST OF OUR LIVES.
パパー
I'LL MEET YOU AT THE GYM TOMORROW. GOOD LUCK, NATE!
おやすみ
YEAH.
YOU TOO.
RIVALS...
A NEW FEELING HAS OVER-COME ME.
SOMETHING I'VE NEVER FELT BEFORE.
KANAKITA IS STRONG... BUT...
...I DON'T WANT TO LOSE TO HIM!!
......TO BE CONTINUED.

STAY TUNED!!!

We hope you enjoyed your selected manga, *Rebound* Volume 7. Tune in two months from now when the tale continues and Johnan's basketball crew might be in for the basketball blues...

Preview for  Volume 8

There are only eight teams left in the fourth round, and the pressure is starting to rise. Kanakita and Johnan are preparing for battle, each trying to work out the strategy that will lead to victory...but in the end, it'll come down to who wants it more! With a tight Zone Defense, Johnan might be able to keep Kanakita from scoring, but how will Johnan's offense get into the key. It may take Nate learning how to shoot outside the arc to push Johnan on to the fifth round.

And now, a commercial break...

ALSO AVAILABLE FROM TOKYOPOP®

**For more
information visit
www.TOKYOPOP.com**

02.03.04T

ALSO AVAILABLE FROM TOKYOPOP®

MANGA

.HACK//LEGEND OF THE TWILIGHT
@LARGE
ABENOBASHI: MAGICAL SHOPPING ARCADE
A.I. LOVE YOU
AI YORI AOSHI
ANGELIC LAYER
ARM OF KANNON
BABY BIRTH
BATTLE ROYALE
BATTLE VIXENS
BRAIN POWERED
BRIGADOON
B'TX
CANDIDATE FOR GODDESS, THE
CARDCAPTOR SAKURA
CARDCAPTOR SAKURA - MASTER OF THE CLOW
CHOBITS
CHRONICLES OF THE CURSED SWORD
CLAMP SCHOOL DETECTIVES
CLOVER
COMIC PARTY
CONFIDENTIAL CONFESSIONS
CORRECTOR YUI
COWBOY BEBOP
COWBOY BEBOP: SHOOTING STAR
CRAZY LOVE STORY
CRESCENT MOON
CULDCEPT
CYBORG 009
D•N•ANGEL
DEMON DIARY
DEMON ORORON, THE
DEUS VITAE
DIGIMON
DIGIMON TAMERS
DIGIMON ZERO TWO
DOLL
DRAGON HUNTER
DRAGON KNIGHTS
DRAGON VOICE
DREAM SAGA
DUKLYON: CLAMP SCHOOL DEFENDERS
EERIE QUEERIE!
ERICA SAKURAZAWA: COLLECTED WORKS
ET CETERA
ETERNITY
EVIL'S RETURN
FAERIES' LANDING
FAKE
FLCL
FORBIDDEN DANCE
FRUITS BASKET
G GUNDAM
GATEKEEPERS
GETBACKERS

GIRL GOT GAME
GRAVITATION
GTO
GUNDAM BLUE DESTINY
GUNDAM SEED ASTRAY
GUNDAM WING
GUNDAM WING: BATTLEFIELD OF PACIFISTS
GUNDAM WING: ENDLESS WALTZ
GUNDAM WING: THE LAST OUTPOST (G-UNIT)
HANDS OFF!
HAPPY MANIA
HARLEM BEAT
I.N.V.U.
IMMORTAL RAIN
INITIAL D
INSTANT TEEN: JUST ADD NUTS
ISLAND
JING: KING OF BANDITS
JING: KING OF BANDITS - TWILIGHT TALES
JULINE
KARE KANO
KILL ME, KISS ME
KINDAICHI CASE FILES, THE
KING OF HELL
KODOCHA: SANA'S STAGE
LAMENT OF THE LAMB
LEGAL DRUG
LEGEND OF CHUN HYANG, THE
LES BIJOUX
LOVE HINA
LUPIN III
LUPIN III: WORLD'S MOST WANTED
MAGIC KNIGHT RAYEARTH I
MAGIC KNIGHT RAYEARTH II
MAHOROMATIC: AUTOMATIC MAIDEN
MAN OF MANY FACES
MARMALADE BOY
MARS
MARS: HORSE WITH NO NAME
METROID
MINK
MIRACLE GIRLS
MIYUKI-CHAN IN WONDERLAND
MODEL
ONE
ONE I LOVE, THE
PARADISE KISS
PARASYTE
PASSION FRUIT
PEACH GIRL
PEACH GIRL: CHANGE OF HEART
PET SHOP OF HORRORS
PITA-TEN
PLANET LADDER
PLANETES
PRIEST

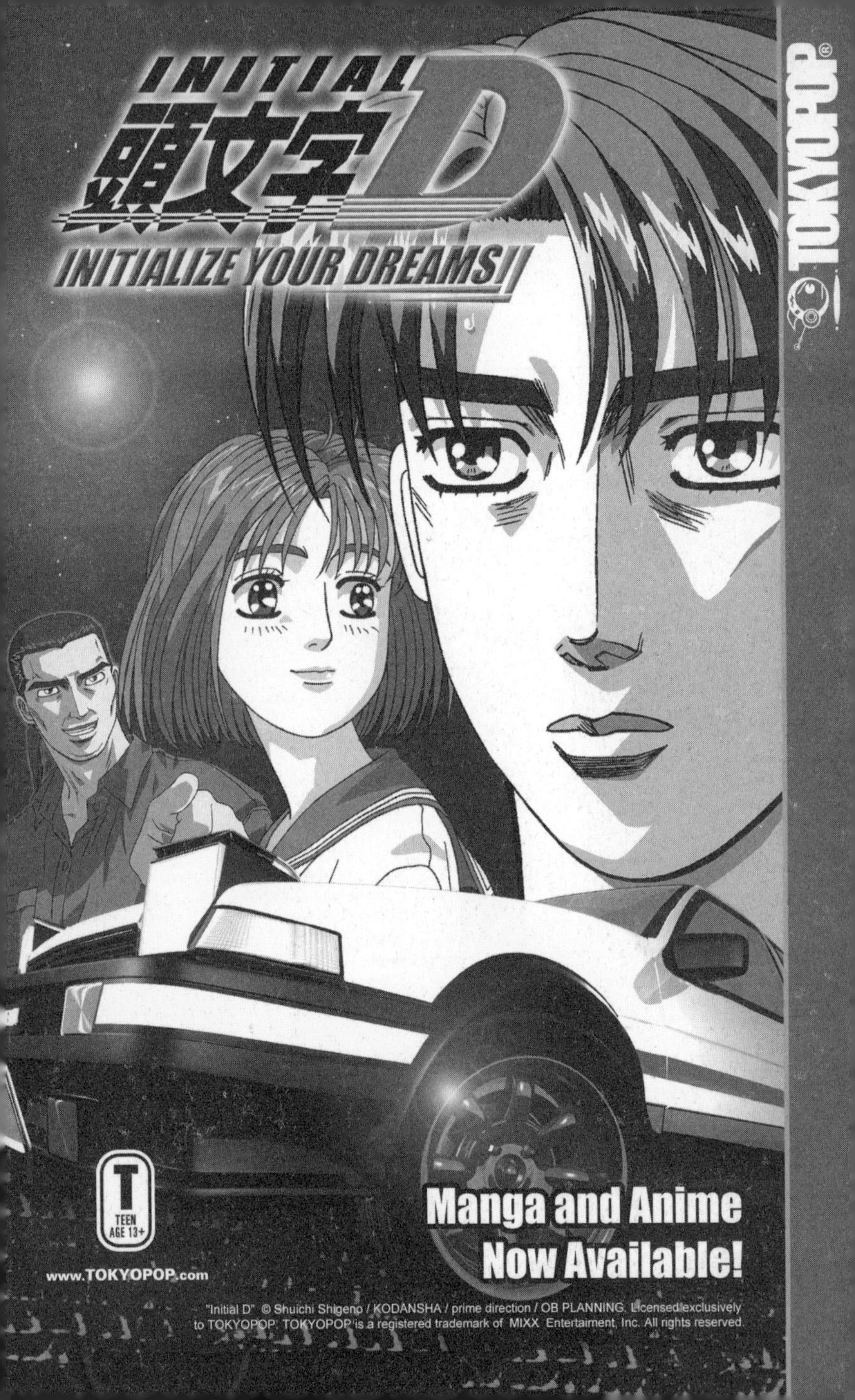
INITIAL
頭文字D
INITIALIZE YOUR DREAMS!
TOKYOPOP®
T
TEEN
AGE 13+
Manga and Anime
Now Available!
www.TOKYOPOP.com
"Initial D" © Shuichi Shigeno / KODANSHA / prime direction / OB PLANNING. Licensed exclusively to TOKYOPOP. TOKYOPOP is a registered trademark of MIXX Entertaiment, Inc. All rights reserved.

PLANETES

By Makoto Yukimura

Hachi Needed Time...
What He Found Was Space

A Sci-Fi Saga About
Personal Conquest

Available at Your Favorite
Book and Comic Stores.

TEEN AGE 13+

www.TOKYOPOP.com

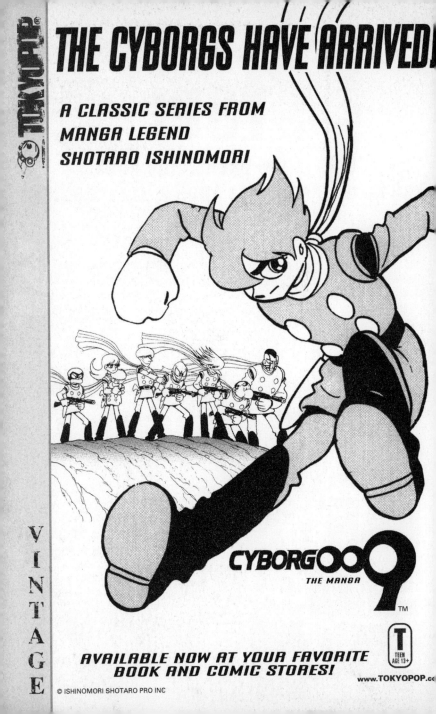

STOP!

This is the back of the book.
You wouldn't want to spoil a great ending!

This book is printed "manga-style," in the authentic Japanese right-to-left format. Since none of the artwork has been flipped or altered, readers get to experience the story just as the creator intended. You've been asking for it, so TOKYOPOP® delivered: authentic, hot-off-the-press, and far more fun!

DIRECTIONS

If this is your first time reading manga-style, here's a quick guide to help you understand how it works.

It's easy... just start in the top right panel and follow the numbers. Have fun, and look for more 100% authentic manga from TOKYOPOP®!